MARXISM, SOCIALISM, INDIAN POLITICS

A View From The Left

Randhir Singh

To the Memory of

Paul Sweezy
&
Harry Magdoff

Marxism, Socialism, Indian Politics
Randhir Singh

First Published 2008
Reprinted 2020

ISBN 978-81-89833-56-5 (Pb)

Published by
AAKAR BOOKS
28 E Pocket IV, Mayur Vihar Phase I
Delhi 110 091, India
www.aakarbooks.com

Printed at
Sapra Brothers, Noida

Contents

Publisher's Note

We have here put together a few of Professor Randhir Singh's recent writings including some excerpts from his recently published *Crisis of Socialism—Notes in Defence of a Commitment*.

The themes are topical and the analysis, as solid as ever, has longterm validity. Though written at different times and occasions, the overriding concern in each case is to get across a basic theoretical understanding of things, a radical strategic orientation as it were, which, in the author's view, is a prerequisite of principled and fruitful tactical resilience in the theory and practice of those struggling for a radical or revolutionary transformation of our society; the lack of such an orientation has invariably made for pragmatic or opportunist and therefore ultimately barren political practice so far as a genuine advancement of our people's interests is concerned. This has meant an awkward repetition of argument and expression now that these writings are being put together in one volume. The author regrets this repetition and seeks indulgence of the reader—though, as he has written elsewhere, 'a justification is not to be entirely ruled out. Gunter Grass has said : "In politics you have to repeat and repeat, like a parrot, ideas you know to be correct and proven as such, which is exhausting—you constantly hear the echo of your own voice and end up sounding like a parrot even to yourself. But this is evidently part of the job, if one is to find any listeners at all in a world so full of different voices", or, I may add, when the noisy voice of those currently dominant in society, seeks to drown all other voices and wants us to forget what was said earlier and has been proved to be true, or forbids what needs to be said and repeated anew today'.

Prof. Singh admittedly writes from the stand point of Marxism or 'Marxism of Karl Marx' as he prefers to call it to distinguish it from 'official Marxism' that once flooded in from Moscow. Of his Marxism, he has written: 'I have no pretensions to scholarship in Marxism. I picked up some on the way and have found it useful not only in my politics, or profession as a teacher, but in living my life as well. This last is not just a formal statement. Knowing Marx does make a difference to what sense you make of life, how you understand, live and act in the world. "Indeed, I must confess that Marx made a man of me", is how George Bernard Shaw once put it'.

Away from the mainstream scholarship or political thinking, Prof. Randhir Singh is recognized as 'one of the major radical intellectuals of our times'. Prof. Dale Riepe (State University of New York) has taken note of him in his *Indian Philosophy Since Independence*, and Prof. T. V. Sathyamurthy (University of York, U.K.) in a critical assessment of Marxist writing in India has written of 'the distinguished exception of Kosambi and Randhir Singh'.

We at Aakar Books feel privileged to publish this book.

K.K. Saxena

In Lieu of a Biodata*

There is a certain inevitability about it. Sooner or later someone was bound to ask me, again, for my biodata.

A 'biodata', now, has been a source of perennial embarrassment for me. For I simply don't have any—I have no credentials at all so far as scholarship in the academy goes. I have only a life to speak of, lived somewhat differently, and on a generous interpretation, maybe a little more meaningfully too. Here, very sketchily, then, is some of the more public part of the story, for whatever it is worth.

Childhood, they say, is important, always and in many ways. For me it was rather a unhappy childhood, very bleak and altogether lonely. I literally lived and survived on books, which partly explains my lifelong love for and involvement with them. This childhood, possibly, also left me with a certain sensitivity for the reality of suffering in the human condition of our time.

Over this childhood loomed large the heroic figure of Bhagat Singh. A morning is still vividly etched on my mind, the morning after he and his comrades were hanged. I was detained, briefly, while passing in front the Lahore Central Jail on my way to the Borstal primary school in the neighbourhood. The army and the police, a surging sea of humanity, tears in each eye and the proud faces, portraits, of the martyrs everywhere—

---

* An 'autobiographical note' written in response to a request for biodata for a felicitation volume (1988).

and the defiant unending cry of *'Inquilab zindabad'*.... That morning was born a dream which, I believe, in some from or the other, has always stayed with me. Years later I was to spend a few months, among the happiest in my life, in the 'Terrorist Ward' of this very prison with some of the surviving comrades of Bhagat Singh—Kishori Lal and others—who had in the meantime joined the Communist Party.

Thus I grew up. And in due course, on the eve of the Second World War, I again came to Lahore, this time for my studies at a college there. My father, a remarkable man in his own mixed sort of way—a brilliant physician and surgeon, profoundly religious and puritanical, with a rather deadly combination of Gandhi and Lenin in his head—sensing the turbulence inside me, his only son, had advised: 'Do anything out there but don't join some illegal organisation'. Predictably, this was the first thing I did on reaching Lahore. Even as I was searching for it, the Communist Party found me. When my father admonished me that I had shown scant regard for the family, I wrote back: 'I have found my real family.' The Communist Party meant this and very much more in those days, to many of us at least. Besides, there was a certain pride in being a Communist. I still remember from those times two lines from the poet C. Day Lewis. A question and an answer, they went something like this:

> Why do we on seeing a Red feel small?
> For he is future walking to meet us—

Fifty years later, badly buffeted, some of this pride yet remains. Incidentally, this is also how I came to Marxism—beginning with whatever Marxism was then available with the Comintern and permitted or possible in our country under the British rule.

Followed years of hectic activity in the students' movement and in the underground with the Communist Party, including entire vacations spent with workers in factories away from Lahore or with peasants in their villages.

We were good students, among the best in the University. I duly qualified for admission to the Medical College. But it was clear that the demands of ever-increasing political work would be impossible to reconcile with those of a study in medicine. I decided to shift to a 'soft' discipline. I was advised that Political Science was, possibly, the easiest subject to get your master's degree in. That, perhaps, is one reason why I could never take it seriously. Later I was to discover that it is also, possibly, the poorest among the social sciences. And if I may suggest, one important reason for its poverty as a social scientific enterprise is its near-universal ignorance of or hostility towards Marxism as social science; though, in recent years, it has not been averse to recognising Marxism as 'political thought'.

Be that as it may, in a couple of years even the pursuit of Political Science had to be given up for full-time work with the Communist Party—on the party wage of, I think, rupees twenty or twenty-five per month. For most of the next five years and more, till after the Partition, I moved around the villages and towns of Punjab, organising people and persuading them to move through their struggle for freedom towards a social revolution in this country, which I believe still needs to be made.

Soon enough I landed in prison, charged with opposition to 'the war effort' of the British Government in India. (Incidentally, it was 'the people's war' period!) Released, after nearly a year's imprisonment, I was for some time put under the usual restrictions on movement, meetings, etc. I filled up the time with a stint on the editorial staff of the Party's Punjabi weekly, *Jang-i-Azadi*. I also started work on a biography of the still active legendary revolutionary, Baba Gurmukh Singh, a fragment of which was later published as *Ghadar Heroes: A Forgotten Story of the Punjab Revolutionaries of 1914-1915* (1945). My professor at the University—he was none other than Dr. J.N. Khosla—who was rather fond of me, insisted that I use this opportunity to at least finish my studies. The Party gave me the required leave for a couple of months, and my professor provided me with the necessary certificate of attendance at classes—which partly overlapped the period I was in prison! I duly took the examination—and was soon back in the villages. (The degree, a first-class-first, was to come in very handy later in my life, at Delhi.)

Came the great popular struggles, the near-revolutionary upsurge of the mid-1940s, the haggling and compromising presided over by Imperialism, the consequent riots, the Partition, and more riots—and Indian independence. A faith had been kept *and* betrayed. Those were glorious yet ignominy-laden years, the years at once of victory and defeat for the Indian people. More specifically, it was the final success, however ambiguous, of a Gandhi and bourgeois-led politics, and a definitive failure, only temporary we thought, of our Communist politics, which included that last adventurist flourish with B.T.R. as well as the heroic struggle in Telengana. One lived, shared and fought through it all—and survived. Some of this experience, intensely personal as well as political and collective, found expression in a small collection of poems in Punjabi—*Rahan Di Dhoor* (1950). In one of these, I recorded:

> A caravan has reached the destination,
> And yet lost its way—

I never wrote poetry again—don't ask me why. Only very recently I have learnt that early in 1951 itself, a distinguished critic had, in a review, hailed my book as a truly significant piece of work. A contemporary scholar even considers it to be the best poetry of that period, though, as he told me, he had difficulty in locating its author!

It would appear that, as in scholarship, so in poetry, and may be in much else besides, I am a genuine 'might have been'.

I came to Delhi sometime after the Partition, having lived with death the previous few months and on the way. Uprooted, a refugee, everything around me, including my politics in a shambles, I sought a new foothold in life—only temporarily, I had then thought, mistakenly. I started teaching at what was then known as Camp College, an institution set up by the Punjab University at Delhi for refugee students and teachers. Even as I began to enjoy my new vocation, the Party, passing through a series of crises, both internal and external, finally opted for 'peaceful', 'parliamentary' ways. And so it came to pass, with other tangible and not-so-tangible factors contributing, that, over a period of time—during which I still edited from Delhi its theoretical monthly in Punjabi, *Sada Jug* (till removed, charged with 'individualism' and 'intellectual arrogance' for refusing to publish a BTR criticism of Mao Tse-tung), and translated *Communist Manifesto* and some more Marx into Punjabi—I just opted out of the Party. [Later, soon after its formation, I was to spend a few years in the Communist Party (Marxist)]. For me the comforting rationalisation was that in our society, after 'revolution-making', teaching perhaps holds the maximum possibilities for a non-alienated life. Here, if you want, but only if you *want*, earning your living can be at the same time living your life. So teaching it was to be for me for the rest of my life. Soon I moved from Camp College to Delhi College, where I was to teach for nearly two decades; then, after a brief stint at Jawaharlal Nehru University, in 1972 I joined Delhi University, rather late in life, as Professor of Political Theory.

Thus it is that having spent some of the best years of my life elsewhere, away from the academy, and the rest only teaching, scholarship has simply passed me by. Hence, as I said in the beginning, 'biodata' has been a perennial embarrassment —for I never managed to acquire one as a scholar. I have no research degrees and no publications except some odd entirely casual exercises, including the book, *Reason, Revolution and Political Theory*, which was an ad hoc response to a provocation in the classroom when my students wanted me to explain and defend an observation I had made. I have had no string of scholars working 'under' me, no fellowships, no research projects, no study or other academic leaves, no 'seminaring', national or international, nothing—not even a visit abroad that has come to certify any sort of achievement or standing as a scholar these days!

Recently, the Indian Council of Social Science Research, perhaps wanting to be helpful, more than once extended me invitations involving 'a foreign visit' each time. Having somehow missed or evaded every such opportunity or activity in the past, I thought, I would make a virtue of it—and declined. Besides, it seemed a bit too late in life for me to now get started on this. Perhaps I also wanted to make certain that there is at least one professor in this country who has not been abroad!

Incidentally, the Council have also very generously offered me a National Fellowship which I have accepted. So I may yet end up as a scholar, though, I am not too sure. For the subject on which I have chosen to write a brief monograph is rather away from what have been my major concerns as a teacher—Western Political Thought, Contemporary Political Theory, Marxism. My subject is so obviously *political*, not 'scholarly'; I seek an understanding of Indian politics which may, it is hoped, help towards 'a more effective people's intervention in what is happening in our country.' What is more, contrary to the current fashions in the world of Marxian scholarship, where 'orthodoxy' is almost a dirty word, and a comfortable and comforting 'post-Marxism' is abroad, I visualise my work as an exercise in Marxist orthodoxy!

If I have, most of the time, done none of the things that scholars are normally supposed to do, I have been, most of the time, busy with what they are normally supposed to keep away from. Which is as well, for life has been such fun this way. I have thus functioned, in the profession and in the university, more as a militant on the Left—even when revising the syllabi in Political Science whenever or wherever I got the opportunity to do so, or putting in a rather noisy plea on behalf of Political Theory in general and Marxism in particular on the campuses of Indian universities. As a militant, the aim was always *hegemony* and not factional or mere economic or organisational gains.

Over the years, teaching and related work apart, I have, along with many others of course, spent a great deal of time helping build up the teachers' movement, fighting for democratic rights and reforms in the university (with the vice-chancellors and against them), carrying on socialist education among workers, students and teachers, including school-teachers, running Marx Clubs and putting together Socialist Groups (one such effort, incidentally, went into the making of the Communist Party (Marxist) on Delhi University campus), writing and publishing pamphlets and bulletins, editing and producing, distributing or circulating journals like *Enquiry*, *Socialist Digest*, *The Marxist Review*, *Monthly Review*, *Science and*

Society and *New Left Review*, campaigning on issues like Vietnam and Czechoslovakia, collecting signatures for Iranian students and others, mobilising and marching for all sorts of popular causes, associating with almost any radical initiative on the campus and every revolutionary venture off it, an association which on occasions, quite understandably, even ended in a love—hate relationship—and so on. That is how it has been for the most part over nearly forty long years.

But if scholarship has passed me by, I have not done too badly as a teacher. At least that is what my students, colleagues, and many others tell me. And I am inclined to believe them; maybe because I very much want to. I have taught in the departments of History, Political Science, and occasionally Philosophy. Students have come to my classes from other disciplines and other universities, from Economics and Sociology, Law and Literature, Mathematics, even Chemistry and Physics. (Perhaps Commerce and Business Management alone have been missing!) And they have given me abundantly of their love and affection, and thoughtful appreciation. This has been compensation enough for whatever I may have missed out on not being a scholar. It was compensation enough especially during periods of bitter conflict and controversy which, inevitably, have been a persistent feature of my long career as a teacher. It is the students who first spoke of 'a legend in Delhi University'. And it is, above all, to them that I trace the real source of an observation Bertell Ollman has made, though it is also expressive of his own characteristic generosity. After his recent visit to Delhi and Jawaharlal Nehru Universities, he writes: 'If I wasn't already over 50, I would probably say something like: when I grow up I want to be a Professor like Randhir Singh.' Yes, teaching has been compensation enough.

At one of the farewell meetings at Delhi University, they questioned me on the subject of my teaching. I responded that, given the 'functional rationality' governing the organised structures of teaching and research, so that scholarly writing is increasingly addressed not to problems or publics but to peers and to prestige and preferment in the needlessly bureaucratised academic professions, and given the growing, and often mindless, specialisation in the social sciences (including Political Science) which is resulting in a situation where fewer and fewer people are hearing more and more about less and less—given all this, a certain lack of conventional academic scholarship can even be an advantage in that it may help one see the social reality as a whole, see the wood and not just the trees, and thus address, as teacher or scholar (or activist), the real problems of society.

Incidentally, I also told them, my students and colleagues, that, for one speaking up for Marxism, my knowledge of Economics is shockingly poor and that I have always regretted it. But this lack, perhaps, has made me that much more sensitive to the humanist, philosophical, and above all political dimensions of Marxism. Of course, I added that 'politics as revolution' is central to Marxism, at least to Marxism as Karl Marx practised it. 'Marx was before all else a revolutionist', as Engels put it.

These are, however, somewhat peripheral considerations. I had gone on to suggest that its strictly academic aspects apart, my teaching could be viewed as a form of 'robinhooding' which, even as it functions within the system, yet seeks to stretch it to its limits. Of course, this 'robinhooding', this functioning as a radical or a Marxist inside the classroom, has its problems and its risks too. The most important problem is that it needs to have a certain quality about it which, above all, demands a genuine and acknowledged familiarity with the mainstream scholarship in the concerned field or discipline, one's reservations about it notwithstanding. Lacking this, it can easily degenerate into vulgar propaganda or empty moral rhetoric. As a student coming from the discipline of English literature, in a complementary reference, once said: 'One needs to have that rare combination of idealism and intelligence.' As for the risks, the most important ones concern the security of job and the denial of promotion. I must admit that I have been rather lucky in this regard. It is true that whenever interviewed, the selection committees invariably turned me down. Yet appointments came, by invitation, including the professorship in 1972, when, incidentally, seeing everyone making a beeline for Jawaharlal Nehru University, I chose instead to opt for the University of Delhi.

'Robinhooding' has its minor risks also. For me it has meant another continuous struggle from the day I started teaching. At the very outset they asked for an undertaking 'not to teach subversion'. Later, they stopped you, again and again, from teaching, or teaching a particular course. For long years, they would let me teach only Plato and not Marx—so that you learn to teach Marx via Plato, which is not only possible but is in some ways far more effective also, for obvious reasons. They can organise harassment and humiliation for you in diverse ways, with the lumpen elements in the academic community thrown in.... One has struggled against all this and *them* all along, and with a reasonable measure of success. My only regret is for the students and teachers who, now and then, had to suffer for their association with me.

There are problems and there are risks. And for better credibility here one must learn to say 'no' to at least some of the innumerable benefits, the cooptive attractions the system has to offer even to a radical teacher, though this 'no' is only of symbolic value. But the most important thing is to be aware of the limitations, even ambiguities, inherent in the very nature of 'robinhooding' as an academic exercise. And for this reason one needs to be very modest about what one is doing or achieving here.

What is more, in so far as it is an exercise *within* the system, it is always in danger of itself becoming a form of cooption into it. In fact, the more you succeed in what you are doing, the more you are also, in an important sense, lending legitimacy to the system as a whole. Such is the dialectics implicit in this mode or style of teaching. That is why its quality is of decisive importance. Even so, how effective it is in its own modest manner, and how it contributes to any qualitative departures in the system, will be determined by other, larger social forces at work in the historical process in this country. We can only recognise and try to help these in whatever way we can.

I will only add that what goes on within the discipline of Political Science or its classrooms, or, for that matter, within the universities and the social science institutes of this country, is only of marginal relevance to the problems and prospects of the Indian people's struggle for a better future. But this is where we work—teachers, students, scholars, all others. And it is axiomatic, for most of us, that we make our efforts where we work, or we shall make no effort at all.

Chapter 1

The Collapse of Soviet Socialism: An Initial Response*

The theoretical conclusions of the Communists are in no way based on the ideas and principles that have been invented or discovered by this or that would be universal reformer.

They merely express, in general terms, actual relations springing from an existing class struggle, from a historical movement going on under our very eyes.

Communist Manifesto

Socialism is young....

The road is long and in part unknown....

To build communism, a new man must be created simultaneously with the material base.

Che Guevara

It is only when people get to the point of seeing that the price of contradictions is yet more intolerable than the price of ending them that they acquire the nerve to go all the way through to a consistent socialist politics....

Once you have decided for revolutionary socialism, not because it is quicker or more exciting, but because no other way is possible, then you can even experience defeat, temporary defeat, such as a socialist of my generation has known, without any loss of commitment.

Raymond Williams

---

* *Economic and Political Weekly*, February 8, 1992.

These are tragic, indeed traumatic times for those who still take their socialism seriously....

A long time ago, even as the modern socialist tradition, inspired above all by Marxism, had just established itself, someone as little suspect of sympathy for any sort of socialism as Ludwig Von Mises described it as the 'most powerful reform movement that history has ever known, the first ideological trend not limited to a section of mankind but supported by people of all races, nations, religions and civilizations'. More recently, even as *The Times* too noticed the truly global reach of the ideas of Karl Marx—'there is no country in which at this moment someone is not discussing Marx's ideas', etc.—Peter Laslett, very far from being a Marxist, pointed out that the teachings of Marx 'have proved more successful than any other set of doctrines which the West has brought forth, swifter and more final in its conquest of the world than ever Christianity was'. In the meantime, even so hostile a critic as Leopold Schwarzschild seemed to sum it all up when he wrote: 'If a name had to be found for the age in which we live, we might safely call it the Marxian era'. And now!....

Many of us had known, even from afar and without ever visiting there, for nearly four decades if not more, that it was bad, in fact pretty bad, in the countries of 'the socialist world' as it was called. We had come to recognise these regimes as, at best, aberrant or deformed versions of socialism as Karl Marx and the classical Marxist tradition had visualised it. Taking our distance, as disappointed but still friendly critics, always hopeful of a change for the better, we had learnt to speak of them, in Rudolf Bahro's more truthful though somewhat ambiguous expression, as countries of 'actually existing socialism', whose crisis, as expressed in domestic and foreign policies, was increasingly seen by us as a negative factor in the development of world revolutionary process, in many ways more decisive for the future of socialism than 'the general crisis of capitalism' that Marxists conventionally, though quite rightly, focused upon. Yes, it was pretty bad there, but it is only fair to confess that even the most knowledgeable amongst us did not know it was *that* bad! For now even the 'actually existing' has ceased to exist in the Soviet Union and Eastern Europe and is in a real crisis elsewhere. As we move into the last decade of the twentieth century, the wreckage around us is already sufficiently comprehensive not only to eliminate the so-called 'Marxist-Leninist' model of socialism as an alternative to capitalism, it has compromised the very idea of socialism, in every one of its forms, Marxist or non-Marxist, be it Trotskyism or Maoism, or reform-Communism, or social democracy, or even whatever anti-Communist socialism is still around in India and elsewhere. The deluge of disenchantment has in fact put a question mark not only on the possibility of any escape from capitalism but on the validity of Marxism itself as the theory and practice of the struggle for human emancipation in our times. As I look back upon my more than fifty years of hopeful involvement with the 'idea of communism', and as today the memory of the heroic struggles of generations of communists and common people for a cause recedes and the reality of broken illusions, wasted lives and bloody sacrifices behind a shattered political model grows on you, one begins to doubt, if only for a while, whether hope will ever again create 'from its own wreck the thing it contemplates'! One almost instinctively turns, once again, to Goethe's injunction, so apt for our troublous times: 'One must from time to time repeat what one believes in, proclaim what one agrees with and what one condemns'.

For me it all began in 1939....

Global capitalism, as imperialism or its fascist variant, driven by the logic of its contradictions, was inexorably moving towards yet another world war, in the process seeking desperately to destroy, as it had sought all along, the barely two-decades old Soviet Union, still struggling to survive and 'build socialism', no matter how one qualified this pioneering effort, then or now. In India, the struggle for freedom was poised to enter its most critical phase and, despite a certain well-justified distrust of its leadership, there was a hopeful turbulence in the atmosphere around us. For me, personally, Bhagat Singh's had been a compelling presence since childhood, and now there was the immediate inspiration of the still-fresh saga of the struggle in Spain—the International Brigades, the finest of writers, poets and artists, across the continents, taking sides and committing themselves to political action against 'war and fascism', their manifestoes speaking the language of 'the revolutionary cause', 'proletarian revolution' and 'the destruction of capitalism', 'the establishment of a workers' government', and so on. And most important of all that fired our radical imagination in that age, that which held together and gave its essential meaning to our idealism, was the continuing reality of Lenin's revolution in Russia—John Reed's *Ten Days That Shook The World*—and its cause now embodied in the Soviet Union; yes, the fabled and forbidden 'land of the Soviets', so distant and yet always so near, the centre of a world-wide fraternity of revolutionaries and the bearer of the promise of *other* possibilities for the oppressed and exploited everywhere, indeed, at last, of a full and truly rich life for the entire humankind. One almost inevitably moved left, to revolutionary socialism which was then gathering unto itself, in Punjab and elsewhere in the country, virtually all the streams of modern India's revolutionary tradition—the legendary survivors of Kartar Singh Sarabha's Ghadarite uprising, old revolutionaries in exile or jails of India and the Andamans, comrades of Bhagat Singh and the battle-scarred fighters from different strands of 'revolutionary terrorism', leaders and activists of the militant peasant and working class movements, left-wing socialists and congressmen, radical young students, poets, artists and intellectuals, and many more. This is how I recorded it in an autobiographical note some years ago:

> And in due course, on the eve of the Second World War, I again came to Lahore, this time for my studies at a college there. My father, a remarkable man in his own mixed sort of way—a brilliant physician and surgeon, profoundly religious and puritanical, with a rather deadly combination of Gandhi and Lenin in his head—sensing the turbulence inside me, his only son, had advised: 'Do anything out there, but don't join some illegal organisation'. Predictably, this was the first thing I did on reaching Lahore. Even as I was searching for it, the Communist Party found me. When my father admonished me that I had shown scant regard for the family, I wrote back: 'I have found my real family'. The Communist Party meant this and very much more in those days, to many of

> us at least. Besides, there was a certain pride in being a Communist. I still remember from those early years two lines from the poet C. Day Lewis. A question and an answer, they went something like this:
>
> Why do we on seeing a Red feel small?
>
> For he is future walking to meet us.
>
> Fifty years later, badly buffeted, some of this pride yet remains. Incidentally, this is also how I came to Marxism—beginning with whatever Marxism was then available with the Comintern and permitted or possible in our country under the British rule.

In fact, we had very little of Marx and Engels, or for that matter Lenin, available to us in those days, and a governmental ban on libraries at Lahore in this regard took care of much of even this little. 'Party literature' apart, Palme Dutt's *India Today* and Stalinist 'summing up' of Leninism in *History of the Communist Party of the Soviet Union (Bolshevik)—Short Course*, in illegally printed or cyclostyled editions, were the staple of our education in Marxism. Sympathetic writing on the Soviet Union was not easy to reach either; though later, with Hitler's invasion and the heroic Soviet resistance to Fascism as the war progressed, a great deal more of the Soviet Union became available. There was the monumental work of Sidney and Beatrice Webb, *Soviet Communism: A New Civilisation*—'In all social history, there has been no such a colossal and so exciting an experiment', they had written. And we noticed that within two years they had withdrawn the interrogation mark they had put against the title in the first edition, published in 1935. The Fabian bias of the Webbs notwithstanding—a certain identification of socialism with statification—their exceptionally well argued and documented writing was at once a recognition of and a tribute to the truly astonishing achievement of the Soviet people and communists in building what they had built—built, I may add, with Stalin and despite Stalin. This achievement retains its rich significance for all socialist experiments of the future. Webbs apart, there was Dean of Canterbury's *The Socialist Sixth of the World*, Joshua Kunitz's *Dawn Over Samarkand*, reports by Nehru and Tagore and so much else on the Soviet Union that we mostly avidly imbibed. So many with impeccable credentials had visited there and assured us with Lincoln Steffens: 'I have been over into the future and it works'. 'A land where utopia was becoming reality', Andre Gide had said—that he later turned a bitter critic was, for us, part of a different story. I can still recall the argument which Eugene Vargas' *Two Systems* had, in its own way, endorsed; namely, that given the massive release of people's creativity which socialism ensures as against its pitiful expression under capitalism (or for that matter under all class-divided societies of the past), it is only a question of time before socialism established its superiority and ultimately triumphed over capitalism. A little later we had that 'strange and frightening story' as *Newsweek* called it, *The Great Conspiracy Against Russia* by Sayers and Kahn—a book which should be compulsory reading for every socialist even today. We learnt, yet again, how bourgeoisie conspired and how it lied when it came to the Soviet Union and Socialism! Voracious readers, we devoured all this and despite all the odds, the illegal or semi-legal conditions of life and work, grew ever more firm in our solidarity with the Soviet Union as the first effective breach in the global capitalist system, and in our revolutionary commitment to the cause of freedom and socialism in India. At the time, nothing, literally nothing appeared impossible to us. As the distinguished historian, V.G. Kiernan, my teacher and comrade of those years, recently wrote to me: 'Yes, those were exciting days we lived through when the dear old Party seemed to be soaring towards heaven'. We indeed lived and functioned in 'the actuality of the revolution' as Lukacs once phrased it.

Today it all seems to be so very long ago. Not that the ideal has not held—the ideal of socialism as the historically necessary negation of capitalism, a free, cooperative and democratic society based on a social, *genuinely* social, ownership of the means of production. It has. Through more than five decades, at Lahore or in Delhi, inside the Party or outside, in one form or another, a certain involvement with the socialist cause has always been there: the early activity in the students' movement, years of full-time open or secret work with the Communist Party, including a stint in jail, writing, editing and translating for the party; or later, after the partition, as a teacher, occasionally as a party member, but always as an ordinary activist, often with an understandable love—hate relationship with the diverse currents or formations of the Communist Left, and so on. Through it all I have held on to the ideal of socialism and to whatever little Marxism I came to acquire, finding it useful, beyond politics, not only in my work as teacher but in living my life as well.

But if the ideal has held, it is also true that today the vision is somewhat blurred, due not so much to the passage of time as to the developments of these past few years which, in their totality, indeed constitute an unprecedented 'crisis of socialism' that demands an explanation, an honest coming to terms with it.

Before I attempt such an exercise, it is necessary to make a point which is often obscured in the current euphoria or despair over what has happened. The era that began in 1917 may in one sense be seen as having ended. But it needs to be recognised that when the balance sheet of this era is finally drawn up it will not be as one-sided as on-the-spur-of-the-moment assessments, improvised by the enemies and often meekly accepted by the much-demoralised friends. This era had its dark chapters. But this era was also a saga of struggle and sacrifice by people unparalleled in history, and its achievements are a revolutionary inheritance that will always inspire the poor and the oppressed everywhere in their struggle for a better life. More specifically, I would like to affirm that the 'crisis of socialism' we are witnessing, though diversely damaging in its consequences, takes nothing away from the historic significance of the world's first socialist revolution or from the achievements of either the pioneering experiment in the erstwhile Soviet Union or the world communist movement—the achievements of 'historical communism', as it is being described in certain epitaph-like pronouncements these days.

The October Revolution, a truly electrifying moment in history, by its revolutionary breaching of the world imperialist system, not only heralded the necessary beginning of the new epoch of transition from capitalism to communism—a fact fully vindicated by the historical experience since then—it also achieved the immediate demolition of 'the prison house' that was Czarist Russia, ending age-old oppressions and freeing vast masses of human beings, peoples and nationalities, within its extensive frontiers. Local variations apart, even when led or supported by the Red Army, the changes in Eastern Europe at the end of the Second World War had similar liberating consequences for the common people in these countries.

This historical truth should not be too difficult to recognise or accept. But the pervasiveness of the crisis, the disillusionment and despair accompanying the collapse of the communist regimes in Soviet Union and Eastern Europe, makes it equally necessary to point out that these post-revolutionary societies have had real achievements to their credit in the period following the initial revolutionary transformations, particularly noteworthy if account is taken of the conditions they had to a greater or lesser degree inherited and the circumstances in which they survived and achieved what they did—economic, social, cultural and political backwardness, massive illiteracy, war, civil war and counter-revolution, continuous imperialist intervention in one form or another and, in most cases, a long tradition of centralised authoritarian rule, often imposed from outside, and so on. The record is far, very far, from being only negative as the hostile critics are busy making out today. In the Soviet Union, for example, it is not merely that its prodigies of industrialisation in the 1930s constitute an incontrovertible argument for the capacity of a planned economy to achieve growth—in a single decade it turned the country into the world's second industrial power and created the powerful Soviet state that survived years of capitalist hostility and encirclement and could take on the full might of world fascism and defeat it, an argument well confirmed by the spectacular performance of the Soviets during the years of reconstruction immediately following the Second World War when, with more than 20 million dead and its lands ravaged and economy wrecked by war, rejecting all imperialist aid, through its own planned, self-reliant effort, the country was rebuilt into the world's other super-power. Still more significant have been the other successes of the first experiment in building socialism: the establishment of the right to work and social security for the working people; the equitable distribution of scarcity and reallocation of resources so as to reduce the economic disparities among different, unevenly developed regions; the rapid elimination of the conditions of extreme poverty and the development of social consumption in health, education and cultural life; the breaching of at least some of the traditional forms of sexism and securing unprecedented participation of women in social occupations and political life; the remarkable initial responses to such difficult and complex issues as national oppression or the protection of nature; and, especially in the early years, the extraordinary flowering of human creativity in every sphere and mass participation of workers and peasants in public life, through their Soviets and otherwise. Even though there were retreats later on, tragic distortions and reversals in many areas, including the catastrophically rapid decay of Soviet democracy, the Soviet Union assured for vast masses of its ordinary citizens a life of material security and moral and aesthetic culture far superior to what even the countries of advanced capitalism have to offer to their common people. In Eastern Europe too, under the communist regimes, there were parallel achievements in economic, social and cultural spheres. These achievements even today have a great deal of explosive potential for the revolutionary process of the future in these countries.

The impact of the Soviet Union and the movements associated with or inspired by it has been no less powerful and profound outside of its borders. And this does not refer only to their decisive contribution to the defeat of Fascism. It is no doubt true that while the communist movement attracted to itself some of the finest minds in the first world—writers, poets, artists, scientists and others—it was generally less influential than 'social democracy' as the latter had come to be. Despite its powerful presence in Italy and France, communism could not shift politics effectively in a socialist direction anywhere in Western Europe, though its heroic role in the resistance movements of occupied Europe gained for it extraordinary prestige and popularity which was eventually frittered away, partly because of the Soviet connection. But there is no denying world communism's immense *civilising influence* on capitalism in the First World, in curbing its structurally inherent predatory logic at home and abroad. The very existence and survival of the Soviet Union over these years, together with the communist, socialist or labour movements it inspired or supported, was a most important factor, of course among many others, in persuading the ruling classes in the West not only to cede ground to anti-colonial liberation movements, especially after the Second World War, but also to make concessions to their own people, to establish and enlarge the elementary democratic rights in capitalist societies. It has been pointed out that social welfare provisions were often at their most generous in the West European states bordering the former Soviet bloc; those instituted at a time when the prestige of the Soviet Union was at its highest in the early post-war period, are even spoken of as 'the fruits of 1945'.

Far more significant in the short as well as the long run, perhaps, is the continuing impact of the October Revolution on a world scale, which the erstwhile Soviet Union, in its own much distorted manner, reinforced. Though the immediately following European revolution was betrayed, suppressed or aborted in different countries, the Russian Revolution survived to be a source of constant inspiration for the anti-capitalist revolutionary movements everywhere. What is more, it ignited the world-wide anti-colonial liberation struggles in the periphery and semi-periphery of the global capitalist system. This way well turn out to be its crowning achievement in history. The pioneering exploits of the Bolsheviks, the seizure of power by the workers, gave hope and courage to millions of downtrodden throughout the world. The salvoes from the battleship *Avrora*, heralding a 'Workers' and Peasants' Government' in Russia, sent out the message of Marxism to the oppressed and exploited in the remotest corners of the earth, and with it came the Leninist summons to militant revolutionary politics, which have since moved vast masses of people to resist and rebel and become effective actors in political life, to make their own more or less successful revolutions in China, Cuba, Vietnam, and elsewhere. It needs to be noted that not all these subsequent revolutions were sponsored from above, and, no matter what happens now or in future, together with the Russian Revolution, they remain the landmarks they have been in the saga of humankind's long struggle for freedom and a better life. The Soviet Union, just as it aided the radical causes and the communist movements abroad, also provided help to people's liberation struggles and a certain support and protection when they emerged as revolutionary regimes. That, increasingly, this aid or help, support and protection, was born not of any consideration for world revolutionary process but of mixed compulsions of own history, ideological legitimacy, or 'national interest' and even *realpolitik*, or plain super-power politics, should not be allowed to obscure the signal Soviet contribution to the anti-colonial liberation in the third world. If the world revolutionary interests came to be subordinated to the interests of Soviet foreign policy, the very existence of that policy often acted as a check on the power and expansion of western imperialism. Certainly, the sweep of post-war decolonisation owed much to the challenge and competition resulting from the need for the Western colonial powers to contend with a powerful and prestigious global rival.

Indeed, without 'historical communism', as it has been called, this world of ours would have been a far more inhuman and hopeless place. Beyond its historically specific achievements mentioned above, to which could be added many more, is a somewhat intangible aspect of the social reality around us today, a general illumination, as it were, that bathes all the failed or successful particularities of our age. You have to take only one quick look around to recognise the living presence of 'historical communism' in the enhanced awareness of humankind the world over concerning issues of human dignity, of justice and injustice, of equality, oppression and exploitation, in the voice and hope the poor and oppressed have come to acquire in our times, in the quality and spread of their struggles for a better life and, above all, in their confidence, despite all the retreats and reverses, that they can fight and win their emancipation....

I am aware of the complexities of the historical processes subsumed in the sketchy account above, aware of the need to make qualifications as also to take notice of the terrible, often needless, price paid for some of the achievements. But as E.H. Carr had written: 'The danger is not that we shall draw a veil over the enormous blots on the record of the Revolution, over the cost in human suffering, over the crimes committed in its name. The danger is that we shall be tempted to forget altogether, and to pass over in silence, its immense achievements'. Carr's warning still holds. And today, when the latter temptation seems to have swamped about everything, the point I am immediately wanting to make is the simple one: there is a great deal to be said, even today, even in this hour of 'defeat', for Lenin's Revolution, for the Soviet Union that was, and for the world communist movement—they have another record which holds promise of other possibilities that may yet be. With the spiritual forces set free by it, the hope and inspiration it remains for the struggling poor and oppressed everywhere, the October Revolution of 1917, a *defining* event in history, may yet come to be more universally assessed the way Goethe assessed the French Revolution. After the defeat of the German forces at Valmy, Goethe had said to officers in bivouac: 'From this place and from today there issues a new epoch in the history of the world, and you can say you were present at its birth'.

But the point made, the fact of 'defeat' retains its overwhelming reality. It may be too early or rash to speak of the termination of the historical process that began in 1917, but *the* issue today is the 'crisis of socialism', dramatically highlighted by the collapse in Soviet Union and Eastern Europe and the stampede backward into the world capitalist system. And this evokes memories of another kind, they come rushing in a welter, filtered through time.

Even as I left home and took the road to life and politics with Marxism, among the very first books I read was one then recently published by a professor of Economics at Lahore, Brij Narain, titled *Marxism Is Dead*. Later I was to learn that periodic pronouncements of this sort are the historic destiny of the doctrine of Karl Marx. One that claimed more than the usual attention and was constantly thrown at us was that symposium by six penitents with communist pasts, *The God That Failed* (as if God ever does anything else but fail, at least most of the time). However, I must confess that never before did such a pronouncement sound so convincing as it does today. And the memories, in their rush, travel over that other territory – the territory of doubt and disillusionment over these fifty long years: the dubious aspects of Stalin's pact with Hitler; the sudden switch to 'Peoples War'—'who lives if Russia dies'—whose ambiguities overnight reduced us from heroes in the freedom struggle to its 'traitors'; the dissolution of the Communist International and the post-war surrender of revolution in Greece and the revolutionary possibilities in Italy and France; the embarrassments of Zhadanov's cultural pronouncements, Stalin's foray into linguistics, and the Lysenko affair; the breaking away of Tito's Yugoslavia; the purges of 1945–52 in the Soviet Union and the trials, purges and executions in Eastern Europe, reminiscent of the Moscow trials, purges and executions of 1934–39, in which perished, as we now fully know, among millions of other 'enemies of the people', more than a million communists, including almost the entire leadership of the Red Army and 1108 of the 1966 delegates present, together with 98 of 139 Central Committee members elected, at the 17th Congress of CPSU (B) held in 1934—'the entire flower of the revolution had been butchered', as E.P. Thompson put it later, decimating whatever was left of the 'Party of Lenin'. (Incidentally, this Congress, held in 1934 and known as the 'Congress of Victors', was hailed by Stalin himself for its 'colossal achievements', for 'the decisive results achieved by socialism in all branches of economic and cultural life', for laying 'an unshakeable foundation of a socialist economic system in our country', and so on and so forth).

It is not that we had no idea earlier of this dark chapter of Soviet history. But we believed Stalin entirely—persuaded as much by the weight of evidence made available on the left in support of the trials as by our knowledge of the then rapidly deteriorating international situation (threat of fascism, betrayal at Munich, collapse of the Spanish Republic, the slide towards another world war increasingly sought to be turned into a war against the Soviet Union, etc.). We were in fact all the time learning, without entirely believing though, something of the barbarism, ruthlessness and terror behind some of the Soviet achievements; if ideals had indeed moved millions of Russian people and communists to heroic endeavour, their actual practice had also caused these people and communists untold pain and suffering. Socialism was acquiring, above all in its lack of democratic freedoms, its arbitrary and cruel exercise of political power, an ugly and inhuman face. This was certainly a contributory factor in the working people of advanced capitalist countries turning away from this socialism, though it retained its attraction for the backward, poverty-stricken countries of the third world where an increasing number of people saw in it the promise of rapid economic development and a better life. For us, however, it was socialism as we believed it to be, and socialism by definition has a human face. Its ugliness in Soviet Russia, whatever part of it we were then willing to see, was credibly attributed to its historical origins—hadn't Marx argued against utopianism and written of the 'inevitable defects' in 'the first phase of communist society' as it emerged from the old capitalist society? In any case our official Marxism was content to explain it all, really explain it away most of the time, as so many 'mistakes' or 'distortions', as unfortunate 'deviations' from 'socialist norms'.... Such 'explanation' was not difficult to accept because we knew, and we were daily reminded of it by irrefutable, ever accumulating, new evidence, how wholly unscrupulous the bourgeoisie was in its hostility to socialism, how it lied and conspired against the Soviet Union. The lies and conspiracies of the bourgeoisie indeed stood between us and the truth. For the rest, we were young and youth has its resilience, an optimism or buoyancy that sees and shines through even the most darkened vistas of the future; our idealism, our faith and commitment, well made up for our ignorance, our lack of information and understanding. Besides, despite everything, Marxism for us was a morality that simply would not countenance ethical justification for crime and cruelties in revolutionary politics, a morality which was daily reinforced by the integrity, the dedication and self-sacrifice of any number of communists immediately around us and in the world communist movement. It was one such, Julius Fucik, our comrade, who had written those *Notes from the Gallows*....

And then, as we thus survived in our revolutionary commitment and faith in the Soviet Union, confirming our worst fears, came Khrushchev's report at the 20th Party Congress, to be followed in regular succession, after the earlier rumblings in East Germany, by Hungary (1956), Czechoslovakia (1968) and Poland (1980), interspersed with the American-backed brutal massacre of over one million communists in Indonesia, liquidating the largest communist party in the non-socialist world, and the near total silence of the entire communist world over it, the violent breach between the Soviet Union and China and further splits within 'the socialist world' and the communist movement, the armed conflicts between countries professing socialism amidst widespread charges that some were taking 'the capitalist road', the military misadventure in Afghanistan, and so on, accompanied all the while by authentic news about the stagnation of Soviet economy and society and the continuing degeneration of the Communist Party and its leadership, the rulers of the Soviet Union—the public bestowal of Soviet honours on Suharto, the butcher of Indonesia or the likes of Marcos being as good a symbol as any of this degeneration.... Such are the memories of doubt and disillusionment over the years. And now, finally, no longer the memories but the harsh contemporary reality, the earthquake of 1989-90 and its tremors at Tiananmen Square, the ignominious collapse of Eastern Europe and then of the Soviet Union itself! 'Defeat of socialism', 'triumph of capitalism', the enemies exult and proclaim. And, once again, 'Marxism is dead'.

'Upturned Utopia' is how Norberto Bobbio has described the recent developments in the Soviet Union and Eastern Europe, and to convey the full tragic meaning of the metaphor, he points out that it was 'the first utopia that tried to enter into history', for it was sought to be raised on a real, material basis. Utopias have been with us for a very long time. Religion, for example, has invariably promised a heaven, up there, to its votaries, especially those who have little or nothing down here on this earth—only its details have varied with the varying historical and even geographical contexts of different religions. And there have been the secular versions too, like *Island of the Sun* in antiquity, or those of Thomas More and Utopian Socialists in our times. But all such utopias, religious or secular, were imaginary, like Plato's in *The Republic* which was, as Glaucon put it to Socrates, true only 'in our words'. These utopias indeed played a socially important ideological role in human affairs, but they did so primarily by virtue of their real significance which lay not so much in the imagined ideal they projected as in the implicit critique they carried of the inadequacies of contemporary society. But the utopia now 'upturned' was different—it had dared to move from the realm of 'words' to that of 'things', and seemed to have succeeded, almost, in giving a real expression to the ideal. And even if, for the moment, we must speak in the past tense, it is well to remember what an ideal it was! Even as it claimed the allegiance of any number of master spirits of our time—a Neruda or Picasso, Joliot-Curie or Einstein, Aragon or Hikmet, Brecht or Faiz, to mention only a few from more recent years—it had also the power to move, more than any other ideal in history, millions below, Fanon's 'wretched of the earth', to heroic action in behalf of freedom and dignity of all on this earth. It had behind it, as Gandhiji once said, 'the purest sacrifice of countless men and women who (had) given up their all for its sake'; they had indeed risked everything they held dear, cheerfully braving the hazards of life-long revolutionary struggles, the prison and exile, torture and death in the extermination camps. It was the inspiration of Bhagat Singh when he chose to 'mount the gallows boldly and with a smile', and of Che Guevara when death surprised him in the jungles of Bolivia. Gabriel Peri, on the eve of his execution by the fascists had spoken of it as 'singing tomorrows' of humankind.

'Upturned Utopia' is an understandable description of what has happened, but as a metaphor it has its limitations too. Taken literally, it can be quite misleading. Not only because it is certainly too early to speak of these matters in the past tense, but far more because it simply was no utopia. As 'actually existing socialism', its problems, contradictions and dilemmas, its very nature, were for long a subject of angry or anxious, friendly or hostile discussion among socialists and Marxists of the world. Trotsky onward, and including Mao Tse-tung's critique and Bettelheim's multi-volume *Class Struggles in the USSR*, there is a whole corpus of authentic socialist criticism of what was being built in these post-revolutionary societies. While most hoped, rather wishfully it is obvious now, for a turn from 'actual' to 'real' socialism, and none even remotely anticipated the present ignoble denouement, the analytic comment was uncompromisingly sharp and the forebodings clearly expressed. More than a decade back, for example, Paul Swezy wrote of the very real possibility that the Soviet Society may have reached 'a dead end... with no visible signs of a way out'. And as long ago as 1949, in an explicit statement of his commitment to socialism—'Why Socialism?'—Einstein had, in his own straightforward manner, thus focused on one of the most crucial issues:

> 'Nonetheless, it is necessary to remember that a planned economy is not yet socialism. A planned economy as such may be accompanied by the complete enslavement of the individual. The achievement of socialism requires the solution of some extremely difficult socio-political problems: How is it possible, in view of the far-reaching centralization of political and economic power, to prevent bureaucracy from becoming all powerful and over-weaning? How can the rights of the individuals be protected and therewith a democratic counterweight to the power of bureaucracy be assured?'

Later, equally specifically, the Marxist economist, Lange, wrote, 'The real danger of socialism is that of a bureaucratization of economic life'. And we had the characteristically pungent and perceptive observation of Kalecki: 'Here in Poland we have successfully abolished capitalism; all we have to do now is to abolish feudalism'—he had thus drawn our attention to the formation of neo-feudal structures of power and exploitation in the post-revolutionary societies, which involved not only the denial of political equality, the socialist sharing of power and freedoms, but also a politically coercive appropriation of surplus from the direct producers, very much akin to the feudal mode of production.

There was plenty of such criticism, and obviously, for these socialist critics there was no utopia in the Soviet Union or elsewhere. It is true, however, that these critics, though socialists or Marxists, were strictly speaking 'outsiders' for official Marxism and the mainstream communist parties, and they were treated as such. It is the 'insiders', those who belonged, who really mattered, and for them it was indeed a utopia realised—they saw or heard or spoke no evil!

But now it has become impossible not to see or hear or speak. And much as I would have liked to avoid it, a nagging question persists, especially for the period after the Khrushchev Report of 1956. What of the hordes of these 'insiders', scholars, academics and writers of all sorts, members of friendship societies or peace, solidarity and sundry other international organisations, leaders and functionaries of the communist parties, and so many others, who visited there year after year, often several times in a year, and yet saw and heard nothing— nothing not merely of the terrible costs of forced collectivisation, the deaths of millions of ordinary Soviet citizens and communists as 'internal enemies', the Terror, the Gulag and the labour camps, the purges and executions of the past, or of the growing chauvinism, national and ethnic antagonisms, gender or minority oppression, drunkenness and religiosity, even racism and anti-Semitism, but more specifically and to the point, nothing of the almost mafia-like degeneration of the Communist Party, producing and putting in power Khrushchevs, Brezhnevs, Gorbachevs and Yeltsins, or the self-serving abuse of their monopoly of power by the new rulers to secure a most corrupt and vulgarly luxurious living for themselves—no different from and in many ways worse and more obscene than what Engels spoke of as 'the senseless luxury and extravagance of the present ruling class and its political representatives' in capitalist society. They saw and heard nothing of the yawning chasm that had come to exist between the rulers and the ruled, the total alienation of the people from the powers that be, their indifference, hostility or contempt for the new rulers, the communist leadership, which, denied other avenues, found eloquent expression in the politically explosive humour of popular jokes. Remember the one about Khrushchev's vulgar flaunting of his material acquisitions before his old mother who, impressed, yet has other memories, remains worried, and fearfully asks: 'But son, what if the Bolsheviks come back?' Or the one where a tired and disgusted citizen leaves his never-ending queue in anger to go and kill Brezhnev, only to return, soon, disappointed, for 'the queue there is much longer', and so on.

Scholars, perhaps, one can understand—and I am not here speaking of the far too many hangers-on or racketeers in the academic business and the business of left politics as well. Their mundane interests apart, compulsions of official Marxism or 'party loyalty', together with the dominant methodological orientations and the 'functional rationality' that has come to govern the organised academic disciplines and research, may well have prevented these scholars from seeking the reality behind the appearances; they simply chose to be 'scholars' first and Communists or Marxists only a long time afterwards. But what about others, above all the leaders and functionaries of the fraternal communist parties and allied organisations, whom Lenin once likened to *inspectors* visiting the Soviet Union for a check-up on what was being done? How come they failed to see what a poet, who was a communist too, saw so early and so clearly, namely, the awesome alienation of the people from their rulers. This is what Bertolt Brecht wrote, way back in 1953, when the first rumblings of the coming earthquake were heard and a workers' uprising was suppressed in Berlin:

> After the uprising of the 17th June
> The Secretary of the Writers' Union
> Had leaflets distributed in the Stalinallee
> Stating that the people
> Had forfeited the confidence of the government
> And could win it back only
> By redoubled efforts. Would it not be easier
> In that case for the government
> To dissolve the people
> And elect another?

The communist rulers in Berlin, however, did the next best thing – they went on to build the Wall!

Whatever the motivations or extenuating circumstances, this stubborn refusal to see or hear or speak, when it was their revolutionary duty to see, hear and speak, constitutes an act of historic complicity on the part of these leaders and functionaries that is crying out for atonement, which must visibly express itself, above all, in a return to communist norms of personal conduct and a better, revolutionary practice of Marxism. One can only hope that they have the necessary honesty and courage, for the sake of their comrades in the ranks and the cause they hold dear. One does not have to be a repentent communist to thus come to terms with our past.*

---

* The author has attempted this in his *Crisis of Socialism—Notes in Defence of a Commitment,* New Delhi 2006. A response to the collapse of Soviet Union's 'actually existing socialism', the book deals with the basic issues of the why and how of this collapse, its implications, and where it leaves the question of socialism in our time.

Chapter 2

Of Marxism of Karl Marx*

The collapse of 'Soviet Socialism' needs to be understood as one historically specific outcome of Marxism, implicating only a particular political practice in the name of Marxism. It must not be understood in any abstract or universal terms, as settling the question of capitalism or socialism for all times, or signalling some final demise of Marxism itself.

In recent years, such ahistorical argumentation has been a regular feature of articles and books in the popular press and academic circles, where it has been fashionable to equate the collapse of the communist regimes not only with the collapse of socialism as such but of Marxism as a social theory or political project as well. This has only helped to accelerate a growing sense of self-doubt and confusion on the part of many radical activists and intellectuals, including socialists and communists not only about the future of socialism, but, more important for my immediate argument, about the viability and future utility of Marxism. Even those who, with Hobsbawm concede Marxism a future as a social theory—'that Marx would live on as a major thinker.. could hardly be doubted'—deny it any future

* A chapter, excerpted from the author's *Crisis of Socialism—Notes in Defence of a Commitment*, this was written in response to a request from two friends, most eminent in the fields of literature and people's theatre in Punjab.

as a political project, positing a disjunction between the two which is quite alien to the classical tradition of Marxism. It is important, therefore, to recognise that while there is unquestionably a linkage between Marxism and 'capital "c" communism' of the erstwhile Soviet-type regimes, it was a *historical* linkage, the two are not interchangeable. Marxism as a social theory and political practice that seeks to understand and change the world is not exhausted with the exhaustion of 'actually existing socialism' of the Soviet Union. Marxism retains its validity and viability as a tradition of social theory within which it is possible not only to do social science—that is, identify real causal mechanisms and understand their consequences—but also do it as an emancipatory project for our times, which remains a socialist project. The collapse in the Soviet Union is a defeat for but not of Marxism. Even as we seek to understand it as one outcome of Marxism, rather of a certain Marxist political practice, we must do so in Marxist terms and recognise its historical specificity, which leaves open the possibility of other, better and more successful outcomes of Marxism or, more specifically, of Marxism as a political project that seeks to build a socialist society.

Marxism as such is not my concern in these notes. But, given the overall nature of the issues involved and the fact that the current crisis has made Marxism all the more a controversial topic where its status as a social theory, and even place on the Left, is being questioned, and far too many are in a hurry to reject it as obsolete for reasons which are in the main unjustified, a digression on the subject will not be out of place—no detailed exploration of what Marxism is or is not, but some general observations and a few substantive propositions which may help clarify issues and sustain the contention that, the damage done by the Soviet collapse notwithstanding, Marxism retains its viability and utility as a vital tradition of social theory and revolutionary praxis.

II

Speaking of the conflict between 'reason' and men's 'interests' and of men 'setting themselves against reason as oft as reason is against them', the seventeenth-century English philosopher Thomas Hobbes once wrote: 'For I doubt not, but if it had been a thing contrary to any man's right of dominion, or to the interest of men that have dominion, *that the three angles of a triangle should be equal to two angles of a square,* that doctrine should have been, if not disputed, yet by the burning of all books of geometry, suppressed, as far as he whom it concerned was able'. History of Marxism is well illustrative of this remarkably insightful observation of Hobbes. Marxism, obviously, is 'a thing contrary to the interest of men that have dominion' in our society, it arose as a challenge to all the established authorities—economic and political, intellectual, ideological or academic. Therefore, hostility and prejudice against Marxism, its misrepresentation or caricature, a conscious and continuous effort to either ignore Marxism or distort and denigrate it, should not be difficult to comprehend. Successive generations of bourgeois social scientists and ideologues have felt the compelling need to 'refute' Marx's ideas yet again, and to make periodic announcements of its death and final demise over the last hundred years and more. As a result, what Maurice Dobb, describing Marx as 'one of the least understood of social thinkers', once said of his method of historical interpretation is indeed true of Marxism as a whole: 'it is usually much easier to state in brief what it is not than to expound its positive claims'. And the situation has been only confounded by the 'faithful' who, from the other side, have often approached Marxism almost as a matter of religious faith. Given the intellectual and moral authority that Marxism as a social theory yet acquired, it has also had to pay the penalty for its 'success'—namely its co-optation by alien elements. Here it has been not so much a question of the rapidly spreading, confused and confusing, use of Marxian language, categories and concepts in bourgeois social and political theory. Really significant is the fact that so much of what has gone by the name of Marxism in recent years has little or nothing to do with Marxism as Marx himself understood or practised it. The current crisis has only reinforced all this, the overt hostility and prejudice, the caricature and misrepresentation, ill-informed oversimplification and generally facile disputation in its treatment that Marxism has always faced. The latest here is the post-modernist 'critique'. Marxism is the 'meta-narrative' that post-modernists most like to scoff at. Marxism is treated at its most skeletal and abstract level, ignoring its materialist and dialectical underpinnings; long-dead or settled themes (such as economic determinism or class reductionism, essentialism, functionalism or universalism, etc.) are flogged into some semblance of life to impose on Marxism impossible rigidities, a positivist closure or completeness, which makes it eminently amenable to refutation, indeed final destruction, analytically and otherwise.

It is important to note that critics' questioning or denial of Marxism has been all too often nihilistic in character, born of an implicit, utterly unscientific, 'all or nothing' attitude, an attitude, it must be added, that has been well-sustained, unfortunately, by the claims the 'faithful' have tended to make for their 'science of Marxism'. Marxism is called upon to provide answers to all questions which a supposedly complete system of thought must provide. And since Marxism does not or cannot, it stands condemned. The focus is not on the positive achievements of Marxism but its limitations, its 'silences' or 'empty spaces', which are indeed there, as they are bound to be, and which the classical tradition of Marxism always recognised. Even the slightest qualification to a basic proposition—and these have to be made in social scientific theory to secure better validity—is interpreted as being self-destructive of Marxism. Indeed, the critics have demanded of Marxism or sought to impose on its theory standards which they demand of or impose on no other social theory and which no social theory has yet been able to attain or can possibly attain. For example, even a knowledgeable critic like Barry Hindess has recently demanded that Marxism must specify 'the precise mechanisms' of the relation between base and superstructure! Such 'precision', needless to say, is not demanded of any other theory in the domain of social and historical analysis where in fact relativism of all sorts is readily conceded. Such precision is in fact impossible in social theory and likely to remain so in future. For, as Goethe put it in his own way: 'theory, my friend, is grey, but green is the eternal tree of life'—an aphorism that was quite a favourite with Lenin, the Marxist. Change and interconnectedness of social being, being what they are, our concepts can never fully hold or grasp the concrete, it always spills over the designated territories; a good enough reason, among others, to reject all claims to absolute truth and the possibility of ever finding or revealing it. This however does not imply lapsing into an unthinking kind of relativism which has literally enveloped the social sciences today, a relativism which, incidentally, refuses to relativise itself. As Adorno has argued, even if a concept is lacking in the sort of 'precision' that is demanded, to be concrete, as expression of truth, it yet needs to establish rational identity with its object. Hence his insistence that the dividing line separating Marxism from the currently fashionable relativising sociology of knowledge is the former's commitment to the 'idea of objective truth'. As Lenin put it: 'the materialist dialectics of Marx and Engels certainly does include relativism, but is not reducible to relativism, that is, it recognizes the variability of our knowledge, not in the sense of denying objective truth but in the sense that the limits and approximations of our knowledge of this truth are historically conditioned.' Postulating *growth* of our knowledge of objectively existing reality, without either attaching finality to our knowledge at any stage or lapsing into vulgar relativism, avoiding both the hard rocks of crude positivism and the swampy morass of relativism, Lenin had written: '*The limits* of approximation of our knowledge to the objective, absolute truth are historically conditional, but the existence of such truth is *unconditional* and the fact that we are approaching nearer to it is also unconditional'—though we shall never reach it absolutely. As Engels put it: 'an adequate exhaustive statement.... the formulation in thought of an exact picture of the world system in which we live, is impossible for us and will always remain impossible.'

This is how we have truth as scientific approximation; not 'the absolute truth', or 'the whole truth', but the truth that is ours which, never finally certain or complete and always open to revision, yet reveals, however partially, genuine aspects of an objectively existing world and thus, however relative is nonetheless objective truth, not saying everything about the whole yet enables us to say something truthful about it as a whole.

III

In understanding Marxism, it helps to remember that Marx was not a professional philosopher, a system-builder, offering us, in the tradition of Plato or Hobbes or Hegel, a more or less complete system of thought. Nor was Marxism ever intended to be a 'positive science', an assortment of statements about past and present facts, or a set of predictions about the shape or timing of future events. Not a 'philosopher' or a 'social scientist', Marx was by vocation a revolutionary, 'before all else a revolutionist', as Engels described him. The major thrust behind his systematic theoretical work (pre-eminently represented by *Capital*) was born of his urge to understand the capitalist social order, the system he wanted to overthrow, and most of his other writing was done as part of his revolutionary, that is, Marxist practice of politics. In so far as his work claims to be scientific, it was never science for science's sake or for peers or policy-makers. It was his commitment to the liberation of working classes that drove Marx to gather together the theoretical and factual knowledge that he could muster at the time into a scientific understanding of history in general and capitalist society in particular, and put it at the service of the emancipatory struggles of his time, which remain our struggles today.

Again, in a most important sense, Marx's theoretical work is 'an unfinished project'. Engels' *Anti-Duhring*, that masterpiece of popular exposition and clarification, written with Marx's collaboration and endorsement, does offer a somewhat systematic account of Marxism, but the fact remains that so much of what Marx—according to the plan briefly sketched by him in his letters and prefaces—expressly wished to write under his own name to ensure a clearer and fuller understanding of his ideas—on philosophy (Hegel), or political theory (the State), or, desperately towards the end, at least 'two or three printer's sheets' on method (Dialectics), and much else besides—remained simply unwritten. Part of the explanation lies in

Marx's life and work as a revolutionary—intense practical activity and involvement with men, politics and movements the world over, besides long years of poverty, privation and ill health, 'the humiliations, torments and terrors, (the) *petites miseres* (small wretchednesses)', as Marx himself wrote, of the daily struggle for sheer physical survival, and always the demands and still more the hazards of a revolutionary's life.... Possibly, the high exacting standards Marx set himself for any serious theoretical work also acted as an inhibiting factor. Engels has told us how 'Marx thought his best things were still not good enough for the workers, how he regarded it as a crime to offer the workers anything but the very best'.

Certainly, an important reason was the inescapably necessary, but near-exclusive concern of the mature Marx with his work on 'Economics' as he called it, which yet remained unfinished—thus, for example, the second and third volumes of *Capital* were later put together by Engels, *Theories of Surplus Value* by Kautsky still later, and *Grundrisse* in different editions has become available outside the archives only in our times. (Incidentally, concentration of Marx's mature efforts on the capitalist economy, the outstanding quality of this work and its preponderance in his published writings, together with some of its strong skeletal propositions and their mostly historically conditioned erroneous interpretations, are among the factors which facilitated the widely prevalent economistic interpretation of Marxism). It also needs to be noted that concerned with all of capitalism, Marx lived long enough to view it only from the vantage point of economics (and that too incompletely) and not politics, ethics, ideology, culture, etc. as well, which could have, apart from providing a fuller understanding of capitalism as a social formation, clarified Marx's thinking on these subjects. Marx's writings, including those on economics are, of course, full of brilliant insights into these diverse aspects of social life, and not only in relation to capitalist society. But these insights, Marx's treatment of philosophy, politics, ethics, literature or culture, in fact the realm of the non-economic in general, remained largely untheorised by him. As a consequence of it all, it is not surprising that there are any number of 'silences' and 'empty spaces', inadequacies and ambiguities, in Marx's work, far too many loose threads, the argument often yielding large questions rather than providing neat answers, and the answers always open to questioning and correction... This is, however, as it should be in any scientific enterprise and does not in any way impair Marxism as a body of thought claiming to be scientific.

IV

Within the corpus of Marx's 'unfinished project' we also need to notice and resolve a problem arising out of the inherent variety and quality of his writings. While we do have an authentic, even if somewhat partial, expression of the view of Marx, as of Engels, in works which were put out under the writer's own control, duly corrected and revised for publication —all of which even so are not comparable to each other and certainly not to a writing like *Capital*—there are other works, the early as well as the latter ones, which lack such authenticity and which have come down to us scattered and translated over a long period of time. And these include writings of all sorts: works written in the form of weekly articles and 'under the immediate pressure of events', as Marx said of his famous *The Eighteenth Brumaire*; unpublished or unpublishable mice-nibbled manuscripts in finished, unfinished or fragmentary form; numerous articles and other journalistic, even 'hack' pieces as Marx called them, which he hated having to write; addressees, proclamations, speeches and statements for particular occasions, situations, organisations or audiences; extensive correspondence with diverse addressees, obviously not intended for the eyes of others; private notes and workbooks, often in a personal 'shorthand' and meant only for the writer's own subsequent use (some of which he may himself find difficult to decipher later on), and so on. Hence the problem, namely, determining the *specific nature* and *theoretical status* of each such writing of Marx and Engels. A good example here is Marx's 1853 articles on India published in *New York Tribune*, which were for long treated by the Indian Communists (like the rest of Marxism then available to them under the British rule) almost as sacred texts, as authentic a statement of Marxist theory as anything else written by Marx, including *Capital*. Written in a period of hunger and deprivation, and deep family distress, on payment of desperately needed £1 per article, these were part of what, for nearly ten years, Marx penned away as weekly dispatches covering the widest field of international politics, on European affairs, on the Far East, on India, on the Crimean War, on the American Civil War, etc. Marx himself said this 'continual newspaper muck annoys me. It takes a long time, disperses my efforts and in the final analysis is nothing'. Of course, we would still do well to remember that this is 'muck' written by a Karl Marx. But for himself Marx had insisted that 'purely scientific works are something completely different'.

The point is that all of Marx's writings cannot be treated on par in terms of their theoretical importance or significance. There is always the need for utmost caution in determining their precise nature and theoretical status in each case for purposes of understanding and assessing Marxism—a caution generally observed only in the breach by the critics who have preferred to take every liberty with the texts of Marx, and often disregarded even by many of the professed followers of Marx himself. 'If people could only read,' Marx used to say; we may well add, they also need to know 'how not to quote Marx'!

Again, precisely because Marx's work has come to us the way it has, that is, not as a body of thought systematised by him, we have yet another quite understandable problem. Of course there is continuous growth and development in the thinking of Marx. But obviously he was not some sort of supra-historical genius who would be always fully consistent in what he said or wrote; and what needs to be recognised is that, revision of earlier positions or perspectives apart, there are different and indeed sometimes inconsistent strands in his writings, in those belonging to different periods or even to the same period. Even the same writing may have propositions carrying different, conflicting implications, some of which certainly facilitated the development of grave deformations of his theory later on. One of the gravest of them, for example, could appeal to many statements in the thought of Marx, particularly in popular or propagandist or polemical writings, which either articulated an economistic view or can be reasonably interpreted in an economistic manner, the most famous being Marx's frequently quoted formulation of the doctrine of historical materialism in the preface to his *Critique of Political Economy*. Such statements came to be emphasised and exaggerated, and thus misinterpreted, by the followers in the half century after his death, as part of the justificatory ideology and political theory of the reformist working class movement, which grew up in the industrialised West in the period of emerging monopoly capitalism. Such emphasis excluded other more representative and more important tendencies in his thought, and simply overlooked the overall dialectical orientation of his thinking to which any kind of 'factorisation' of social life is alien. Marx, with Engels, rejected the 'metaphysical mode of thought' as the latter called it, which is 'one-sided, limited, abstract', studies things 'in isolation, detached from the whole vast interconnection of things' and thus, 'cannot see the woods for the trees'. For Marx, as with Hegel, 'the truth is the whole'. Which, however, does not rule out a consideration that goes beyond the question of dialectical or 'metaphysical' orientation in social theory, or of assigning importance to different aspect of social reality or practice. As V.G. Kiernan has suggested, 'the most formidable intellect cannot work at full stretch on human problems except passionately and all original and intense thought must be one-sided; the eye that sees every aspect of the question sees none of them vividly'. 'Passionate' is indeed the word to characterise Marx's theoretical engagements; and it is probably this very passion which infuses his writings with their continuing relevance, just as it also accounts for Marx's ideas and aspirations for humanity at moments outrunning the historical evidence.

Be that as it may, 'economism' was not the dominant thing in Marx, ever. It is not just his insistence that 'the proletarian needs his dignity more than he needs bread', or that 'the realm of freedom', truly *human* freedom, for him lay 'beyond the sphere of actual material production (where) begins that development of human energy which is an end in itself.' Most to the point here is that Marx's theory as well as lifelong practice were for the most part informed by the ideas so succinctly set forth in the *Theses on Feuerbach,* which are thoroughly anti-economistic and speak up for 'revolutionising practice', for human beings changing their circumstances. If anything, as a revolutionary doctrine, Marxism accords primacy not to economics but politics; politics is the cutting edge of the social revolution it argues for. Very early, Marx saw the weakness of Feuerbach's preoccupation with philosophy in that 'he refers too little to politics'. For Marx himself, philosophy had to be realised through politics. This conviction remained central to Marx's lifelong practice as a revolutionary. His emphasis on 'economy' does not refer to any so-called 'economic factor', but to the economic structural basis of society which can be transformed only through revolutionary politics.

V

The economistic tendency within it is suggestive of another important consideration in understanding Marxism of Karl Marx, namely, its intellectual as well as historical context. The former involves bearing in mind what he was variously arguing with, for, or against—notably Hegelian philosophy, classical political economy and contemporary socialism. Thus, for example, if Marx and Engels sometimes put the sort of emphasis they did on 'the economic side' of things, or 'the economic base', tending to set the intellectual or ideological 'superstructure' too far apart from it, it should be remembered that they were polemicising not only against the dogmas of conventional historiography but also the not insignificant threat of philosophical idealism. Accepting part of the blame for 'more stress (being laid) on the economic side than is due to it', Engels himself wrote, 'we had to emphasise the main principle in opposition to our adversaries who denied it' which, he added, gave 'our adversaries a welcome opportunity for misunderstanding and distortions'. Engels specifically disavowed the tendency to economism in Marxism, even though, on occasions, he still succumbed to it.

The historical context of Marx's theoretical work was the nineteenth century and his writing in what he called 'only a little corner of the world—Europe'. This does impart his work a certain Euro-centricity, though some of it is not without its historical justification, for that is where the epochal transition from feudalism to capitalism was most manifest. Yet Europe was only 'a little corner' of the world for him. In his now well-known letter to the editorial board of the Russian periodical, *Otechestvenniye Zapiski,* in response to a critic, 'honouring me too much' as he said, Marx specifically disowned any claims of having provided a 'master key' or 'universal passport' of 'a general historico-philosophical theory, the supreme virtue of which consists in being super-historical'. Rejecting the very notion of such a theory, he insisted that *Capital* contained 'my historical sketch of the genesis of capitalism in Western-Europe', and it must not be metamorphosed into 'an historic-philosophic theory of the general path every people is fated to tread, whatever the historical circumstances in which it finds itself.' And we now know, better than before, that his earlier interest and work apart, the later Marx was primarily busy exploring, in relation to Russia and its backwardness, problems which are today our problems in the third world. Marx's earlier writings, including *Capital,* have their penetrating insights into capital's iniquitous expansion outward and he had more than once pointed to the ravages wrought by capital as it travels abroad. Now he was *beginning* to think in terms of a dialectical relation between the advanced and the underdeveloped countries where capitalism does not spread by creating a homogenised system in the image of the advanced countries that led the way, but rather creates a polarised global system between the developed and the underdeveloped areas so that the two are dialectically interrelated as parts of a single whole but not homogeneous parts and not ones that are ever going to become homogeneous. No doubt Marxism is an offspring of Western-centred thought but what needs to be recognised is that it had, especially as Marx himself was shaping it in his later years, the potential to transcend its European origins and to become a truly universal world outlook—as arguably it indeed became in the twentieth century.

Let me conclude with the basic point of my argument so far on how one needs to go about understanding Marxism. Rich, multiple, and tirelessly creative as Marx's work is, it has its 'silences' and 'empty spaces', and—like all living reality—its contradictory aspects. But to focus on these 'silences' or 'empty spaces', or to abstract any one of its different or contradictory aspects at the expense of ignoring either its context or its place in his thought as a whole is to distort and misunderstand his Marxism. As Gramsci once suggested, what is important is not 'single casual affirmations and isolated aphorisms' but 'the Leitmotiv', 'the rhythm of the thought as it develops'; the need is to look for those 'permanent' or stable, mutually consistent elements that go to constitute the 'essential coherence' of Marx's thought. Describing Marxism as 'a new conception of the world' as also the 'philosophy of praxis', Gramsci wrote that its essential coherence is to be sought 'not in each individual writing or series of writings but in the whole development of the multiform intellectual work in which the elements of the conception are implicit'.

VI

Marx was, of course, very much—as much as anybody else—a 'child of his time' (to borrow an expression from Hegel). This not only involves the implications of not looking for answers in his work which either do not exist or which are not at any rate to be found there, it also involves recognising that Marx too, like anybody else, carried his share of 'the mud of his times', including, for example, a certain gender blindness and ecological short-sightedness. He very much belonged to his age, even as he was, here as elsewhere, in his own magnificent manner, moving beyond it. Immediately important is to notice the fact that it was an age excessively confident of itself, drunk with the achievements of modern science. Marx was not immune to its intellectual or cultural ethos, its language or idiom. It had its impact on his work. And one important negative consequence was that Marx's thought did not always transcend the bourgeois-positivist model of the social science of his time, based on an arbitrary and unqualified extension to the social and historical sphere of the epistemological paradigm of the natural sciences, with its laws, its determinism, its purely objective predictions, linear development, and so on, all expressed in the strong, confident, even dogmatic language of the second half of the nineteenth century. This tendency, however minor, indeed expressed itself in Marx's social scientific work and was, during certain phases of subsequent historical development, pushed to its logical conclusion by a certain kind of Marxism, which besides a certain Eurocentrism, came to be characterised by an entirely unjustified evolutionism, by scientistic, economistic and deterministic interpretation of Marx's theoretical and political writings. Plekhanov and Kautsky are good examples here. 'Economism' in its scientistic expression emerged as the most grievous deformation within Marxism.

Such indeed was the Marxism which came to be dominant in the Second International, where the pursuit of Marxism as 'science' led to a disastrous loss of revolutionary perspective, its replacement by a complacent concern with 'the historical necessity' at work in the socio-economic processes; 'irresistible natural necessity' having made socialism 'something inevitable' (Kautsky), this Marxism simply turned its back on the other necessity, which is yet a free choice, namely, a revolutionary struggle for socialism. In our own times, we have had efforts such as Althusser's, for example, to 'rescue' Marxism in rigorous structural terms, highlighting the scientific credentials of Marxism as against its revolutionary as well as humanist interpretation. The need for epistemological correctness and rigour in matters of Marxist theory and practice is obvious. But to privilege Marxism's scientific potential in such structural, economistic and deterministic terms has only reinforced an earlier tendency and given rise to a most misleading, dogmatic, scientistic Marxism, with its slogans about 'invincibility' of the 'science of Marxism' (or 'Marxism-Leninism'), heard from time to time, and somewhat more loudly these days among desperate, die-hard 'official' as well as 'ultra-left' Marxist circles. By claiming too much for Marxism, without any serious consideration of what really makes it a scientific doctrine, such 'friends' or 'defenders' of Marxism not only give its 'enemies' an easy and welcome opportunity to attack and denigrate Marxism, but also deny themselves access to the immense social scientific potential Marxism really has, and thus fail 'to confront the reality around them with reason' in a truly Marxist manner. To repeat what I have said earlier, if Marxism was indeed *that* kind of science, surely socialism would not have been in *this* kind of mess today. A tribute to the deserved but in some ways dangerously ambiguous prestige that Marxism has come to acquire in our times, among friends and foes alike, such scientism together with the claims that have been made in its name, is absolutely alien to Marxism of Karl Marx.

Here mention may also be made to an associated ideological deformation where Marxism remains 'invincible' simply through a lazy refusal to confront reality. Instead of being used for the methodological investigation of reality through theory and practice, Marxism is misused as a defence against that very reality. There is reference to the total situation, 'the system' as it is conveniently and most superficially called, but no 'concrete analysis of concrete conditions' which Lenin described as 'the living soul of Marxism'. Every conceivable problem is straightway attributed to capitalism, it is seen as the cause of it all, every evil on earth. The argument begins and ends with 'capitalism is to blame!'—a formulation which well serves as a defensive mechanism, a talisman as it were, against the demands of reality. Deprived of its critical subversive power, Marxism turns into an affirmative doctrine, digging behind a series of stereotyped statements or exorcisms which, in their abstraction, are as irrefutable as they are devoid of truth. The commonplace nature of such Marxism renders it politically harmless. In the absence of concrete analysis of a concrete problem, any effective, that is, truly revolutionary intervention here and now is ruled out—a situation which is often accompanied by what can only be described as revolution-mongering, appeals for revolution against 'the system', where revolution itself becomes an empty formula, the ideological mask of passivity.

VII

It is not my concern here to discuss the nature of Marxism as social science or for that matter, the nature of social science itself as a scientific enterprise, which would need to include a consideration of what is valid and not so valid in the conventional critiques of positivism and how Marxism is scientific without being positivist. (In the name of rejecting 'positivism'—now reduced to a vague and pejorative epithet—what is often rejected is any kind of scientific understanding of society.) I will also concede that dogmatism, a deterministic necessitarianism, has a certain usefulness in sustaining faith when the movement is weak, a persecuted minority, or is faced with defeat. Speaking of what he described as 'the fatalistic conceptions' of 'the philosophy of praxis', that is, Marxism, Gramsci wrote:

> When you don't have the initiative in the struggle and the struggle itself comes eventually to be identified with a series of defeats, mechanical determinism becomes a tremendous force of moral resistance, of cohesion and of patient and obstinate perseverance. 'I have been defeated for the moment, but the tide of history is working for me in the long term'. Real will takes on the garments of an act of faith in a certain rationality of history and in a primitive and empirical form of impassioned finalism which appears in the role of a substitute for the Predestination or Providence of confessional religions.

But whatever its usefulness for sustaining faith in difficult times, or partial justification in certain periods of history, such dogmatism, evolutionist or determinist interpretation of Marxism, or 'revolutionary fatalism' as Gramsci called it, surely can never be a long-term support for sustenance and growth of the movement. On the contrary, it has, and can have, only dangerously negative consequences for the movement, because, apart from its inherent passivity, such dogmatism not only means a refusal to study the ever-changing concrete situations, or obscuring of live issues, choices or alternatives before the movement, it has also involved all sorts of problematic claims concerning 'necessities' of history, exclusive possession of 'truth', much too precise predictions and provisions of 'the correct party line', and the infallibility of the leadership on the ground that their decisions reflected the objective working of natural laws, provided by the 'science' of Marxism—'laws of history', or those most dubious 'laws of socialism'—which enabled Foucault even to argue, no matter how mistakenly, that Gulag, as he puts it, is not the consequence of an unhappy mistake but the effect of the 'truest theory in the political order'. It is with good reason that Gramsci, the Marxist revolutionary, had argued for the need to 'pronounce a funeral eulogy' upon such scientistic-deterministic Marxism, and its usefulness for a certain period in the history of the movement notwithstanding, urged us 'to bury it with all due honours'.

Alien as all this was to his Marxism, Marx had found the doctrines of his scientistic, evolutionist disciples in Russia, Plekhanov and others, 'boring' and had expressly dissociated himself from these Marxists. If Lenin's break with their evolutionist-determinist politics was in the authentic tradition of Marxism of Karl Marx and made for the success of the October Revolution under Bolshevik leadership, the scientistic economism of the other parties of the Second International only resulted in the failure of the post-First World War revolutions in the rest of Europe, with disastrous consequences for the future of socialism, not only in Europe but elsewhere too; this failure was a vital factor in the growing deformation and ultimate demise of socialism in the Soviet Union.

VIII

It is worth noticing here that an important proximate, as well as ultimate, possibly the most decisive factor behind the demise of Soviet socialism was the scientistic-economistic deformation of the post-Lenin Marxism in the Soviet Union which, while allowing for a certain kind of even spectacular economic progress, left it essentially incapacitated for coping with the entirely unanticipated situation resulting from the survival of the post-First World War European revolution only in a single, backward and beleaguered country, Russia. I will return to this issue in some detail later. Immediately I would only like to make a brief comment on this deformation which soon found expression in the Stalinist canonisation of Marxism, its reduction, as Roger Garaudy put it, to 'a dogmatic pseudo-scientific positivism dressed up as dialectic'—with its scholastic codification of the three principles of materialism, the four laws of dialectic and the five stages of historical materialism (that is, development), etc., creating 'the procrustean bed on which science and creativity were multilated'.

Stalinist canonisation of Marxism, with its monopolistic claims for itself, became a new orthodoxy which not only came to be identified with Marxism in the public mind and established itself as 'official' Marxism for the world communist movement, it also made possible an easy transition to Marxism being treated, not as the critical social theory it is, but as a religion, something to be invoked on high and holy days, the official preachers providing Soviet rulers appropriate quotations for every occasion from classics of Marxism, now treated as so many sacred books. Reduced to a legitimising ideology for the established social order, this Marxism was utterly incapable of understanding or changing the world which in the Soviet Union meant, above all, effecting a genuine transition to socialism. And it posed no problems, indeed facilitated matters, when Soviet rulers found it convenient to convert to a new ideology, the capitalist gospel according to Milton Friedman.

One aspect of this new 'orthodoxy' in the Soviet Union deserves to be particularly mentioned. Scientism of this orthodoxy, in tandem with the persistent 'economism' within Marxism, which now acquired a new life by the needs or demands generated by the economic backwardness of Russia, found expression in a rigidly structuralist, entirely undialectical, implementation of Marx's *metaphorical* model of base and superstructure, that refused to consider the superstructural dynamics, contenting itself with a vague theory of a determining economic base and a derivative superstructural realm, and ending up almost literally as 'a theory of productive forces'. The dialectic of freedom, which lies at the very heart of Marxism of Marx was trivialised and lost except for apologetic academic exercises or plain propaganda purposes. This could not but lead to grave deficiencies in Marxist theory and practice in the Soviet

Union, apart from the damage this theoretical deformation caused in the allied communist movements elsewhere. ('A bad and dangerous model', E.P. Thompson called it, 'since Stalin used it not as an image of man changing in society but as a mechanical model, operating semi-automatically and independently of conscious agency'. Against this mechanistic interpretation and use of Karl Marx's metaphor, Thompson, while in no way denying the place of 'objective determinations' in historical process, argued for restoration of the authentic Marxist project as one of freeing humanity 'from victimhood to blind economic causation, and extending immeasurably the region of choice and conscious agency'.)

To question scientism in Marxism, the scientistic emasculation or mangling of Marxism, by both its supporters and detractors, is not to deny the scientific credentials of Marxism but to assert them by focusing on how precisely it claims to be scientific, what indeed it has to offer as a critical science of society, with careful attention to certain long-standing misuses of the word 'science'. Marxism is, and needs to be, scientific in its philosophical foundations and commitment to criticism and continuing verification and development of its main principles, postulates and conclusions. It is a living and creative theory that continuously interacts with the reality of the world around it and with the rest of contemporary thought, and grows with the growth of scientific and historical knowledge.

IX

It is important to recognise that Marxism of Karl Marx is a remarkably open body of thought, open in the best *scientific* sense of the word. Of course, in humankind's centuries-old effort to understand society and to change it for the better on the basis of this understanding, Marxism is possibly the most ambitious exercise, so far, ambitious not only in the extraordinary sweep and power of its explanatory theory, its truth, but also in its actual historical achievement. At the same time, Marxism is very modest in its claims and extraordinarily open in its orientation, contrary to the conventional belief, the familiar caricature of

Marxism as a rigid, closed system already in possession of 'the truth', a set of sacred scriptures as it were—a caricature compounded of its opponents' distortions and misinterpretations and nurtured, it must be conceded, by certain trends within Marxism itself that we have already noticed. Enlightenment's notion *'De Omnibus Dubitandum'* ('Doubt Everything') was Marx's favourite methodological principle. Almost every major work of Marx has 'critique' either in its title or subtitle. That is the way he thought you had to approach problems. Engels not only wrote: '(our) dialectical philosophy dissolves all conceptions of final absolute truth, of a final absolute state of humanity corresponding to it. For it nothing is final, absolute, sacred', but also made it a point to state that all knowledge—the Marxist theory not excluded—'contains much more that is capable of being improved upon than that which cannot be improved upon, or is correct'.

Aware of the intrinsically irreducible historicity of their own work and of programmes getting 'antiquated', Marx and Engels, in claiming truth (some truth, that is) for themselves, always postulated a continuous growth of human knowledge and understanding. In a statement remarkable for their age, the Darwinian age drunk on its achievements of science, or 'reason' as they also called it, and breaking sharply with the received philosophical tradition, from Plato to Hegel—which, in Marx's words, again and again sought 'to settle all problems for all time' and regularly demanded: 'Here is the truth! Here you must kneel'—the founders of Marxism proclaimed: 'we are but little beyond the beginning of human history, and the generations which will put *us* right are likely to be far more numerous than those whose knowledge we—often enough with a considerable degree of contempt—are in a position to correct... the stage of knowledge which we have now reached is as little final as all that have preceded it'. It is this self-critical, 'correction'—demanding spirit of Marxism that was underlined by Rosa Luxemburg, when, referring to the second and third volumes of *Capital*, she wrote: 'they offer more than any final truth could: an urge to thought, to criticism and self-criticism, and this is the essence of the lessons which Marx gave the working class'.

And it is precisely this critical spirit underlying Marxism which gives its essential meaning to Engels' adjuration to followers to 'not pick quotations from Marx or from him as if from sacred texts, but think as Marx would have thought in their place'. He had insisted that 'it was only in that sense that the word *Marxist* had any *raison d'etre'*...

This scientific resilience, this openness to 'correction', is really the strength of Marxism and not its weakness, except to religious minds. Behind it lies an explicit assumption about the growth of human knowledge, the endless human quest to acquire a better, more true, understanding of the world. To question the signature of Marx in the course of this quest, to seek to 'put *him* right' if need be, is not to deny Marx but to enter into the freedom of his Marxism.

X

Marxism was open in its origins: it arose, as is well known, acknowledging its debts—a 'critical settling of accounts' Marx called it—to English political economy, German philosophy and French socialism. It is, and needs to remain, open to new ideas, to new data and experience, competing insights and bodies of learning, to newer fields of enquiry. Marxism must continue to learn from other intellectual traditions, confront them not merely for the sake of critique and dismissal but drawing out elements to enrich itself, just as it does so through corrections, rectifications and criticisms inspired by its own experience and social practice. To be able to grow and develop as a living creative theory, Marxism has to recognise that it 'cannot generate all its intellectual capital out of its own resources', as V.G.Kiernan has put it; it must be receptive to what may possibly be secured from competing theories. Equally, if not more, Marxism needs to be self-conscious and self-critical about its own inadequacies and responsive to new challenges and demands. It is only such an open and honest, self-critical and creative Marxism that can remain current and relevant, and survive to play its vital role in the ongoing struggles and the struggles that lie ahead, as people persist with their quest for a just and humane, an egalitarian social order to replace capitalism.

There is an aspect to the new challenges and demands which is important enough to be specifically noticed. It is that Marxism today needs to respond to problems of the present-day world which were not recognisably the problems in Marx's time, especially those raised by the 'new social movements' as they are called, the struggles around such issues as feminism, ecology, democracy and human rights, rights of national, religious and ethnic minorities, race and caste oppressions, oppression of dalits and tribals communities, and so on. Not that these issues or struggles are alien to Marxism or that Marx and Engels were unfamiliar with or uninfluenced by them, or had nothing to say about them, at least most of them. On the contrary, even as it is, these issues or struggles carry the imprint of Marxist thought on them, many of those involved have belonged to Marxist parties or are familiar with Marxism, and many more are turning to it as they learn from their experience and recognise the need to articulate their struggles with class struggle. Even so, the fact is that these struggles have developed outside of or remained generally neglected by the organised socialist movement led by Marxists (or, for that matter, by others). That such struggles should have developed outside its ranks can even be seen as a sign of the bankruptcy of the socialist movement in recent times. Today these struggles and issues involved have acquired an importance all their own and call for a specifically new and positive response from Marxism. This is what Marxist openness of theory and practice immediately demands.

XI

Having argued on behalf of 'openness' in Marxism, a word in defence of 'orthodoxy', properly understood as a commitment to basic principles, will perhaps not be out of place, especially in view of certain recent developments within or around Marxism, or at its 'frontiers' as the 'going beyond' fraternity likes to claim.

'Openness' is integral to Marxism, and its value is almost impossible to overrate today in view of the long and persistent tradition of a certain other practice of Marxism, which has been 'officially' or otherwise, dogmatic, sectarian or scientistic, even to the point of reducing Marxism to a political catechism, the ossified 'commonsense' of the average Party cadre, or an ideological device for legitimising Communist Party leaderships and the erstwhile communist regimes. It is necessary to argue for 'openness' in the context of all this and so much else that has disfigured and stultified Marxism in our times, resulting in repeated failures to respond effectively to the changing historical situations and to particular national conditions. But then 'openness' is not a value in itself, a self-evident or self-validating good. And at a time when anything and everything has claimed the fashionable mantle of Marxism or Marxism of some hyphenated kind or the other, and in the name of 'openness' even a surrender or falsification of basic Marxist positions has been passing for Marxism, a certain orthodoxy, a commitment to 'Marxism of Karl Marx', I believe, is not only in order, it is necessary, if one would take the issues of socialist theory and practice seriously. In other words, the 'open' character of Marxism notwithstanding, there are basic, principled Marxist positions which cannot be abandoned without ceasing to be a Marxist.

Not a closed or finally definitive theory, certainly not one forever sealed and delivered at the death of Marx, or that of Lenin or Mao or anyone else for that matter, Marxism is yet not so open that anything goes—a room you can enter by an open door and leave by another, at will, and remain a Marxist all the while. This has been quite a phenomenon in recent years, with such Marxists either unaware or refusing to see that in 'further developing' Marxism, they have been really exiting from it. That they have generally preferred to call themselves 'post-Marxist' is understandable. 'Marxism' lends intellectual and moral prestige and, as mentioned earlier, 'post-Marxist' has a nicer ring to ears than the alternative 'ex-Marxist'. (This, incidentally, provides a good example of Hayakawa's distinction between 'purr' and 'snarl' words, the value-load that language itself invariably carries, something that 'value-free' or 'ethically neutral' fraternity in social sciences is oblivious of.) The new tag however cannot hide the truth that in fact Marxism has been abandoned. If the critics, saving themselves the trouble of engagement with particular issues or debating the empirical validity of this or that Marxist concept—which would after all require a developed knowledge of not vulgar but authentic Marxist traditions—are happily busy pulling the ontological or epistemological carpet out from under Marxist or any other radical thinking as such, so many on the Left, knowledgeable and serious scholars otherwise, too have been engaged in similar or parallel exercises of their own, thus adding their own 'Marxist' endorsement to the familiar proclamation of the 'obsolescence' of Marxism. In ridding themselves of the sin of 'orthodoxy' and revising earlier 'Marxism' to make Marxism suitable for our post-modern times, they have been simply revising Marxism out of existence and doing so as Marxists, or as they prefer to describe themselves as 'post'- or 'neo'- Marxists. We have already noticed how this 'revision' or 'updating' of Marxism has often meant only a regression into social democratic non-Marxism or, further down, into the long-discredited bourgeois orthodoxies of yester years. That they have chosen to describe all this as 'going beyond' Marxism, only reminds us of what Sartre had said. Stating that 'Marxism is the ultimate possible horizon of our age', he had added, 'and attempts to go beyond Marx frequently end up *falling* short of him.' For Sartre it cannot be otherwise. As he put it:

> The periods of philosophical creation are rare. Between the seventeenth century and the twentieth, I see three such periods, which I would designate by the name of the men who dominated them: there is the 'moment' of Descartes and Locke, that of Kant and Hegel, finally that of Marx. These three philosophies become, each in its turn, the humus of every particular thought and the horizon of all culture; there is no going beyond them so long as man has not gone beyond the historical moment which they express. I have often remarked on the fact that an 'anti-Marxist' argument is only the apparent rejuvenation of a pre-Marxist idea. A so-called 'going beyond' Marxism will be at worst only a return to pre-Marxism; at best, only the rediscovery of a thought already contained in the philosophy which one believes he has gone beyond.

XII

Before I note Marx's concern for theory and affirm a few of the basic positions in Marxism which, for the present at least, cannot be surrendered or revised without ceasing to be Marxist, there is another aspect of the recent developments within Marxism that deserves to be taken note of.

While 'official Marxism', religiously dogmatic in theory and unashamedly revisionist in practice reigned supreme in the politics on the left, often serving only as a legitimising ideology in the 'socialist world' and the communist movement, the post-Second World War period saw Marxism acquire a new lease of life in the academies of the West. As the centre of Marxist scholarship came to be displaced from Germany and the South-European countries to the United States and England, mid-1970s onwards there was an unprecedented growth, a virtual deluge of Marxism in these countries—numberless philosophical and exegetical works, politically-desiccated culture studies, and a variety of Marxisms—'Analytical', 'Neo-classical', 'Game Theoretic', 'Rational Choice', etc. This certainly filled up a few 'empty spaces', lighted up some dark corners, clarified many unresolved issues and made for greater rigour in Marxist theoretical debates. But whatever the gains, it was a deluge of academic or 'theoreticist' Marxism which was in the main a shift away from the traditional or core concerns of classical Marxism as a critical social theory and a revolutionary doctrine. Marxism became an academic discipline, a subject for study in the universities. An academic or professional Marxism (as Luxemburg called it), it did the same kind of things as the ordinary academic scholarship and came to share a lot of features or weaknesses of the mainstream academic world: divisions into fields, kinds of specialisations, self-serving scholasticism, needless apparatuses—more for credential than intellectual purposes—circular references to authorities, complaisant self-citations, elaborate vocabularies and involved, near-incomprehensible manners of expression including, as one comment has it, 'standards of writing that would have left Marx or Morris speechless', and so on. Even outside the universities, it came to acquire similar academic, fragmentist and scholastic features. The significant fact is that whatever its strength or weakness, unlike 'official' Marxism, which it scoffed at and rejected, this Marxism had no ties at all with Left political movements at home nor any links with liberation struggles or other emancipatory movements stirring in the third world. Some sort of 'intellectual Marxism' that Trotsky once spoke of, 'a Marxism which ends only in thinking and not acting', this Marxism was and remains essentially impotent politically.

This is how Douglas Dowd saw the situation in the early 1980s: noticing that 'the years since the Second World War have unquestionably produced more people in the United States who see themselves as Marxists, more Marxist periodicals and books, more university and other classes taught by Marxists... than at any time in US history', he wrote:

> But in the same years, and despite growing widespread cynicism, skepticism, despair, and anger of ordinary working people concerning various aspects of the society (though seldom 'the system'), the upsurge of Marxism has just unquestionably coincided with—not, one trusts, caused—a noticeable decline in the overall political effectiveness of the Left in the United States, and an associated dimming of prospects here for even a mildly improving, let alone a democratic socialist society. The Marxists, mostly out of, or still connected with, universities, tend to function like a suburban swimming pool: self-contained and self-purifying.

More recently, John Saville has written:

> There are more Marxists in Britain today than there have ever been; there are more socialist books on the shelves than at any previous period; and there are serious journals of the Left. The gap, however, between socialist theory and socialist practice continues to widen, and while we are not yet in the American situation, where an annual meeting of 3000 socialist scholars can meet in New York with almost no impact on practical politics, we do seem to be moving, albeit slowly, in the same direction.

And we have the cryptic comment of a sympathetic observer, Hugh Stretton, which has a relevance beyond its bare statement:

> I do not believe the workers of the world can expect much benefit from the feuds which entangle some contemporary Marxists in

> the concerns of Althusser, Habermas, and other obscure but rigid elaborators of Marx.

Confirming this, we have Alan Sokal's most recent 'why confession' as he calls it:

> I am an unabashed old Leftist who never quite understood how deconstruction was supposed to help the working class.

XIII

With the collapse of the Soviet Union the situation is obviously not the same, it is changing, though not necessarily for the better. But this paradoxical phenomenon of Marxist scholarship flourishing in countries where there seems to be less class consciousness and less of an organised Left movement, of Marxism becoming a theory without movement, does continue to have a certain relevance, even if of a negative sort, for the present and future of Marxism. It is not my concern here to explore this phenomenon in any detail. A reaction away from 'official Marxism' and the communist movement guided or misguided by it, could be one possible cause for it. Maybe 'functional rationality' that comes to govern organized academic disciplines has something to do with it—intellectual fashions emerge and are driven by peer group considerations and a competitive logic, which even when it involves shifts within, even displacement and succession, yet keeps scholarship away from substantive concerns. There could also be the more important impact of the failure of the Left at home, the disastrous experience of Marxist-led regimes in the third world, and the continuing, eventually terminal, crisis of the communist regimes in the Soviet Union and East Europe. The absence of an effective political organisation capable of coordinating the whole range of political oppositional struggles against capitalism, including that at a plausible theoretical level, was certainly a factor in the situation. All this and more that can be said in this connection explains but does not justify. In a somewhat justificatory explanation we have been told: in reactionary times Marxism has become the province of intellectuals operating without any popular base in society and has lost its bearings. But the fact remains that this Marxism has offered little or nothing by way of guidance or sustenance to people struggling against these reactionary times as Marxism has indeed done, and not lost its bearings, in other such times. Perhaps there has been safety too in staying away from politics and political struggle. Scholars are not known to be immune to such or similar considerations.

Whatever the explanation or justification for it, this Marxism, a theory without a movement, is a significant phenomenon within Marxism. It has been quite influential in its own way, finding adherents even among the academic and intellectual circles in the far-off lands of the third world. Its real importance perhaps lies in providing, understandably enough, a breeding ground for post-Marxism, when it was not itself already post-Marxist. What is more, those who came to Marxism via this route, in the West or the East, have generally made an easy and natural transition to post-modernism—and carried its political impotence with them. (Incidentally, how you come to Marxism is an important question—via this academic Marxism or 'official' Marxism once sanctioned by Moscow, via Lenin or Mao, or, more recently, Rosa Luxemburg or Gramsci, or for that matter via Stalin or Trotsky and the Fourth International. They have all contributed to Marxism, some more and better than others. But it is still best to come to Marxism via Marx and Engels).

Marx sure would have difficulty in recognising a Marxism that is all theory and no movement, just as he would have in recognising that other scripture-quoting 'official Marxism' with its scientistic 'Brahmanical' concern for 'ideological purity'. Much is made of the scholarship involved in this Marxism and there is no denying it either. But a revolutionary, Marx was a scholar too, a 'man of science' as Engels put it. And typical of this 'man of science' is his response to the news of the great run his theories were then having in the Czarist Russia. On December 14, 1882, Karl Marx, old, sick and dying, thus wrote to his daughter Laura Lafargue:

> Nowhere is my success more delightful to me; it gives me the satisfaction that I damage a power which, besides England, is the true bulwark of the old society.

Yes, *damage* is the word. One wonders how much of recent Marxist scholarship can claim this quality for itself?

A distinguished Marxist himself, G.E.M. de Ste Croix once wrote of 'the disastrous developments of Marx's thought by many of his followers'. We have noticed some of these in the preceding pages. Of his disciples in another age—the French Marxists of the late 1870s—Marx had said: 'All I know is that I am no "Marxist".' He would have felt much the same about quite a few 'Marxists' of our own, more recent times. As the German poet Hans Magnus Enzensberger says in his moving short poem, *Karl Heinrich Marx* :

I see you betrayed
by your disciples:
only your enemies
remained what they were.

XIV

A concern for theory has been central to the authentic Marxist tradition. As a scientific as well as revolutionary doctrine, it visualises the relationship between theory and practice as a dialogue, a dialectical relationship in which theory guides practice but is modified and enriched by the experience offered by practice. That is how it grows in truth and this truth matters. Theory cannot act as a guide to practice—subject to modifications imposed on it by practice—unless it offers a true account of the nature of the social world. Marxism emerged and saw itself, and still sees itself, not as anything complete, perfect or final, but as the most adequate, preeminently true and fertile theory for the emancipatory practices of our time.

Marxism's concern for theory has to be noted and emphasised not only for its intrinsic importance but also because, along with proclamations of 'obsolescence' or 'death' of Marxism, it has been claimed that 'there is no such thing as Marxism', and in support is mentioned Marx's revelation of his own non-Marxism. This is Marx's often cited statement which we have just noticed: 'All I know is that I am no "Marxist"'. The citing seems to have accelerated in recent years, it is doing the rounds today in seminars and conferences, learned articles and books, and espoused by an increasing number of Marxists gone 'open-minded' in order to gain respectability and acceptance among their bourgeois peers. This rather pointed quip is one of the most misunderstood and misleading of the quotes from Karl Marx. In betraying its utter ignorance of Marx and Marxism, the misrepresentation here only lends substance to Marx's complaint: 'Yes, if people could only read'! Aware of the power of 'thought'—'As soon as the lightening of thought has struck deep into the virgin soil of the people, they will emancipate themselves and become men'; or again, 'Theory becomes a material force once it has gripped the masses'—Marx was extremely sensitive to matters of theory, his own and that of his opponents, and waged a lifelong struggle in defence of his own ideas not only against his opponents, but also un-understanding followers. This quote is precisely an expression of this sensitivity and thus means the very opposite of what it is made out to be by hostile critics or 'open-minded' and ignorant friends. Marx's expression is really a comment on the then prevalent 'so-called "Marxism" in France', 'an altogether peculiar product', according to Engels. Marx felt compelled to tell his son-in-law, Paul Lafargue, face to face, that he and other French Marxists of the late 1970s had not understood his theory and politics. A comment on the incapacity of would-be disciples to understand his ideas, what the quote really means is this: if what you people are putting out is Marxism, then I am no Marxist! Commenting on parallel misunderstandings or misinterpretations of Marxism, Engels had once written of 'how not to translate Marx'. Here we have a good example of 'how not to quote Marx'.

[Another example that immediately comes to mind and is important enough for a disgression is the notoriously common misunderstanding of Marx regarding his reference to religion as 'opium', where a completely out-of-context sentence is quoted to foist a vulgarly instrumental, Voltairean view of religion on Marx. What Marx says is entirely different from, if not opposite of, what is attributed to him, and what he says is part of no theorisation on religion proper, only a brief reference in a fragmentary piece of writing where Marx is 'settling accounts' with his predecessors. Marx is here concerned with redefining the object of philosophy. Philosophy must criticise not religion (as Feuerbach and others would have it) but the real world, of which religion is merely the 'halo'. With Marx, not critical thought but the revolutionary transformation of society will emancipate mankind. Here is the relevant extract from Marx's *A Contribution to the Critique of Hegel's Philosophy of Right*:

> The foundation of irreligious criticism is: *Man makes religion*, religion does not make man. Religion is indeed the self-consciousness and self-esteem of man who has either not yet won through to himself or has already lost himself again. But *man* is no abstract being squatting outside the world. Man is *the world of man*, state, society. This state and this society produce religion, which is an *inverted consciousness of the world*, because they are an *inverted world*. Religion is the general theory of this world, its encyclopedic compendium, its logic in popular form, its spiritual *point d'honneur*, its enthusiasm, its moral sanction, its solemn complement and its universal basis of consolation and justification. It is the *fantastic realization* of the human essence since the human essence has not acquired any true reality. The struggle against religion is therefore indirectly the struggle against *that world* whose spiritual *aroma* is religion.
>
> *Religious* suffering is at one and the same time the *expression* of real suffering and a protest against real suffering. Religion is the sigh of the oppressed creature, the heart of a heartless world and the soul of soulless conditions. It is the *opium* of the people.
>
> The abolition of religion as the *illusory* happiness of the people is the demand for their *real* happiness. To call on them to give up their illusions about their condition is to *call on them to give up a condition that requires illusions*. The criticism of religion is therefore in *embryo* the *criticism of that vale of tears* of which religion is the *halo*.
>
> Criticism has plucked the imaginary flowers on the chain not in order that man shall continue to bear that chain without fantasy or consolation but so that he shall throw off the chain and pluck the living flower. The criticism of religion disillusions man, so that he will think, act and fashion his reality like a man who has discarded his illusions and regained his senses, so that he will move around himself as his own true sun. Religion is only the illusory sun which revolves around man as long as he does not revolve around himself.

> It is therefore the *task of history, once the other-world of truth* has vanished, to establish the *truth of this world*. It is the immediate *task of philosophy*, which is in the service of history, to unmask self-estrangement in its *unholy forms* once the *holy form* of human self-estrangement has been unmasked. Thus the criticism of heaven turns into the criticism of earth, the *criticism of religion* into the *criticism of law* and the *criticism of theology* into the *criticism of politics*....

Marx's brief reference here is characteristically profound in its understanding of religion as a 'spiritual' phenomenon. (Elsewhere, his Marxism is fully accommodative of the *historical emergence* of religion as the ideology and practice of several significantly progressive or radical social movements). Marx's criticism of religion is, in effect, a criticism of our world—this 'vale of tears', its 'real suffering' and 'human self-estrangement' —and a plea for a different, changed world, no longer heartless or soul-less, with human beings, having thrown off their chains, able to 'pluck the living flower', that is, fulfill themselves right here on this earth. In practical-political terms, Marx's view is a demand that the criticism of religion must become criticism of the society that makes religion both necessary and possible. It is a demand for a just and truly humane social order.]

Digression made, let me return to the issue under discussion, namely, Marx's sensitivity in matters of theory. This sensitivity is, of course, indicative of the importance of theory in Marxism as a revolutionary doctrine, and the importance Marx himself attached to his theories. But I have drawn attention to it primarily to point out the fact that there *is* such a thing as Marxism, that we can legitimately speak of an authentic Marxist tradition. It has its 'empty spaces' and 'silences', its share of anomalies and unresolved problems, and contradictions too. But all this notwithstanding, it has its basic propositions which hold together as an eminently self-consistent body of thought and which cannot be abandoned without ceasing to be Marxist. No doubt Marxism has suffered several serious, though by no means fatal, political defeats, but none of its basic positions have been refuted, let alone replaced by those offered by any more powerful alternative or successor. Marxism continues to be not only a viable, indeed a robust, social scientific research programme, but its core insights remain indispensable to any serious emancipatory project for our times which, insofar as it has to be in opposition to and a negation of capitalism, can only be socialist in its proximate direction and ultimate outcome. Rosa Luxemburg's claim, however, strong or monopolistic it may sound these days, is still substantially true: 'no socialism... outside of Marxist socialism'. At the very least, no emancipatory struggle in this capitalist era can ignore or bypass Marxism and yet hope for success.

XV

Critiques of Marxism, of course, continue, suitably sophisticated to be in tune with the times, that is, with the fashionable post-Marxist or post-modernist trappings. There is the occasional insightful writing, but most often only a rehashing of the old, much-too-tired themes: Marxism is scientistic and monadic (and, therefore, also authoritarian), it is determinist and teleological and class reductionist, its objectivism is denial of the role of the subjective, and so on. If, oblivious of the dialectics of men and circumstances in Marx—that Marx so well expressed in his early *Thesis* on *Feuerbach*—Karl Popper once condemned Marxism as the most dangerous 'Historicism' (which denies the importance of 'human will, consciousness and intelligence', regards ideals as largely impotent or irrelevant, and reduces man to 'a pawn', 'a somewhat insignificant instrument in the general development of mankind'), and about the same time, Michael Oakeshott denounced Marxism for exactly the opposite reasons, as a most dangerous 'Rationalism' (which gives high importance to man, his reason and freedom of action, to the role of ideas and ideals as human beings go about making their own history), armies of such straw persons continue to be set up and duly annihilated as Marxism, by positing new or resurrecting old rigid oppositions between men and circumstances, between freedom and necessity, between objectivism and subjectivity, between strict inevitabilism and indeterminacy, between monadic, linear causality and non-causality, between single agency and unstructured multiplicity, between scientism and rejection of science, and so on—all of which is alien to the materialist dialectics of Marx and which Marxism rejects. Characteristic of the current criticism, post-Marxist or post-modernist, is its near-exclusive preference for a supposedly 'philosophical' attack on Marxism. More than questioning substantive Marxist propositions and analytic concerns, or denying particular historical materialist postulates, such as the systemically *capitalist* nature of the modern industrial order, which is hardly to be denied, the critics have sought to undermine, if not wholly reject, the philosophical basis of Marxism as an explanatory enterprise. In the currently fashionable post-modernist philosophical disputes, conducted in its own incomprehensible or obfuscating jargon, to accuse any theory of working with concepts described as 'reductionism', 'essentialism', 'functionalism' or 'universalism' is deemed sufficient to dismiss it entirely. And the 'modernist' theory that most prominently stands accused of committing these four 'methodological sins' is Marxism. The critics' analyses which question and reject these concepts have consistently refused to face the fact that these concepts, properly used, are literally integral to any useful form of intellectual activity. Indeed, without some version of these 'four sins of modernist thinking', as they have been called, the very notion of explanation in social theory cannot be sustained. Used not in a crude or vulgar but properly nuanced and sophisticated manner, they are simply inescapable in any searching explanatory endeavour. Of course, insofar as certain practitioners of Marxism have been guilty of their crude or vulgar use, such Marxism is deserving of criticism. But it seems that even the best of critics, including many sympathetic ones, have generally preferred to go in search of only vulgar Marxism—or what Sartre once called 'lazy Marxism'—in order to secure credibility for their attack, rather than confront the authentic Marxist tradition, which I have chosen to describe, somewhat symbolically, as 'Marxism of Karl Marx'. In which case they may have well hit upon what really needs to be done, and is also worth doing, namely, going to Marx not to find what is not there or is flawed, dated or gone vulgar, but to discover what his Marxism nevertheless offers as a critical social theory. And it has a great deal to offer, far more than any other tradition of thought in our or any other times. Again, it is this which accounts for its strength and continuing relevance.

Criticism is welcome, even of the mistaken kind. A reminder of the deformations, of what has gone vulgar, compels us to look within for the tendencies which too have contributed, and seek rectification. But surely this does not mean replacing 'lazy Marxism' with a still more lazy 'post-Marxism' or 'post-modernism'. The real task lies elsewhere. It is to recover the classical tradition of Marxism, its basic positions or components as they emerge from the vital and mature works of Marx (as of Engels) and his lifelong practice, and the works and practice of followers who remained 'fidel' to him.

These positions ranging from a most general view of the world and man's place in it, of human life and destiny, to particular principles or doctrines, concerning philosophy, science, economics, politics and ethics, culture, art and literature, and so on, are not an eclectic affair. They are interrelated and cohere together in a way that gives Marxism its distinctive identity as a body of scientific thought which retains its validity and relevance today. Open and undogmatic methodologically, skeptical in the true scientific sense, this Marxism yet cannot accommodate anything and everything, certainly not the various forms of currently fashionable hyphenated Marxisms. Its basic positions, as already stated, cannot be abandoned without ceasing to be Marxist. They can only be abandoned if the growth of our knowledge so decrees. As I said at the beginning, Marxism as such is not my concern in these notes. It would suffice for my purpose here to offer, even at the risk of being charged with dogmatism or oversimplification, a bare statement of some, only some, of its basic positions as I understand them.

XVI

Marxism, with its twin philosophical premises of materialism and dialectics as formulated and interpreted by the founders—to be distinguished from 'official' Marxism's 'dialectical materialism', 'that dreadful term', as Althusser was once compelled to call it, which surely put generations of young and old Soviet citizens off Marxism and bored or frightened as many away from it elsewhere—provides the basis for any viable scientific world view today. Its materialism accepts the reality of the world 'just as it exists without any foreign admixture', as Engels put it, or as Einstein saw it: a law-governed 'world of things existing as real objects'. This is a world existing independently of our knowledge, and the objectivity of ideological or socio-cultural constructions in no way contradicts the materialist postulate concerning the chronological and ontological primacy of being over consciousness. For dialectics, viewed in its most general form, this world is a complex, multi-level, evolving world of contexts, connections, contradictions and processes, a 'whole vast interconnection of things' that is constantly changing, 'coming into being and passing away', evolving through contradictions and conflicts, the interaction and interpenetration of various, often contradictory, components. It is a world whose dynamic of self-development accommodates not only quantitative changes, but qualitative leaps as well, transformations and counter-transformations in which realities are at the same time preserved and transcended in ways that seem to defy logic, unless one's logic is dialectical. Integral to a dialectical materialist world view are the beliefs that this world is knowable, that is, can be rendered intelligible within a unified framework of principles, that 'all science would be superfluous if the appearance, the form, and the nature of things were wholly identical' (Marx), that 'the truth is the whole', and while the search for truth is unending, and absolute truth is out, there is genuine growth of our knowledge (as of mortality too) in the course of human history.

Philosophy as our most general way of looking at and making sense of the world is of utmost importance for how we live, think and act in the world. And literally everyone has, and has to have, a philosophy. There is none so poor as not to have philosophy of his own and none so rich either as to be able to do without one. As A.E. Taylor has pointed out, 'we have no choice whether we shall have a philosophy or not, but only the choice whether we shall form our theories consciously and in accord with some intelligible principle or unconsciously and at random'. In other words, the only real choice is to have a philosophy as rational and scientific as we possibly can make it, that is, as much in correspondence with the nature of things in general as our current stage of knowledge allows—and this is precisely what Marxism as a philosophy offers. It is indeed *the* philosophy for our times; at the very least, Marxism has to be central to any sane way of looking at and acting in the world today. As a corollary of its revolutionary politics, Marxism accepts the obligation to, as Mao said, 'liberate philosophy from the confines of the philosophers' lecture rooms and text books and turn it into a sharp weapon in the hands of the masses'.

We may here notice the way Paul Baran has put the argument. Speaking of Marxism as 'an intellectual attitude or a way of thought, a philosophical position', he has described its 'fundamental principle' as 'continuous, systematic, and comprehensive confrontation of reality with reason.' Not that this principle originated with Marx and Engels. It has been central to all progressive thought in history and there already existed a great philosophical tradition which centred on the critique of reality in the light of reason and whose aim and purpose was to seek out and establish the prerequisites or conditions for the growth and development of human beings. 'Yet it was left for Marx and Engels to make a decisive step forward in this centuries-old effort at confronting reality with reason. They translated the notions of both reality and reason from the metaphysical abstractions and idealistic assertions—the forms in which they appear in most-pre-Marxian thought—into living, concrete categories of real, continuously moving, continually changing, human existence.' That is, they put them on a basis at once materialist and dialectical. As such, Marxism by no means implies a dogmatic finding as to what defines reason or what constitutes reality at any given time. For it, the task of any fruitful intellectual endeavour is, as Baran puts it:

> to define and continuously redefine the meaning of reason, to assess and continuously reassess the structure of reality—confronting systematically the one with the other, pointing out

> the shortcomings of the concrete, specific reality in terms of equally concrete, equally specific standards of reason. Remaining realistic because it derives its frame of reference from the study and observation of the attained stage of historical development, and retaining the courage to be utopian because it sets its sights on the not yet realized but already visible potentialities of the future, such intellectual effort performs an overridingly important function: it serves as a guidepost to the next steps in mankind's forward movement.

This is precisely the task that Marx carried out for his times which are our times too; that is, he confronted the reality of capitalism with reason to provide us a guidepost to the next step, which is socialism in humankind's forward movement. Marx's *Capital* is an exemplary exercise in the use of the dialectical materialist method where, moving from appearance to reality, from form to substance, from immediate external relations to deeper lying inner interconnections, he explores 'the hidden structure' or 'the inner physiology' of capitalism to explain—and explanation, not description, however impressive, is the essence of a scientific theory—how capitalism emerges and functions as a system (a systemic whole), and what possibilities, both positive and negative, it holds for the future of humankind. Marx's is an explanation and prognosis that still holds.

XVII

This brief reference to Marx's achievement in *Capital* should make it clear that Marxism, its comprehensive materialism embracing both the physical and social realms, believes in the universality of scientific endeavour. Science illuminates the natural world. However differently and relatively less adequately, but using fundamentally similar though specifically different methods, science can do the same for the social world. In historical materialism, which can well be regarded as its hard core as a science, Marxism has provided so far the most adequate intellectual tools for such a social scientific enterprise, for illuminating the structure and dynamics of social formations, the movement of society in its historical development.

It may be noted that historical materialism itself was not a principal focus of Marx's theoretical investigations. Its theory was developed over a long period, beginning with some of his (and Engels') early writings and particularly while inquiring into the genesis and working of capitalism. Like basic theories in science which are about the whole of a certain subject matter, historical materialism is a theory about history as a whole. As such, it is potentially applicable to, or has as its potential subject matter, any part of history, but it does not in itself contain any assertions about the latter—it is the job of those who use the theory as a tool for research to produce such assertions. The crux of the theory, its central principle is the simple proposition that human beings obtain the material conditions of their existence through specific and historically variable relationships with nature and with other human beings, and that the nature of these relationships, constituting as they do 'the economic structure', 'the real foundation' of society, is the most basic fact about any form of social organisation. Speaking of Marx's achievement here, V.G. Kiernan has pointed out: 'Much as Columbus and those who came after him convinced men once for all that the earth was round, Marx brought recognition of an order and priority of relationships among all human concerns.' Or, as Raymond Williams has put it: 'It is true that there are forms of material production which always and everywhere precede all other forms (in society)... The enormous theoretical shift introduced by classical Marxism—in saying these are the primary productive activities—was of the most fundamental importance.' With historical materialism Marx indeed opened up the continent of social sciences, as Althusser stated it years ago. Sweezy and Magdoff have rightly stressed: 'Historical materialism as first formulated in the *German Ideology* and later extended and developed in the *Critique of Political Economy* and *Capital* is the firm foundation on which all that is best in social sciences has been and continues to be based.'

Historical materialism remains central to any viable science of society. Marx and Engels advanced the general proposition that 'the mode of production must not be considered simply as being the reproduction of the physical existence of the individuals. Rather it is a definite form of expressing their life, a definite mode of life on their part.' Making a more specific reference to social relations of production as the economic 'base' which 'determines' the superstructure of a social formation, Marx thus located the source of its structural dynamics which also makes for the centrality of class struggle in historical process: 'It is always the direct relationship of the owners of the conditions of production to the direct producers... which holds the innermost secret, the hidden foundation of the entire social structure'...

It should be clear, therefore, that Marx's view of the place and role of 'economy' in society is no recognition of the so-called 'economic factor', often vulgarly read into historical materialism. This recognition as economic interpretation of social life and history, is as old as Plato and is a commonplace of bourgeois social science today. Marx's is an entirely different, differently precise and specific argument. Viewed in a Marxist, that is, historical materialist perspective, a society or social formation is not just an aggregate or random togetherness of parts, factors, levels or instances. It is a complex and differentiated social whole or *'totality'*, a historically structured interdependence of parts, which is loaded by predominance in the long run of one part within it, the economy—'the mode of production' with its 'social relations of production', the *economic-structural base*—and whose existence is characterised by *contradictions* (principal or structural, and other equally specific secondary ones within and between various parts) that account for its dynamics, its concrete *overdetermined* historical development—the whole shaping and expressing itself through the parts, and the parts, even as they represent and bear the signature of the whole, constituting, in their interrelatedness, the specific unity that makes it a whole, *the* whole and no other, that is, a particular society or social formation.

The social existence or historical development, in this view, is not to be understood in any reductionist or determinist manner. 'Determination by the economic' (Engels' phrase) is no economistic determination. 'The concrete', as Marx himself put it, 'is the product of many determinations', it is 'overdetermined', as Althusser later phrased it. Nor is 'determination by the economic' unique. It is essentially a *correspondence,* and, therefore, variable. For example, speaking of 'the political form of the sovereignty-dependence relationship', that is, 'the specific form of the state', Marx wrote: '...due to innumerable different empirical circumstances, natural conditions, relationships among races (tribes, & c.), outside historical influences, etc., the same economic basis—same in terms of the main conditions—can show endless variations and gradations in the phenomenon, which can be made out only by analysis of these empirically given circumstances.' In other words, the *determination* involved, insofar as we must use this term, is neither simple or straightforward, nor unique, and nor a matter of any reductionism; it is something far more complex and problematic, realised on an economic base but through any number of interactions and mediations, horizontal, vertical and across each other, and allowing for other, base-corresponding, possibilities—unless, of course, what is involved is a revolutionary, that is structural transformation of the economic base itself. The non-economic parts, aspects or instances of a social formation, generally referred to as 'superstructure', along with their contradictions, are not some immediate or epiphenomenal manifestation of the economic base. On the contrary, they may have, and often do have, an autonomous, irreducible, historically specific existence of their own. But this is an existence of dialectical, determined and determining, relationships to each other and to the social whole, and the dynamics of this existence, the working out of their contradictions is, in an asymmetry of reciprocal influence, most decisively conditioned by the basic economic contradictions, the structural logic of the economic base. This conditioning, again, does not rule out or in any way foreclose *real* choices, or possibilities for human action, only these arise and exist within the necessities and constraints of the given objective situation, above all, the economic-structural situation, which sets their context, outer limits and parameters. The economic defines, as it were, the terrain, the 'conditions of existence', the horizon of the non-economic, including, I would like to add, the political.

It is within the necessities and constraints of the given objective, economic-structural situation, within this 'determination by the economic in the *first* instance', that men choose and act, and whatever happens, every complex historical effect or outcome, is *ultimately* determined by the activity of men in pursuit of their aims or purposes.

Hence also the primacy of politics, not economics, in Marxism. It is not merely that historical materialism accommodates or incorporates the subjective side of things, which, after all, is also a part of real life, produced like everything else that matters to us, as a philosophy of praxis, Marxism puts subjectivity, willed human action that is politics, at the centre of social practice for our times (At least that is how Marx himself, unlike so many Marxists in recent years, understood and practiced Marxism throughout his life). Given a Marxist understanding of society as a structured whole, and the crucial place or role of 'economy' in it, any fundamental change in society involves as a necessary, though not sufficient, condition a changing of its economic structural base. And this is possible only through a politics of revolution. That is why Marx spoke up for revolution as 'the highest form of class struggle'. This is how politics, *as revolutionary politics,* has primacy in Marxism. But this primacy does not in any way contradict the other, better known, Marxist proposition about 'the base determining the superstructure', it only calls for its better understanding. The obvious implication of our argument is that in the absence of politics changing 'the economic base' of society, the logic of this base shall assert itself and, in howsoever different ways, 'determine' superstructure, reducing politics itself to something superstructural in its essential character and outcome. Such is the dialectics of economy and politics, of science and revolution, in the social theory of Karl Marx.

XVII

Marxism certainly, though in its own specific manner, emphasises the special role of 'the economy' in society—and without this emphasis Marxism would be theoretically indistinguishable from conventional or any other sociology, including the post-modernist sociology of discursive relations. But this does not make Marxism either 'determinist' in politics, or 'reductionist' in its explanation. For Marxism, 'men make their own history', and in so far as they cannot make it except under given circumstances or objective conditions, structurally constituted or determined by the relevant mode of production, revolutionary politics, gives them the freedom to transcend or transform them. As for 'reductionism', one must recognise the difference between explanation that is reductionist *and* explanation. It is integral to the very act of explanation that some things are picked out as important, given prominence over others, in terms of their effect or influence. Otherwise there is no explanation, only aggregates of things, disparate elements, or descriptive fragments—and this surely does not take one very far. In fact, a notion of explaining the events of one domain in terms of those seen to be important enough from another domain is basic to what we mean by an 'explanation'. Marxists pick out economy, economic or class structure, or classes, for prominence or importance for the simple reason that they consider them to have, with their exceptionally powerful effects in society, the necessary explanatory potential for the purpose they have in view. Again, to see some things as important is not to see them as the *only* ones. The real issue here is not the possibility of explanation or Marxism's reductionism—which is now a very tired theme and only betokens political prejudice or philosophical illiteracy—but the empirical validity and achievement of this scientific, that is, explanatory hypothesis of Marxism, relative to what bourgeois social theory has to offer in explaining the world around us and the worlds past. In any unbiased assessment the latter can well be envious of the Marxist record.

The record certainly allows us to affirm that historical materialism as a theory about the dominant, not the only or exclusive, lines of social and historical causation has been deservedly validated as the most fruitful in the field, that the metaphor of base and superstructure, as metaphor and not a rigidly structuralist, mechanistically interpreted formula, is a theoretically viable one, that the concept of 'economic structure' has a well-justified explanatory pre-eminence in scientific understanding of social phenomena, that causal determination of social and cultural life by economic structures, without excluding interaction, is a valid general proposition, that class and economic structures do have powerful effects, both shaping and constraining, on ideas, ideologies and culture, on institutions like the state and political and other practices in society, that class is not just another 'identity', it is a *structural* constituent of a social formation and therefore class questions are central to revolutionary politics and to any pro-people social transformation or reconstruction of society, that class structural positions are indeed the primary, not sole or exclusive, historical determinants of social and political identities and alignments, of institutions, ideologies and politics, and that, as Ralph Miliband has put it: 'when all is said and done, Marxism as class analysis handled with due care, remains an instrument of unsurpassed value in the interpretation of social and political life, and in the explanation of phenomena which, in other hands, remain unexplained or misunderstood'.

XIX

The concept of class, ambiguities of the argument over its definition notwithstanding, remains central not only to explaining historical processes, but to the possibilities of human emancipation. At issue is the fact of class struggle as the motive force of history. If a grasp of the dynamics of class struggle is essential to understanding politics, it is even more so for pursuit of revolutionary politics. And this does not mean any kind of class-reductionist politics. Classical Marxism, even as it laid a historically specific emphasis on the role of the working class, yet visualised the proletarian movement (as, for example, in *Communist Manifesto*) as 'the self-conscious independent movement of the immense majority, in the interest of the immense majority.' This obviously implies drawing together a whole range of other classes against the bourgeoisie, which indeed was a key concern of Marx whenever he touched on the role of peasantry or petty bourgeoisie in the revolutionary process of his time. Understood and defined not in narrow economistic or reductionist but pluralist terms, class struggle, or struggles if you like, remain central to any genuinely emancipatory project of the present or the future. Philosophical presuppositions of Marxism such as materialism and dialectics are important as is its explanatory enterprise of historical materialism, but the insistence upon the viability and relevance of Marxism in practical terms means insisting upon the centrality of class struggle. Class struggle is indeed the conceptual linchpin in as much as it is here that Marxists and socialists have to fight for the truth they believe in.

It can be legitimately argued that Marx overestimated the revolutionary potential of the working class. Whatever the reasons, the European proletariat can be said to have failed, on the whole, to live up to his expectations—though an European revolution did occur and the Russian proletariat under Bolshevik leadership certainly vindicated Marx. Also, important changes have occurred in the conditions, composition and structure of the working class since Marx's days. Economic globalisation and technological change has not only increased the political power of capital, it has also weakened the working class everywhere, not the least in the mother countries of capitalism. There is also the historical experience of the failed or successful revolutions and revolutionary struggles of the twentieth century, as also of the more recent 'new social movements'. All this and more make it abundantly clear that the agency for a socialist transformation has to be specifically multiple and more inclusive, according to the situation in different countries. But apart from the fact that this view is not entirely alien to Marx, as even a cursory look at his political writings would reveal, it does not in any way exclude the vital role of the working class in the struggle against global capitalism and, the past failure notwithstanding, it may still have a decisive role to play in the emancipatory struggles of the advanced capitalist countries. The working class everywhere continues to have an objective interest in socialism. I may add that, in line with Marx's view of the working class, it is rational to speak of the objective interest of a class or classes, that the victims of capitalism anywhere have an objective interest in socialism, and that among its victims, the structurally significant class or classes have more radical or revolutionary potential than others and, therefore, a possibly privileged role in struggling for and effecting a socialist transformation. This also means that in so far as it is the contradictions of capitalism (and allied exploitative structures) which generate the conditions and forces for socialist politics, the need is to analyse these contradictions and locate the main or worst victims of the extant exploitation, the class or classes with the strongest possible interest in a socialist transformation, who, having gained the requisite revolutionary consciousness—'won the theoretical awareness of their loss', as Marx put it—shall be the driving social forces of socialist or socialism-oriented struggles. It is indeed the task of the socialist movement to bring in and foster revolutionary consciousness among these classes as also to develop appropriate programmes, politics and organisation to help them pursue their struggles more effectively and purposefully. If the point is to actively change the world, not merely interpret it, then Marxism is above all about using class analysis to understand the ongoing socio-economic and political processes, and pursuing *class struggle* for realisation of *historically* possible *emancipatory* goals, which goals in their immediate or ultimate definition today can only be socialism as Karl Marx visualised it.

XX

At the core of Marxism, best illustrative of its scientific character and continuing relevance, lies Marx's critical analysis of capitalism, its structure and contradictions and the laws of its movement, which, as he foresaw, almost inexorably led to its worldwide extension, a global domination of capital, even as its structural logic simultaneously manifests itself, in each society and across societies globally, in the tendency towards accumulation of wealth and affluence at one end and poverty and misery at the other. Marx's empirical analysis of capitalism is suffused with a profoundly perceptive ethical critique of capitalism, drawing attention to the inherent inhumanity of its origins, existence and worldwide expansion, its manifold, historically specific alienations, and the 'barbarism' that its market-based regime of private property and profit-making ultimately portends. Against the pitiable, fragmentary and alienated existence which is the lot of human beings under capitalism where all the truly *human* senses are swamped by a historically transient substitute sense, the sense of property, and 'the more you *have*, the less you *are*', Marx pointed to the historically possible ideal of a 'truly rich human life', of human beings appropriating the world with all their glorious human senses, 'the realm of freedom ...beyond the sphere of actual material production (where) begins that development of human energy which is an end in itself.'

Marx certainly underestimated capitalism's potential for growth and development, but his framework for understanding the capitalist system remains as illuminating as ever. His empirical and ethical critique of capitalism still holds, as does his argument that, an inherently irrational system, capitalism yet prepares the necessary, though not sufficient, conditions for a transition to a more rational social order, a socialist, ultimately communist, society. Whatever may have happened to socialism in the former Soviet Union, Marx's argument for socialism, seen essentially as a negation or transcendence of capitalism, has lost none of its legitimacy or force, and the abolition of capitalist production relations remains the strategic goal, a necessary but not sufficient act within the project of emancipatory social transformation, defining as it were the fundamental moment, the decisive point of revolutionary rupture in the epochal process of transformation from capitalism to socialism.

The current 'triumph of capitalism' is often cited as the reason for Marxism having become 'dead' or 'obsolete'. The critics seem to be in an unseemly hurry. Marxism, given the extraordinary achievement of Marx's *Capital*, can well be defined as the science of capitalism none of whose fundamental theses have been refuted so far. Therefore, it is simply incoherent to celebrate the 'death of Marxism' in the same breath with which one announces the definitive triumph of capitalism. The latter would rather seem to augur a secure future for the former, leaving aside the matter of how 'definitive' its triumph could possibly be. In other words, the very fact that Marx, more than any other human being, then or now, devoted his life to explaining the reality or logic of capitalism and his achievement here remains unrivalled, ensures that Marxism can neither die nor go obsolete so long as capitalism lasts. Capitalism has 'triumphed' to become, post-Soviet collapse, a truly global or universal system, such as it has been never before. Leaving aside the vitally important associated issues—the universalisation of capitalism's systemic logic of accumulation, profit-maximisation, competition and commodification, the universalisation of its polarisations of rich and poor, exploiters and exploited, and a sharpening of its contradictions and destructive as well as self-destructive tendencies—the immediately relevant point is that its 'triumph' has made capitalism all the more important as a system whose working we need to understand. And this makes Marxism not dead or obsolete but all the more relevant today, indeed more relevant than ever before.

This relevance is already asserting itself. 'Spectres of Marx', says Derrida, continue to haunt neo-liberalism, and not a few of those who still speak of 'failure of communism', have been writing of 'the ghost of Marx' hovering 'over the global landscape, perhaps with a knowing smile; the gross conditions that inspired Karl Marx's original critique of capitalism in the nineteenth century are present and flourishing again'. BBC News Online, running a cyberpoll to find 'the thinker of the millennium', found Marx at the top. It is going to be no different in the new millennium. Towards the end of the eighties in the last century, even as the communist regimes collapsed in Eastern Europe, the *New Yorker*, 'an upmarket magazine for sybarites of world over', celebrated the occasion with an article entitled 'Triumph of Capitalism', whose argument reverberated worldwide, setting off a new round of hosannas to capitalism and pronouncements of 'the death of Marxism'. Less than a decade later, towards the end of 1997, in a bout of futurology, bringing together a series of articles around the theme 'what's next?', the same *New Yorker* went looking for the 'next most influential thinker', and the article, written by one who is no Marxist, now or ever before, was entitled 'The Return of Karl

Marx'! It concluded: 'His (Marx's) books will be worth reading as long as capitalism endures'. Yes, Marx is going to be with us so long as we live in a capitalist society.

[It is interesting to note how the above article came to be written by its author, John Cassidy. This is how *Monthly Review's* 'notes from the editors' reported it: John Cassidy is self-identified as an Oxford-educated friend of "a highly intelligent and level-headed Englishman whose career has taken him ... to a big Wall Street investment bank." Visiting with his friend at the latter's Long Island summer home during the early summer, the two discussed the economy and speculated on how long the current financial boom would last.

"To my surprise, he brought up Karl Marx. 'The longer I spend on Wall Street, the more convinced I am that Marx was right', he said.

"I assumed he was joking.

'"There is a Nobel Prize waiting for the economist who resurrects Marx and puts it all together,' he continued, quite seriously, 'I am absolutely convinced that Marx's approach is the best way to look at capitalism.'

"I didn't hide my astonishment. We had both studied economics during the early eighties at Oxford, where most of our teachers agreed with Keynes that Marx's economic theories were 'complicated hocus-pocus' and Communism was an 'insult to our intelligence.' ...Nonetheless I decided that if my host, with all his experience of global finance, reckoned Marx had something worthwhile to say, perhaps it was time to take a look."

So he did the rounds of second-hand bookstores and picked up what seems to have been a reasonably representative collection of Marx's writings and took them along with him as reading matter on his August vacation.

The result is the *New Yorker* article mentioned above].

So much for the more basic Marxist positions. I have already touched on some of these earlier and may return to others later in my argument. Here, in conclusion, I would only add that with its scientific world view, its powerful dialectical-analytic method, the depth and sweep of its explanatory theory, historical materialism, the continuing validity of its analysis of capitalism, the exceptionally rich humanism of its ethical commitment, and the unqualified sanction it provides for struggles of the exploited and oppressed everywhere, for revolutionary politics in behalf of socialism, there is enough to be said for Marxism to justify Sartre's aphoristic summing up. He had spoken of Marxism as the *necessary* philosophy of our time.

XXI

A contrasting reference to the mainstream, if I may so describe it, 'bourgeois' social science will help clarify the nature and achievement of Marxism as social science. A somewhat detailed discussion of the subject will be found in my *Reason, Revolution and Political Theory*. Here I will only make a few very brief and general but basic observations. The claim is not that Marx's social theory fully accounts for all social phenomena, or that it has answers to all our problems, or that there is any finality to the answers this theory itself provides. There are no such claims, promises *or* pretentions in Marx. On the contrary, as we have already noticed, Marxism has its 'silences' and 'empty spaces', its contradictions and any number of unresolved tensions: for example, between determinism and contingency, structure and agency, individuality and sociality, spontaneity and organisation, and so on, which tensions, I may add, are an intrinsic part of ever-changing real life. On its own Marxism often yields large questions rather than provide neat answers. Its own strength rather lies in highlighting questions or problems as no other social theory does and in suggesting better ways of understanding and resolving them, in theory as well as in practice. The claim is that Marxism offered and remains a superior mode of analysis of our social world, better than anything that bourgeois social theory has to offer. It is not merely that 'Marx's combination of insight and method permanently altered the manner in which reality would thereafter be perceived', as Heilbronner once put it, it is that none has provided, so far, a better method of understanding this reality, the reality of society and historical processes. It is in this sense that Marx opened up the continent of social sciences, as

Althusser stated it years ago. But there is also a more specific and substantial claim. It is that guided by his dialectical method, Marx's own exploration of this continent (which he saw as a never-ending enterprise) has gained for us knowledge of the structure and dynamics of the contemporaneously dominant social formation, capitalism, better than anything that bourgeois social theory can claim for itself. In fact, whatever be its other achievements, here bourgeois social science has signally failed to deliver. And for reasons which make for a direct contrast with Marxist social science.

In his masterly survey, *Science in History*, J.D. Bernal has pointed out that it is 'a very dangerous thing to look too closely into the workings of one's own society'. For this may well bring out its arbitrary, irrational and unjustifiable features. This 'dangerous thing' is what Marxist social science has always attempted and the dangers involved are precisely what has pushed bourgeois social science persistently in the direction of *apologetics*. If *truth* indeed be *the* concern of social science, then in the kind societies we have—class-divided and unequal, more or less iniquitous and oppressive—doing social science, search for truth, cannot but be, essentially, a subversive exercise, dangerous for those who have 'dominion' in society, as Hobbes put it long ago. Hence Bernal's argument that 'the backwardness and emptiness of the social sciences are due to the overriding reason that in all class societies they are inevitably *corrupt*'. The corrupt or apologetic character of bourgeois social science as a whole has been facilitated or reinforced, and justified as well, by its philosophical orientation or 'Methodology', which has been, in the main, a modernised version of 'the metaphysical mode of thought' which Engels had found wanting as 'one-sided, limited, abstract' because it studies things 'in their isolation, detached from the whole vast interconnection of things and, therefore, not in their motion, but in their repose; not in their life, but in their death.' He had added: 'in considering individual things it loses sight of their connections; in contemplating their existence it forgets their coming into being and passing away; in looking at them at rest it leaves their motion out of account...

it cannot see the woods for the trees.' Seeking to become a *science* in our times, social science modelled itself *uncritically* on modern natural science, rather as the latter appeared to be in its period of 'adolescence', as it came up in opposition to 'rationalism' and 'religious metaphysics' of late medieval scholasticism, emphasising the essential empirical basis of science and value-free nature of scientific knowledge. As a consequence, the practice of mainstream social science came to be early characterised by 'the fetishism of Empiricism' and the accompanying fetishism of 'fact-value dichotomy' or 'ethical neutrality'. Focusing on 'facts' in opposition to traditional social theorising, dismissive of the latter as so much value-laden metaphysics ('spooks', etc.) it developed a distrust of generalisation or theory, failing to understand that science, in its maturity, is not factual or descriptive statements but *explanatory* theory, a knitting together of the empirical and the rational. An universally admitted 'hyperfactualism' followed where 'the immediately observable, measurable fact' was soon 'the Moloch', as Paul Baran called it, 'which is always seeking to devour analytic thought in contemporary social science'; 'a social science of the narrow focus, the trivial detail, the abstracted almighty unimportant fact' is how C. Wright Mills described it. It spoke with Robert Dahl, an eminent practitioner himself, of 'the rapid development of the social sciences, with their rigour and empiricism', and even boasted of 'the intellectual revolution brought about by the development of logico-experimental reasoning', but was yet admittedly 'concerned often with a meticulous observation of the trivial'. As Rogow reported it: 'The data stand mountain high, with fresh increments arriving quarterly (when the Journals appear) alongside molehills of generalization and theory'. This essentially quantitative output, certainly had (and still has) its 'molehills' of theory, its undoubtedly valuable 'little truths' about contemporary society, but no 'big truth', that is the truth about the whole that is the capitalist system, no explanation that could take one behind 'appearances' to the 'nature of things', be it capitalism itself or the reality of things under capitalism. This reality indeed often took this social science 'by surprise' as, for example, eminent mainstream scholars, Easton, McWilliams, Schaar, Lowi, among others, have openly admitted for Political Science. Thanks to its 'metaphysical' mode of thought or 'abstracted empiricism', this social science invariably missed the woods for the trees. Its 'value-freedom' or 'ethical neutrality', the insistence on sticking to description and explanation, whatever 'little' explanations it had to offer, and eschewing prescription—'There is always a demand that the professor of the social sciences shall become a political eunuch' is how George Catlin saw it—only betrayed rank philosophical illiteracy in that it was a multiple failure to recognise that while truth in natural science is by and large politically neutral, in the social science of a class-divided society truth, any worthwhile truth that is, not only is and cannot but be partisan, it can even be political dynamite; that a description or explanation invariably has a value slope, even if the values remain unacknowledged; and that the very use of language, given its inescapably value-loaded nature in human sciences, forbids any kind of ethical neutrality. (This raises a most difficult problem for any genuine social scientific enterprise, including the Marxist. But its discussion, including the question of proper response, is beyond the scope of what I am here concerned with.)

Recognition of its inadequacies and the accompanying loss of relevance, even when dressed up as yet another 'revolution in social science', has not made for any significantly new or radical departures in practice. Insofar as a reaction away from 'hyperfactualism' has meant a turn to theory, it is not scientific theory that *explains* through concepts which are concepts *of* the world—'explaining the world by itself', as Engels once phrased it. The proliferating 'concepts' and 'conceptual frameworks' simply stand apart from the real world. 'Towards a theory of...' that academic research is flush with is a promise that only beguiles for there are no genuine arrivals. In Oran Young's words, 'a theology of concepts' has come up, confronting as it were 'the world of facts'. 'Fetishism of the concept' replaces or supplements the 'fetishism of Empiricism', each in its own way ensuring that we do not learn much about man and society, the social world we inhabit. Even the welcome shift from facts to their interconnections has engendered a 'systems theory' which, as used in social analysis, has been generally a formal or classificatory exercise with little or no *explanatory* value. As for 'ethical neutrality' the only real advance here, amidst a fashionable agnosticism about values, seems to be the admission that this 'neutrality', hid and still hides, from others and often from themselves as well, the social scientists' unstated commitment to the values dominant in their, that is their own bourgeois society.

❖

As knowledge became the domain of academics, the academic disciplines got organised into separate social sciences (where students study power in political science, social class in sociology, the market in economics, and so on)—an essentially artificial separation that performed a conservative detotalising ideological function in opposition to Marxism's radical 'totalising' concern with society as a whole. Under the constant pressure of capital's imperatives and determinations, intellectual production got further fragmented into countless specialisms within each discipline, to the detriment of any comprehensive understanding of social reality. That any such understanding is possible was itself 'ruled out of court', indeed exorcised, with the help of pseudo-philosophical argumentation over 'holism' ('wholeism'), now reduced to a swear word. The ultimate consequence is a situation of ever-growing, often mindless specialisation, where fewer and fewer people are now hearing more and more about less and less, and all the time woods continue to be missed for the trees. Contrasting this empiricist orientation of contemporary social science with the holistic and deep-penetrating thrust of Marxism, which seeks to go behind 'the appearance' to 'the nature of things', David McLellan has written: 'the huge development of the social sciences in the century since Marx's death has often brought with it results that are thin in two respects: first in the vertical sense of being produced inside a narrow specialization by scholars who know more and more about less and less, and secondly in the horizontal sense that they spring from a preoccupation with the surface phenomena of society, so easily available for observation and quantification'. This 'thinness', the failure to 'interconnect' and to reach down and question the basic assumptions of the system as a whole, obviously makes for apologetics and conservatism in social science, facilitating, as not a few scholars have pointed out, its easy degeneration into 'scientific applauding of official policies and defaults' (C. Wright Mills), 'footnoted rationalization and huckstering of these policies' (Neal Houghton) or plain 'capitulation to the status quo' (Christian Bay), etc.

Individual exceptions are of course always there, but no social science discipline today is free from being thus 'corrupt', as Bernal phrased it. Certainly not Economics, that crucially important domain of social inquiry. The discipline has its quota of handmaidens and cheerleaders for capitalism and its 'free market', and a host of others doing 'applied economics' for the ruling establishment, the most 'skillful' of these landing the Nobel Prize in Economics. But really significant is the way the discipline, its 'pure theory' as they call it, has been moving steadily away from explanation of the real world towards formalised axioms and model-building with only a precarious bearing on actuality. There is a wholesale shying away from the classical concern with the working of the system as a whole. Nowhere is this more evident that in the country at the centre of global capitalism, the United States, where a 'mathematical obscurantism' seems to have taken over. More and more a 'good economist' is defined by the economic profession 'as someone with daunting mathematical skills'. Eminent economists have expressed concern over what is happening. Leontief has said: 'Departments of Economics are graduating a generation of idiot savants, brilliant at esoteric mathematics yet innocent of actual economic life.' Kenneth Arrow has famously remarked that the profession has 'tended to shy away from the grandest themes. The fundamental questions of economic change, the theme of Schumpeter's work, are not discussed'. The apologetic nature of it all has also not gone unnoticed. Heilbronner and Milberg, writing of 'the crises of vision in modern economic thought', have noted 'the failure of mainstream economics to recognize the presence of the underlying social order'. 'The best guarded secret of the profession', they say, is 'the inextricable entanglement of economics with capitalism', which secret 'is not even known to all economists'. The mainstream economics, according to them, has moved from 'ideology to apologism' in recent times.

❖

The institutionalisation of social science activity in the academy and the research institutes has also had the almost unavoidable consequence of strengthening the apologetic or status-quoist bias of social science studies. The institutional success or success within the institution becomes the major concern, which increasingly ties them down to doing 'policy research' for the ruling establishments, that is, finding means to their ends without any questioning of those ends. The social scientist becomes a 'specialist' or an 'expert' who, taking the existing order of 'facts' for granted and existing order of 'values' as somehow beyond rational inquiry, questions or deals with the prevailing state of affairs solely within the limited, unrelated area of his immediate preoccupation. No longer an intellectual but only an intellect worker, as Paul Baran put it, he turns 'a *technician*'—'typically the faithful servant, the agent, the functionary, and the spokesman for the capitalist system'—whose preoccupation is with 'the job in hand', with 'the rationalisation, mastery, and manipulation of whatever branch of reality he is immediately concerned with' and not with 'the meaning of his work, its significance, its place within the entire framework of social reality'. 'His "natural" motto is to mind his own business, and... to be as efficient and as successful as it is possible'; 'he is not concerned with the relation of the segment of human endeavour within which he happens to operate to other segments and to the totality of the historical process'. 'The concern with the whole' which as 'holism' is in any case deemed unscientific, is not his concern and thus 'he *eo ipso* accepts the existing structure of the whole as a datum and subscribes to the prevailing criteria of rationality, to the dominant values, and to the socially enforced yardsticks of efficiency, achievement and success'. Taking an agnostic view of the ends themselves, he makes a fetish of 'ethical neutrality', of his abdication *qua* social scientist, expert or scholar of all 'value-judgments', an abdication which 'amounts in practice to the endorsement of the *status quo*, to lending a helping hand to those who are seeking to obstruct any change of the existing order of things in favour of a better one.'

What is involved here is an aspect of contemporary social science which may be specifically noted: the way its professed 'substantive rationality' has come to be virtually swamped or displaced by 'functional rationality', to borrow the two terms from Karl Mannheim. 'Substantive rationality' implies a concern with the substantive issues, the reality behind the 'appearance' of things, an effort to *interconnect*, that is, relate whatever specific areas one is working in to other aspects of human existence, a recognition that 'the truth is the whole' and that 'the seemingly autonomous disparate and disjointed morsels of social existence under capitalism—literature, art, politics, the economic order, science, the cultural and psychic condition of people—can all be understood (and influenced) only if they are clearly visualized as parts of the comprehensive totality of the historical process', and above all an awareness of the larger ends and purposes of society and the implications of one's own work in relation to them. With social science disciplines and associated intellectual activities growing into professions, organised structures of teaching and research to make a living, these considerations have all too often given way to a 'functional rationality'. Scholarship is increasingly fashion-driven, addressed not to problems and publics but to peers and to prestige and preferment in the increasingly bureaucratised academic professions or research set-ups. The professional or peer group compulsions to stay noticed and the 'publish or perish' syndrome leads to a constant search for novelty, formal and empty ingenuity, laboured exercises in originality, all sorts of irrelevant pedantry and repetitive writing. Research agenda are formulated, even invented, with an eye to lucrative outside funding, reputation, book sales or marketability and similar other considerations. 'Invisible colleges' and 'repute systems' come up to set standards and certify the quality of work done. Theories are valued not for their content in terms of truth or knowledge or any kind of larger social usefulness but, as Hugh Stretton has said, 'for themselves, for their qualities of novelty or intricacy or elegance or mathematical interest', or even as tests of loyalty including 'cliquish academic loyalties'; they indeed become 'consumption goods' for the use of producers themselves, serving the social purposes of the disciplines and the people who generate them rather than the social purposes of the society at large. In short, the 'substantive rationality' which, necessarily in association with a certain degree of courage, ought to govern and characterise a genuine social science or any worthwhile teaching and research, has simply lost out in the way bourgeois social science has come up and grown to its so-called maturity in our time. It is significant that the overall irrelevance of this social science has been a major topic of discussion in recent years, even among its proponents and practitioners.

At its best this social science can certainly be said to have 'served society', which, however, is not the same as 'serving truth'. Morgenthau's sharp comment here has a relevance that goes beyond the discipline he is referring to: 'it is the measure of the degree to which political science in America meets the needs of society rather than its moral commitment to the truth that it is not only eminently respectable and popular, but—what is worse—that it is also widely regarded with indifference'. At its worst, social scientists have been co-opted into 'the establishment' as, for example, David Apter has confirmed for America and Joseph La Palombaras has wondered how they can rebut the charge that 'western social science is not much more than thinly veiled bourgeois ideology'. Not unoften, this social science has sought to hide its poverty and mediocrity behind esoteric sophistication and elaborate vocabularies of weird and unintelligible jargon—'socspeak' Malcolm Cowley called it—which has led Stanislav Andreski to even write of 'social sciences as sorcery'. Not an inapt description, considering the overall obscurantist ideological role of much of bourgeois social science in our society. One does not have to deny the substantial achievements of bourgeois social science in certain areas to, at the same time, substantially agree with Bernal that 'much social science is merely the putting of the current practice of the trades and professions into learned language', or is science 'only by courtesy or for examination purposes'. Chomsky indeed well summed up the situation when, recognising the overwhelmingly apologetic character of modern social science, he once described its practitioners as 'a secular priesthood'!

XXII

A last word before I leave the subject of Marxism as a social science. Marxism did not arise as a social science for peers or policy makers, it is social theory at the service of the exploited and the oppressed who are yet wanting to struggle for a better life. A struggling people will not get very far without some substantial knowledge of the structures they need to overthrow for their emancipation and a sense of direction in their struggle. This is what Marx sought to provide. For a better grasp of his theory we have tried to relate Marx to his times and to some of the subsequent history of Marxism. But for its effective practice, we also need to relate Marx's theory or received Marxism to our times. This makes it a legitimate object of reflection and criticism, all the more so because of the political defeat it has suffered. The failure of the socialist enterprise in the Soviet Union has certainly precipitated an intellectual crisis for Marxism. But it is only religious dogmatism which is impervious to reality that sees in an intellectual crisis nothing but threats to its own certainties. Marxism does not have to do that. Anyway, Marxism never had any 'certainties' of that sort. For it the crisis is also an opportunity, to reflect on itself and to rectify. New challenges have to be met—a failure here will only result in ossification and ultimate atrophy of Marxism. Rectifications are indeed called for. But this does not mean analytical regressions or obfuscations of hyphenated Marxism, or 'making sense of Marx' that puts a question mark on Marxism itself, or 'reconstruction' of Marxism that reconstructs it out, or simply lapsing into social democratic theory and practices. The task is, if I may again put it that way, a recovery of Marxism of Karl Marx, a garnering of the resources of its classical tradition for facing the new situation and the tasks that lie ahead. In other words, in coping with the current crisis we don't in any way have to abandon the basic framework of Marx's theory. This framework remains the overall horizon of our activity, our orientation, not for any dogmatic reasons but for the simple fact that it remains the right orientation, that its basic thrust embraces the whole epoch of transition from capitalism to socialism. And if, and insofar as we indeed go 'beyond Marx' in our enterprise, we go with him and not against him or away from him.

XXIII

Marxism is science, it is also about revolution. I have spoken of the dialectics of science and revolution in Marxism. This dialectics is not only a matter of *theory* guiding revolutionary practice, it also involves a commitment to revolution—which Marx once described as 'the conversion of all hearts and the raising of all hands in behalf of the honour of the free man'. This commitment, for Marx, always implied the recognition of moral consciousness as a vital agency of revolutionary change. A matter of head, revolution with Marx is a matter of heart also. Underlying Marx's theoretical work throughout was a proud and passionate ethical commitment, the motivating force of the moral choice he had made early in his life to stand up for 'humanity'. His was a vision or dream, a dream born of reality but a dream nevertheless, 'Traum' Marx called it, that looked beyond capitalism to a society in which 'the free development of each is the condition for the free development of all', where all human beings are fulfilled by equality and freedom and a truly rich human life. Communist utopianism? Maybe, but a legitimate utopianism, based as it was on Marx's recognition of 'free conscious activity' as 'man's species character' and his awareness of the range of possibilities inhering in human nature which we cannot imagine today, not only because of the way capitalism has blighted our essential humanity and distorted our vision but even more because we are, according to Marx, still living in our 'pre-history'. Marx saw communism as the *beginning* of the history of a liberated humankind. Human liberation was the vision Marx pursued throughout his life and he saw capitalism barring the road to it when its own productive achievements had at last made its realisation possible. This is how Marx, 'the man of science', was also a revolutionary and an advocate of class struggle.

That scholars in recent years have sought to divest Marx of this 'Traum', his 'image of the future', his revolutionary commitment and advocacy of class struggle, and reduce him to just another savant, even run-of-the-mill humanist philosopher, or turn his revolutionary doctrine into a modern metaphysics, is generally known. But the real damage here has come from within, above all from scientism and economistic deformations in the post-1880 Marxism as a whole, whose one consequence has been, as expressed by E.P. Thompson, 'the subordination of the imaginative utopian faculties within the Marxist tradition: its lack of moral self-consciousness or even a vocabulary of desire, its inability to project any images of the future, or even its tendency to fall back in lieu of these upon the utilitarians' earthly paradise—the maximization of economic growth'. There is the need, therefore, to recover what Ernst Bloch called the visionary 'warm stream' which always flowed alongside the 'cold stream' of Marx's political economy, to recover, in other words, the utopian vision, moral consciousness and ethical commitment of classical Marxism. One cannot but reiterate what Thompson concluded in his vindication of utopianism of William Morris, which was also the utopianism of Karl Marx : 'What Marxism might do, for a change, is to sit on its own head a little in the interests of socialism's heart'. In this 'heart' lies the secret of Marx's life-long hostility to capitalism and his equally life-long pursuit of revolution. It is important that Marxism's claims as social science are not so recognised as to evade, obscure or push out of sight the fact that Marxism is also about revolutionary transformation of the present-day capitalist society.

Marx was, by vocation, a revolutionary, as Engels emphasised in his famous grave-side speech on the death of Marx. Philosopher, economist, historian, and so much else, Marx was indeed 'the man of science' said Engels. He had however immediately added: 'But this was not even half the man... for Marx was before all else a revolutionist... Fighting was his element. And he fought with a passion, a tenacity, and a success such as few could rival'. Marx recognised for himself and for others the liberating quality of practical activity, the purifying power of revolutionary action in transforming the very nature of those involved in it. Teodor Shanin is very right in insisting that revolutionary ethics was as central as his historiography to Marx's political judgment and to practice flowing from it. It is this ethics, a fighting commitment to the cause of social revolution, and the moral passion that went with it, which gives its special quality to Marxism of Karl Marx, and enables us to make sense of his life—full of the trials and hazards of the life of a revolutionary, its political defeats, factional struggles and repeatedly dashed hopes as well as years of personal poverty and privations, 'the humiliations, torments and terrors, the *petite miseres* (petty wretchednesses)', as Marx himself put it, of the struggle for sheer physical survival which did grave damage to his wife's health and his own and were a contributory cause of the death of a daughter and two sons, years when he had no money to pay rent or buy medicine or even coffin for a dead child, when his daughters were out of school because their winter shoes were with the pawn-broker, when for days the family fed on bread and potatoes and at times even these were not available.... And all this while Marx refused those other easily available 'soft options'—'steadfastly rejected the temptation to save himself in the peaceful harbour of some bourgeois career', his biographer Mehring has proudly written, 'although he might have done so without dishonour'. This life is simply inexplicable in terms of conventional scholarship, of 'science' or 'reason' or any 'theory of historical development', of some 'pure logic'. It had an altogether different logic to it, one which underlay all of Marx's theoretical work and his life-long struggle, the logic of a revolutionary commitment, of the clear-eyed choice Marx had made in the fight between the people and those who oppress and exploit them. And he had chosen to stand by the people.

❖

In an essay Marx wrote for his school-leaving examination in 1835, 'A Young Man's Reflections on the Choice of a Career', he stated that working 'only for himself' one can 'become a famous scholar, a great sage, an excellent imaginative writer (*Dichter*), but never a perfected, a truly great man'. Instead, Marx himself opted for a life 'that is most consonant with our dignity, one that is based on ideas of whose truth we are wholly convinced, one that offers us largest scope in working for humanity'. This option, which soon matured into a clearly defined revolutionary commitment, stayed with Marx throughout his life. Early in his youth, asserting that 'man is the highest being for man' he spoke up for 'the categorical imperative to overthrow all conditions in which man is a humiliated, enslaved, despised and rejected being'; later, about the time he finished writing *Capital*, to complete which he had sacrificed, as he said, his 'health, happiness and family', Marx wrote to a friend: 'I laugh at the so-called "practical" men with their wisdom. If one chose to be an ox, one could turn one's back on the sufferings of mankind and look after one's own skin'; towards the end, as we shall see, he stood up with the revolutionaries of the People's Will in Russia, against his own evolutionist disciples there.

It needs to be clearly understood that this moral option or choice, this revolutionary commitment, which was indeed the only absolute principle that governed the life and work of Karl Marx (and which his dialectics allowed), was not a matter of any scientific or historical analysis, knowledge of 'laws' or 'stages', or any 'inevitabilities' of history or 'predictions' about the future, etc. On the contrary, it entailed a seemingly 'romantic' but necessary boldness in pursuit of revolutionary possibilities. That is how, for example, even as Marx foresaw (in *Communist Manifesto*) the coming 'bourgeois revolution' in Germany, he also saw it as 'the prelude to an immediately following proletarian revolution'. And when this 'bourgeois revolution' indeed occurred, he proclaimed it 'our interest and our task' to seek 'to make the revolution permanent... until the proletariat has conquered state power'. Marx failed in Germany, but seventy years later, exactly as Marx had wanted, Lenin succeeded in Russia though I must add, to fail again, through unworthy successors, another seventy years later. Such success or failure in struggle, in the epochal process of transition to socialism, however, is not my concern at the moment. The issue here is the commitment and conduct of Marx as a revolutionary, which for Marx also entailed contempt for the philistines who, as he wrote to an old friend, 'consider people like you and me as immature fools who all this time have not been cured of their revolutionary fantasies'. Told of a contemporary having 'mellowed with age', his response was a disdainful 'oh, has he?' 'To fight' was his 'idea of happiness' as he confessed to his daughter Laura, and to the very end Marx's sympathies always lay with fighters and revolutionaries, whatever be the 'small print' of their creeds. Marx had only scorn for the 'know-all' types, the doctrinaire theorisers including Marxists, his own followers, when on scientific or theoretical grounds they questioned, criticised, rebuked, or abandoned revolutionary struggle.

We know that Marx had tried to persuade the workers of Paris, for good reasons, not to venture on a revolution. But once they did so he hailed them for 'storming heavens' and stood up magnificently in defense of the Paris Communards against their enemies and calumniators. Again, even as he persistently warned against utopianism and Blanquism in the movement, he was scornfully dismissive of socialists within his own party in Germany who 'keep themselves within the limits of the logically presumable and of the permissible by the police'. Yet again, when the issue was joined between on the one hand the revolutionaries of the People's Will—the indigenous revolutionary organisation of his times in Russia, remembered for its insurrectionary politics and heroic defiance of the Czarist state—who postulated an immediate Russian revolution and the possibility of 'revolutionary leaps' which may ensure Russia 'bypassing the stage' of capitalism on its way to a just society, and on the other Marx's own 'disciples' in Russia—Plekhanov and others—whose strictly evolutionist Marxism saw history as constituted by necessary stages and postulated the necessity of a capitalist stage in Russia's advance to socialism, and, therefore, criticised the populist revolutionaries in the name of Marxism and scientific socialism, Marx came down loud and clear on the side of the revolutionaries of the People's Will. He found these revolutionaries, on trial for life, not only right in the essentials of their stand but 'simple, objective, heroic'. Theirs was, Marx wrote, 'not tryannicide as "theory" and "panacea" but a lesson to Europe in a "specifically" Russian historically inevitable mode of action, against which any moralizing from a safe distance was offensive'. Marx always spoke admiringly of human qualities of these revolutionaries and to the end he and Engels consistently referred to them as 'our friends'. In contrast, Marx spoke of the 'boring doctrines' of the evolutionist disciples and referred to them derisively as 'Russian capitalism admirers' (Incidentally, later on, Lenin too seems to have shared Marx's deviation on the Russian question. During and after 1905–07 revolution, he was accused of leaning towards populism, that is the Russian revolutionaries, by some of his associates and adversaries).

❖

Marx never countenanced scientistic, evolutionist, or economic determinist deformations of Marxism. On occasions, a legitimate Marxist recognition of the 'historically progressive' character of certain phenomena (men/women, movements, economic developments, etc.) has been deemed excuse enough to speak up for them and to eulogise and extend support to them in a manner as to go soft on the exploiting classes, even to the point of rallying behind them in the name of Marxism. Marx would have none of such political opportunism. It was on this issue that he, along with Engels, broke publicly with the Lassalleans in Germany and later, as we have seen, spoke with unconcealed scorn of 'Russian capitalism admirers'. Marx was always allergic to and contemptuous of such doctrinaire or, shall we say, 'scientific' Marxism. If Marx sought to discover the necessity underlying a contemporary socio-historical process, it was to establish the objective context or terrain of his own political struggle and define its revolutionary thrust. When he recognised the historical progressiveness of certain roles or developments, it was as *fait accompli*, without approval but with all their advantages and drawbacks, so as to make the best possible use of the new starting points or opportunities provided by them for the prosecution of his own political purpose, his uncompromising struggle aimed at overthrowing the system of exploitation and oppression that is capitalism—be it 'progressive', 'self-reliant' or any other. In this sense, Marx's practice of science was always subject to the logic of his political position, the choice he had already made in the fight between the people and those who oppress and exploit them. And, as we have already said, he had chosen to stand by the people. This choice, a revolutionary political position, was for Marx not a matter of scientific analysis—economic, social or historical; it was, as it has always been for revolutionaries, simply taking of sides in the ongoing class war.

In a brief but brilliant exploration of the life and work of late Marx, drawing our attention to this particular aspect of Marx as a revolutionary and, more specifically, to his expression of solidarity with the Russian revolutionaries, Teodor Shanin has written:

> It has been the way of many sophisticates of marxology to scoff at such utterances of Marx or to interpret them patronisingly as 'determined rather by... emotional motives' (an antonym, no doubt, of analytical, scientific or sound). To understand political action, especially the struggle for a socialist transformation of humanity, as an exercise in logic or as a programme of factory building only, is utterly to misconstrue it, as Marx knew well. Also, he shared with the Russian revolutionaries the belief in the purifying power of revolutionary action in transforming the very nature of those involved in it—the 'educating of the educators'. The Russian revolutionary populists' concern with moral issues found ready response in him. Moral emotions apart (and they were there and unashamedly expressed), revolutionary ethics were often as central as historiography to Marx's political judgment. So was Marx's distaste of those to whom the punchline of Marxist analysis was the adoration or elaboration of irresistible laws of history, used as the license to do nothing.

XXIV

The collapse of the Soviet Union has caused, however temporarily, a retreat from Marxism. Another consequence has been the resurgence of old and elaboration of new alternative theories. All sorts of essentially Right-wing ideologies have come to flourish. Old orthodoxies have been resurrected and ancient prejudices and superstitions argued for in modern and supposedly scientific ways. 'Culture' and 'civilisation' and their so-called 'clashes', are invoked to explain history rather than be explained by it and in an exercise of racial pseudo-science, not only is the reality of imperialism obscured but its crimes are justified as the product of cultural 'incompatibility'. 'Identity politics' and 'communitarianism' are the new catchwords; obscuring the reality of iniquitous class structures within and around the identities or communities and the 'mud of the times' invariably carried by them—for example, 'the coercions and inequities', in Amartya Sen's words, 'that many traditional communities standardly impose on less privileged members (such as women, or female children, or those belonging to the lower tiers of the collectivity)'; they are so theorised as to persuade the victims of capitalism and imperialism to accept and stay happy with their 'difference' in place of equality and liberation they need to struggle for. Multi-culturalism is hawked around, an inverted though disavowed racism, which is at the same time a safe, eminently marketable form of identitarianism in the academy and outside in the politics of the elites; its valoring of the separate and exotic 'other' as an authentic self-enclosed community, far from countering the proclaimed universality of capitalism only obscures the fact that the capitalist market is today homogenising and destroying, indeed McDonaldising cultures everywhere. And so on. Of these supposed alternatives, there is one that I would like to take a quick notice of—the rather 'in-fashion' post-modernism which is particularly influential in the Left intellectual circles in the West and has acquired adherents worldwide. Loud in proclaiming the 'end' or 'obsolescence' of Marxism, it has even claimed to be a replacement of and advance over Marxism, (or 'traditional Marxism' as its ex-Marxist adherents would have it), and thus, to be the most advanced radical social theory of these, our post-modernist times. Critics from the other end have seen post-modernism as, in some ways, the most dangerous of the forces currently threatening the survival of the socialist project inasmuch as it threatens the project from within, given its origins, the nature of its criticism, and the significant ex-Marxist presence in it. Post-modernism's rhetoric of rupture and discontinuity renders wrong everything you thought you ever knew and the accompanying fragmentation of time, space and historical experience is supposed to liberate us from the mistaken modernist notions of reason, knowledge, history, morals or progress, and, above all, the dead hand of 'meta-narratives'. The best or rather the worst, typical, representative of this mistaken 'modernity', they say, is Marxism and its socialist project. As it is, traditionally conditioned, coerced or persuaded to under-reach themselves as they have been in class-divided societies, people always had a hard time seeing beyond their most immediately visible oppressors or hopes for the future. Post-modernist thinking, with its distrust of so-called 'meta-narratives', simply reinforces such myopia. That is how, for post-modernism, capitalism *is* and socialism *can never be*...

❖

It is a point of interest that, as noticed above, quite a few of the original or leading post-modernists, who have thus argued against Marxism or socialism, were once (around 1968) themselves Marxists or near-Marxists. Some in France were Maoists, even 'more Maoist than the extreme Maoists in China' or, like Lyotard, members of the '*Socialisme ou barbarie*' group. They believed in what they were willing to call socialism. This draws our attention to a certain psychological aspect to this post-modernist episode in the intellectual biography of the Western Left intelligentsia. Post-modernism has certainly a great deal to do with capitalism; scholars like Jameson and Harvey have seen it as a cultural expression of late capitalism and Hawkes—old-fashioned enough to be still a believer in concepts like 'false consciousness'—has even defined and dismissed post-modernism as 'nothing more than the ideology of consumer capitalism'. But surely there is more than a grain of truth in the view which, taking cognisance of its noticeably significant French origins, has seen post-modernism as a passing, even if somewhat lasting, fad of French intellectuals (typically the survivors of the 'sixties generation'—professors in the universities that flourished during the post-war boom, and their students), who having lost their revolutionary faith, have taken refuge in a nihilistic skepticism rather than come to amicable terms with the bourgeois world in which they live and whose benefits they enjoy. Or perhaps, they have found it *psychologically* the most comforting way of coming to terms with this world and succumbing to it.

But a fad or whatever else originally, post-modernism is a significant mode of thought today which has much to do with the failure of the 1960s movement in France, the disappointment at the world not turning out quite as expected by the putative revolutionaries. If students and intellectuals were supposed to be the agents of revolution, the failure here was obviously no one's failure but their own. But, as Ellen Meiksins Wood has written, 'some took a different lesson from that failure. Instead of simple despair, they lapsed into a kind of hubris, an odd sort of defeatism combined with extreme intellectual arrogance: having given up on any social transformation, they shifted the terrain of "revolution" to the academy, to the academic politics of the text, replacing revolution by postmodernist deconstruction and "transgression"'; Politics was transformed 'into a disembodied academic exercise... instead of social revolution carried out by popular struggles, you get textual deconstruction carried out by intellectuals, as if this were the most subversive activity possible.' This however did not obviate the need of these erstwhile radicals for making a direct peace with the established order. But, given that they were among the beneficiaries of the relatively successful capitalism of the period of the post-war boom, with all its consumerist pleasures, and that their radical engagement was only skin deep, this did not pose much of a problem. That the post-war boom was *atypical* and with its end in the 1970s capitalism showed itself to be what it *normally* is did cause a degree of troublesome disorientation of consciousness but there was no serious loss of faith in capitalism's ability to deliver as it had done in the recent past. As their youthful political optimism of yesteryears gave way to a kind of 'libertarian pessimism', it could be easily combined with a near-conservative acceptance of the inevitability of capitalism, which later equally easily merged with the 'there is no alternative' chorus of the post-Soviet collapse years. Capitalism was not so bad after all, especially in its more exotic consumer forms. Much change in any case is not possible, only 'little recits' are, so goes Lyotard's discourse against 'grand narratives'. 'Radicals like everyone else', Terry Eagleton has written, 'can come to hug their chains, decorate their prison cells, rearrange the deck chairs on the *Titanic* and discover true freedom in dire necessity.'

❖

Though it does not exhaust the issues involved, the most important context of post-modernist ideas, in terms of their origins, appeal and later spread, is the desperate situation of general disorientation on the Left, a situation that appears to be unique in history, what with the ultimate exhaustion of the world communist movement and European social democracy, the collapse in the Soviet Union and China rolling along the capitalist road, the failure and abandonment of autonomous development in the third world and the harshest form of 'free market' capitalism as the implacable reality for the foreseeable future. Never before have ideas of justice and equality seemed so utopian, and socialism so far away.

In the satirical first chapter of his *The Illusions of Post-modernism*, Eagleton invites us, using a rhetorical device dear to postmodernists, to imagine a world in which the Left has suffered a crippling political defeat. This is how Colin Mooers has summarised it:

> In such a world one would expect that big ideas like 'social totality', 'class system', and 'mode of production' would become suspect, in part because the only kind of political activity around would seem to be restricted to the cracks and crevices of the system. The grand political projects of yesterday would have given way to an apparently more feasible and sensible 'micropolitics.' One could visualize a new politics celebrating the fragmentary and the ephemeral aspects of life emerging, or perhaps 'a new somatics' in which the body (but definitely not labouring ones) would be seen as the primary site of struggle and resistance. In the realm of knowledge one could imagine the belief taking hold that not much of anything could really be known for sure about the world—which

> raises the sticky question of how one would know that such a belief was true in the first place. If all scientific and other forms of knowledge had been levelled to the common denominator of 'culture', with no culturally produced 'discourse' any better than another, one could equally conceive of many well-intentioned people at a loss to justify why democracy might be preferable to, say, fascism. When political horizons shrink, 'rigorous, determinate knowledge is rather less in demand when there seems no question of full-blooded political transformation'.

The world Eagleton depicts is, of course, not fictional but entirely real. It is the depressingly familiar post-modernist intellectual and political landscape inhabited, Mooers says, 'by much of what is left of the Left.' As Eagleton himself puts it: 'Part of the power of postmodernism is that it exists, whereas how true this is of socialism these days is rather more debateable. *Pace* Hegel, it would seem at present that what is real is irrational, and what is rational is unreal.'

Post-modernism does not just exist or exist as a form of thought among the 'leftist' or 'progressive' academics. It has spread far and wide, its modern 'New Age' anti-rationalism finding allies in traditional irrationalism and obscurantism (ancient superstitions, religious fundamentalisms, etc.) and its theories any number of purveyors and practitioners among the supposedly up-to-date philosophers and social scientists, though, significantly enough, natural scientists have refused to be seduced by them. Much of ex-Marxism, often via post-Marxism, has found its way into post-modernism, and similarly disillusioned or otherwise complacent or conservatively inclined intellectuals everywhere, in the West as much as in the third world, have flocked to it as the very latest in social theory. For the time being at least, post-modernism is so ubiquitous and influential as to be the intellectual *fashion par excellence*. That post-modernism has spread so fast and far is a matter for social historians to explore. But the power of fashion apart, surely it has something to do with its animus against Marxism (however ambiguous it may be at times), and even more its unambiguous surrender to what *is*, that is, capitalism and its current triumphalism—a surrender made all the more attractive or comforting by the seemingly avantguard sophistication of post-modernism. It only needs to be added that the success, such as it is, of the post-modernist theory is largely parasitical because, as a contemporary has put it, 'it rests on its proponents' claims concerning the obsolescence of Marxism, and it is this which enables the post-modernists to position themselves as the most advanced radical social theorists'!

The language is abstruse and esoteric, almost incomprehensible, the 'discourse' inaccessible except to the initiates. Rhetoric of 'discontinuity' notwithstanding, there is continuity of assumption with the jargonised modernist thought that to be readable or comprehensible is to be superficial, to be not theoretical, certainly not theoretically profound. It is supposed to be a theory but there is no agreement among the proponents, let alone the critics, what precisely 'post-modernism' is. Its practitioners are in fact inclined to be rather disdainful of any such systemising or self-consistency seeking enterprise. Our difficulty in comprehending and assessing post-modernism critically is compounded by the fact that it has emerged generally, and as an influence on the Left, in almost inseparable association with a variety of other intellectual and political trends, including 'post-Marxism' and 'post-structuralism'. We have already noted something of what post-modernism is about. We will take another, closer look at it, including a look at the themes secreted in its interstices—which themes, even as we reject post-modernism, must be the concern of any serious socialist today—before concluding our argument over post-modernism and the original, main issue of Marxism.

Post-modernism covers an 'ill-defined complex of ideas ranging from art and architecture to the social sciences and philosophy, even the natural sciences'. But, as the name itself suggests, the basic thrust of post-modernism is a 'rupture' or 'discontinuity' with the 'project of modernity' which is seen to have its origins in the Enlightenment, though it came to fruition only in the nineteenth century. The so-called Enlightenment project is supposed to represent 'rationalism, technocentrism, the standardization of knowledge and production, a belief in linear progress and universal, absolute truths', a whole lot of such or similar ideas, values and beliefs, which are said to have gone into the making of the so-called project of modernity. Post-modernism is professedly a reaction to, and the rejection of this project.

The post-modernist interpretation of Enlightenment or the so-called 'project of modernity' is not my concern here. I will readily concede that there is a great deal to be criticised in the Enlightenment theories of history and progress, its view of science or technology, knowledge or truth, or reason itself whose excesses indeed spawned 'some petrified and tyrannical versions', as Feyeraband has described them. Its optimism or general hopefulness, however justified then or even now, could be charged with a certain lack of sensitivity to the complexity or *dialectics* of human situation and processes of social change. Certainly much went wrong in the working out of the principles of the Enlightenment. At the same time, it can be legitimately argued that much of what went wrong, or is wrong in the current situation, is traceable not to 'the process of Enlightenment' as it has been called, but to the incompleteness or distortion of this process under capitalism. For example, the reduction of reason to what is purely technically feasible, where the cause really lies in the way our modern *capitalist* societies are organised. Even otherwise the culprit is not 'reason', or for that matter science and technology *per se,* but rather the objectives towards which they are directed, so that the blame really lies with those wielding power in our societies who set these objectives—attack on rationality, science and technology, it may be noted, is welcome to these wielders of economic and political power, for it helps conceal the real cause, the social-structural relationships on which their power is based. A great deal more along these lines could be said in defence of the Enlightenment without denying what was wrong or has gone wrong with it. But more to the point is the fact that not only is all this only a small part of the story but that it soon came to be criticised from within, long before the arrival of post-modernism. Marx himself, for example, was profoundly aware of the limits or deficiencies of the theoretical baggage carried from Enlightenment. He certainly rejected any linear view of history or human progress.

Even as he hailed the spectacular productive achievements of capitalism—'wonders far surpassing Egyptian pyramids, Roman aqueducts and Gothic Cathedrals'—he continually emphasised the degradation and destruction it involved—'human progress (resembling) that hideous pagan idol who would not drink the nectar but from the skulls of the slain'—and pointed to the explicitly non-linear choice ahead which Rosa Luxemburg phrased as the alternatives, '*socialism* or *barbarism*'. In other words, Enlightenment or 'modernity' so-called had within them a strong critical tradition—'*De omnibus dubitandum*' ('Doubt everything') was a key notion with Enlightenment—which, over the years, questioned almost all the 'evils' now being ascribed to them by post-modernism. Aberrations, even serious aberrations, were there; but on the whole and at its best it was a tradition of positive, rational scepticism, a scientific scepticism if I may so call it, that helped us gain better knowledge of reality around us and improve our modes of getting things chosen and done—it could even be viewed as reforming the Enlightenment with the methods of Enlightenment. Post-modernism is, in its own way, rooted in this sceptical tradition within 'modernism'. But what has now happened is that in its 'new turn' (as one of its leading lights, Laclau, has called it), scepticism has been pursued, dogmatically, to its ultimate conclusion in a nihilistic rejection of the tradition of Enlightenment itself. As Eagleton has defined it: 'Postmodernism is a style of thought which is suspicious of classical notions of truth, reason, identity, and objectivity, of the idea of universal progress or emancipation, of single frameworks, grand narratives or ultimate grounds of explanation. Against these Enlightenment norms, it sees the world as contingent, ungrounded, diverse, unstable, indeterminate, a set of disunified cultures or interpretations which breed a degree of scepticism about the objectivity of truth, history, and norms, the givenness of natures and the coherence of identities.' Looking at it as a natural scientist, Alan Sokal has described postmodernism as 'an intellectual current characterized by the more-or-less explicit rejection of the rationalist tradition of the Enlightenment by theoretical discourses disconnected from any empirical test, and by a cognitive and cultural relativism that regards science as nothing more than a 'narration', a 'myth' or a social construction among many others'. Post-modernism makes a virtue of almost every anti-Enlightenment idea or perspective. The result is a pervasive political paralysis and ideological impasse.

Marxism, as the most worthy heir of the Enlightenment, seeks to find a perspective and purpose for human life by an inquiry into the functioning of human thought and action. Postmodernism, in its omnibus denial of the Enlightenment, makes no such inquiry, and says it cannot be made in a manner that at the end of it all the post-modernist view of life looks very much like what Shakespeare put in the mouth of Macbeth: 'a tale told by an idiot, full of sound and fury, signifying nothing'.

❖

Post-modernism sees the world or social reality, when it is at all willing to see it, as essentially fragmented and indeterminate, a realm of the contingent, the ephemeral and the discontinuous, where the only thing possible is delight in the chaos of life as if it were some kind of game. The social is not to be conceived either in terms of possessing unproblematically 'real' empirical characteristics, or in terms of constituting a structured totality. The very notion of structure or structural connections is denied. There is no such thing as a social whole or structured processes accessible to human knowledge and therefore to purposive human action, only a bricolage of difference, identity and social multiplicities, so diverse and flexible that it can be rearranged as you like by discursive construction. A dominant theme has been the denial of capitalism as a 'structured' and 'totalising' whole with its own systemic unity and 'laws of motion'. The constitutive relations of capitalism are at best only one personal 'identity' among many others, no longer in any way 'privileged' by their historic centrality. Capitalism, therefore, is simply unamenable to any 'causal analysis'. Structures and causes are all replaced by fragments and contingencies, and an absolute indeterminacy. There is an uncritical eclecticism that celebrates particularity and multiplicity for its own sake. What exists are only disconnected, anarchic and inexplicable *differences* or particularities. There are only so many different kinds of power, oppression, identity, etc. and of course, as many or more 'discourses' about them.

Causality and therefore the very possibility of causal analysis, is rejected. There can be no social science as it has been traditionally conceived—and in extreme cases perhaps, no science at all. What is deemed possible and advocated is a 'deconstructed', restless, indeterminacy of analysis. There is historicity of knowledge, but no historical knowledge or any objective truth. Marxism is ruled out and so is any other attempt at systematic explanation of social or historical conditions. Not only have we to give up any idea of intelligible historical processes or causality but along with it, evidently, any idea of 'making history'. One distinctive feature of the post-modernist 'new turn' is its rather loud rejection of 'totalising' thought in all its forms, the so-called 'meta-sagas' or 'meta-narratives'. And significantly enough, privileged for attack here are the universalistic, emancipatory 'meta-narratives', the projects for a general 'human emancipation', which are typically represented by Marxism and its project of socialism. It is argued that any broad movements for social change, general emancipatory struggles for equality and liberation, inevitably lead to new forms of repression and oppression. What is possible and permissible are only particular struggles, on particular issues or against particular oppressions, only a fragmented politics of 'difference', and 'identity'.

The post-modernist 'deconstructed' indeterminacy of analysis is carried into the realm of morals with similar nihilistic or near nihilistic consequences. We cannot be sure of any rational values. We simply cannot or do not have any general moral principles, let alone ones that should be universally defended as between human beings, communities and traditions. There is an unequivocal denial of the possibility or the desirability of universal values, ambitions or aspirations. The irreducible historicity of values (as of knowledge), interpreted in terms of a theoretically most flawed relativism, is so emphasised by post-modernists that, their protests notwithstanding, the end result is, and on their argument can only be, an undeniable moral nihilism, where there is only multiplicity of values (as of truths) and no rational way of choosing or deciding between them.

❖

Post-modernism may be disdainful of confronting fundamental issues or evasive about its philosophical premises, but it has come to sport what can only be described as idealism, its own specifically new form of philosophical idealism, the idealism of 'discourse', and at one more remove, of 'language' that 'discourse' cannot do without and is therefore reducible to. An idealism of the subjective kind, it has an obvious flavour of solipsism about it.

As the argument proceeds, social reality, seen as fragmented and indeterminate, is soon dissolved into 'discourse'. Since there are no historical conditions or connections, limits or possibilities, only arbitrary juxtapositions, conjunctures and contingencies, only discrete and isolated fragments or differences, if anything holds it all together, gives it meaning or coherence, it is only the logic of 'discourse'. What is involved here is not merely a detaching of thought (or ideology) from any basis in social reality, its autonomisation, but its self-sufficient independence and domination so that social reality itself is now constituted by thought or 'discourse'. Social reality is nothing objective, only a field of discursivity, a discursively constructed idea about it. In the ultimate analysis, it is a situation where language is all.

This however is nothing new, no post-modern 'discontinuity' with the past. A long time back, in *The German ideology*, Marx and Engels had written: 'Language is the immediate actuality of thought. Just as philosophers have given thought an independent existence, so they were bound to make language into an independent realm'. Philosophers have been at it, or preparing the ground for it, before, during and after Marx's own time. Plato's 'theory of ideas' as an exercise in 'reification of concepts' was a significant beginning, and Hegel's massive act of similar reification was thus noticed by Marx: 'To Hegel, the life-process of the human brain, i.e., the process of thinking, which, under the name of "The Idea", he even transforms into an independent subject, is the demiurgos of the real world, and the real world is only the external phenomenal form of "The Idea"'. Of the more recent 'Age of Analysis', Barrows Dunham has written: 'Whereas philosophers had once speculated boldly about the universe as a whole, they now preferred the safe latitudes of language. They began as seers, and they dwindled into grammarians.' Cutting itself free from the material world, philosophy in 'modern' times has not been without its devotees who have so focused on language as to not only question the objective validity of social concepts but even treat social problems as a matter of language and syntax—as if struggle against fascism, for example, involved no more than a definition of terms.

It has been a long journey for such idealism in Western philosophy. But it can be said that the destination or denouement has been now reached with post-modernism—a slide down the road from reality to discourse to language. Language is not merely an independent realm but an all-pervasive force, so omnipresent and dominant as to overwhelm and exhaust all that was supposed to be an objectively existing social reality. Language is all we can know about the world, and we have access to no other reality, none whatsoever except language or discourse. Once again matter has disappeared, this time giving way to the immateriality of communication, where everything is discourse and discourse is everything. Our very being, our identities or 'subjectivities' are constituted through discourse or language. Our 'language' or 'discourse', or 'text'—the jargon varies but not the message—defines and limits what we are, what we see or know, what we can imagine or do. It is all a matter of the way in which we are positioned by words in relation to other words. Oppression and exploitation, things like rape or deaths in police lock-ups and fake encounters, are really a matter of the way in which they are defined, rather 'constituted', linguistically—this is the only reality they have, or can even hope to have. So goes this new idealism.... That this idealism serves the established order or the power-that-be, is obvious. But it is equally a self-serving philosophy for the intellectual whom it privileges against fellow human beings. He is the one who discourses, or can discourse in the best deconstructionist-solipsistic manner.

❖

Post-modernism is very much *a la* mode at the moment, *the* fashion in the academy and elite intellectual circles elsewhere. And the power of fashion is great. But to say this is not to be dismissive about it. For fashion, in philosophy or social theory at least, is never something merely frivolous or fortuitous. It is always a true and revealing thing. And post-modernism in its spread is truly revelatory of the disillusionment caused by the collapse of the socialist project in our time, the seeming failure of the long-term promise of the Enlightenment and the consequent succumbing of the intellectual to the established order. But, as stated earlier, while political defeat on the Left is indeed its major context, it does not exhaust the significance of post-modernism. It is also a response to an equally real something else, the real situation as it has come to be in contemporary capitalism. As Jameson, along with many others, has pointed out, post-modernity corresponds to 'late capitalism', a new multinational 'informational' and 'consumerist' phase of capitalism. Postmodernism is the cultural-ideological expression of this phase, its own kind of answer to the needs and requirements of the new situation. It has also been argued that postmodernism is playing a contradictory role in the current phase of capitalism: compatible with, even celebratory of certain aspects of capitalism's current *zeitgeist*, especially its rampant consumerism, it has also rather aggressively exposed its several flawed aspects. And the argument is not entirely lacking in validity. This however is not the subject I want to pursue here. Important for my immediate purpose is the fact that postmodernism has, in its own way, raised or highlighted questions that we need to consider and incorporate into any analysis of what is wrong with the world today, if we would find really adequate or effective answers to its problems. In other words, secreted in the interstices of the basic thrust of postmodernism are themes which, reflecting as they do the real conditions under contemporary capitalism, are, therefore, also the themes with which people on the socialist Left must come to terms. This is how Ellen Meiksins Wood has listed the more important of these themes especially as they have found expression on the 'postmodern' Left:

> a focus on language, culture and 'discourse' ... to the exclusion of the Left's traditional 'economistic' concerns and the old preoccupations of political economy; a rejection of 'totalizing' knowledge and of 'universalistic' values (including Western conceptions of 'rationality', general ideas of equality, whether liberal or socialist, and the Marxist conception of general human emancipation), in favour of an emphasis on 'difference', on varied particular identities such as gender, race, ethnicity, sexuality, on various particular and separate oppressions and struggles; an insistence on the fluid and fragmented nature of the human self (the 'decentered subject'), which makes our identities so variable, uncertain, and fragile that it is hard to see how we can develop the kind of consciousness that might form the basis of solidarity and collective action founded on a common social 'identity' (such as class), a common experience, and common interests—a celebration of the 'marginal'; and a repudiation of 'grand narratives', such as Western ideas of progress, including Marxist theories of history…

Postmodernists have tended to lump these themes together in a dismissal of Marxism, rather what they allege Marxism to be. But as Wood has insisted, Marxists do not need to deny the importance of at least quite a few of these themes: 'For instance, the history of the twentieth century could hardly inspire confidence in traditional notions of progress, and those of us who profess to believe in some kind of "progressive" politics have to come to terms with all that has happened to undermine Enlightenment optimism. And who would want to deny the importance of "identities" other than class, of struggles against sexual and racial oppression, or the complexities of human experience in such a mobile and changeable world, with such fragile and shifting solidarities? At the same time, who can be oblivious to the resurgence of "identities" like nationalism as powerful, and often destructive, historical forces? Don't we have to come to terms with the restructuring of capitalism now both more global and more "segmented" than ever before? For that matter, who is unaware of the structural changes that have transformed the nature of the working class itself? And what serious socialist has ever been unconscious of the racial or sexual divisions within the working class? Who would want to subscribe to the kind of ideological and cultural imperialism that suppresses the multiplicity of human values and cultures? And how can we possibly deny the importance of language and cultural politics in a world so dominated by symbols, images, and "mass communication", not to mention the "information superhighway"? Who would deny these things in a world of global capitalism so dependent on the manipulation of symbols and images in a culture of advertisement, where the "media" mediate our own most personal experiences, sometimes to the point where what we see on television seems more real than our own lives, and where the terms of political debate are set—and narrowly constricted —by the dictates of capital in the most direct way, as knowledge and communication are increasingly in the hands of corporate giants?'

But, most important, Wood immediately adds:

> We don't have to accept postmodernist assumptions in order to see all these things. On the contrary, these developments cry out for a materialist explanation. For that matter, there have been few cultural phenomena in human history whose material foundations are more glaringly obvious than those of postmodernism itself. There is, in fact, no better confirmation of historical materialism than the connection between postmodernist culture and a segmented, consumerist, and mobile global capitalism. Nor does a materialist approach mean that we have to devalue or denigrate the cultural dimensions of human experience. A materialist understanding is, instead, an essential step in liberating culture from the stranglehold of commodification.
>
> If post-modernism does tell us something, in a distorted way, about the conditions of contemporary capitalism, the real trick is to figure out exactly what those conditions are, *why* they are, and where we go from there. The trick, in other words, is to suggest historical explanations for those conditions instead of just submitting to them and indulging in ideological adaptations. The trick is to identify the real problems to which the current intellectual fashions offer false – or no – solutions, and in so doing to challenge the limits they impose on action and resistance. The trick, therefore, is to respond to the conditions of the world today not as cheerful (or even miserable) robots, but as critics.

And no theory provides better weapons for the needed critique and true solutions to the real problems of the world today than Marxism.

❖

Post-modernism, with its denial of objectivity and causality and overall explanatory agnosticism, its embrace of an indeterministic concept of complexity and ultra-relativism in matters of truth and morals, its overriding historical cynicism and fear-laden contempt for modernist 'meta-narratives', all of which really adds upto a rejection of everything that purports to offer anything resembling *answers*, can obviously provide no answers to the problems that the modern, or shall we say post-modern, world confronts. Its claim to be a radical rupture with the past only betrays its lack of historical sensitivity which makes it sublimely oblivious of everything that has been said so many times in the past and condemns it to conscious or unconscious repetition of old themes. Even the epistemological skepticism, the assault on universal truths and values, which is so crucial a part of this current intellectual fashion, has a history as old as philosophy—post-modernism has only so pursued it as to reach altogether nihilistic conclusions. That science or morals are a social or historical product is turned into an argument that all theories or moral principles, thus conditioned, are equally valid or invalid, and the categories involved valid only as objects of discourse. Concepts indispensable to any worthwhile social theory, 'universalism', 'essentialism', 'functionalism' and what they misdescribe as 'reductionism'—which like all such concepts need to be used with care and sophistication—are attacked and rejected as 'the four methodological sins' of modernism, and Marxism is held to be the worst culprit. The uniqueness of things is used to deny the possibility of general theories about anything. Particularity is celebrated without realising that it is self-defeating because any account at the level of the given particular can be undercut by some more particularistic analysis. We can never actually know when any particular is particular enough, and in any case the smallest significant particulars you can think of—groups, selves, experiences, thoughts, words, events, actions—are themselves inevitable *abstractions* from countless further particulars. In fact, without a more general or universal theory it is impossible to tell when to stop or make sense of particularities. And these 'universalising' theories, all the time moving from the particular to the general, have embodied immense imagination and scientific capacities and helped us reach ever closer to the nature or truth of things. 'Essentialism' is considered a major methodological sin when it is simply indispensable to any realist thinking about complex entities and processes. Without some coherent notion of what is central, that is *essential* to a thing which makes it, as a specific unity of parts or particulars, *the* thing and no other, and without which it would be literally unrecognisable as that type of thing, it is impossible even to speak of any particular thing (for example, an 'identity' that post-modernists are otherwise so loud about), or postulate anything explanatory about its being, behaviour or functioning. 'Functionalism' is questioned when, positing a certain kind of 'why' questions of its subject matter, 'making sense' of how things came to be what they are, explaining the emergence, persistence or rationale of the more concrete practices, institutional arrangements or ideological phenomena in terms of, for example, the way in which they comply with the needs or logic of interests of classes in society, functional explanation has its intellectual validity and value and remains, not an all-purpose affair but a legitimate *part* of any adequate, reasonably comprehensive causal explanation. As 'reductionism', what is rejected is the act integral to any explanation where some things are picked out as important and given prominence over others in terms of their effects or influence—otherwise there is no explanation, only 'disparate fragments' or 'aggregates' and their *descriptive* statement. What is entailed here, as I have argued earlier, is a failure to distinguish between explanation that is reductionist *and* explanation. These vital concepts are so interpreted or misinterpreted by post-modernists as to cover and reject not just simplistic or lazy explanations but any kind of serious causal analysis or general explanatory enterprise.

❖

That this epistemological skepticism stops short of nihilism in practice only means that, at this level at least, it is impossible to wish away social reality and some knowledge to cope with it, however fragmented a view one takes of both; the fragments are yet the sites where human beings live and act. Postmodernism thus is not entirely bereft of knowledge. Its 'fragmented knowledge' has produced some keen insights, well-suited for narrowly defined specific types of tasks, even when any 'big picture' or 'meta-narrative' is ruled out. This is welcome and to be acknowledged. But there is an interesting aspect to it which also cries out to be noticed. Its 'rhetoric of ruptures' notwithstanding, post-modernism here is very much like the modernist (mainstream or bourgeois) social science, governed as it has been by quantitative empiricism and mindless specialisation, where its narrow focus and piecemeal approach, and distrust of generalised explanatory theory, have led it to study only relatively unrelated, particular parts, areas or problems of contemporary social and political life, and thus helped it avoid 'big issues' concerning the basic character of society as a whole and the general direction of its movement, and thereby also evade the issue of large scale social change. Neither modernist social scientists, nor post-modernists, however, would be willing to accept that in turning away from 'grand theory' in one case and 'meta-narrative' in the other, they have both come to deal with 'small potatoes' only and avoid the 'big issues'. The former assume away the big issues, whereas the post-modernists claim that big issues do not exist or that they are impossible to understand. If modernist social science *adjusts* itself to existing social reality, that is, the established social order, in one way, post-modernism does it in another, its own post-modernist way.

The adjustment has been facilitated in both cases by their respective stances on the question of values. Bourgeois social science's treatment of values as somehow beyond rational inquiry or validation (and the accompanying fetishisation of 'value freedom' or 'ethical neutrality') is paralleled by post-modernism's ultra-relativism in matters moral or cultural. It should not be difficult to see that in both cases, notwithstanding their occasional expression of dissatisfaction, or disillusionment, with the current state of affairs, this in effect amounts to an endorsement of and submission to the currently dominant moral and cultural values of bourgeois society. The two incidentally, also share in obscuring this adjustment and submission to bourgeois social order by their linguistic practices. Critical of unnecessary obscurity and jargon of modernist discourse, post-modernism has created a parallel obscurity of hermeneutics, deconstruction and textual nihilism. Once again, triviality of content is often in sharp contrast to complexity of form, obscurity of presentation a substitute or compensation for the lack of substance. 'Post-modern gibberish' of 'the latest lunacies of Paris culture', Chomsky has called it. A critic has written of 'the more obscure, relativistic cant put out by post-modernism', and as an example referred us to Jacques Derrida's *Spectres of Marx: The State of the Debt, the Work of Mourning and New International*!

Post-modernism's fascination for obscurity in thought and expression is well-illustrated by the now famous 'Sokal affair', the unorthodox and admittedly uncontrolled experiment carried out by Alan Sokal, Professor of Physics at New York University, to show up the kind of work that has proliferated under the banner and influence of post-modernism. Alan Sokal self-identifies as 'a stodgy old scientist who believes, naively, that there exists an external world, that there exist objective truths about that world, and that my job is to discover some of them', adding: 'If science were merely a negotiation of social conventions about what is agreed to be "true", why would I bother devoting a large fraction of my all-too-short life to it?' And the experiment was a parody he wrote under the forbiddingly pompous title, 'Transgressing the boundaries: Towards a transformative hermeneutics of quantum gravity', which was then accepted and published by the prestigious American cultural studies journal, organ of American post-modernists, *Social Text* (1996). As later explained by Sokal himself, the parody was constructed around quotations from eminent French and American intellectuals—a veritable pantheon of contemporary 'French theory' including Gilles Deleuze, Jacques Derrida, Felix Guattari, Luce Irigaray, Jacques Lacan, Bruno Latour, Jean-Francois Lyotard, Michael Serres and Pul Virilio, and many leading American academics in Cultural Studies and related fields—about the alleged philosophic and social implications of mathematics and the natural sciences. The passages may have been absurd or meaningless, but they were nonetheless authentic. Sokal's only contribution was to provide a 'glue' (the 'logic' of which was admittedly whimsical) to join these quotations together and praise them. The article, its supposedly erudite but nonsensical jargon apart, was brimming with absurdities and blatant non sequiturs. The whole thing, as Sokal later said, was a 'melange of truths, half-truths, quarter-truths, falsehoods, non-sequiturs and syntactically correct sentences that have no meaning, whatsoever'. In addition, it asserted an extreme form of cognitive relativism: after mocking the old-fashioned 'dogma' that 'there exists an external world, whose properties are independent of any individual human being and indeed of humanity as a whole', it proclaimed categorically that 'physical "reality", no less than social "reality", is at bottom a social and linguistic construct'. By a series of stunning leaps of logic, it arrived at the conclusion that 'the pi of Euclid and the G of Newton, formerly thought to be constant and universal, are now perceived in their ineluctable historicity'. The rest too was in the same vein.

Published in a special issue of *Social Text* devoted to rebutting the criticisms levelled against post-modernism and social constructivism by several distinguished scientists, neither the editors of the journal nor any of the post-modern fraternity recognised that it was a parody and a hoax till, a few months later, Sokal himself revealed the truth, provoking a firestorm of reaction in both the popular and academic press, earning Sokal, along with protests, the thanks from many scholars and researchers in the humanities and social sciences for what he had done. Incidentally, the 'affair' provoked this delicious observation from a commentator, Katha Pollitt:

> the comedy of the Sokal incident is that it suggests that even the post-modernists don't really understand one another's writing and

> make their way through the text by moving from one familiar name or notion to the next like a frog jumping across a murky pond by way of lily pads.

❖

Possibly the most important thing to be specifically noted in postmodernist social theory is its cognitive relativism, which throws into question any effort at scientific understanding of social reality, dismissing it as vulgar positivism, and has obviously nihilistic consequences in the sphere of morality or ethics. There is not just an emphasis on discourses (or language) as opposed to the facts to which these discourses refer, but a rejection of the very idea that facts exist or that one may refer to them. All facts are contingent and socially, indeed intellectually, constructed, and all discourses are merely 'stories' or 'narratives', none more objective or truthful than another. All are 'equally valid' as descriptions or analyses of the real world (assuming that one admits the existence of a real world). Writing of 'the rise of "postmodernist" intellectual fashions in Western universities, particularly in departments of literature and anthropology, which imply that all "facts" claiming objective existence are simply intellectual constructions... that there is no clear difference between fact and fiction', Eric Hobsbawm has insisted that there is a difference 'and for historians, even for the most militantly anti-positivist ones among us, the ability to distinguish between the two is absolutely fundamental'. Postmodernism does not recognise such 'fundamentalism' or 'dogmas'. It so emphasises the historicity of knowledge as to confuse the questions of origins with those of truth or validity and is wary of and rejects any assessment of social reality that claims to be based on truth, going beyond what is currently accepted as 'good in the way of belief'—which, it should be obvious, is established by media, business interests, governments, by the powers that be in our society. In denying any real foundation for knowledge or truth, the post-modern scepticism permits at best only interpretation, 'fiction', as some would call it. It may with Foucault claim that in holding this view one need not 'go so far as to say that fictions are beyond truth'; but such concession is only verbal and ritualistic, a homage that the good old 'concept of truth' yet exacts from the post-modern sceptic. What in effect ensues is a pragmatism which, as with Richard Rorty for example, contends that the only kind of truth that counts is the power to enter into meaningful conversation with the members of one's own interest group, or 'interpretive community' who share the same 'good in the way of belief'. We have already noticed how its recognition of the undoubted historicity of values, combined with a refusal to admit any other validating principles, leads post-modernism to sport an ultra-relativism which denies the very possibility of any universal values like equality, fraternity, justice, etc. What needs to be further recognised is that its cognitive relativism, where 'nothing explains anything and everything is simply a matter of perspective' and the 'concept of truth' is irrelevant, has the consequence of making it even more nihilistic in the matter of values or moral judgments than would be the case otherwise. We are indeed left with no values at all, not even the otherwise permitted, historically conditioned particular values, though we were still without any rational criteria to evaluate them, to choose or decide between them. As Norman Geras has argued:

> If there is no truth, there is no injustice. Stated less simplistically, if truth is wholly relativised or internalised to particular discourses or language games or social practices, there is no injustice. The victims and protesters of any *putative* injustice are deprived of their last and often best weapon, that of telling what really happened. They can only tell their story, which is something else. Morally and politically, therefore, anything goes.

Of course, one cannot insist that there is just one true image of a person or description of an event or state of affairs. Different angles of vision and personal beliefs, different political, cultural or other purposes, different linguistic and conceptual frameworks, will shape and colour the content of any description or narrative, yielding a plurality of possible representations of whatever is the subject at hand. Yet there is, for all that, a way things were down there, a reality constraining the range of adequate description, interpretation or explanation, the basis for a more or less true, relatively but nevertheless objectively true, description, interpretation or explanation. Post-modernism's cognitive relativism, pushed this way or thus far, simply blocks this last kind of judgment and thus opens the door wide for a moral relativism which is ultimately destructive of all values–though many of the post-modernists are in the habit of denying that they are relativists at all.

❖

Post-modernism claims to be a radical social theory, it not *the* radical social theory for our postmodernist times. Many who would still be on the left have even seen it as a replacing advance over Marxism. But its basic thrust and detailed principles or positions are destructive of any kind of radical politics. We have already noticed its emphasis on the fragmented nature of the world and human knowledge, and the impossibility of any emancipatory politics based on some kind of 'totalising' vision. The view that there are no systems and no history susceptible to causal analysis rules out any possibility of getting to the root of many powers that oppress us, and with it any aspiration to some kind of serious united opposition for general *human* emancipation. The fragments alone can be the sites of our struggles, and the most we can hope for is a lot of particular and separate resistances, an oppositional politics fragmented and parcellised into many disconnected pieces. Radical politics has been traditionally seen as having to do with the overarching power of classes or states and opposition to them. This is now effectively pushed out of consideration, giving way to the fractured struggles of 'identity politics', 'new social movements', or even the 'personal as political', to a reformist politics devoid of any overarching political or social vision. Instead of a radical departure, we once again witness the much proclaimed post-modernist 'rupture' ending up as a continuity. For this is surely not very different from those traditional forms of liberal 'pluralism' which denied that there was any concentration of power or systemic source of domination in capitalist society, and argued in defence of a 'pluralist politics'. It would appear that the new post-modernist discourse is 'post-modernist', rather 'anti-modernist', only in its rejection of modernism in one of its forms—Marxism, while adopting the old universalist language of another—liberalism, the ruling form of the modernist project.

A significant aspect of post-modernist social theory, which more than anything else exposes its real nature and pretensions to radicalism, is the way it treats the question of capitalism. Rooted essentially, even if ambiguously, in 'the golden age' of post-war capitalism, the 1960s, post-modernists have accepted an ahistorical notion of a capitalism that delivers, and failed or refused to see it historically and as it actually exists and works —an essentially irrational economic system, full of inherent contradictions and problems and, despite current triumphalism, in deep crisis everywhere. In the words of Ellen Meiksins Wood, 'the postmodern sense of epochal novelty depends on ignoring, or denying, one overwhelming historical reality: that all the ruptures of the twentieth century have been bound together in a single historical unity by the logic—and the internal contradictions—of capitalism, the system that dies a thousand deaths.' The in-fashion post-modernist philosophers have been busy deconstructing literally everything in sight, except what really counts, that is, capitalism.

Post-modernism's self-description and the form of periodisation it relies on—modernity transiting, 'rapturously', to post-modernity—obscures the most important part of the way the things really were, and are, out there, that is, the historical development and actuality of capitalism. And the way its epistemological scepticism has gone on to question and throw out all notions of 'structure' or 'system', or 'totality', capitalism is simply 'off limits' for purposes of study and analysis as a structured whole or a system—least of all as an irrational, exploitative system whose accumulative logic puts its disfiguring mark on everything within its reach, which reach, via market, extends far beyond our economy, politics, morality, culture, etc., into the deepest recesses of our social and personal life—'though we may forget about totality', Eagleton has written, 'we may be sure that it will not forget about us.' That 'totality' remains forgotten and capitalism as a totalising system can hardly be said to exist in postmodern discourse, has an obvious implication. If you cannot even *think* capitalism as a system, you cannot understand or criticise it, let alone oppose it. You may as well lie back and enjoy its consumerist and other pleasures—which is indeed what most post-modernists are doing.

The denial or rejection of anti-capitalist politics as old-fashioned, out-of-date left politics, or a dangerous 'totalising' or 'universalist' enterprise, has its inevitable fallout. When the irrationality of the structural logic of capitalism comes to threaten people with its multiform consequences and problems, which are neither understood nor opposed, and which mess up and disorient even the alternative politics of 'identity' and 'new social movements', which, in any case, as with the conventional old politics, does not take you very far in this situation, a 'capitalism is off limits' approach can only lead to cynicism and depoliticisation, if not outright reaction.

There are those who have hoped for post-modernism having the same politicising effect on young people today that existentialism had on youth in the West in the 1960s and early 1970s. But so far the evidence has been only to the contrary. Deep epistemological scepticism and profound political defeatism have gone hand in hand in post-modernism, pointing the way to disillusion, apathy and inactivity. The capitalist social order today tends to produce and reproduce political apathy. Culture of depoliticisation is a hallmark of monopoly capitalism which infects even the most oppressed sections of society. Post-modernism feeds into monopoly capitalism's culture of depoliticisation. The claims to be a radical social theory, however, persist. But, as Michael Ryan, in a book written sometime back to find common ground between Marxism and post-modernism, noted: 'millions have been killed because they were Marxists; no one will be obliged to die because she/he is a deconstructionist.'

Post-modernism does have a certain sophistication to its critique of 'modernism so-called' including Marxism, though critics have also seen it as a 'hairsplitting philosophy', as Marx in his time described the early 'dissection' of Hegelian philosophy. It has revelled in proclaiming Marxism to be dead and buried, but scholars, in a way similar to Marx and Engels' characterisation of new German philosophers in the opening paragraphs of *The German Ideology*, have found it generating much noise but little understanding. While it certainly knows that all is not well with the world, post-modernism indeed offers little to help make it a significantly better place, only some petty, fragmented interventions and a sophisticated way of making peace with its many wrongs. This is so primarily because post-modernist theory precludes even the notion of capitalism as a system—and this at a time when the world is being shaped, rather mis-shaped, by global capitalism as never before, both at the centre and in its semi-peripheries and peripheries. It is indeed amazing that for all its rhetoric against 'meta-narratives', post-modernism fails or refuses to see the ongoing 'meta-narrative' of our times, that of capitalism, and does so when continuing beyond its historical time, capitalism has exhausted its creative potentialities and is now a bearer of only destructive possibilities for the future of humankind.

❖

Post-modernism rejects 'meta-narratives' of human emancipation, and views 'fragments', all that is there to social reality according to it, as the only possible spaces for any kind of 'emancipatory' politics. In doing so post-modernism does tap some real concerns or causes of our time—democracy and decentralisation of power, economic and social justice, environmentalism, feminism and sexual liberation, human rights, rights of ethnic groups and minorities, and so on—but without providing any effective answers to the problems involved. The task here is to understand the historical material conditions that block the realisation of the objectives which these concerns or causes represent and the kind of transformations that would make their realisation possible. But any serious effort of this nature is bound to take us back to capitalism and its systemic logic. And here post-modernism, far from being a help, is in fact a positive liability; its fragmentation of both theory and practice and refusal to see the systemic nature of capitalism only weakens our capacity to understand and to resist capitalism, which is a necessary, though not sufficient, condition for a successful pursuit of the above-mentioned concerns or causes.

It needs to be noticed that there is nothing particularly 'post-modernist' about these concerns or causes which post-modernism claims as its own. If anything, they are quintessentially 'modernist'. Most of them are deeply rooted in Enlightenment values—a humanist pride in our existence, faith in reason, science and knowledge, hopefulness about a future of progress and a world fit for every human being, etc.—and all of them long part of the general history of the socialist Left, and still central to its struggle for a more humane society which it believes socialism to be. A failure to see this is yet another evidence of post-modernism's remarkable insensitivity to history which also accounts for this supposedly radical theory's deafness to the reactionary echoes of its attack on the Enlightenment and its values.

It has been suggested that while both sides of the twentieth century's ambiguous history, its horrors and its wonders, have played a part in forming the post-modernist consciousness, the horrors that have undermined the old idea of progress are less important in defining the distinctive nature of today's post-modernism than are the wonders of modern technology and the riches of consumer capitalism, so that 'post-modernism sometimes looks like the ambiguities of capitalism as seen from the vantage point of those who enjoy its benefits more than they suffer its costs'. It is surely pertinent to note that, questions concerning capitalism and post-modernism apart, of the more worthwhile benefits that people in the privileged positions have enjoyed in the West and elsewhere, not a few have accrued from a pursuit of the Enlightenment values, which pursuit is supposed to have continued as a questionable feature of modernity. In other words, those denouncing Enlightenment and modernity have been beneficiaries of the very values they so blithely denounce today. These privileged post-modernist elites may well disown, condemn and reject these values now, but the overwhelming mass of common humanity the world over, suffering from injustice and exploitation, poverty, disease and ignorance, all sorts of economic and social backwardness, can ill afford to do so. They have indeed refused to abandon these values. As O'Neill has rather cryptically remarked: 'No, it is not these people who have abandoned idealism, universalism, truth and justice. It is those, who already enjoy these things who have denounced them on behalf of the others.'

The people need to defend and uphold Enlightenment values in full recognition of the fact that even though it had nothing to do with many of them, capitalism, in its contradictory progress has both sustained and destroyed these values and that in its current phase it subverts and destroys them more than ever before. If 'modernity' has indeed anything at all to do with these values, then modernity is well and truly about over, terminated by capitalism. Enlightenment too could be declared dead, almost. May be socialism will revive it. Be that as it may, the vital fact is that the reality generating the world's most serious problems, today and for our future, has a name and it is not modernity but capitalism. And post-modernity is no answer to it. The antithesis to capitalism is not post-modernism, it is socialism.

❖

The material, moral and cultural crisis of our times, further underlined and accelerated by the Soviet collapse, has found its response in various forms of backward-looking philosophies, newer versions of old Right-wing ideologies, religious and other fundamentalisms. These have flourished the world over, even when they have no answers to the real problems of the common people. The backward parts of the world have been having more than their share of reactionary theories and practices. The economically and technologically advanced Western world, while having its share of these, has pre-eminently responded with a supposedly forward looking social theory of its own, post-modernism, which, however, is not without its almost inevitable weak or loud, despairing or hopeful, echoes among the academics and intelligentsia of the backward parts. This theory too has little understanding of and no answers to the problems the common people face, and is an ally of reaction in its own way. But it has a feature which perhaps, for good or ill, could be regarded as distinctively its own: political impotence. Professing an epistemic skepticism, explanatory agnosticism and historical cynicism, it has generated new orthodoxies of relativism and revived or reinforced many old ones, to provide a way of seeing, knowing and acting in the world where we are informed that to speak of 'reality' is ancient folly, that 'the way the world is no particular way at all, if indeed we can know enough about it in the first place even to assert that', that there is no 'objective truth' any longer, nor any values or ideals that can be rationally defended or validated, that all social analysis is blinded and indeterminate and, therefore, all action beyond a timorous reformism a dangerous adventure, that there are no structures to break or causes to espouse, the 'system' or 'economic structures' that radicals seek to change are, theoretically speaking, simply non-existing, that all this, and whatever else there is, is real only as 'object' for discourse and 'discourse' is all that is left to us to engage in, indeed the only worthwhile activity for those who are really knowledgeable about things or feel concerned about them. No wonder it has been suggested that Chinese rulers could well have distributed copies of Derrida, Foucault or Laclau to the protesting students and workers at Tiananmen Square. This would have surely dispersed them more easily and rapidly than water cannons or bullets. They would have read and realised the futility of it all, repented their waywardness and returned home peacefully, to the safety and pleasures of post-modernist discourse!

Post-modernism is hardly the philosophy or social theory to help us confront the hard and harsh realities of the contemporary capitalist world. It simply does not have the resources for that. It came up very much as a fashion, and fashions change. It is very likely that a decade or two from now, it will no longer be the major point of reference it is today, especially among certain elite intellectual or academic circles. Its political impotence or defeatism apart, it is too feeble philosophically to have anything like the intellectual staying power of Marxism it claims to replace and to which people will soon turn, or return, if for no other reason than the one adduced by Althusser:

> the feebleness of current theoretical thinking is such that the mere reappearance of those elementary but necessary ingredients of authentic thought—rigour, coherence, and clarity—will at a certain

> point contrast so markedly with prevailing intellectual attitudes that all those who are bewildered by what has happened are bound to be struck by them.

Marxism, however, has a great deal more to offer than just 'rigour, coherence, and clarity', only a body of 'authentic thought'. It has its acknowledged achievements of theory and practice, its scientific potential, ethical commitment, and failures notwithstanding, a long tradition of successful revolutionary politics and, above all, an overriding contemporary relevance, where capitalism is in a long-term structural crisis which, precisely because of its current 'triumph', makes capitalism more desperate and dangerous than ever before, indeed a threat to the very future of humankind. Marxism has weightier reasons for people, including radical intellectuals, turning, or returning, to Marxism.

XXV

It is now universally recognised that the world is in deep trouble. And there is no assurance that it can eventually transcend its current crises. Marxists are, thankfully, far from being the only ones striving nowadays to tell the truth about the world and act on the truth which is theirs. But if the challenge is seen as anything more than finding more or less effective answers to its isolated problems, if it is to articulate a programme of action, both inspirational and practical, whose analysis of the world is holistic enough to go to the roots of its troubles in order to identify the barriers, material-ecological as well as social-structural, that need to be overcome to find truly effective and lasting answers, then it seems inconceivable that this can be done without turning to Marxism—at the very least, without assigning a major role for the Marxist tradition. Of course, this Marxism can neither be the ancient 'official' Marxism or the recently fashionable 'post-Marxism'. It will be authentic Marxism that, conscious of its limitations, is open, in the spirit of its classical tradition, to other critical and non-complacent currents of thought and action, and, conscious of its adequacies, in the spirit of the same classical tradition, is orthodoxly firm in commitment to its basic principles. It will also need to have the capacity to digest and transcend its costly defeats, particularly the recent collapse of the regimes calling themselves Marxist.

More than anything else, it is this political defeat, and not any theoretical refutation, which is the fundamental cause of the current retreat or recession of Marxism. A theoretical refutation of Marxism has indeed not been forthcoming; critics have been happy demolishing, as always, only strawmen, or vulgar and 'lazy' Marxism. The authentic Marxist tradition remains alive and relevant as ever. A dialectical-materialist orientation still helps us in understanding the world and our place in it, and resolving knotty philosophical problems—which also have important implications for our political theory and practice—concerning the relations between being and consciousness, change and determinacy, the general and the particular, the relative and the absolute, the concrete and the abstract, the internal and external in causation, concerning partisanship and objectivity of science, and so on. Historical materialism together with Marxist analysis or critique of capitalism is still the most powerful framework available for understanding and spotlighting the constraints and possibilities in the current world disorder, though it does not predict, or for that matter promise, human survival and transcendence, which is ultimately a matter of effective human intervention. To speak of the end or *final demise* of Marxism is to betray a wishful prejudice and rank ignorance of the intellectual and political history of our time. As Norman Geras has put it:

> Judged as an intellectual tradition of the kind of breadth and wealth that this one has encompassed, the very question of its end is comical. No less. Of no other intellectual tradition of remotely comparable achievement would such a question even be posed. With historical materialism, Marxism contributed fertile analytical resources to our understanding of history. It mounted a powerful critique of the evils of capitalism. And it set itself to seeking forces for, and ways of, challenging and overcoming them. This is to say nothing of what it offered more generally to the whole culture of a century and more through a legion of thinkers, writers and artists. The celebration of its end is at best wishful thinking and at worst a form of intellectual intolerance.

Geras' statement on Marxism as a critical intellectual tradition makes a point which is important enough to bear repetition in this summing up of my argument concerning Marxism, a point which is also a more specific reason why Marxism remains relevant and need have no fears about its survival. Historical materialism, as the historical and theoretical basis of Marx's critique of capitalism, thereby also provided for the theoretically and politically ambitious liberationist project of classical Marxism: a socialist transition to a communist future for humankind. Marxism, in its anti-capitalist thrust, is the critical science of human emancipation. Yes, if you like, the meta-narrative of science in the service of human emancipation in our time. Within Marxism as a theory and its authentic practice which has linked it to radical or revolutionary popular movements all over the world, two elements have been central: the aim to critically understand the present-day societies where exploitation and inequality continue to exist; and the intention to go beyond criticism of the present in order to build a new society, an exploitation-less society of freedom and equality. Hence Marxism's rejection of capitalism and the argument for its negation in socialism, a call to replace capitalism with a more rational and humane social order. This call to replace capitalism has lost none of its urgency today. For this reason alone, if nothing else, the body of theory that underlines and addresses this call remains as vital and relevant now as it ever was.

The first historically-effective response to this call, the effort to build socialism in the Soviet Union, has no doubt failed. Socialists will long continue to debate this failure, even argue whether it was a massive setback or the disappearance of a liability. They certainly need to analyse and understand this failure, to digest the experience of this political defeat. But the failure of this particular project or even of a whole epoch of such projects, can have no bearing on the need for socialism or on the validity of the theory which articulated that need and continues to do so. The socialist project was conceived, as a way of overcoming the power of capital, a very long time before the Soviet Union came into being; it remains with us for the same reason after the Soviet Union has ceased to be. As has been well put, 'the real ground of socialist politics was never the existence of the Soviet Union but rather the existence of capitalism'. Indeed, aware that things there had gone grievously wrong, some of us could be said to be socialists despite the Soviet Union.

Socialism always was, and remains, about capitalism. It is, as it always has been, the specific antithesis to capitalism. As long as there is capitalism, the socialist project will have a solid historical foundation, it will remain on humankind's agenda for the future. Of course, after what has happened, there is need for a better, perhaps more precise, understanding of what socialism and the struggle for socialism entails—for instance, what its transitional forms or routes are going to be in different parts of the world or what the practice of revolutionary socialist politics today involves, especially in countries with bourgeois democratic regimes, etc. It has to be an understanding which is fully sensitive to our skeptical times, and adequate enough to cope with the new, unanticipated situation in the world where the first experiment in socialism has failed and capitalism has re-acquired its global domination.

Such or similar renewals of socialist understanding are certainly needed but they are purposeful only within Marxism and not without it. Marxism, in its basic propositions, remains the necessary theory for understanding, criticising and struggling against capitalism as it exists today and works out its logic of accumulation at its centres and in the peripheries. It is all the more necessary because of the renewed global domination of capitalism, which has meant increased economic exploitation of the people everywhere, more ruthless plunder of human and natural resources of the earth, a worldwide moral, cultural and ecological devastation, and all sorts of regressive and disintegrative developments that have followed in its wake—this domination and its displacement or delegitimisation, however partial or temporary, of the socialist alternative and hope has surely something to do with the new resurgence of more or less sophisticated reactionary philosophies, aggressive promotion of a rapacious, consumerist individualism, the murderous outbreaks of chauvinistic nationalism and racism, xenophobic tribalism and homophobia, religious and other fundamentalisms, and 'terrorism'. That the renewed ideological hegemony of capitalism presently prevents people from seeing all this is a fact. But the situation is changing with every passing year. The objective reality of it all is daily pressing itself into the consciousness of the people. And as people learn through their experience, they will find Marxism helping them to put the right meaning into it, to penetrate the thick veil of bourgeois and associated reactionary ideologies and see the truth of this world, the real source of their misfortunes, and act accordingly.

The world is acknowledgedly in deep trouble today, plagued by a myriad problems. Insofar as it is the world of global capitalism, Marxism remains indispensable for those who would confront these problems with any hope of success. I will only add that this world is populated not only by lovers of capitalism, or its mere victims, or by 'cheerful robots' as C. Wright Mills called them, but also, and increasingly, by some very angry human beings, those still fighting under the darkened skies for a world fit for everyone. Marxism is where they will find the necessary intellectual weapons for their struggles.

What is at stake in the current crisis, therefore, as I stated in the beginning, is not Marxism, whose necessity and future as a critical intellectual tradition and theory of socialism, are well-assured, but the present and future of socialism *in our time*, and this is my basic concern in these notes.

Chapter 3

Socialism—A Negation of Capitalism*

There is a dream, an image of the future in Marx, a certain utopianism, born of a realist understanding of the possibilities of the emerging material conditions and those inhering in the nature of human beings; it is this element in his social theory which makes the meaning, the range and scope of his prophetic sounding statements well worth serious exploration. But Marx is not even remotely a utopian thinker. In Marx's social theory there are no blueprints of the society of the future, no pronouncements about its geographical location or inevitable arrival according to a given time-table. There is no futurology, no predictions about the shape or timing of future events, no determinism of this sort in Marx. Marx's socialism was not a Platonic intellectual construct given in advance, a well-elaborated vision of a 'good society' to be pursued by men of goodwill on this earth. He simply had, as Marx repeatedly insisted, no readymade Utopias to offer. It has been fashionable, especially in recent years, to decry Marxism as an idealistically utopian or messianic doctrine. But Marx himself explicitly rejected *such* utopianism. His work has no elaborate programmes or proposals as to how the future socialist society should work. A concern with such blueprints was indeed a

* A Chapter excerpted from the author's *Crisis of Socialism–Notes in Defence of a Commitment.*

characteristic of Utopian Socialists who sought, according to Marx's expression, 'to boil the pots of the future' and predesign the concrete forms of the transition to a 'classless society', and whom Marx most categorically dissociated from. Describing such blueprints, their 'new social systems', 'best possible plan(s) of the best possible state of society' as 'sentimental socialistic day dreams', 'pure phantasies', 'castles in the air' or 'pocket editions of the New Jerusalem', Marx and Engels saw them to be 'foredoomed as Utopias', though they yet delighted in 'the stupendously grand thoughts and germs of thought that everywhere break out through their phantastic covering'. Admiring both their commitment and contribution to the cause, Marx and Engels took note of the extenuating 'historical situation' that conditioned these early founders of socialism: 'to the crude conditions of capitalistic production and the crude class relations corresponded crude theories'. Their dissociation from such utopianism in fact occurred quite early in their own commitment to socialism. In *The German Ideology,* Marx clearly stated that 'Communism is for us not an ideal to which reality will have to adjust itself.' The *Communist Manifesto,* even as it paid its much noted extraordinary tribute to capitalism, concluded with a lengthy and very sharp critique of all then-existing conceptions or doctrines of socialism. Arguing against their utopian, ideological or doctrinaire character, Marx insisted that socialism is not to be cooked up by thinkers in their studies, it should arise from the real movement or historical process going on in society.

This movement or historical process was the development of capitalism. It is Marx's critique of capitalism centred on its mode of appropriation of surplus value from direct producers, which was the point of departure for his theory of socialism. It defined the basic character of socialism as a negation, 'the real other' of capitalism. Its necessary but not sufficient condition was freedom from capitalist exploitation, its expropriation of surplus value, and this involved as a minimum condition the abolition of private ownership of the means of production and its replacement with social ownership. This, admittedly, would be merely the starting point of socialism whose possibilities, some of these truly amazing, would unfold through its actual existence, though Marx did indicate a few which, even when visualised for a somewhat distant future, may appear implausible or utopian to men or women without vision among us, conditioned, trained and persuaded to under-reach themselves as they are in our class divided, scarcity-driven societies. At times there is indeed the somewhat simplifying hope that once capitalism is swept away, the problems of production or of law or culture, or of political organisation, will be easily manageable, but Marx was on the whole aware of not only the new society inevitably carrying the 'defects' or 'birth marks' of the old capitalist society, from which it emerged, but also that human social powers are cumulative, dialectical and various and that in a socialist society some forms of complexity may be removed but others will be added, posing problems for those actually called upon to build socialism. But these were not *his* problems. He saw socialism as the first phase of communism which marks the end of human 'pre-history' and the beginning—not an end of any kind as it is commonly misrepresented—of 'truly human history' in Engel's expression. But as to the organisation, the institutions, technologies or culture of this 'new historic form', as he called it, Marx had, beyond the sketchiest outline, little or nothing to say.

Marx himself, on his own, simply refused to speculate about the problems that might arise on the soil of the 'new historic form'. He saw it 'intimated' by development of capitalism but, given his perspective of scientific socialism, the question of how to get from the negated world of capitalism to the realm of the merely 'intimated' new historic form played no part in Marx's theoretical project. He indeed scorned those who engaged in such 'speculations about the future' and even considered this a diversion from the real tasks of the day. Though his early metaphorical insistence in this regard—an idea later reiterated on several occasions—that 'they (the working class) have no ideals to realise, but to set free the elements of the new society with which old collapsing bourgeois society itself is pregnant' is not free from problems or difficulties of formulation which made it easily amenable to misunderstanding. Meszaros has aptly commented:

> The difficulties concerned the objective constituents of social change on both sides of the equation: the strategies aimed at setting free 'the elements of the new society' on the one hand, and the prospects of development of 'old collapsing bourgeois society' on the other. People tended to read Marx's metaphor with optimistic one-sidedness which ignored its implicit warning: namely, that pregnancies of old wombs often result in miscarriages or badly handicapped offspring.

II

The problems of transition to socialism were never discussed by Marx in detail. The issue, with all its bewildering practical dimensions as we now know, was not an acute historical challenge in Marx's life-time, given the lease of life and new vitality capitalism acquired, above all, on the ground of its imperialist expansion. There are only scattered references to it in different writings of Marx and Engels concerned primarily with characteristics of socialism as a transitional society between capitalism and communism (which they regarded as the goal towards which history was moving). The most important single document of classical Marxism here, that is, on the subject of construction of a new socialist society, is Marx's *Critique of the Gotha Programme*—really Marx's marginal notes to the programme of the German Workers Party, published by Engels after Marx's death, sixteen years after Marx wrote them. (It is interesting to note that sixteen long years had to elapse before Marx's critical notes could be published—in the German Marxist journal, *Neue Zeit*—and even then at the insistence of Engels and only after some bitter fight against powerful opposition and with the omission of 'a few sharp expressions and judgments' and choice of 'milder expression' in some places. Initially, Karl Kautsky, editor of the *Neue Zeit*, along with its publishers, was reluctant to publish this document. And later, some of the Party leaders even tried to withdraw the journal from newsstands. Nor did it all end there. For, following the publication, Engels found himself isolated from his closest German followers, and the 'socialist bosses' continued their attacks to which Engels had to respond defensively in a letter to Kautsky: 'If we dare not say this [the criticism] openly today, then when?' Marx himself had ended his criticism with the cryptic phrase: *dixi et salvavi animam meam* (I have spoken and saved my soul). It indicated the strange difficulties under which Marx had to write his remarks in the first place—as remarks addressed in strictest confidence to a mere handful of friends: 'only to absolve his conscience and without any hope of success', as Engels later admitted. The radical scepticism of Marx's cryptic phrase at the end of his *Critique* bears witness to his feeling of unease over the newly emerging negative trends in his Party and the working class movement in Germany.

To return to Marx's notes, the very title is significant. The only time Marx is drawn into making a somewhat detailed, yet all too brief, comment on the subject, it is as a critique of his own party or followers in Germany for their confused and shoddy thinking over several issues which also included that concerning the socialist society of the future—a critique distinguished for 'the ruthless severity' and 'mercilessness' typical of Marx in mattes of theory. Among the chief purposes of this text was a challenge to propagandist but misleading claims; the contention that labour is the sole source of all wealth is met by insistence that nature is as important, and the claim that workers should receive the full fruits of labour is met by itemisation of the prior charges that should be made for investment, for the further development of material productive resource, etc. Several significant issues are touched upon, but Marx makes no effort to sketch out how the socialist economy should function; he has hardly anything useful to say about the socialisation and coordination of production. Marx, who wrote a great deal about development under capitalism, offers no theory of economic development under socialism. Perhaps such a theory was redundant in view of his belief that socialism will be built in highly developed countries and economic development was the historical task of capitalism. Perhaps there was also the assumption that the rationality of applying labour to social need will become readily apparent once the veil of commodity entitlement has been lifted, or that the unmet human needs he could see around him require no very complex economic or other assessments and decision making. The fact remains that in line with Marx's view of scientific socialism, the *Critique*, while it indeed clarified and settled many issues, offered no blueprints, nor any directions about giving a practical shape to his theories in this regard. There is not a word about the construction of socialism, about its forms of economic and political organisation, about any other institutional structures of a socialist society, etc. As Engels was to say about his and Marx's overall position later, in 1893: 'Pre-set opinions regarding details of the organisation of future society? You won't find even a hint of them in our works'. But if founders of Marxism did not offer any blueprints of the socialist society of the future and if at all, rarely discussed its characteristics, there is at least one firm statement they made which is most relevant for purpose of my argument in these notes. They more than once expressed the view that socialism is not to be understood as a distinct form of society, like capitalism, one existing in its own right. Instead, they always treated it as a transitional society between capitalism and communism, as the first or lower phase of communism, in every way a transitional period between capitalism and communism ; it is communism which Marx as well Engels saw as the society superseding capitalism, the goal towards which humankind was moving as the society of the future.

Marx deliberately refrained from offering any vision or blueprints of a socialist society of the future. With him the most a theory can and must do is to describe the conditions necessary for emancipated forms of life for its time. Characteristic of Marx, therefore, was his concern with the present, with capitalism as it had then emerged as a mature system, and with the future only as it was likely to grow out of this present. It is the historically specific and unique contradictions and possibilities of capitalism that put socialism on the agenda. For Marx, capitalism creates the necessary conditions for socialism, as a more rational and humane form of society that is likely to and must supersede it as the next step in the historical progress of humankind. It is only in this sense that, not a vision or a blueprint, socialism emerges as a historically privileged form of concrete economic, political, ethical and cultural practice for our times. For Marx, thus, the key task was to understand the ongoing historical process that was capitalism, to discover and lay bare its law of motion, its contradictions and inherent irrationality that made a transition to socialism *necessary*, and to locate the social forces which would make such a transition *possible*. For the rest, he struggled all his life—'sacrificed all my fortune to the revolutionary struggle', as he himself once said—guiding and helping such forces to realise this possibility in the historically specific conditions of his time. While it was possible for Marx to be precise about what must be abolished or superseded, that is capitalism, he obviously would not do what is impossible and impermissible for his mode of thinking, that is to draw up, like the Utopians, precise or detailed pictures of socialism in advance. He simply refused to compose such 'music of the future' as he himself put it. This precision or detail, the socialist organisation and management of society, is a matter for the succeeding generations, their concrete social praxis, to work out. The responsibility for the concrete carrying out of the socialist liberationist project, for shaping their own destiny, can lie only with them, the men and women of the future. It is their task. It is thus that they will 'make their own history'.

That Marx and Engels never offered any blueprints, or shared in the loose usage of the term 'socialism' current in the nineteenth century, or at times, like others, even used 'socialism' and 'communism' interchangeably, does not mean that they had nothing worthwhile to say about this society of the future. On the contrary, they do provide us with a reasonably coherent idea of what they understood to be socialism. This is not only clearly expressed in several places in their writings, in passages which are full of flashes of insight as well as more mundane propositions, about the kind of society they thought would and should succeed the capitalist society. It is most explicit in their critique of capitalism—for, as already indicated, Marx's socialism was not just another vision of a good society, it was above all a negation of capitalism in a most comprehensive manner, its dialectical transcendence—a negation and transcendence of not only its economy but its ethics, politics, ideology, culture, indeed its mode life as a whole. (In this regard Marx himself spoke of 'Aufhebung', which is a complex historical process of 'supersession-preservation-raising to a higher level'.)

We may therefore well take a quick look at Marx's critique of capitalism to not only notice the continuing validity of this critique but also, more immediately relevant, get some insight into how socialism was visualised in classical Marxism.

III

Holding that 'the anatomy of civil society is to be sought in political economy', Marx focused his attention on the study of capitalist economy in order to understand the dynamics of the capitalist social order. It is to this task that he devoted the better part of his working life and most of his mature efforts. The result was a truly prodigious contribution to knowledge. So great was this achievement that, aided by the tendency of his followers to erroneously attribute an influence to the different social spheres in proportion to the treatment accorded them in Marx's published writings, it soon gave rise to the view, which still persists, that Marx was primarily an economist and Marxism's chief concern is with matters economic only. Marxists in the West, coming after Marx, lent their support to this view, as it came to be well-manifested in the economistic interpretations and 'scientism' of the Second International. This, however, is not our concern at the moment. Immediately important is to notice that, at a time when the advent of capitalism was being either celebrated for its tremendous economic or productive achievements, *a la* Adam Smith and others, or condemned for the truly disastrous consequences of its unrestrained industrialism by morally sensitive writers of the age—Carlyle, Ruskin, Morris, Dickens, among others—it was the distinction of Marx to recognise both the historical achievement of capitalism as well as its inherent irrationality and inhumanity, and therefore the transitory character of the new mode of production.

'The bourgeoisie, historically, has played a most

revolutionary part' Marx pointed out in the *Communist Manifesto*: 'It has been the first to show what man's activity can bring about', creating 'more massive and more colossal productive forces than have all preceding generations together'. 'What earlier century had even a presentiment that such productive forces slumbered in the lap of social labour', wrote Marx. (In view of the scientific and technological revolutions of out times, this could be said to be true of Marx's own century, though Marx himself can be seen as looking forward to such revolutions to provide the necessary material basis for what he visualised as communist society of the future). Marx sought to locate the driving force behind this unprecedented productive achievement of capitalism. In doing so, in a truly remarkable intellectual effort, Marx laid bare 'the economic law of motion', the structural logic of capitalism, which Adam Smith's benevolent interpretation had wished away as the 'hidden' or invisible hand of 'Providence'. The essence of capitalism, Marx argued, is the self-expansion of capital, an expansion whose norms are unashamedly quantitative. As he put it: 'Accumulate, accumulate! That is Moses and the prophets! ... Accumulate for accumulation's sake, production for production's sake; by this formula classical economy expressed the historical mission of the bourgeoisie and did not for a single moment deceive itself over the birth-throes of wealth'.

This self expansion or accumulation of capital takes place through the production and capitalisation of surplus value, produced by the expropriated proletariat, who now produces for capital and not for the satisfaction of its own or anyone else's needs. It is thus that capitalism, in Marx's words, 'establishes an accumulation of misery corresponding with accumulation of capital'. The accumulation of capital goes hand in hand with 'the expropriation and pauperisation of the great mass of producers', wealth and affluence at one end is accompanied by poverty and deprivation at the other. Speaking of 'the absolute general law of capitalist development'—such laws for Marx are always 'laws of tendency'—Marx wrote: 'Accumulation of wealth at one pole is, therefore, at the same time, accumulation of misery, agony of toil, slavery, ignorance, brutality, mental degradation, at the opposite pole, i.e., on the side of the class that produces its own products in the form of capital'.

Capitalism, without doubt, is no longer what it was in the nineteenth century when Marx wrote this; it has undergone many important changes. Certainly in its later development, this structurally inherent tendency in capitalism has been somewhat, but only somewhat, curbed in the countries of advanced capitalism, by the working class resistance, by state intervention generally in the long-term interests of capitalism itself, by the historically determined emergence of the welfare, rather welfare-warfare state. But the dualism in society that Marx noticed, the outcome of the structural logic of capitalism, has persisted and tended to grow (despite 'welfare' which remains reversible, is always resisted and has been again, as often in the past, under capitalist attack in recent years). As the French saying has it, 'the more it changes, the more it remains the same'. Capital accumulation, often generalised as economic growth, remains the holy grail which dominates capitalism's working, economic discourse of its ideologues, and public policy of capitalist states. And the consequences are necessarily dualist, always and everywhere, within countries and across them globally.

For Marx, the tendency of capitalism to generate wealth at one end and poverty at the other, whether on the national or international scale is a consequence of the exploitative socio-economic relations on which it is based. These exploitative socio-economic relations continue to constitute capitalism even today. The laws of capitalist accumulation still impose themselves, in Marx's words, 'as an external coercive force' on the capitalist, and poverty amidst affluence remains the characteristic feature of all capitalist societies in our times. As Harry Magdoff has written:

> New features of twentieth century capitalism—such as the growing role of monopoly capital, imperialism, internationalization of production and finance, and the spread of the welfare state in the center—affected but did not change what was essential in the laws of motion discovered long ago by Karl Marx. Despite the great advances in science and technology, major wars, and other historic developments, one feature of capitalist development

> prevailed; the forces of production expanded side by side with the growth of misery; the gap between wealth and poverty among and within nations continued to widen.
>
> The reason for this consistency is that there is a logical connection between the system's achievements and its failures. The market system under the guidance of the profit motive generates an urgent need for capital to accumulate, which by the inner necessity of the system leads to capital's exploitation of most of the people on the planet and of the planet itself. This interconnection is at the heart of capitalism's laws of motion: underlying tendencies which, even though approximate and modified by historical developments, assert themselves as a blind, elemental force, independent of the aims and decisions of those active in the economy.

It was part of Marx's critique that while transition from feudalism to capitalism represented a tremendous advance towards a more rational condition of humankind, the inherent irrationality of capitalism itself, as a system of private property and profit-based market economy, would warp and hinder further economic and social progress. Hence the transitory character of capitalism. The structural logic of capitalism, its accumulative process generating wealth and poverty at opposite poles, inevitably leads to recurring crises of 'over production'—people's purchasing power again and again failing to match the increasing production that capitalists put in the market. As Marx wrote in the *Communist Manifesto*:

> In these crises there breaks out an epidemic that, in earlier periods, would have seemed an absurdity—the epidemic of over production. Society suddenly finds itself put back into a state of momentary barbarism; it appears as if a famine, a universal war of devastation had cut off the supply of every means of subsistence; industry and commerce seem to be destroyed; and why? Because there is too much civilisation, too much means of subsistence, too much industry, too much commerce.
>
> And how does the bourgeoisie get over these crises? On the one hand by enforced destruction of a mass of productive forces; on the other by the conquest of new markets and by the more thorough exploitation of the old ones. That is to say, by paving the way for more extensive and more destructive crises and by diminishing the means whereby crises are prevented.

Marx saw these crises as an expression of 'the revolt of modern productive forces against the property relations that are the conditions for the existence of the bourgeoisie and its rule', and therefore indicative of the need to overcome and abolish these property relations to make possible production geared not to profit in the market place, but to satisfaction of people's needs.

'Crisis of overproduction' or excess-capacity has been a perennial tendency in capitalism. Such slumps or crises at regular intervals—except under exceptional circumstances such as war or accelerated preparation for war, for example—have been a characteristic feature of capitalism from at least 1825 on, with capitalism's internal mechanisms becoming increasingly inadequate to cope with them, making it necessary for the capitalist state to intervene to save capitalism, as it were, from the capitalists; left to themselves, capitalists would have most probably destroyed capitalism a long time ago. In exploring this essential irrationality within capitalism, Marx saw and defined the basic contradiction of this mode of production as a contradiction between its socialised production and private, that is capitalist, appropriation so that, under capitalism it becomes difficult, and increasingly impossible to use the available or potential productive resources either fully or for the good of society, for human welfare as a whole. The huge disparity between its 'colossal' productive capacity and the quality of life it delivers is indeed the most obvious fact about capitalism today. Hence the Marxist argument for *socialist* relations of production and appropriation, for socialism as a more rational and humane social order; in its economic aspects, a 'free society of associated producers' making a democratically planned use of its social and material productive resources for common human welfare.

Aware and appreciative of the creative drives of capitalism, Marx was remarkably prescient about its destructive drives or potential in the long run, and his prognosis here was thus summed up by Rosa Luxemburg: 'either an advance to socialism or a descent into barbarism'. Again, Marx has been more than vindicated. Barbarism of sorts has already emerged as an important aspect of the social, political and moral-cultural life of contemporary capitalist societies. And capitalism's potential for wholesale barbarism is today more than visible in the imperialist politics of the capitalist powers, the United States' stockpile and use of weapons of mass destruction and 'Star Wars' programmes ('Strategic Defence Initiative', 'missile defence system', 'Falcon', etc.) and in the ecological disaster which, thanks to the structural logic of capitalism, its insatiable accumulative drive, now looms large over the future of humankind. The issue 'socialism or barbarism', implicit in Marx's prognosis, is indeed more urgent today than when Marx first sounded the warning. (I will have more to say on this subject later in these notes.)

It is characteristic of Marx's critique of capitalism, in fact of his entire mode of thinking, which does not recognise the conventional, academically fashionable disjunction between 'is and ought', (fact and value), that even as he analysed the structurally inherent contradictions of capitalism, its essential irrationality and its consequences, he also recognised capitalism as generating, in the course of its historical development, the necessary prerequisites of a more rational and humane social order—not an external idea or a vision imposed on history but a projection or extension, so to speak, of trends and patterns within capitalism itself. Of course, socialism itself cannot take root and grow within the confines of capitalist society as capitalism had done under feudalism. But capitalism has a characteristic historical role which not only makes possible but guarantees the existence of a different road to its transformation. Capitalism creates the *objective* material basis for socialism in the social productive forces it develops but now increasingly fetters in their use for human welfare, and it simultaneously brings into existence the *subjects* of history, the political and ideological force needed to carry out the necessary revolutionary transformation. This social force Marx located in the proletariat which even as it is essential to capitalism for its accumulation process, is also its essential victim, and one that is rapidly gaining a 'theoretical awareness' of its real situation. As capitalism grows, so does the proletariat, and the very process of capitalist development prepares the proletariat for its historical role. As Marx wrote: 'What the bourgeoisie therefore produces, above all, are its own grave-diggers. Its fall and the victory of the proletariat are equally inevitable'. It is this understanding of a most important aspect of the internal dynamics of capitalism that underlies Marx's insistence that 'Communism is not... an ideal to which reality (will) have to adjust itself (but) the real movement which abolishes the present state of affairs'.

That is how Marx visualised the necessity as well as the possibility of a transition from capitalism to socialism in the countries of advanced industrial development, with their mature productive basis and proletarian presence. And it is here, not his analysis of capitalism or argument for socialism—both of which remain as valid and relevant as ever—but his historically specific prognosis concerning the necessity and possibility of socialism in the advanced capitalist countries, that history, as it were, played a trick with the doctrine of Karl Marx, whose one major consequence is the current crisis of socialism. But of this later.

IV

Socialism as negation of capitalism of course means a thorough-going transformation of property relations and abolition of private profit as the organising principle of production, a genuine, not merely formal or juridical social ownership of the commanding heights of the economy and democratically planned use of social-material resources for human welfare. These are, however, necessary rather than sufficient conditions for socialism, and certainly not a description of socialism. For Marx the negation involved very much more than such necessary transformation of economic arrangements, 'the subordination of (people's) common social productivity as their (own) social power', as he put it.

'The mode of production', according to Marx, 'must not be considered simply as being the reproduction of the physical existence of the individuals. Rather it is a definite form of expressing their life, "a definite mode of life" on their part'. Capitalism as a mode of production, for example, completely subordinates human needs to the reproduction of exchange-value in the interest of capital's expanded self-realisation, which makes it pre-eminently a system not only of accumulation, but of commodification as well, which in its immediate working and ultimate outcome seeks to commodify every aspect of social life or human existence. In socialism, as Marx wrote in *The Poverty of Philosophy*, humans must change 'from top to bottom the conditions of their industrial and political existence, and consequently *their whole manner of being*'. Central to this changed 'manner of being' is the end of a private-property-governed and commodified existence, the 'unfreedom' of capitalist social order and the beginning, in Marx's words, of 'free individuality based on the universal development of the individual' in a socialist society. In other words, socialism is a society ensuring the 'free development' of its members, 'the associated producers', enabling them to realise their human powers, needs and capacities in as rich, untrammelled and all-round manner as possible. It is by the unleashing of actual productive forces that these human powers and capacities are bred and only by transformation of the social relations of production that the conditions in which they can flourish all-round can be created.

This draws our attention to an aspect of Marx's argument concerning capitalism that we need to notice for the light it throws on his idea of socialism, rather the *revolutionary humanist ambition* of his idea of socialism. This is the ethical and aesthetic-cultural dimension of his critique of capitalism, expressing a concern that everything Marx wrote is suffused with, and is in fact a distinctive feature of his social theory. Though this dimension never came to be theorised by him—unlike the economics of capitalism—Marx's humanist concern is an ever-present motivating force in his work as a thinker and a revolutionary.

Underlying Marx's humanist concern in his view of man, of man's *essential* humanity, his intrinsic being or immanent nature, the evolution-produced special property as a human being that, beyond the 'mere bodily' or 'mundane' activity and needs which in his own way he shares with other living beings, distinguishes man from them, his 'species-being' as Marx called it. Marx expressed this *differentia specifica* of man in such phrases as 'conscious life-activity directly distinguishes man from animal life-activity', 'free conscious activity is man's species character', 'freedom is thoroughly the essence of man', conscious and purposive activity that 'distinguishes the worst architect from the best of bees', etc. This is how Marx viewed human nature in general, which then comes to be modified in each historical epoch; his species-distinctive capacity being determined and developed but more often also limited, curtailed, mutilated or perverted in the course of his socio-historical development, more specially under capitalism.

Speaking of Marx's *Capital,* Che Guevara had once pointed out that 'the magnitude of this monumental achievement of human intelligence is such that we are often oblivious to the profoundly humanist (in the best sense of the word) nature of its interests'. In other words, Marx's humanist concern was an integral part of his critique of capitalism as an economic system. Apart from several brilliantly insightful passages on the human condition under capitalism, *Capital's* vocabulary on the subject is characterised by an indignant and relentless use of such terms as 'brutalizing', 'alienating', 'monstrous', 'savage', 'ghoulish', 'bestial', 'inhuman', and so on. Marx's humanist concern is equally well expressed in several sharp passages of the *Communist Manifesto*. But this concern—what is man?, how capitalism limits, distorts or damages his essential humanity? and what can man become? —is somewhat more elaborately stated in his early writings. Its most explicit expression is in Marx's *Economic and Philosophical Manuscripts of 1844,* with its focus on human condition, the alienated existence of human beings, in capitalist society. And Marx's argument of 150 years ago today stands more than vindicated. Witness to it is the extraordinary interest *Manuscripts* have evoked, and the endorsement its argument has received, in our times, especially in the countries of advance capitalism, making *Manuscripts* one of the half-a-dozen most discussed writings of the post-second world war period. Apropos non-Marxist western scholars' interest in this and related writings of Marx, it is interesting to note that while some of them have indeed shown a real desire to understand him and written with sympathy and perception, not a few have sought, some of them so very desperately, to so focus on these writings as to separate Marx from himself and from Marxism—to separate the young Marx from the old, the 'idealistic', 'freedom-loving' Marx of *Economic and Philosophic Manuscripts* from the supposedly cynical and disillusioned Marx of *Capital,* Marx the humanist from Marx the revolutionary and an advocate of class struggle, Marx from Engels, and, of course, from Lenin and Mao Tse-tung and any radical movement; he was now their own humanist and 'Western' Marx, having nothing to do with revolution or 'the East'.

At the heart of Marx's ethical and aesthetic-cultural critique of capitalism lies his deep concern for humanity, its present condition and possible future. Central to his argument is the idea (particularly expressed, along with *Manuscripts of 1844,* in his other early writings such as *On the Jewish Question, Contribution to the Critique of Hegel's Philosophy of Right, The Holy Family,* etc.) that man, stripped of 'his human essence' when he first fell into the class of exploited, faces 'the destruction of all humanity' in him under capitalism. The process of capitalist exploitation, with its attendant 'greed and the war between the greedy—competition', not only holds the entire society, the capitalist as well as the worker, in its irresistible compulsive grip and at the mercy of 'the blind forces' of the market, it also transforms free creative self-activity of man into alienated labour, and reduces man himself to a commodity. It 'estranges man from nature, from himself, his own active functioning... from his *universal essence*.....It makes his *essence* into a mere means for his existence.... (and results in) the alienation of *man* from *man.*' Capitalism tears up 'all genuine bonds between men' and replaces them by selfishness, dissolving 'the world of men into a world of atomized individuals, hostile towards each other'. It leaves 'no other nexus between man and man than naked self-interest, than callous "cash payment"' and resolves 'personal worth into exchange value'. The very things which were once 'communicated, but never exchanged; given, but never sold; acquired, but never bought—virtue, love, conviction, knowledge, conscience, etc.'—now become marketable and pass 'into commerce'; 'the *divine* power of money' overturns and confounds 'all human and natural qualities' in the marketplace. There comes to be generated a savage lust for money and property, a maniacal obsession with the accumulation of capital, a veritable fanaticism of appropriation. Amassing wealth becomes the supreme object of human endeavour and the final criterion of human success. The emphasis is on acquisitiveness and the only success that matters is the success of the market place, resulting in 'that whole system of appetites and values' which 'with its deification of the life of snatching to hoard, and hoarding to snatch' leaves, as Tawney wrote, 'a taste as of ashes on the lips of a civilization which has brought to the conquest of its material environment resources unknown in earlier ages, but which has not yet learned to master itself'. And all this leaves man, even the so-called rich man of capitalism, 'ever poorer as a *man*', robbed of real life and crippled in his inner being.

Marx, in line with his mode of thinking, took a historical view of the growth of needs and desires of human beings as one aspect of the general development of human nature, which is also the subjective aspect of the growth of human powers and capacities. With the development of our powers and capacities new needs emerge; and the growth of new needs spurs the development of new powers. As Marx saw this process, it is 'the absolute working out of (man's) creative potentialities, with no presupposition other than the previous historic development', which makes 'this totality of development,' i.e. the development of human powers as such 'an end in itself', not to be measured on any *predetermined* yardstick. Human development in this perspective is the growth of human capacities and powers, the actualisation of human potentialities, the self-development and self-realisation of human beings. This however must not be understood in any utilitarian or hedonistic manner. Central to the growth of human powers and capacities is the development of the specifically human faculties, the creative, aesthetic faculties of human beings, their 'glorious human senses'. For Marx, like the evolution-produced five physical senses, these too are 'the work of all previous history'. Marx wrote: 'The most beautiful music has *no* sense for the unmusical ear, because my object can only be the confirmation of one of my essential powers.... For the same reasons the *senses* of social man are *different* from those of non-social man. Only through the objectively unfolded wealth of human nature can the wealth of subjective *human* sensitivity—a musical ear, an eye for the beauty of form, in short, *senses* capable of human gratification—be either cultivated or created.'

This is surely suggestive of an infinite future of creation and cultivation of 'the wealth of subjective *human* sensitivity,' of specifically human senses, which is really the same as human nature all the time *becoming more human*. And the important point is that, for Marx, the exercise of these naturally and historically produced specifically human senses—the sense for music and poetry, art, science and history, love, justice and compassion, and so on—constituted the very essence of a truly human appropriation of life and nature, a genuinely rich human life. That is how, in pointing out the alienating, depersonalising and dehumanising consequences of capitalism, Marx particularly focused attention on the fact that for all the glorious human senses, whose active and concrete exercise alone constitutes the true content of a genuinely rich human life, capitalism substitutes a single abstract sense, the sense for property, a particular, historically transient, substitute sense which plays havoc with human personality and plunges man, in the words of Ladislav Stoll, 'into the terrible inner sickness of a dehumanised world'. Marx wrote: 'In place of *all* these physical and mental senses there has ... come the sheer estrangement of *all* these senses—the sense of *having*. The human being had to be reduced to this absolute poverty in order that he might yield his inner wealth to the outer world'. 'The more you *have*', said Marx, 'the less you *are*'. Hence his insistence that 'the transcendence of private property is therefore the complete *emancipation* of all human senses and attributes'. He spoke of communism, 'the *actual* phase necessary for the next stage of historical development in the process of human emancipation and recovery', 'as the positive transcendence of *private property* as *human self-estrangement*, and therefore as the real *appropriation of the human essence* by and for man; communism therefore as the complete return of man to himself as a *social* (i.e., human) being—a return become conscious, and accomplished within the entire wealth of previous development.' Marx added: 'What is to be avoided above all is the re-establishing of "Society" as an abstraction *vis-à-vis* the individual. The individual *is the social being*. His life ... is therefore an expression and confirmation of *social life*.' Marx is an individualist in the basic sense that his ultimate vision was a society where every individual could be a fully human being, where, as Marx himself put it, 'the free development of each is the condition for the free development of all'.

What this 'free development', the above-mentioned 'transcendence of human self-estrangement' means, what Marx meant when early in his life he wrote (in *Economic and Philosophic Manuscripts of 1844*) that 'communism equals humanism', and towards the end spoke (in *Capital*, Vol. III) of 'the true realm of freedom' which makes possible 'that development of human power, which is its own end', what vision of the genuinely rich human life lay behind his life-long struggle for socialism—this has been well expressed by Ladislav Stoll. Pointing out that 'in place of many-sided, active, concrete appropriation of life and the world, through which the individual says not only "I see, I hear, I smell, I taste, I touch", but also, "I work, I study, I love, I admire, I struggle for a happier tomorrow"—in place of all this wealth of emotion capitalism makes one single emotion supreme: "I *have*!"', Stoll writes:

> The truly human way of appropriating the world's riches is that by which man really overcomes the world, in other words, with all his senses, concretely. And here it is not a question only of the five physical senses, for unlike the animals man has a whole series of glorious human senses, not only the senses of sight, hearing, smell, taste and touch, but also a sense for music, a sense for poetry, a sense for the plastic arts, a sense for science, a sense for mathematics, a sense for history, crystalography, etc. etc. It is only when a man begins to satisfy the needs of these glorious human senses, which one and all are the product of historical development, that he can appropriate to himself all the beauties of the world and become genuinely rich.

In a related comment on Marx's *Manuscripts of 1844*, Erich Fromm has written:

> Socialism, for Marx, is a society which permits the actualization of man's essence, by overcoming his alienation. It is nothing less than creaing the conditions for the truly free, rational, active and independent man; it is the fulfilment of the prophetic aim: the destruction of the ideals ... For Marx, the aim of socialism was freedom ... based on man's standing on his own feet, using his own powers and relating himself to the world productively.

V

An aspect of Marx's analysis of capitalism, which deserves to be specifically noticed, is his brilliant anticipation of what we have come to recognise as 'consumerism', an increasingly dominant and deeply disturbing and destructive bane of life in contemporary capitalist societies, which Marx castigated as the 'true norm' of capitalism. Marx saw human nature as modifiable in history. He had written: 'Our desires and pleasures spring from society, we measure them, therefore, by society and not by the objects which serve for their satisfaction. Because they are of a social nature, they are of a relative nature'. And however arisen, they continue to be modified, gain or lose in importance, with changing social conditions. Take, for instance, such pathological phenomena as greed or selfishness. Capitalism did not invent them; they are deep in human nature, related as they are to elementary infantile structures and the overall determining situation of *scarcity* which has characterised civilisation throughout and so far. But capitalism has undoubtedly magnified their role in ordinary life, and, unlike its predecessor feudal or other pre-capitalist social formations, which had the (Christian or analogous) grace to condemn greed or selfishness, capitalism even celebrates them. For Marx, therefore, 'consumerism' is not a matter of human nature as such, of its so-called insatiable appetites, but of a human nature desired, moulded and manipulated by capitalism as a market-based system of private property and profit making. Capitalism invariably tends, via profitability in the marketplace, to drive a wedge between human *needs* and human *wants*, and to proliferate the wants in a manner that, as Baran once said, 'people steeped in the culture of monopoly capitalism do not want what they need and do not need what they want'. Capitalism irresistibly gives rise to consumerism which is essentially the artificial, market determined and mediated, stimulation of consumption for private profit under capitalism. In an extended comment, with an opening reference to socialism, Marx wrote in the *Manuscripts of 1844*:

> We have seen what significance, given socialism, the *wealth* of human needs has, and what significance, therefore, both a *new mode of production* and a new *object* of production have: a new manifestation of the forces of *human* nature and a new enrichment of *human* nature. Under private property their significance is reversed: every person speculates on creating a *new* need in another, so as to drive him to a fresh sacrifice, to place him in a new dependence and to seduce him into a new mode of *gratification* and therefore economic ruin. Each tries to establish over the other an *alien* power, so as thereby to find satisfaction of his own selfish need. The increase in the quantity of objects is accompanied by an extension of the realm of alien powers to which man is subjected, and every new product represents a new *potency* of mutual swindling and mutual plundering. Man becomes ever poorer as man.... *Excess* and *intemperance* come to be (capitalism's) true norm... the extension of products and needs falls into *contriving* and ever-*calculating* subservience to inhuman, refined, unnatural and *imaginary* appetites....

Marx added:

> and no eunuch flatters his despot more basely or uses more despicable means to stimulate his dulled capacity for pleasure in order to sneak a favour for himself than does the industrial eunuch —the producer—to sneak for himself a few pennies... He puts himself in the service of the other's most depraved fancies, plays the pimp between him and his need, excites in him morbid appetites, lies in wait for each of his weaknesses....

VI

For Marx, the abolition of capitalism and the establishment of socialist economy does not by itself usher in a 'truly human society', it only makes it possible. Material fulfilment is for him only the condition, the necessary basis, and not the sum, of man's 'spiritual', that is, 'truly human' fulfilment. The vision which underlies his whole work from the early 1840s to the end is the vision of 'human emancipation'. His life and struggle was a plea to replace the pitiable, fragmentary and self-alienated existence, which is man's lot in a class-divided and exploitative society that is capitalism, with a truly rich human life; it was an assertion of life abundant against mere existence. Socialism opens up the possibility of this abundant life. More than ending the economic exploitation of a capitalist market system, it will make for direct cooperative socio-economic relations between people such that they cease to be alienated from the product of their labour, from nature and their fellow human beings, and from themselves. And as socialism transits to communism, with the productive forces further developed, all the springs of collective wealth flowing freely, labour become not merely a means but prime necessity of life, and the personality-diminishing excesses of division of labour eliminated, the way will be open for the full flowering of man's creative potentiali-ties, his glorious human senses, for 'the unfolding of man', 'the all round development of the individual', as Marx put it.

Early in his life, this is how Marx saw this 'unfolding' or 'all round development', or looked beyond the reduction of human work to dictated 'mindless detail task' that division of labour under capitalism entails:

> as soon as the division of labour comes into being, each man has a particular, exclusive sphere of activity, which is forced upon him and from which he cannot escape. He is hunter, a fisherman, a shepherd, or a critical critic, and must remain so if he does not want to lose his means of livelihood; while in a communist society, where nobody has one exclusive sphere of activity, but each can become accomplished in any branch he wishes, society regulates the general production and thus makes it possible for me to do one thing today and another tomorrow, to hunt in the morning, fish in the afternoon, rear cattle in the evening, criticize after dinner, just as I have a mind, without ever becoming hunter, fisherman, shepherd or critic.... (No longer a human being needs to be) exclusively a painter, sculptor, etc.... In a communist society there

> are no painters, but at most people who engage in painting among other activities.

In another celebrated passage, now towards the end of his life, Marx saw socialism in its transition to communism as humankind's transition to 'the realm of freedom' which according to him lies beyond material pursuits, beyond all activity geared to economic needs. He wrote:

> ...The realm of freedom actually begins only where labour which is determined by necessity and mundane considerations ceases; thus *in the very nature of things* it lies beyond the sphere of actual material production. Just as the savage must wrestle with nature to satisfy his wants, to maintain and reproduce life, so must civilised man, and he must do so in all social formations and under all modes of production.... Freedom in this field can only consist in socialised man, the associated producers, rationally regulating their interchange with nature, bringing it under their common control, instead of being ruled by it as by a blind power; and achieving this with the least expenditure of energy and under conditions most favourable to, and worthy of, their human nature. But it nonetheless still remains a realm of necessity. Beyond it begins that development of human power which is an end in itself, the true realm of freedom, which, however, can blossom forth only with this realm of necessity as its basis.

The aspirations or vision that Marx here sets forth is in fact as old as civilisation; it is there, for instance, in Plato and Aristotle, though its realisation, then and afterwards, was seen possible only for a few. Marx put more substance into this aspiration and sought its realisation for *all* human beings. In other words, economic activity was, throughout, deemed to have meaning only if it serves something other than itself. For Marx this is activities 'valued as an end in themselves' (as he phrased it in the *Grundrisse*), which for him is indeed 'the true measure of wealth'.

A first condition for such a shift of balance in human activity from 'the realm of necessity' to 'the realm of freedom' is obviously a reduction in socially necessary labour time that economic activity involves. Society would have to be able to produce sufficient to satisfy the necessities of material existence without absorbing all the time and effort of its people. Marx saw this becoming a distinct possibility, for the first time, with the productive achievements of capitalism (and those he visualised under socialism). Compared with the means these achievements put at our disposal, 'the theft of somebody else's labour time, on which wealth now rests, appears a miserable base', wrote Marx. To take 'working time as the standard of wealth,' Marx argued, 'is to base wealth on poverty, ...reducing time as a whole to working time and degrading the individual to the simple role of the working man, dominated by his labour.' This was becoming no longer necessary, and the possibility existed for moving towards a qualitatively different society in which, as Marx put it, 'the surplus labour of the masses will no longer be the condition for the development of general wealth as the leisure of the few will cease to be the condition for the full development of the human brain.' Herein lay the hope and promise of the future, a real basis for Marx's vision of a transition from the realm of necessity to the realm of freedom where there is 'free individuality' and 'the development of human power is an end in itself'. Here at last, in Marx's famous 1859 formulation, the 'pre-history' of humanity ends and its 'history' begins. For Marx, it is this beginning that socialism represents.

It has been fashionable in a society vitally interested in persuading its victims to underreach themselves, to decry and dismiss Marx's vision of socialism as something 'utopian', a 'romantic' or 'millennial' dream. One can only ask such critics or sceptics to shed their myopia and look at the world around them with a little less prejudice and more courage, for utopian or not so utopian for his age, Marx was remarkably prophetic for us; his vision is very much a realistic proposition today with the magnificent possibilities now being opened up for humankind by the scientific-technological revolutions of our time—provided, of course, these revolutions are used not for stoking up the furnaces of private profit and privilege, or making wars, as it is bound to be under capitalism, but for the benefit of humanity at large which socialism may not guarantee but certainly makes possible.

VII

Socialism, as Marx visualised it, is a negation of capitalism, its transcendence in the strict sense of Marxian dialectic. It is a new society different from and beyond the bourgeois society, operating according to radically different principles. In its material or economic structural basis, with the dissolution of private property and supersession of the *capitalist* market, it is 'a society of free and associated producers', 'whose social relations are subordinated to their own collective control', making them masters of their own lives and destiny; it will have put an end to that separation of the direct producers from the conditions of production which is one of the basic characteristics of capitalism. This is the essential meaning of replacing the private with 'social ownership of the means of production'—social not in a formal sense or juridically ordained but, as Marx had insisted, 'in its *real* configuration'. Unlike capitalism, which treats people as a means for the expansion, 'the self-expression', of capital—the root cause of its manifold contradictions and evils—socialism, according to Marx, is 'an association of free men, working with the means of production held in common, and expending their... labour power in full self-awareness', 'a society of civilised cooperators' in Lenin's words, for whom the means of production, indeed all human and natural resources, are simply the means for satisfying genuine human needs, for shaping an ever better and fuller life for themselves. With social ownership of the means of production and the accompanying allocation of resources by 'conscious plan', instead of by 'the blind forces' of the market as under capitalism, it becomes possible to move towards greater equality and the eventual elimination of classes, of state as coercive public power, and of invidious distinctions between manual and mental labour and between city and country. In its ultimate outcome it will also mean replacement of all money and commodity relations by direct human relations and the ending of 'the enslaving subordination of the individual to the division of labour', thus ensuring 'the all round development of the individual' and, the way we have noticed earlier, a non-alienated, 'truly rich' human life for all. As Marx himself put it: 'In place of the old bourgeois society, with its classes and class antagonisms, we shall have an association in which the free development of each is the condition for the free development of all'.

Such briefly was Marx's view of socialism—a view born of a masterful socio-historical analysis and lit up, as everything with Marx always was, by the touch of a certain *Traum* (*Dream*) that he carried with him throughout his life. A vision, it was yet rooted in real life; profoundly insightful of the present, it was remarkably prophetic about possibilities of the future, the promise as well as the threat it holds, both of which have today already become compellingly real, confronting humanity with possibly the most momentous choice of its long history: 'socialism or barbarism'. And it is this view of the situation that helps us understand how socialism was also a programme of struggle for Marx who was always disdainful of ideas and thoughts not carried into praxis.

VIII

Insofar as socialism is born of and validated by Marx's critique of capitalism—socialism as the necessary and possible negation of capitalism—it bears restating that nothing that has happened since the days of Marx vitiates or refutes the essentials of his argument. The socialist critique of capitalism in terms of its economic irrationality and the inequality and alienation it generates, has lost none of its sharpness. As we have already noticed, a certain curbing of capitalism's predatory structural logic has indeed been possible in the countries of advanced capitalism, not the least because of the powerful *civilising* influence of the sheer presence of 'actually existing socialism' (which is not to deny the decisive part played by the working class struggles). State has been compelled, often in the interests of the continued existence of capitalism itself, to provide some protection to people against capital's worst depredations. But while some of its worst expressions may have been thus taken care of and some forms altered, primarily in the more advanced parts of the capitalist world, the basic irrationality and inhumanity is even today, as in the days of Marx, a characteristic structural feature of capitalism in every capitalist country, North or South, and on a global scale. In some ways it has been even more pervasive, pronounced and threatening in our times.

Marx's analysis and critique of capitalism, his prognosis has indeed stood up well at the level of essentials and often even at the level of details. There has been the increasing concentration and centralisation of capital, the massive merger movement into ever larger financial and industrial conglomerates and the increasing subordination of national competitive capital to global, multinational corporations, making 'globalisation' another buzz word of our times. There have been increasingly severe recurrent economic crises. An unprecedented 'degradation of work', as Braverman calls it, has occurred and labour has become ever more alienating. There is a pervasive moral and cultural disorientation which is nowhere better manifested than in the emergence of 'alienation' as a major and ever-worsening phenomenon in contemporary capitalist societies. Alienation under capitalism is today far more pronounced, far more inclusive and monstrous, than when Marx first wrote about it. It has found varied expression in man's growing sense of anomie and estrangement, of isolation, loneliness and homelessness, of hostility and frustration. The so-called advanced capitalist societies are today sick with these and a hundred other social and psychic ailments born of the essential irrationality of capitalism, sick with apathy and boredom, with 'other-directedness', conformism and self-abasement, with insanity, drugs and crime, all symptoms of 'the terrible inner sickness' of an 'acquisitive society' that has lasted too long. Witness to it all is the massive and still mounting literature on these pathological themes in countries of advanced capitalism. Countries on the periphery or semi-periphery of the global capitalist system are suffering from parallel, in many ways worse, somewhat lumpen or comprador, consequences of the historically specific capitalisms they have spawned in the post-colonial era—material, moral and cultural consequences of which are today all too painfully evident in their economy, politics and social life, in their steadily degenerating codes of moral and social behaviour.

As Marx foresaw, capitalism has grown and expanded to become a *deadly* serious business. Constituted, essentially, by class exploitation, capitalism is today more than just a system of class oppression, of economic inequalities and iniquities. It is a ruthless totalising process which seeks to shape our lives in every conceivable sphere, everywhere, in the relative opulence of the capitalist North as much as in its impoverished peripheries, subjecting all social life, through the manifold power of capital, to the abstract requirements of the market, commodifying life in all its aspects. This makes a mockery of all our values, all our aspirations to autonomy, freedom of choice and democratic self-government, all that is good, decent and worthwhile in life. Marx had noticed this at the very beginning of modern capitalism and warned us. Today his warning rings more true than ever before. As does the warning about its overall destructive potential in the long run.

Such being the case, regardless of what has happened to the so-called 'socialist world' or is likely to happen to what is left of the old communist or socialist movements, the struggle against capitalism and for socialism will go on—in a sense it could even be said to have truly begun now that capitalism has really attained a global reach. The socialist project is not dead. It bears repeating that this project arose out of opposition to capitalism; the ideas of socialism are basically a negation of capitalism. Therefore so long as capitalism exists, socialism too continues to be. It is true that the Russian Revolution did not hold, its socialist project has failed. But capitalism remains and therefore the socialist project remains. The collapse of 'actually existing socialism' is certainly not the end of socialism. It is indeed myopic, historically as well as politically and morally, for socialists anywhere to either abandon Marx's argument for socialism or reduce it to a search for 'capitalism with a human face', some version of social democracy that better realises the publicly stated ideals and values of contemporary bourgeois society—something that has itself become problematic, if not impossible. (Incidentally, social democracy is what the theoretically and politically bankrupt Soviet leadership of *glasnost* and *perestroika* days aspired for, only to be inevitably abandoned for lumpen capitalism by its successors).

The real issues for people's politics everywhere today lie not with Marx's argument for socialism, they arise only *after* it; they concern the struggle for socialism. And one thing that can be averred with any certainty amidst the current flux of human affairs is that, capitalism being what it is, it is the issues concerning this struggle which will soon assert themselves in the capitalist world, if they are not in different ways already doing so. The historically significant question today is neither the so-called triumph of capitalism, nor abstract explorations into the future of humankind, but the concrete need, in all societies of capitalism, at the centre or in the periphery, for a politics that seeks to move, slow or fast, depending upon the moral and material resources available in each case, against and away from capitalism in a programme that aims at socialism, at a more or less prolonged transition to socialism. Really important and decisive for our times are the issues relating to the politics of social transformations for which socialism remains the programmatic vision that inspires and guides.

IX

The construction of socialism, or communist society proper, itself constitutes a long period of transition. That is how Marx visualised it. He had also pointed out: 'what we have to deal with here is a communist society, not as it has developed on its own foundations, but, on the contrary, just as it *emerges* from capitalist society; which is thus in every respect, economically, morally and intellectually, still stamped with the birth marks of the old society from whose womb it emerges'. But, as we have already noticed, Marx simply refused to speculate about the economic or political organisation of this society of the future. If there is little in Marx or Engels about its economic structure beyond some very general propositions, there is even less about its political arrangements. But there is one issue concerning the politics of this transition which Marx touched upon when he spoke of the 'dictatorship of the proletariat' that needs to be considered, however briefly. It is necessary to do so, not only because of the intrinsic importance of the issue, or because there is a great deal of unnecessary confusion over it among friends and foes of socialism, but above all because whatever the problems with the 'administrative command economy', Soviet central planning or Soviet economy as a whole, properly understood, that is not in isolation from economic-structural or class issues, a decisively important source of Soviet crisis and cause of the ultimate collapse of socialism in the Soviet Union lay, not in the realm of its economy, but here in the realm of its politics, its failure to practice the 'dictatorship of the proletariat' as Marx and Engels, and following them Lenin himself visualised it.

The book on 'the State' originally planned by Marx—as the sequel to *Capital*, it was supposed to develop the political implications of Marx's global theory—never came to be written; it is an important missing dimension of his unfinished theoretical project. Marx did stipulate a *political form* (the proletarian state) under which the transition from the old to the new society was to be accomplished, a transitional state—'the political form of social emancipation', 'the Communal form of political organisation'—which was not a state in the conventional sense and destined to ultimately wither away. But the stipulation was not even sketched, let alone fully worked out. Amidst the scattered reference to the political problems of a transitional socialist society and a few general observations on the Paris Commune, what stands out is Marx's concept of the 'dictatorship of the proletariat', its untheorised status a source of much confusion and abuse among friends and foes of socialism.

Marx recognised that 'every provisional state set up after a revolution requires a dictatorship and an energetic dictatorship at that'; a proposition well testified to by the historical experience of the successful bourgeois revolutions of the past—in England in the seventeenth century (Cromwell), and in America (Washington) and France (Robespierre's Jacobins) in the eighteenth—as well as by the successful (e.g. the Bolsheviks in Russia) or failed (e.g. Social Democracy in Germany) revolutions of the twentieth century. Accordingly Marx specifically noted in the *Communist Manifesto*, that with a socialist revolution, after raising itself to 'the position of ruling class', 'the proletariat will use its political supremacy' to make 'despotic inroads on the rights of property and on the conditions of bourgeois production', to 'centralise all instruments of production in the hands of the state', that is, of 'the proletariat organised as ruling class', 'as a means of entirely revolutionising the mode of production'. It is important to note that Marx saw this proletarian rule as the establishment of democracy. As the *Manifesto* put it: '...the first step in the revolution of the working class is to raise the proletariat to the position of ruling class, to win the battle of democracy'.

Viewing capitalism and communism as two distinct societies, each existing in its own right, Marx saw the emerging socialist polity as a transitional period between capitalism and communism in which classes would necessarily persist for a long time, classlessness being a feature not of socialism but of the higher stage of communism. Therefore this period will be characterised by contradictions and conflicts, by class struggle in diverse spheres as its motive force right upto the achievement of a classless and stateless society. In Marx's social theory, any government in a class society, regardless of its specific form—be it democratic or any other—is essentially a dictatorship of the ruling class over the ruled classes. And this is how he visualised the 'dictatorial' state during this transitional period. For Marx, it was to be a regime which, while dictatorial towards the old exploiting classes would be the broadest kind of democracy for the workers and the people in general, much more democratic than the most liberal of bourgeois democracies, extending to the working people all those civil rights and political freedoms through whose exercise alone they could transform themselves into new human beings capable of building a new society. It is in *this* specific context that he spoke of the 'dictatorship of the proletariat'. He wrote: 'Between capitalist and communist society lies the period of the revolutionary transformation of the one into the other. There corresponds to this also a political transition period in which the state can be nothing but the revolutionary dictatorship of the proletariat'.

What needs to be understood is that this was a statement about the essential *social content*, the class character of public or political power in a transitional socialist society—just as, for Marx, even the most democratically organised bourgeois state, in this sense, is yet a 'dictatorship of the bourgeoisie'. 'Dictatorship' here is not something opposed to democracy as the conventional view has it. Laski, for example, recognised this in his own way, when apropos this concept he wrote: '...neither for Marx nor for Engels was it an anti-thesis of democracy; for them, its anti-thesis was the "dictatorship of the bourgeoisie" which, as they believed, obtained in every country, even when concealed by formally democratic political institutions, so long as the ownership of the means of production remained in middle class (*sic*) hands'.

In other words, Marx's was not a statement about form of government, its institutional structure or organisation, its parties or politics, or for that matter any specific 'dictatorial' policies to be pursued. Marx had in fact warned against confusing the 'state' with the 'government machine'. As the absolute political power of the proletariat, exercised by it as a class for self-emancipation and emancipation of the people in general, the 'dictatorship of the proletariat' had no implications at all of a totalitarian dictatorship of a party, group, or individual, such as it ultimately came to be in the Soviet Union and elsewhere in the regimes of 'actually existing socialism'. In fact, it was visualised as so devoid of repression or domination in relation to 'the immediate producers' and the overwhelming majority of the people, that it was to be, in Engels' celebrated phrase, 'no longer a state in the proper sense of the term'; as 'a *state*', according to Marx and Engels, it was to begin to wither away as soon as it was established.

Nevertheless, 'dictatorship of the proletariat', has remained one of the most misunderstood and mispracticed concepts in Marxism. Marx never elaborated upon it, perhaps he never found it necessary to do so. In any case he never had the time to do so. As we have already noticed, his proposed work on 'the State' never came to be written and much of what he said or wrote on the state, politics, party, democracy, etc. never came to be theorised by him. But he was always deeply suspicious of state power. He opposed 'setting the state "free"... as in Russia', and wrote: 'Freedom consists in converting the state from an organ superimposed upon society into one completely subordinate to it, and even today forms of the state are more or less free to the extent that they restrict the "freedom of the state".' I don't need to enter into any detailed discussion of this subject here. For my purpose it would suffice to draw attention to one *decisive* expression of Marx's view of the 'dictatorship of the proletariat' in his brief comment on the Paris Commune of 1871. He regards the Parisian Communards—Marx's 'heaven-stormers'—as the pioneers of such 'dictatorship'. Marx saw the Paris Commune, despite its limitations or inadequacies and short duration, as a workers' state in action, an example of the *rule* (or 'dictatorship') of the proletariat. Describing it as a self-liberating 'working-class government', he assessed it as 'the political form at last discovered under which to work out the economic emancipation of Labour'. Marx noticed the extraordinary advance in *democracy* which Commune represented both as a form of government and in the measures it carried out. Commune, wrote Marx, 'supplied the Republic with the basis of really democratic institutions', though he recognised, especially in view of the brief duration of the Commune, that its measures 'could but betoken the tendency of a government of the people by the people'.

The Commune, elected in a general election, destroyed the old military-bureaucratic bourgeois state apparatus, suppressed parliamentarism, and substituted it by people more directly governing themselves with binding mandates (*mandat imperatif*) on delegates to representative bodies; it 'got rid of the standing army and the police', replacing one with people at arms and turning the other into a responsible, 'at all times revocable agent of the Commune'; it abolished bureaucracy and put in its place an elected civil service, all its officials—administrative, judicial, educational and any other—to be elected on the basis of universal suffrage and subject to recall at any time at the demand of the electorate, their salaries at par with the wages of the working people; it divested the police and clergy of their political influence, and so on. Its view of national organisation, which Commune had no time to develop, involved decentralised democratic structures so that, in Marx's words, 'the unity of the nation was... to become a reality by the destruction of the State power which claimed to be the embodiment of that unity, independent of, and superior to, the nation itself, from which it was but a parasitic excrescence'.

Crucially important in the measures of the Commune, which covered the Commune members themselves, was the concern for effective safeguards or barriers against corruption, place-hunting, coercion or arrogance of the state officials and their own deputies, making difficult, if not impossible, the emergence of any privileged bureaucratic elite. As if half-aware of the bureaucratic threat that could arise in the future, Marx and Engels were at great pains to underline the measures that the Commune had undertaken to guarantee a socialist revolution against the recrudescence of bureaucratic power. Even as Marx praised the Communards for their 'Revolution against the *state* itself', and welcomed the 'amputation' of the 'merely repressive organs of the old governmental power' (the army and the police) and the return of the state's 'legitimate functions' to the democratically elected and modestly compensated, responsible agents of society, he wrote: "Nothing could be more foreign to the spirit of the Commune than to supersede universal suffrage by hierarchic investiture'. There was no room here for any *nomenklatura* or bureaucratic rule which became the dominant feature of government and politics in the erstwhile Soviet Union. The Parisian workers sought to make impossible *ex ante* the rise of a special caste (bureaucratic or any other) standing above and opposed to the people that was later the source of so-called 'deviations' and 'distortions' and so much else that went so grievously wrong in the Soviet Union. Severely critical of the 'statist superstition' of the German Social Democrats, it was precisely this significance of the Commune that Engels underlined when he approvingly wrote of the measures taken by it 'against transformation of the state and the organs of the state from servants of society into masters of society—an inevitable transformation in all previous states'. For Marx and Engels, the Paris Commune was and remained the model of a 'dictatorship of the proletariat' as they had visualised it. Two decades after the Commune arose and was soon drowned in blood by a most ruthless bourgeois counter-revolution, in a sharp rejoinder to the rather shallow critics of their concept, Engels wrote: 'Of late, the social-democratic philistine has once more been filled with the wholesome terror at the words: Dictatorship of the Proletariat. Well and good, gentlemen, do you want to know what this dictatorship looks like? Look at the Paris Commune. That was the Dictatorship of the Proletariat.' It needs to be specifically noted that Marx not only saw the extraordinarily democratic Paris Commune as the model of 'the dictatorship of the proletariat', a 'thoroughly expansive' political form for a socialist transition, but, insofar as class struggle continues throughout the *transitional* period, Marx also viewed it as affording 'the rational medium in which that class struggle can run through its different phases in the most rational and humane way.'

It will not be out of place to mention that Lenin understood 'dictatorship of the proletariat' exactly as Marx and Engels did. He argued for it in his *State and Revolution* and sought to practice it—'Soviets' being its new historical form—in the immediate aftermath of the revolution he led in Russia; though it all withered away and perished too early and too fast. The how and why of it we shall explore later. The fact to be immediately noticed is that 'dictatorship of the proletariat' soon become 'the great absence' in the historical experiment of 'building socialism' in the Soviet Union. This is what R. Khasbulatov, himself a servant become master, and a latter-day accomplice in the final decay, degeneration and collapse of the Soviet experiment, in an earlier, honest moment wrote: 'If the Soviets had really become the organs of power, if the regime of the dictatorship of the proletariat and peasantry had really been organised, Stalinism would never have existed... The paradox of socialism consists in the fact that the concept itself of the proletarian dictatorship was discredited without ever being applied in the USSR'. That this observation betrays rank ignorance of Lenin and the early Soviet history only shows up the kind of leadership Stalinism ultimately spawned in the Soviet Union.

X

I would like to conclude this rather scrappy account of how Marx and Engels thought about socialism, the values and ideals which, according to them, socialism embodied, with a brief discussion of an implication of this account for what was built and has now collapsed as socialism in the Soviet Union. The implication is that if such indeed was socialism as visualised in classical Marxism, such its economic and political values and ethical-aesthetic ideals, then it can be legitimately argued that what was built in the Soviet Union was not socialism; and this has raised an issue that needs to be noticed and taken care of, before I proceed with my discussion of more substantive themes.

That what was built in the Soviet Union, or later imposed or more or less copied in East Europe, was not socialism as Karl Marx or the classical Marxist tradition had visualised it, was common knowledge for a pretty long time, except in official communist circles; it had compelled even its friendly critics, willing to give it every benefit of doubt, to speak of it as only 'actually existing socialism', though 'formerly existing socialism' would be, perhaps, more appropriate now. Scholars had argued about it previously and now any number are busy pointing out that it 'ran counter to what socialism has meant to all shades of socialist thought', that it was indeed not socialism at all. We are informed that it was 'not socialism as historically understood, for example, by Marx, involving a democratically controlled economy and a state subordinate to society', that it was 'very far from socialism—a form of society where the associated producers are the masters of the process of production, a society based on the largest economic, social, and political democracy, a commonwealth liberated from all class, ethnic, and gender exploitation and oppression', that it was 'at best an authoritarian welfare state', or something 'closer to what Marx dismisses as "crude communism"', and so on.

The failure of 'actually existing socialism', really a non-socialism according to these critics, has therefore, most naturally, given rise to a response which needs to be taken note of, for it is widely shared on the Left including knowledgeable scholars and even activists, who would still defend and speak up for socialism. It has been argued that since the 'socialism' in question had little or no relation to the real thing, the socialism of Karl Marx, but was only propagated and sought to be legitimised as such by the powers that be, the question of failure of socialism simply does not arise; to talk either of failure or 'crisis' of socialism is, strictly speaking, irrelevant. Far too many on the Left, especially Marxologists among them, have been opting for this response. We are told that 'socialism has not failed because it has not been tried', that socialism 'was not tried—or rather, socialism as the attempt by the majority to establish democratic control of economic life was not tried, only control of society by the State bureaucracy was', that 'what never even existed cannot be said to have failed', that 'one cannot die before being born', that 'Communism is not dead, it is not yet born—the same applies to socialism', that to speak of failure 'is a grotesque misrepresentation of facts, because socialism was not even started... not even the first steps were taken', that 'only what has lived can die, that socialism therefore could never die in the East', and so on. And if this response is deemed a sufficient answer to the 'enemies' of socialism who incessantly speak of its 'failure' or 'crisis', its 'friends', the 'official' communists and others, who have complained of 'dismantling' of socialism in the erstwhile Soviet Union and Eastern Europe, are told that it is not possible to dismantle something which does not exist. And that is that.

It is significant that the overwhelming majority of theoretical contributions sustaining this position have been made in the developed capitalist countries, which, however, is not to deny that such argumentation has its validity, it certainly has an empirical basis and theoretical coherence. Nevertheless, for socialists it is a very weak response. Whatever its attraction as an easily scored propaganda point for the academically inclined, it cannot be acceptable to those who take their socialism seriously or are actively involved with the movement, because of the theoretical as well as practical implications of this response. Since 'socialism' in the Soviet Union was not really socialism—an ideal still to be realised—and since it had nothing to do with genuine Marxism, the implications are that its record or failure poses no particular problems for socialists, least of all for those of Marxist persuasion, that the collapse in the Soviet Union does not in any way compromise the socialist cause and therefore there is no need or obligation on the part of such believers in genuine socialism to undertake a rigorously critical reappraisal of this truly agonising historical experience. They only need, as so often in the past, to differentiate themselves and take their distance from this 'fraudulent' socialism and proclaim that, despite everything, real or true socialism is alive and well and as destined to triumph as ever—an argument or political position which, bypassing all the difficult demands of the objective situation and revolutionary praxis, generally ends up either constructing 'visions' of 'true socialism' and appealing in its name, or persuading people of the historical necessity, indeed inevitability, of socialism.

The validity of this argument, such as it is, does not save it from being an argument of utter political poverty. If ever there was an argument that preaches only to the already persuaded, this is it. Those who have experienced or rather suffered this 'socialism', far from getting converted now, will not find even consolation in being informed that it was not socialism at all, certainly not real socialism—they have already turned, for the time being at least, to Yeltsins and their ilk in their midst, to the magic of the capitalist market and authoritarianism of its 'democratic politics', while those in opposition would rather be damned than speak again of socialism, 'real' or any other. For others, elsewhere, this argument amounts to a self-defeating denial of a historic experiment carried out in the name of socialism, simply because it did not take place strictly according to the book. An evasion of the real and difficult issues raised by the failure of this experiment, it is a politically impotent response, and plain bad tactics for those genuinely committed to the cause of socialism. It is wholly unrealistic to believe that the damage done to the idea of socialism by what has happened in the erstwhile Soviet Union can be wished away by abstract theoretical exercises or faithful assertions on behalf of real socialism, its inevitability or invincibility.

It would simply not do for Marxists or serious socialists to disclaim any association with or responsibility either for the October Revolution or the state and socialism which issued from it. The current appellation, usage and vocabulary of socialism, as of Marxism as revolutionary theory and practice, is so deeply embedded in this historical context that the attempts to change or bypass it, to escape its contemporary historical predicament through its denial or abstract exercises in Marxism or socialism, are not only sterile, they could even be harmful to the struggle for socialism in the coming years. The October Revolution and most other revolutions which followed in *its* wake were genuine socialist revolutions with deep roots in an international movement going back to mid-nineteenth century and they were won with the support of tens of millions of people, won and defended by the heroism and sacrifice, dedication and ingenuity of millions of communist or socialist men and women the world over. Parties which led the revolutionary struggles successfully, by and large did so under the banner of Marxism and their leaders were for the most part seasoned Marxists whose mission in life was to overthrow an unjust and exploitative system and to replace it with one based on the principles of socialism as expounded by Marx and Engels and their followers in the late nineteenth and early twentieth centuries. And these leaders, Lenin onwards, appealed to Marx, sought to organise support for their new regimes on the basis that they were Marxists, and at the subjective level, no matter how mistaken, believed that, in a difficult and unexpected situation, they acted in furtherance of the socialist cause as they understood it; and for the most part, at least till recently, their political credentials were accepted by a powerful, even if somewhat stagnant international movement. These leaders had every intention of creating a new social system along the lines suggested, though never elaborated, by Marx in the nineteenth century. And the concerned regimes, again under Marxist inspiration, regardless of the nature of what ultimately came to be built, were explicitly committed to building socialist societies, which was well expressed in their initial and at least some of the later achievements, in economic development as well as in matters of job security, education and healthcare, of social security in general and a cultured life for all. Whatever their success or failure in implementing the classical Marxist or socialist programme, their effort certainly implicated, in some degree, any politics that chooses public ownership and planning as a means and popular welfare as a goal. They certainly came to provide an alternative model of development with impressive achievements to its credit and several features of great appeal to the masses of impoverished and exploited people in what has come to be described as the third world. It is through the October Revolution and the establishment of a state of the Soviets that the crucially important message of Marxism and militant revolutionary struggle reached the vast masses of these poor people in the periphery of the global capitalist system. And like so many others the world over, they identified the countries of 'actually existing socialism' as socialist and Marxist. It is as such that these countries were admired and condemned, vigorously defended and viciously attacked, for seventy odd years in case of the Soviet Union. These years had witnessed a global spread of communist movement and socialist ideas, producing organisations, parties, and individuals by their tens of millions all over the world who identified with the Soviet Union—they looked to it as supporters, as forgiving or gullible friends, as apologists—and did so as socialists or communists. Many of them supported it as Marxists, just as not a few criticised and opposed it, even died for their opposition, as Marxists (which, incidentally, means that not all Marxists and *a fortiori* not all socialists are answerable for the terrible Soviet deformation of the socialist idea). This support and opposition in the name of Marxism implicates the Marxist doctrine in what has happened in the Soviet Union in a manner that no one who cares for Marxism or socialism can afford to ignore. To deny or refuse to see all this—the authentic revolutionary socialist origins and Marxist associations of the Soviet Union, its complex and turbulent, at times heroic history in pursuit of the socialist idea, its professed aims and ambitions, the not inconsiderable initial success and some at least of later achievements, its place in the world socialist movement over these seventy odd years, etc. and the implications of it all for the future of socialism, for the struggle for socialism that continues—is not only falsification of history, it is also bad socialist politics. However we assess it, the Soviet experience is part of our heritage as socialists. We cannot simply deny or disown it, or cast it away so easily. If it is a dream gone sour, it was yet our dream.

The assessments of course vary and the debate will continue for long. There are those, the old 'faithfuls', who till the end believed that what obtained in the Soviet Union was indeed socialism, albeit with some 'deviations' and 'distortions'. To many others it embodied, in however distorted a form, a genuine and at least partially successful effort to build a socialist society, which had a great deal to be said for it and was worth defending. As a somewhat sympathetic summing up we have Isaac Deutscher's suggestive epigram: 'Socialism in a backward country is backward socialism', though it must not be interpreted too literally. Not a few have seen it, with Stefan Heym, as 'pioneering socialism', humankind's first experiment with socialism as society of the future. That it was some kind of capitalism is a mistaken view, but there is no denying that in terms of the classical socialist tradition, it was anything but socialism. Certainly, it was not our model—no so, at least for a pretty long time. But as the argument goes on about what was built as socialism in the Soviet Union, there is no escaping the fact that its spectacularly ignominious overnight collapse will haunt any socialist project in the world for decades to come and continue to demand that we understand what has happened and come to terms with it, for our own sake and even more to be able to explain to the skeptical why and how the society we continue to struggle for will be different from the recently demised 'socialism'.

On a world historical scale, what the demise of this 'socialism' means is that the first world-wide effort to overthrow the world-system of plunder and oppression which is capitalism has not succeeded, leaving the world at the near-absolute mercy of global capitalism with its exploitation and inequities at home and abroad, its unequal exchange relations, debt-slavery and profit-maximising allocation of resources and dictation of economic policy the world over. Global capitalism, with its massive economic and military might survives as the only international system and its victims, the people everywhere, are left without an international movement with a strategy or perspective or, for the time being it seems, even the goal of overthrowing capitalism.

This is indeed the essential meaning of the Soviet collapse in the short run. This is not to suggest, however, that there are not those among us, men and women, who would, if not question this, certainly retain their perspective, who do not think that capitalism is either inevitable or rational, or that greed is the highest organising principle for social life, who still believe that a humane, cooperative and supportive society, a superior way of life, more rational, creative and fulfilling as well as more democratic and egalitarian, is possible. Such men and women are there the world over, more numerous than many in this moment of defeat and despair think—and their numbers will only grow with the passage of time. Significant anti-capitalist movements still exist the world over, many of them influenced by the communist tradition. And soon there will be many more. People in the advanced West, no longer distracted by 'the ugly face' of Soviet-style socialism, may see better, now, the ugly face of capitalism that is becoming daily more viciously visible and yet turn to socialism as Karl Marx had visualised. The working masses in the erstwhile 'socialist' East, in their progress from 'bull-shit Marxism' of Brezhnevs and Gorbachevs to 'bull-shit liberalism' of Gorbachevs and Yelstins and their successors, through their own troubles and turmoils, may yet learn to struggle for their real interests, for a socially just and democratic society born as much of their historical experience as the teachings of Karl Marx. And in the years and decades to come, as in the past, the world historical revolutionary process may well continue to proceed via the poor and oppressed of the third world, for the same reasons as before, though against heavier odds; and as these people confront the choice 'socialism or peripheralisation', they may yet again seek and find inspiration, guidance and sustenance for their struggles in the doctrine of Karl Marx. The struggle against capitalism and for a just and egalitarian social order is far from over.

Surely it does not help to be told that the October Revolution was premature, or that it was no socialist revolution, or that the socialism just demised was just a non-socialism and no more. Nor should critical reflection content itself with simply denouncing its evident denial of democracy, bureaucratic degeneration and loss of ideals, or with the making of better visions of the socialism of the future. It will also not do to explain the failure in the Soviet Union as the fault of evil men, blaming it all on Stalin in the first place and secondarily on a corrupted *nomenklatura*, with due roles assigned to Khrushchevs, Brezhnevs and Gorbachevs of the Soviet Communist Party. And certainly it is neither desirable nor possible to pass by the experience of 'historical communism', as it has been called, as something without significance to those who would today seek to construct a socialist alternative to capitalism. What is needed is a properly serious Marxist analysis of what went wrong; its absence can only harm the socialist cause—not only will the much-needed lessons remain unlearnt, the interpretations of the enemies of socialism will go uncontested and gain acceptability. In fact, the socialist left will have no credibility unless it comes to terms with what has happened, with honesty and clarity, and above all, courage this demands. It has to be a ruthlessly critical analysis of why socialist revolutions of our times have ended the way they have, in new forms of class society, or a 'socialism' that has collapsed so ignominiously, an analysis which does not avoid difficult or painful issues by idealistically defining them out of socialism.

There has to be an honest appraisal not only of errors, which generally do have a certain qualified admissibility, but also crimes committed in the name of socialism, which can never be condoned. The distinction is important. Errors, it has been pointed out, 'are misjudgements in the service of our agreed-upon program, unnecessary compromises or pompous refusals to compromise, faulty estimates of our progress and the enemy's weakness, passive acceptance of capitalist ways of doing things in the hope that they could be domesticated to socialist ends'. Crimes, on the other hand, 'are violations of socialist democracy, socialist legality, revolutionary humaneness, and that fierce honesty which is basic to the commitment to liberate and mobilise the collective intelligence of all the oppressed. Crimes are the debasement of Marxism to apologetics, the use of force to settle disagreements within the revolution, the covering up of corruption'. There is, of course, truth in the claim that the criminal episodes of Soviet history are not socialism but distortions of socialism. But it is well to remember that not socialism but *distortions* of socialism, they are yet distortions *of* socialism, which compels us to think of what in our theory and practice made socialism vulnerable to crimes.

Only a bold confrontation with history in Marxist fashion, a willingness to 'think as Marx would have thought in (our) place' can enable us to make fresh beginnings in our struggle and be equal to the tasks of the day: to defend the gains of more than 150 years' struggle for socialism, acknowledge the reality of the current defeat in a responsible, self-critical manner, evaluate the reasons for it, draw the necessary lessons and regroup and prepare for the next wave of revolutionary upsurge, which may be sooner than most people, friends and foes of socialism, think. It is an agenda for years and even decades and yet an agenda for here and now.

Chapter 4

On the 50th Anniversary of India's Independence— A Marxist Argument*

> To borrow from Tom Paine's metaphoric rejoinder to Burke's attack on the French Revolution, admiration for the 'plumage' of India's 'national development' should not prevent us from seeing its failure in 'the dying bird'. The world indeed looks very different from below, when the poor and oppressed of 'our nation' look at it.

The most important fact of modern times, over the past few centuries, is the 'meta-narrative' of capitalism which is still on, more dominant globally than ever before, and more lethal too, for it is now a capitalism living beyond its historical time, its creative achievements all behind it and only destructive potentialities ahead, a threat looming large over the future of humankind, reminding us of what Marx foresaw and Rosa Luxemburg later formulated as the prophetic poser: 'socialism or barbarism'. The structural logic of capitalism, the law-like tendencies of its capital-accumulative process, which Marx explicated, have meant uneven and unequal development

---

* *Mainstream*, November 1, 1997. Based on the author's *Five Lectures in Marxist Mode.*

within and across countries, generating wealth and affluence at one end and poverty and deprivation at the other (even when, under certain temporarily favourable circumstances, this is somewhat curbed in the advanced centres of capitalism). Worldwide, the inexorable consequence has been a gap between the centre and the periphery of global capitalism, an ever-widening gap between wealth and poverty at the two poles. Hence a worldwide struggle against capitalism, which in the periphery meant a struggle to get out of this global system in order to be at all able to build a better life for the common people.

A major breakthrough in this struggle occurred (as anticipated by Marx and Engels) in the aftermath of the First World War—an Europewide revolution, triggered off by the Russian Revolution. But of this only the revolution in Russia survived—elsewhere it was let down by social democracy and strangled by capitalist counter-revolution—leaving Lenin and the Bolsheviks confronting a totally unanticipated situation, and a problem: what does their poor and backward country do in the midst of global domination of capitalism? History had played a trick on the doctrine of Karl Marx: instead of socialism being built on a base provided by the economic, political and cultural achievements of capitalism, a backward country was called upon to build it. Lenin saw this as a struggle where 'defeat' was a distinct possibility, and wrote: 'struggle, and struggle alone, decides ... how far we shall advance'. But the struggle, particularly after Lenin's early departure, was not adequate enough. A deeply deformed socialism was built and now, seventy years later, a finally defeated Russia has been sucked back into global capitalism. What has happened was not inevitable. But the fact remains that we are now left with the 'experience (that) will benefit other revolutions', the least that Lenin had hoped for in the event of defeat, and the still unsettled question: what does a backward or a relatively backward country like ours do to advance the interests of its people in a situation of global domination of capitalism?

❖

Modern India and its struggle for freedom is a 'meta-narrative' within the global meta-narrative of capitalism. Before 1947, we were part of a global system well-integrated into a world market economy. We were globalised, but we did not like it. Our globalisation then also had a name, imperialism, and we struggled against it, precisely because it meant—by virtue of its structural logic—accumulation of wealth in England and poverty in India. Like other third world countries, we wanted to get out of this globalisation to be able to opt for an independent, self-reliant development in the interests of our common people. Herein lay the essential meaning of our long struggle for freedom.

❖

We won our freedom in 1947. To understand what really happened in this historic event, it helps to think of what did not happen at the time. There was no revolutionary overthrow of the British imperialist rule in India, no accompanying economic or social or even political revolution. The Gandhi-bourgeois-led freedom struggle (a defensible and better description than any other) ended in a compromise and settlement with imperialism which transferred political power from the foreign rulers to the Indian rulers, leaving the old socio-economic and state-bureaucratic structures largely intact which, in turn, with all their structural compulsions, became the basis for the post-colonial 'national development'. This development has carried the full impress of the way freedom was finally 'won' in 1947.

❖

The post-colonial rulers in India, having gained power in the state, went on to set up a 'national project' of self-reliant economic development to supplement the recently won political freedom with the more important economic freedom for the Indian people. The Soviet Union was seen as an example of successful state intervention in the economy (which the Indian bourgeoisie itself deemed necessary), the Cold War allowed the new rulers a certain manoeuvrability of action, and Nehru's 'socialistic pattern of society' soon provided the necessary ideological underpinning for the post-colonial process of national reconstruction, with its focus on the state sector to build up the economy, affirmative action for the most disadvantaged sections of society and economic growth in general which was to benefit the people at large. The project was not lacking in vision and it soon had significant achievements to its credit. But despite Nehru's awareness of the 'terrible costs of not changing the existing order', this project was no radical break with 'the existing order', vindicating Marx who had, in his analysis of the failed German revolution of 1848, already said that henceforth the bourgeoisie could not be relied upon to make success of even a bourgeois democratic revolution.

❖

The Nehru era was the golden age of India's national project, though it was never without its critics. The slogan was 'growth with equity and distributive justice'. Acting as 'the executor of the economic necessities of the national situation', in Engels' words, the Indian state indeed ensured growth in the economy but the hope for equity and distributive justice to people was largely belied. The years that followed revealed the inherent limitations of the Nehruvian national project and saw its rapid disintegration. The structural logic of 'the existing order' prevailing, the economy was soon 'some strange kind of corrupted capitalist growth', as Romesh Thapar saw it, or 'a type of capitalist development in the interests of a narrow section of Indian society', as V.K.R.V. Rao put it. As it finally came up, it could be more firmly described as a state-supported India-specific capitalism which reminded one of Marx's observation about countries which

> suffer not only from the development of capitalist production but also from the incompleteness of that development. Alongside of modern evils a whole series of inherited evils oppress us, arising from the passive survival of antiquated modes of production with their inevitable train of social and political anachronisms. We suffer not only from the living but from the dead.

As capitalism, its structural logic meant unequal and uneven development in the country as a whole—the near-universally recognised 'two nations' (the rich and the poor) and 'internal colonialism' (in relation to the country's more backward parts). As for its specificity, this is how I put it sometime back:

> Its historical specificity has given it a strong comprador and lumpen character, presided over as it is by a bourgeoisie born old without ever having known youth, with none of the possible virtues of youth and all the vices of old age. Here all the exploitative and oppressive evils of belated capitalist development, semi-feudalism, bureaucratically-corrupt public sector and bloated bourgeois politics daily enter into and reinforce each other. All pervasive black money, flourishing as a parallel economy, only intensifies the structural biases of a white money of scams and swindles, even as it serves to sustain, with help from politicians, policemen and sundry state functionaries, an essentially illegal, secular or communal, *mafiosi-led* parallel political polity, which has today come to acquire an almost legitimised coexistence with the formally legal state in large, especially urban, parts of the country. A long time ago, apropos the essentially *secondary* character of such capitalist development, Karl Marx had written: 'as is well known, secondary diseases are more difficult to cure and, at the same time, ravage the body more than original ones.'

Outside of economy, it was soon a case of the 'state as private property', and any kind of power in the state a means of 'rapid private accumulation'; on official admission, even of the funds directly allocated for poverty alleviation, only 'the leakage', a bare fifteen per cent, reached the people—the state in India far from being a part of any solution, itself became a part of almost every problem. Democracy, fought for and won by the people, still valuable to them, and throughout defended by them against subversion from above, yet only vindicated Bagehot's classic observation about its being 'the way to give the people the greatest illusion of power while allowing them the smallest amount in reality', even as it also served to legtimise the ruling class domination in society. 'Democratic politics' itself, once practised as 'Hindu Undivided Family', as economic problems surfaced, steadily degenerated into an utterly unscrupulous, no-holds-barred infighting among the beneficiaries of the system for power and pelf in the state, where, as they violated the rules of their own game, it was now truly the end justifying the means, literally any means; it was Malraux's 'politicians' politics' in its worst sense.

The national project was fast ending up as a class project but not recognised as such. It had its beneficiaries, and there was a consensus of the arrived and the complacent about it. Nationalism too had its uses, the emerging reality could be obscured in its name. Such was the domination of the ruling class ideas that even those who saw capitalism, saw its more as our very own 'national economy', and, together with faith and force of habit, this ensured the prevalence of the view that the 'national project' was still on. But the project was already faltering. In any case there was nothing much in its achievements for the vast masses of the common Indian people. To borrow from Tom Paine's metaphoric rejoinder to Burke's attack on the French Revolution, the 'plumage' of India's 'national development' was yet that of a 'dying bird'. The world looked very different from below, when the poor and oppressed of 'our nation' looked at it. However, the definitive collapse of the national project was still in the future.

Mid-1960s onwards, the post-colonial national project in India floundered and fast degenerated, its economic crises underpinning and moving in step with the crises of the political system, 'democratic politics' and all that. If India's 'national economy' generated any number of potentially explosive issues, its 'national politics' regularly turned these issues into problems, problems into running sores and these sores into tragedies for the Indian people, in Punjab, Kashmir, almost everywhere. By the end of the 1980s the national project was virtually over. Soon enough a dead-end economic crisis or financial bankruptcy of sorts, produced by the previously pursued policies, coincided with the defeat of the Soviet Union in the Cold War and its eventual disintegration, depriving the Indian ruling classes of whatever little manoeuvrability they still had and leaving them more vulnerable than ever before to the offensive of a recharged global capitalism. Given the strong comprador or lumpen strain inherent in their character, led by their major political formation, the Congress-I, with their other political formations in tow, they succumbed, and hiccups and protests over 'level playing field' notwithstanding, opted for what is turning out to be a junior partnership within the global capitalist system. As beneficiaries of growth during the Nehru era and afterwards, and now with a substantial economic strength of their own, 'globalisation' also provides them with new avenues of profit making at home and abroad. Therefore, this 'succumbing' can also be seen as a natural progress for Indian capitalism. India was again globalised, this time through a largely voluntary submission of the Indian rulers. The national project finally and definitively collapsed in 1991.

❖

The evidence of this collapse is there in the disintegration of values and degradation of life all around us, in the continuing poverty of our people and growing consumerism of the elites and a society at once cynical and fearful about the future. It is there in official statistics and pages of the private media and so-called 'national mainstream' which, bearing the impress of India's corrupt and corrupting, somewhat lumpen capitalist development, is an increasingly dirty affair—corrupt, communal and criminalised, a repressively homogenising mainstream. The evidence is there in the visionless and so obviously laboured efforts of the powers that be to flog a tired and flabby patriotism into some semblance of life in this fiftieth year of India's independence, including Colgate-sponsored selling of *Vande Matarams* on the television by hordes of India's VIPs and VVIPs. And this evidence is pathetically present in the impotence (or is it hypocrisy?) of the supposedly 'stirring' calls being made on the occasion—in Parliament for a 'second freedom struggle' and by the Prime Minister to 'begin the struggle for economic freedom'! One wonders what these past fifty years have been about. A Finance Minister took India back into globalisation, asking us not to be afraid of the East India Company, opened up India to the multinationals, on the dishonest plea that 'the nation has been living beyond its means' —'nation' indeed, when a good majority of our people have simply no means to live and most others none to indulge any 'living beyond'! His successor, more honest and ideologically committed, has been publicly pleading with the former globalisers in London to come back to India for another equally long stay (and then gone to town with this pleading in Washington and elsewhere): 'You came to India and stayed for

200 years. Now come prepared to invest and stay for another 200 years, and there will be huge rewards'. The post-colonial national project is indeed over and done with.

❖

Capitalism is today so powerful and pervasive as to have become invisible, and it is all the more powerful for being invisible. You no longer mention or recognise it. It is there, but without a name as it were, a harmless, nay benevolent, phenomenon called 'globalisation', recently arrived on the world scene to help the poor and backward countries out of their problems. Globalisation, nevertheless, has a proper name, capitalism, its world economy or market is a capitalist world economy or market. Harvard economist Robert Reich's phrase 'secession of the successful', is vividly expressive of a crucial feature of any capitalist market society. Globalisation of India means that the 'successful' of Indian society, the ruling elites of India, have decided to 'secede' from the common Indian people. A capitalist market society is also a case of 'the economy is doing fine, the people are not', as a President of Brazil once reported it in Washington. Therefore, the Indian economy may do 'fine' (with its growth rates, etc.) but, given its structural logic, the Indian people will not; for them the consequences of the current globalisation are not likely to be much different from those of the globalisation they had struggled hard and long to finally escape in 1947. Their peripheralisation this time could well be much worse.

❖

The ruling classes of India have, through their different political formations, decided to 'secede' from the people and opted for 'globalisation' as their strategic option for the future. The Indian people yet again face the question, whose full implications were somewhat obscured in 1947 due largely to the interim successes of the Soviet Union: what do they do in the current situation of global domination of capitalism? The historical experience in India and elsewhere in the third world makes it abundantly clear that they will find no answers in capitalism, national (including the one now, in effect, sought by the RSS and its *Swadeshi Jagran Manch*) or globalised. The choice for them remains socialism or peripheralisation. This is not to posit socialism as achievable today or tomorrow, or even the day-after for that matter, but to posit it as an alternative strategic goal, as the principle governing people's politics which links together their immediate, ongoing and emerging struggles in an ultimate project of revolutionary transformation of our society, as the goal of a long transitional process, whose specifics and speed will depend upon the objective material conditions and the nature and balance of the class forces involved at each stage of the struggle for the ultimate objective. Immediately, it means saying 'no' to globalisation. This is not to argue for any kind of 'autarky' in economic development but to pose the issue of whether this development will be governed by *external* imperatives, those issuing from the requirements of the world capitalist market (export-led growth, etc.) and the associated consumerism of the rich, or primarily by *internal* imperatives, those flowing from an assessment of our own resources and the needs of our common people.

The issue, in other words, is that of priorities: development for what and whom? Is it to satisfy the basic needs of the people or the consumerism of the elite in our society? The argument is for a pro-people socialism-oriented autonomous development which draws on our own strengths, our domestic resources and capacities, including those of the hard-working poor who still remain the most creative and productive in our society, a development which gives the common people, in both urban and rural areas, a positive stake in the economy and mobilises them for building a better society and, let me add, for the inevitable struggle against global imperialism and its local allies or partners. This has to be the alternative strategic option of the Indian people.

❖

Technological backwardness is often pressed as an argument to counter the plea for such autonomous economic development in a third world country. Here, apart from the fact that in India at least we are not that lacking in either technology or the talent for it, we need to overcome the widely prevalent fetishism of science and technology, which at times (as, for example, with

Nehru and his 'temples of modern India', etc.) has even gone to the extent of expecting them to do the job of a social revolution, which they simply cannot. As with economics so with technology, the question again is one of priorities: technology for what purpose? Once this question is asked, the argument for getting access to the most modern Western technology, via globalisation—even if that was certain which it certainly is not—loses much of its force. If the purpose is to satisfy the consumerist hunger of the privileged part of our population with the most modern gadgets and designs, and the goodies of the West, then rushing into globalisation indeed makes some sense. But if the purpose or priority is to meet the needs of all the people for decent food, clothing and shelter, clean water, proper sanitation and health protection, education and cultural opportunities, and the like, then devoting scarce resources to the most modern technology is simply wasteful, because there is little in the latest technology of the West that could make a significant contribution. In fact what is most useful and relevant in technology, Western or otherwise, for improving the way of life of the masses, is widely known; moreover, most of it is already available at home and what else is needed, is obtainable in the normal course of managed trade.

A socialism-oriented autonomous economic development as a strategic option for our people is premised on *politics* (that is *people's politics*) and not *'the market'* commanding the economy (which, however, does not rule out an useful role for the market). If such development is necessary in the interests of our people and they have no choice but to attempt it if they would avoid peripheralisation, with the people *really in power* it is also possible. The failure of the world's first experiment in socialism notwithstanding, there is much in the socialist experience of our time to help guide this attempt and be hopeful about it: for example, in the still unparalleled achievements of the early years of the post-revolutionary societies in Russia and elsewhere despite their economic backwardness, in Cuba's struggle to build socialism and save the gains of its socialist revolution, in Lenin's socialist project during the few years that he survived the October Revolution, in the experience of the 'Mao years' in China, and so on. An uncharted territory, we can still enter it with confidence.

❖

The crux of the matter is *people's power in the state*, their 'political supremacy' in society, as Marx put it. Not phoney 'empowerment' from above, but people fighting and winning power for themselves through their own struggles is central to securing a pro-people economic development in the country. 'National politics' of the day is almost exhausted so far as promotion of people's interests is concerned, it is today virtually parasitic on these interests. The traditional or mainstream left, content all these years to operate only on the terrain of bourgeois politics, has finally lost out to it, and does not seem likely to recover its original commitment to revolutionary politics or socialism. But life continues to stir on the ground, the terrain where the real struggle for people's power begins—some old radical initiatives persist and many new ones are emerging everywhere, involving women, dalits, tribals, minor nationalities, ethnic or religious minorities, human rights, ecological concerns, etc; any number of popular struggles at local levels are on. They all face serious problems of theory and practice. The people will surely have to go through the hard and painful school of experience, and survive the all too many wrong battles they are misled into fighting, before they learn to fight the right battles of their own. But learn they will. Globalisation itself, as it proceeds apace, will clarify as nothing else could, the real issues of Indian economy and politics—the issues of class divisions and exploitation, of the rich and the poor within the nation—and thus help people see through the ruling class politics of different varieties and come to a politics of their own, articulate their diverse struggles with a class-based people's politics, at both local and national levels, and confront the strategic option of the ruling classes, globalisation, with their own strategic option of a socialism-oriented autonomous economic development in the country. They will need to do so, the alternative is only their further peripheralisation within the global capitalist system.

❖

The post-colonial national project may have collapsed, and, in terms of their objective interests, the paths of the ruling elite and the people may have diverged as never before, but nationalism yet remains a very strong sentiment among our people. Many of those who would agree with me may still regard the struggle for a socialism–oriented autonomous economic development as a national struggle, a continuation, as it were, of the Indian people's earlier national struggle for freedom. Contributing to the confusion here is the increasing use or popularity of the concept 'national popular', in academic and political circles on the left. This calls for a brief comment and clarification.

Nationalism, however 'ambiguous' an identity, and undoubtedly a powerful social, political and ideological force in our times, is yet a historical phenomenon with class and society-specific character, potentialities and limitations, and, therefore, capable of manifesting itself in diverse forms. Located as we are in the third world and with the still alive, though much faded, memories of our long struggle for freedom, we in this country are conventionally inclined to see nationalism as a liberationist force or ideology. But this is not always or necessarily the case with nationalism. With the ruling classes in the normal pursuit of their interests, or when faced with situations of crisis, nationalism has often taken all sorts of anti-people, imperialist or statist or racist or fascist forms, providing ideological support to ruling class politics, their political domination at home and abroad. In our own country, more particularly in recent decades, nationalism has been used by our post-colonial rulers to cover up or find alibis for their defaults, to conceal the social reality of our much-divided and exploitative society, to divert people away from their real concerns and mobilise them behind ruling class politics. One political formation of the ruling classes has even come up with a Hindu-chauvinist nationalism, 'cultural nationalism' as they call it, to gain popular support and in the name of *swadeshi* better defend and promote the interests of India's 'national' capitalism.

Nationalism in India before 1947 was indeed progressive;

under a different, more advanced class leadership and programme, it could have been radical, even revolutionary. It was progressive because it aimed at resolving the basic structural contradictions of Indian society, congealed in imperialism, whose resolution alone could clear the path for Indian people's struggle for a better life. The struggle to resolve these contradictions, against imperialism, was our national struggle for freedom. But after 1947, with the post-colonial rulers having facilitated a historically specific form of capitalist development in the country, the basic contradictions that now need to be resolved to clear the path for Indian people's continuing struggle for a better life lie *within* the nation, and their resolution is a matter of struggle within, against the Indian ruling classes; therefore, strictly speaking, this struggle cannot be viewed simply as a national struggle. In fact, Indian people's continuing struggle against imperialism, globalisation's neo-colonialism, too is now a part of this new struggle within, and not a continuation of the old pre-1947 anti-imperialist struggle, because the neo-colonialist 'integration', rather enhanced integration of India into the global capitalist economy, is now occurring by the grace of, through the opportunities provided by, indeed at the invitation of, the new rulers at Delhi. Nationalism or a national perspective only obscures this most basic of all issues facing the Indian people.

Thus, the struggle for a people's strategic option as against 'globalisation' that the Indian ruling classes have opted for, the struggle for a socialism-oriented autonomous development—which alone can also be an ecologically sustainable development as against a globalised Indian capitalism, subject to the capital-accumulative or profit-making imperatives of the market—is not a national struggle as such, nor a continuation of the earlier national struggle in India, though it can and may be seen as its transcendence in a strictly dialectical sense, that is, a struggle that carries forward the best traditions and hopes of the earlier liberationist struggles of the Indian people. It is in its basic character a class struggle in the proper Marxian sense which eschews its narrow economistic or reductionist interpretations. No doubt a great deal of tactical resilience is necessary in relating it, theoretically as well as practically, to the obviously important question of nationalism. But even if this struggle is viewed as a national or 'national-popular' struggle of the Indian people, it cannot but be fighting the 'anti-nation within the nation', as the Latin-Americans have learnt to call it, or 'rescuing the nation' from its ruling classes, or, as Marx would have put it, the people 'establishing itself as *the* nation', and thus remains, in its essential content, a class struggle; it cannot be a collective struggle of all Indians for a common goal, for the goals within have sharply diverged. The national task, recovering India for its people, is now, as it were, also a class task of the Indian people. Such has to be the perspective of the Indian people's struggle against globalisation and for a better life today.

Chapter 5

'The Return of Karl Marx'*

It is kind of the Foundation for Social Responsibility to have invited me for this talk in their series on 'Creeds for the New Millennium'. It would have been a grievous mistake if, in deference to current fashion, they had left Marx out of this series. But I have accepted the invitation with much diffidence. I am no scholar of Marxism. The years when one gets started on scholarship of any kind, I, like many others of my generation, had left home and studies to chase a different dream in the freedom struggle and the communist movement—the dream of a social revolution which, I believe, still needs to be made in our country. I did, then and later, pick up some Marxism and have found it useful to me in my profession as a teacher and in living my life, but I have always remained aware of my inadequacy to speak on the subject of Marxism. Part of diffidence is also due to the venue—India International Centre, its overall ambience, the atmosphere heavy with the smugness and sanity of its 'Saturday Club' and 'opinion makers'... How does one speak here of the lifelong insanity that was Karl Marx calling for 'revolution, the conversion of all hearts and the raising of all hands in behalf of the honour of the free man'? The most important reason for my diffidence, however, is the nature of the subject itself.

---

* A Talk, *Mainstream*, May 5, 2001.

Way back in the seventeenth century, the English philosopher Thomas Hobbes had pointed to the rulers' hostility to truth—even geometrical axioms—if it ran counter to their interests. In his characteristically pungent manner, he had written: 'For I doubt not, but if it had been a thing contrary to any man's right of dominion, or to the interest of men that have dominion, *that the three angles of a triangle, should be equal to two angles of a square*, that doctrine should have been, if not disputed, yet by the burning of all books of geometry, suppressed, as far as he whom it concerned was able'. (That is how the burning and banning of books—and suppression of truth—has been such an important part of our civilisational progress and seems to have got a new lease of life under the present dispensation in our country). Now, Marx's truth has obviously been 'a thing contrary to the interest of men that have dominion' in our societies. Therefore he has never lacked enemies who have been busy 'refuting', misrepresenting and vulgarising him over the last hundred years and more. But Marx has suffered equally, perhaps more, at the hands of friends—they have brought much grist to mills of the enemies through their dogmatism, scientism, economism and much else besides. In his moving short poem *Karl Heinrich Marx*, the German poet Hans Magnus Enzensberger has written:

> *I see you betrayed*
> *by your disciples*
> *only your enemies*
> *remained what they were.*

Between enemies and friends a whole range of Marx's ideas—on philosophy and history, economics and politics, ethics and culture—has come to be distorted and vulgarised. Two of the easiest examples that immediately come to mind are what Marx is supposed to have said regarding religion and 'opium' or 'the dictatorship of the proletariat'. 'If people could only *read*', Marx used to say. Maurice Dobb, the eminent Marxist economist who was also a good Marxist, had once suggested that it is much easier to say what Marxism is not than to state what it is. The collapse of the Soviet Union, of what they had built there in the name of Marxism, has made the situation worse confounded, adding to the already formidable difficulties of speaking on the subject of Marxism.

❖

I am not here going to chase any controversies or attempt any kind of comprehensive treatment of Marxism as I understand it. Constraints of time alone make that impossible. Mine will be a modest response to the theme of this series and I will try to make it relevant to what is happening around us in the world at large and in our country. I will advance a few basic propositions but will not be able to either offer explanations, or make qualifications, which is always necessary in social scientific thinking to secure better validity for one's propositions. I will raise more questions than provide answers. The aim is to share with you a general sense of what Marx was after and the hope is that at least some among the younger people present here learn to ask the right kind of questions of the reality around them, for in the final analysis this is indeed what Marxism of Marx is about.

I am sure many of you are intrigued by the title I have given to my talk—'The Return of Karl Marx'. Let me assure you that there is more to it than 'good old dogmatism', or 'at best, misplaced optimism' as even some 'friends', now hopeless about me, have suspected. Towards the end of 1980s, as the communist regimes collapsed in Eastern Europe, the *New Yorker*, an upmarket magazine in the United States, celebrated the occasion with an article by Robert Heilbronner entitled 'Triumph of Capitalism', whose argument reverberated worldwide, setting off a new round of hosannas for capitalism and renewed pronouncements of 'the death of Marxism'. The argument was seriously flawed but that is not my concern at the moment. The immediately important fact is that less than a decade later, towards the end of 1997, in a bout of futurology, bringing together a series of articles around the theme 'what's next?', the same *New Yorker* went looking for the 'next most influential thinker', and the article written by John Cassidy who is no Marxist, now or ever before, was titled 'The Return of Karl Marx'! (Cassidy felt persuaded to write the article when a friend, having reached the highest positions in the US corporate world told him that it was just as Marx had seen it). The article had concluded: 'His (Marx's) books will be worth reading as long as capitalism endures'. Cassidy is right. I will only underline that none, before or after him has studied and analysed capitalism better than Marx and that he has indeed been prophetic in his analysis of capitalism. Hence his continuing relevance for our time and the need for us to turn or return to Marx for a viable creed for the new millennium.

Marx is relevant because we are living, nationally and globally, in a world of capitalism. Of course, capitalism today is not as Marx saw and studied it in the nineteenth century. It has undergone changes, important changes, since then, and it is necessary to recognise them for understanding, and struggling against, contemporary capitalism. But as Raymond Williams once warned, in taking note of what has changed in capitalism, we must not make the mistake of underestimating everything that has not changed. And this 'everything', above all, includes the structural logic of capitalism, the law-like tendencies of its capital-accumulative process which, as Marx explicated, have meant unequal and uneven development within and across countries. Within countries, even when somewhat curbed in the advanced centres of capitalism—which curbing however remains reversible as the current dismantling of the 'welfare state' in the West shows—these tendencies have had the consequence of generating wealth and affluence at one end and poverty and deprivation at the other. Worldwide, the inexorable consequence has been a gap between the centre and the periphery of global capitalism, an ever-widening gap between wealth and poverty at the two poles. This exploitative structural logic of capitalism is as much at work today as it was when Marx first studied and analysed capitalism. In fact it is all the more at work now as, with globalisation, the world is more capitalist today than it has been for a long time—a reality that bourgeois ideology seeks to obscure through its myth-making over 'globalisation'.

In tandem with the somewhat waning 'Post-', 'Globalisation' is the fashionable buzzword these days. It is as if something is happening that has never happened before. As if a whole new epoch of benevolence and prosperity for all has opened in human history, an epoch in which things like capitalism, imperialism, exploitation, and therefore socialism, are all a matter of the past. And there is supposed to be no alternative to what is happening as 'globalisation'. But all this is only ideological mystification, so much 'globaloney', as it has been called. Capitalism has been from the very beginning a globalising system. Adam Smith knew it and you will find its sharpest, and literally prophetic, expression in the *Communist Manifesto,* where Marx wrote of how 'the need of a constantly expanding market for its products chases the bourgeoisie over the whole surface of the globe', how it 'must nestle everywhere, settle everywhere, establish connections everywhere', how it has 'established the world market' and 'through its exploitation of the world market given a cosmopolitan character to production and consumption in every country', how it 'batters down all Chinese walls' and 'compels all nations to adopt the bourgeois mode of production, i.e., to become bourgeois themselves', and so on. 'Globalisation', thus, is nothing new, no new epoch in the history of humankind. It is only another phase in the process of capitalist expansion, of course with its own more or less important specificities.

❖

The most important specificity to be noticed about the current phase of globalisation is its radical departure from the way capitalism existed during the previous period of post-war boom, the 'golden age' of capitalism. Capitalism of this period was marked by Keynesian strategies of moderate macro-economic regulations and the accompanying limits on capital's unending thirst for more profits, collectively known as the 'welfare state', which, incidentally, saved capitalism from its own self-destructive tendencies—as manifested, for example, in the Great Depression—and also helped it acquire a much-needed 'human face', against the internal and external threat of socialism. The onset of a structural crisis of capitalism, which gives every sign of being irreversible, has changed all that. The 1970s saw the world economy going into a downturn that has worsened through every recession since; the gap between business cycles is getting smaller, barely does recovery begin, the growth falters. 'Globalisation', with its neo-liberalism, is essentially a response to this structural crisis of capitalism and signifies a return, as it were, from an atypical to typical capitalism, from the aberration that was the post-war 'golden age', to a period of normal, 'free-market' capitalism. For capital to remain 'competitive' in the global market, Keynesian state interventions in the economy have to go. Nor can capitalism now afford to wear a 'human face'; with the threat of socialism having receded, perhaps, it also does not need to wear it any more. State must revert to its traditional way of serving capitalism, that is, it must now act as the main agent of globalisation. And this is indeed how state is now acting. It is ironic that at a time when the world is behaving, so to speak, in a most Marxian manner, all sorts of wise men have taken to proclaiming the obsolescence of Marxism. Far from being obsolete, Marxism has become all the more relevant today for those in search of a viable creed for our time.

Strictly speaking, Marxism is not a creed, 'a system of beliefs', as the term is conventionally understood or defined. Though, friends and enemies have tended to treat it like one; Marxists themselves have ever so often behaved like 'believers' and it was virtually reduced to a state-religion in the erstwhile Soviet Union. No creed-maker or builder of a philosophical system, Marx was, by vocation, a revolutionary as Engels emphasised in his famous grave-side speech on the death of Marx. Philosopher, economist, historian, and much else, Marx was indeed 'the man of science', said Engels. He had, however, immediately added: 'But this was not even half the man.... For Marx was before all else a revolutionist'. This was a choice Marx had made quite early in his life. In an essay Marx wrote for his school-leaving examination in 1835, 'A Young Man's Reflections on the Choice of a Career', he stated that working 'only for himself' one 'can become a famous scholar, a great sage, an excellent imaginative writer (*Dichter*), but never a perfected, a truly great man'. Instead Marx himself opted for a life 'that is most consonant with our dignity, one that is based on ideas of whose truth we are wholly convinced, one that offers us largest scope in working for humanity'. This option, which soon turned into a clearly defined revolutionary commitment, stayed with Marx throughout his life. Early in his youth, asserting that 'man is the highest being for man', he spoke up for 'the categorical imperative to overthrow all conditions in which man is a humiliated, enslaved, despised and rejected being'; later, about the time he finished writing *Capital*, to complete which he had sacrificed, as he said, his 'health, happiness and family', Marx wrote to a friend: 'I laugh at the so-called "practical" men with their wisdom. If one chose to be an ox, one could turn one's back on the sufferings of mankind and look after one's own skin'. It is this revolutionary commitment, the moral choice he had made to stand up for 'humanity' or 'mankind' that underlay Marx's theoretical work, and the outcome was no creed for the faithful to believe in and uphold, or a closed system of philosophy already in possession of 'the truth', as the enemies have often caricatured it.

In a statement remarkable for his age, the Darwinian age drunk on its achievements of science, or 'reason' as they also called it, and breaking sharply with the received philosophical tradition, from Plato to Hegel—which, in Marx's words, again and again sought 'to settle all problems for all time' and regularly demanded 'Here is the truth! Here you must kneel'—Marx (together with Engels) proclaimed: 'we are but little beyond the beginning of human history, and the generations which will put *us* right are likely to be far more numerous than those whose knowledge we—often enough with a considerable degree of contempt—are in a position to correct ... the stage of knowledge which we have now reached is as little final as all that have preceded it'. *'De Omnibus Dubitandum'* ('Doubt Everything') was Marx's favourite methodological principle, and it is significant that so many of his writings, including Capital, had the word 'critique' in their titles. And it is precisely this critical spirit underlying Marxism of Karl Marx that was later expressed in Engels' adjuration to followers to 'not pick quotations from Marx or from him as if from sacred texts, but think as Marx would have thought in their place'. He had insisted that 'it was only in that sense that the word *Marxist* had any *raison d'etre*'. That is how what Marx has left behind is no creed, no 'system of beliefs' for the faithfuls to uphold and proclaim, but, most importantly, a method of thinking, a *critique* of capitalism, the unjust and inhuman society he wanted overthrown, and the vision of a just and truly humane society beyond capitalism born of this critique—a society which capitalism has not and, because of its structural logic, cannot achieve. It is this legacy of Marx which is today central to the making of a viable 'creed'—if we must use the word—for the new millennium.

Not a creed, Marx did have a vision—'traum' as he called it—of a good society for our times. Marx recognised 'free conscious activity' as 'man's species being' and had a rare awareness of the range of possibilities inhering in human nature which we cannot even imagine today because of the way capitalism has blighted our essential humanity and distorted our vision. He looked forward, beyond capitalism, to a society in which 'the free development of each is the condition for the free development of all', where all are fulfilled by equality and freedom, and a truly rich human life. But Marx's vision was not the usual compendium of high ideals, a string of 'oughts' divorced from 'is', making demands upon the individuals to live up to abstracted values and add up to constitute a good society. Marx rejected idealist utopianism, the making of the blueprints of an ideal society. He refused, as he said, to 'compose music of the future'. Unlike most other visions, Marx's vision was grounded in the objective reality, in the conditions then coming into existence which were for the first time making it possible for humankind to move beyond the inevitably exploitation-based, scarcity-ridden class civilisations of the past, to move beyond its 'pre-history', as Marx called it, to history proper of humankind. Marx saw these conditions as created by capitalism. In his famous tribute to capitalism's extraordinary productive achievements in the *Communist Manifesto*, he wrote: 'What earlier century had even a presentiment that such productive forces slumbered in the lap of social labour?' Marx saw such development of 'productive forces', creation of a material basis for socialist/communist society of the future, as the historical task of capitalism. But Marx also saw capitalism as denying, or making impossible, the realisation of new possibilities now opening up for humankind. In other words, Marx's vision of a good society beyond capitalism was born of his critique of capitalism; not a blueprint, socialism for Marx was a negation of capitalism.

In the course of this critique, even as Marx noticed, along with the productive achievements of capitalism, its destructive material consequences as a class-exploitative system, Marx drew attention to the moral and cultural ravage capitalism wreaks upon humankind. He noted that man, stripped of his 'human essence' when he first fell into the class of the exploited, faces 'the destruction of all humanity' in him under capitalism. The process of capitalist exploitation, with its attendant 'greed and the war between the greedy—competition', holds human beings, the capitalists as well as the workers, in its compulsive grip and puts them at the mercy of 'the blind forces of the market'. It transforms free creative self-activity of man into alienated labour and reduces man himself into 'a commodity'. It 'estranges man from nature, from himself, his own active functioning'. It alienates 'man from man'. Capitalism tears up 'all genuine bonds between men', and dissolves 'the world of men into a world of atomized individuals, hostile to each other'. It leaves 'no other nexus between man and man than naked self-interest, than callous "cash payment"', and resolves 'personal worth into exchange value'. Every aspect of human life is commodified and the very things which were once 'communicated, but never exchanged; given, but never sold; acquired, but never bought—virtue, love, conviction, knowledge, conscience, etc.—' now become marketable and pass 'into commerce'. 'The *divine* power of money' overturns and confounds 'all human and natural qualities' in the market place....

In pointing out the alienating, depersonalising and dehumanising consequences of capitalism, Marx particularly focused attention on the fact that for all the glorious *human* senses, whose concrete and active exercise alone constitutes the true content of a genuinely rich human life, capitalism substitutes a single historically transient abstract sense, *the sense for property*, which plays havoc with human personality and plunges man into what has been well-described as 'the terrible inner sickness of an acquisitive society'. As Marx put it: 'In place of *all* these physical and mental senses there has come the sheer estrangement of *all* these senses—the sense of *having*. The human being had to be reduced to this absolute poverty in order that he might yield his inner wealth to the outer world.' For Marx the so-called rich man of capitalism was 'ever poorer as a man', robbed of real life and crippled in his inner being. Marx wrote, 'the more you *have*, the less you *are*', and insisted that 'the transcendence of private property is therefore the complete *emancipation* of all human senses and attributes'. He spoke of communism, 'the *actual* phase necessary for the next stage of historical development in the process of human emancipation and recovery', 'as the *positive* transcendence of *private property as human self-estrangement*, and therefore as the real *appropriation of the human essence* by and for man; communism therefore as the complete return of man to himself as a *social* (that is, human) being—a return become conscious, and accomplished within the entire wealth of previous development'. Marx adds: 'What is to be avoided above all is the reestablishing of "society" as an abstraction vis-à-vis the individual. The individual is the *social being*. His life ...is therefore an expression and confirmation of *social life*.'

❖

Marx made a distinction between the 'realm of necessity' and the 'realm of freedom'. He noted the inescapable fact that in all societies, material production is necessary to maintain life. 'Just as the savage must wrestle with nature to satisfy his wants, to maintain and reproduce life, so must civilised man, and he must do so in all social formations and under all possible modes of production'. Marx saw this, the realm of material production, as the 'realm of necessity'. The choice here is between the capitalist and the socialist ways of carrying out material production, that is, between producing according to the capitalist criteria, 'the pseudo-moral principles', as Keynes once put it, 'which have hag-ridden us for 200 years (and) by which we have exalted sóme of the most distasteful of human qualities into the position of the highest virtues', or, as Marx advocated, producing according to socialist principles, that is, as 'associated producers, rationally regulating their interchange with nature ... with the least expenditure of energy and under conditions most favourable to, and worthy of, their human nature'. For Marx, however, 'it nonetheless still remains a realm of necessity'. The 'realm of freedom' lies beyond it, it 'begins only where labour which is determined by necessity and mundane considerations ceases; thus, in the very nature of things it lies beyond the sphere of actual material of production'. Marx characterised it as 'that development of human energy which is an end in itself, the true realm of freedom, which, however, can blossom forth only with the realm of necessity as its basis'. That is how socialism or communism for Marx has a material basis, but it is *not* material fulfilment. What true human fulfilment, 'the realm of freedom' and its 'blossoming forth' mean has been well suggested by the Marxist philosopher, Ladislav Stoll. Pointing out that 'in place of many-sided, active, concrete appropriation of life and the world, through which the individual says not only "I see, I hear, I smell, I taste, I touch" but also "I work, I study, I love, I admire, I struggle for a happier tomorrow"—in place of all this wealth of emotion, capitalism makes one single emotion supreme: "I have"', Stoll has written: 'The truly human way of appropriating the world's riches is that by which man really overcomes the world, in other words, with all his senses, concretely. And here it is not a question only of five physical senses, for unlike the animals man has a whole series of glorious human senses, not only the senses of sight, hearing, smell, taste and touch, but also a sense for music, a sense for poetry, a sense for the plastic arts, a sense for science, a sense for mathematics, a sense for history, crystallography, etc. It is only when a man begins to satisfy the needs of these glorious human senses, which one and all are the product of historical development, that he can appropriate to himself all the beauties of the world and become genuinely rich.'

❖

Such was Marx' vision of our future—and it was no idealist utopia. It was firmly grounded in the possibilities then existing and maturing in the womb of society—possibilities which now stand enhanced many times over by the scientific–technological revolutions of recent times. Marx had hoped for the realisation of his vision in countries where capitalism had created the necessary material basis for it, that is, in the industrially advanced countries. But history played a trick on Marx's hope. Of the European revolutions at the end of the first world war—which Marx had anticipated—only the revolution in Russia survived. Instead of socialism being built on a base provided by the economic, political and cultural achievements of capitalism, a single backward country was called upon to build it, and build it in the midst of a most hostile global domination of capitalism. Lenin recognised the predicament and, possibly, had the potential to make a creative Marxist response to this entirely unanticipated situation, a response which, to put it in Marxist terms, involved simultaneous development of productive forces and building up of socialist relations of production as the basis of a new society. Lenin saw this as a struggle where 'defeat' was a distinct possibility, and wrote: 'Struggle and struggle alone, decides, how far we shall advance.' But the struggle, especially after Lenin's early departure, was not adequate enough. Logic of backwardness, compulsions of sheer survival, scientistic Marxism and economism in theory ('theory of productive forces'), flaws in the character of men who led—all taking their toll, what got built was a grievously deformed socialism. And now, seventy odd years later, a finally defeated Russia has been sucked back into global capitalism. What has happened was not inevitable, but it has happened, leaving the world more capitalist than ever before. But, for this very reason, as I have argued earlier, also making Marxism more relevant than ever before.

Since India is a part of this capitalist world and, with our rulers opting for 'globalisation', is becoming still more a part of it, this relevance does not exclude India. Therefore, before I conclude, a quick reference to our own situation today will not be out of place.

It is not much remembered these days that we were very much a globalised country not so long ago. Before 1947, we were part of a global system, well-integrated into a world market economy. We were globalised, but we did not like it. Our globalisation then also had a name, imperialism, and we struggled against it, precisely because it meant—by virtue of its structural logic—accumulation of wealth in England and poverty in India. Like other third world countries, we wanted to get out of this globalisation to be able to opt for an independent, self-reliant development in the interests of our common people. Herein lay the essential meaning of our long struggle for freedom. It is significant of our rulers today that those presently in power or their forbears, when not in opposition to this struggle had little to do with it, and those now in opposition, claiming to be successors of Gandhi and Nehru, have long forgotten what this struggle was about and would like us all to do the same.

Freedom won—a transfer of power from foreign to Indian hands which however left the old socio-economic and state-bureaucratic structures largely intact—our post-colonial rulers set up a 'national project' of self-reliant economic development to supplement the recently won political freedom with the more important economic freedom for the Indian people. But it only led to the development of a state supported India-specific capitalism and, passing through crises and producing tragedies for the people mid-sixties onward, finally collapsed in 1991. In such matters, the subjective concerns of leaders or rulers matter —but only marginally. More decisive are the necessities of the objective material conditions. In the absence of revolutionary politics, which changes these conditions, the economic-structural basis of society, it is the logic of this basis that prevails. That is how for all Gandhi's love and concern for the Indian people, which to him meant, above all, the impoverished peasantry of India—'the semi-starved masses ... slowly sinking to lifelessness', as he put it—it is not Gandhi's peasant but, metaphorically speaking, a Birla who inherited India in 1947;

and for all his awareness of the 'terrible costs of not changing the existing order', Nehru's 'socialistic pattern of society' ended up as India-specific capitalism. Hence also the ultimate collapse of the 'national project' of self-reliant economic growth in the interests of the Indian people.

The evidence of this collapse is all over the place. It is there in the disintegration of values and degradation of life all around us, in the continuing poverty of our people and growing consumerism of the elites and a society at once cynical and fearful about the future. It is there in official statistics and pages of the private media, in our' two nations' and 'internal colonialism', and the so-called 'national mainstream' which, bearing the impress of India's corrupt and corrupting, somewhat lumpen capitalist development, is increasingly, a dirty affair—corrupt, communal and criminalised, a repressively homogenising mainstream. The evidence is there in the visionless and so obviously laboured efforts of the powers-that-be to flog a tired and flabby patriotism into some semblance of life that characterised the celebrations of the fiftieth anniversary of India's independence and included a Colgate-sponsored televised selling of *Vande Matarams* by hordes of India's VIPs and VVIPs. And the evidence is most pathetically there in the impotence (or is it hypocrisy?) of the supposedly 'stirring' calls made on the occasion—in Parliament for a 'second freedom struggle' and by the Prime Minister to 'begin the struggle for economic freedom', which left us wondering about our 'first freedom struggle' and what the past fifty years were about.

❖

The post-independence 'national project having finally collapsed, India's ruling classes, through their major political formations, have gone in for 'globalisation' as their strategic option for the future. Having benefited from the state-supported capitalist development of the past, they now see their interests as lying with the free-marketeering global capitalism. But the historical experience in India, and elsewhere in the third world, makes it abundantly clear that the Indian people will find no answers to their problems in capitalism, national, as built under Nehru in the name of 'socialistic pattern' or now advocated by the RSS in the name of 'swadeshi', or globalised that the ruling elites have opted for. There is much noise over 'growth rates' and 'trickle downs'. 'Trickle down' occurs but rarely, and at best remains, as Galbraith once described it, feeding oats to horses so that some of it passes down to the road for the sparrows! As for 'growth rates', this is how a former President of Brazil once reported about his country in Washington: 'the economy is doing fine, the people are not'. Therefore, the Indian economy may do 'fine' (with its growth rates, etc.) but the Indian people will not. For such indeed is the structural logic of capitalism as a market-governed economy. This logic also makes for 'the secession of the successful' as the Harvard economist Robert Reich has phrased it. 'Globalisation' as an option means 'the successful' of our society, its ruling elites, have decided to 'secede' from their market-wise 'unsuccessful' fellow countrymen, the common Indian people. This is not a matter only of economic policies and their outcome for the people. The 'secession' is as much visible in the values, concerns and life-styles of the Indian elites, in the 'culture' splashed across television screens and the coloured supplements of 'national' newspapers, and in the pitiful protests of the 'cultural nationalists', cabinet ministers downwards, who want a market-economy but not the market morality and culture that necessarily come with it.

The ruling classes having chosen 'globalisation' as their new strategic option, our people are confronted with the task of defining and struggling for an alternative strategic option of their own. This, however, is not a subject I can pursue here. Immediately I will only say that Marxism can help our people better understand what has been and is now happening our country, and thus also help them define and struggle for a strategic option of their own. It is certainly time that leaders on the left and in the people's movements begin to think and act as Marx would have thought and acted in their place.

❖

Let me conclude with a briefest of brief final statement. Marx was optimistic about the future of socialism. But he was no determinist. There are no inevitabilities or guarantees of victory in Marx. Even as he insisted in the *Communist Manifesto* that 'the history of all hitherto existing society is the history of class struggle', Marx had immediately added that this struggle 'each time ended, either in a revolutionary reconstitution of society at large, or in the common ruin of the contending classes'. He had hailed the productive achievements of capitalism. But he had also pointed out both the damage capitalism regularly inflicts upon man and nature and its long term destructive potential which Rosa Luxemburg well summed up in her prophetic poser: 'socialism or barbarism'. Capitalism living beyond its historical time indeed spells a future of barbarism for humankind. It could be a nuclear holocaust that its politics has threatened for half a century or the almost certain ecological disaster which—the noise over so-called 'sustainable development' notwithstanding—capitalism's accumulative logic now portends. Barbarism of sorts is in fact already creeping upon us, in India and worldwide, if only we are willing to see. As Engels put it, 'history is about the most cruel of all goddesses'. History has been cruel, so far at least, to Marx, to Lenin and Mao, as also to Gandhi and Nehru and many others besides. It can well be cruel to all of us. But then, as Marxism has it, in human affairs nothing is inevitable till it happens. We can fight back and reject the future the masters are making for us. In the final analysis it is how we struggle and fight back that will decide our future. We can still make the new millennium *our* millennium.

Chapte 6

Talking of a Few Forgotten or Forbidden Things *

There has been some confusion among friends over the subject of my lecture this evening. The Hindi translation has even suggested that I am going in for an exercise in nostalgia. Not difficult to understand. After all, what else is left to do for people like me who have known better times when the country was not so misshapen politically and its Left politics had some real bite to it, when so many of its well-meaning VIPS had not yet attained to secular sainthood or degenerated into statesmen. A brief introduction to what I am going to speak about is, therefore, in order and I seek your indulgence for the way it is mixed up with an issue of strictly personal nature.

I

Invited to deliver this lecture I was happy and felt privileged to be associated with a function in memory of my friend, late Professor Jaidev, but I had reservations about speaking on the occasion. I belong to an age or generation when we learnt certain ways of thinking and acting and therefore speaking about things which are so out of fashion these days. It was an age when, like so many others of my generation, I left home and studies to chase a dream in the freedom struggle and the communist

* Professor Jaidev Memorial Lecture (September 28, 2002), published in *Mainstream*, March 15, 2003.

movement, spent time in jail with Bhagat Singh's surviving comrades, worked with them and those giants of human beings, the Ghadrite babas from the aborted uprising of 1914-15, in pursuit of freedom from the imperialist rule and a social revolution in the country. The unrealised concerns of those days not only remain relevant, the issues they raise today are a matter of life and death for our people. Yet, platitudinous reference on ceremonial occasions or at election times apart, serious consideration of these concerns or issues has come to be regarded as 'old fashioned', as being out of sync with our 'post-modernist' globalised times. The public discourse is so overwhelmingly dominated by the supposedly more relevant new concerns or issues that, speaking as 'a communist with a small "c"', to borrow that most helpful self-description from E.P. Thompson, has often left me feeling as an 'outsider', a 'dinosaur', as it were, from another age. Earlier this year I confessed as much at the Lady Shri Ram College. That there was an affectionate protest from the students and teachers was reassuring. There is also the inspiring example of friends like Paul Sweezy and Harry Magdoff (at the *Monthly Review*). I am also aware of the small constituency which is there for what I have to say. Yet *that* feeling is never entirely absent. Also, for me it has been important that the wood is not missed for the trees, that is, the basics have to be clearly stated and understood to make proper sense of the details (which however is not to in any way underestimate the latter's importance, for that is the level at which life is lived and the reality has to be ultimately grasped and engaged with). This necessarily involves repeating at least a few basic things and I have been finding this repetition a rather unpleasant experience. Accordingly, I expressed my reluctance to speak on this occasion and eventually got away with the evasive promise to 'think it over'.

Then I ran into something which helped towards more balanced thinking in the matter. It was the report of a dialogue (in 1999) between two most distinguished persons of our time, the Nobel laureate for literature Gunter Grass and the world-famous sociologist Pierre Bourdieu—men, so to speak, on my side of the barricades. They saw what is happening in the world in the name of neo-liberalism as 'simply a return to the methods of nineteenth-century Manchester liberalism, in the belief that history can be rewound', 'a conservative revolution, as the term was used between the wars in Germany—a strange revolution that restores the past but presents itself as progressive, transforming regression itself into a form of progress'. And, they noted: 'It does this so well that those who oppose it are made to appear regressive themselves. This is something we have both endured: we are readily treated as old-fashioned, "has-beens", "throwbacks"... (even) "Dinosaurs".' They were nevertheless agreed that one must continue to speak, use all means to make oneself heard. Grass had even this comforting thought for me: 'In politics you have to repeat and repeat, like a parrot, ideas you know to be correct and proven as such, which is exhausting —you constantly hear the echo of your own voice, and end up sounding like a parrot even to yourself. But this is evidently part of the job, if one is to find any listeners at all in a world so full of different voices,' or, as I then thought, when the noisy voice of those currently dominant in society seeks to drown all other voices and wants us to forget what was said earlier and is known to be true, and forbids what needs to be said or repeated anew today.

Needless to say, when the invitation to deliver this lecture was later renewed, I readily agreed and decided to speak of 'a few forgotten or forbidden things'.

II

What I am going to say, therefore, is not an exercise in nostalgia over any past. It is an exercise in theory concerned primarily with the present and future of our people. During the heady, rebel days in the late 1960s, students of Paris used to ask of everyone who would address them to first tell them: 'Where do you speak from?' For every speaker inescapably speaks from a particular philosophical-political standpoint and owes it to his audience to publicly state it. It is only fair to admit that I am going to speak from the standpoint of Marxism, not 'official Marxism' of any kind but Marxism of Karl Marx, rather Marxism as I understand it. I have no time now to spell it out. Immediately

I will only say that while Marxism is undoubtedly an offspring of Western-centred thought, it needs to be recognised that it had, especially as Marx himself was shaping it in his later years, the potential to transcend its European origins and to become a truly universal theory—as it indeed became in the twentieth century. Very much more than historical materialism and critique of capitalism, Marxism has been and remains everywhere the most adequate theory for pro-people revolutionary politics in our times. Working people have fought their most heroic battles, won their greatest victories, even made revolutions, under its banner. Those who would struggle for the interests of the poor and oppressed in our country, who seek a radical social transformation of our society, cannot afford to be indifferent to, ignorant or dismissive of Marxism.

I will speak of a few, and only a few, things which have been forgotten or forbidden, that is, pushed out of public discourse in the consensus that India's dominant classes have currently built around their ideology—an ideology is seldom, if ever, all of one piece; generally it is constituted by many ideas, doctrines, systems of dogma and philosophies which seemingly compete and are even in conflict with each other, but are socially or politically supplementary—to reinforce their domination in society. Which things, therefore, need to be remembered and put back into public discourse if Indian people's interests have to be advanced. Given the constraint of time, I will be advancing bare propositions in most cases, with little or no explanation (or qualifications which are necessary to secure better validity for them). If the argument therefore appears to be crude or simplified—which it most certainly is not—immediately I will only hazard the consideration that crudeness and simplification, at times, help to make the truth of things more visible. Evidence for my argument is there all around us, if only we are willing to see—only a little reason and ability to interconnect are needed. Theory, let me finally add, does not directly yield a political programme. This is a task for the activists on the ground. Theory provides understanding, a perspective or sense of direction. A struggling people will not get very far without some substantial knowledge of the structures they need to overthrow for their emancipation and a sense of direction in their struggle. This is what Marxism, as I suggested earlier, best provides.

III

Marcuse has said somewhere that the success of a system is when it makes alternatives unthinkable. With the collapse of the Soviet Union—it need not have collapsed, but it did—this is the success that capitalism achieved, or seemed to have achieved in the immediate aftermath of the Soviet collapse. What was built as socialism in the Soviet Union was not socialism as it is visualised in the classical Marxist tradition. Its grievously deformed character had compelled so many of us to speak of it as 'actually existing socialism'. It nevertheless betokened a possibility, the possibility of escape from the essentially predatory system that is capitalism, and therefore symbolised socialism as an alternative to capitalism. Its failure in the Soviet Union was seen as the 'triumph of capitalism', rendering socialism, for that matter any other alternative to capitalism, unthinkable. It was not only that 'there is no alternative' to it, capitalism was now so universal as to become virtually invisible. Not just escape from it, even to see or *think* capitalism became impossible. Even as capitalism, become truly global, was penetrating to the very heart and soul of social life and nature, capitalism, its critique or search for an alternative disappeared from public discourse.

The reality of capitalism catching up, the euphoria over 'triumph of capitalism' is long over in the advanced capitalist world. But it is still resonant in the 'silences' of the public discourse in India and in the Indian ruling elites' secular or communal commitment to 'economic reform' as they call it. Capitalism or 'market society' is taken for granted, for them it is the only possible mode of existence. Even as the reality of a third world capitalism is painfully there all around us, not only is socialism forgotten (except for occasional denigration), even a discussion of capitalism is conspicuously absent. In the consensus built around the establishment ideology, to *think* capitalism remains decreed out of fashion. It is important therefore that capitalism, its critique and the question of a socialist alternative are put back into public discourse. Today, more than ever before we need to *think* capitalism, to talk about it. It may be added that this is best done with Karl Marx, for he, more than any other human being, then or now, devoted his life to explaining the reality or logic of capitalism and his achievement here remains unrivalled.

Such is Marx's achievement here that he will be with us so long as we live in a capitalist society. It is noteworthy that dismissed as obsolete a few years ago, Marx is already back in the West. 'Spectres of Marx', says Derrida, continue to haunt neo-liberalism, and not a few of those who still speak of 'failure of communism', have been writing of 'the ghost of Marx' hovering 'over the global landscape with a knowing smile; the gross conditions that inspired Karl Marx's original critique of capitalism in the nineteenth century are present and flourishing again.'

Marx is not only back but is going to be there so long as capitalism lasts. Towards the end of eighties, in the last century, as the communist regimes collapsed in Eastern Europe, the *New Yorker*, an upmarket magazine in the United States, celebrated the occasion with an article by the eminent economist Robert Heilbronner titled 'Triumph of Capitalism', whose argument reverberated worldwide, setting off a new round of hosannas for capitalism and renewed pronouncements of 'the death of Marxism'. The argument was seriously flawed but that is not my concern at the moment. The immediately important fact is that less than a decade later, towards the end of 1997, in a bout of futurology, bringing together a series of articles around the theme 'what's next?', the same *New Yorker* went looking for the 'next most influential thinker', and the article, written by John Cassidy who is no Marxist, now or ever before, was entitled, 'The Return of Karl Marx'! Cassidy felt persuaded to write the article when a friend, having reached the highest positions in the US corporate world, told him it was just as Marx had it. The article had concluded: 'His (Marx's) books will be worth reading as long as capitalism endures.'

IV

Capitalism has to be brought back into our public discourse because the world we are living in is a capitalist world. The Soviet Union has collapsed and the cause of socialism has received a worldwide beating. But capitalism remains. It needs to be understood and alternatives have to be sought.

Capitalism today is, of course, not as Marx saw and studied it in the nineteenth century. It has undergone changes, important changes, since then, and it is necessary to recognise them for understanding, and struggling against, contemporary capitalism. But as Raymond Williams once warned, in taking note of what has changed in capitalism, we must not make the mistake of underestimating everything that has not changed. And this 'everything', above all, includes the structural logic of capitalism, the law-like tendencies of its capital-accumulative process which, as Marx explicated, have meant uneven and unequal development within and across countries. Within countries, even when somewhat curbed in the advanced centres of capitalism—which curbing however remains reversible as the current dismantling of the 'welfare state' in the West shows —they have had the consequence of generating wealth and affluence at one end and poverty and deprivation at the other. Worldwide the consequence has been imperialist expansion and a gap between the centre and the periphery of global capitalism, an every-widening gap between wealth and poverty at the two poles. This exploitative structural logic of capitalism is as much at work today as it was when Marx first studied and analysed capitalism. In fact it is all the more at work now as, with globalisation, the world is more capitalist today than it has been for along time—a reality which bourgeois ideology seeks to obscure through its myth-making over 'globalisation'. This myth-making or ideological mystification, 'globaloney' as it has been called, seeks to suggest as if something is happening which has never happened before, as if a whole new epoch of benevolence and prosperity for all has opened in human history, an epoch in which things like capitalism, imperialism, exploitation, and therefore socialism, are all a matter of the past. It needs to be clearly understood that 'globalisation' has a proper name, capitalism, global capitalism in its current phase of development.

Capitalism has been from the very beginning, by its very nature, a globalising system. Adam Smith knew it and you will find its sharpest, and literally prophetic, expression in the *Communist Manifesto*, where Marx wrote of how 'the need of a constantly expanding market for its products chases the bourgeoisie over the whole surface of the globe', how it 'must nestle everywhere, settle everywhere, establish connections everywhere', how it has 'established the world market' and 'through its exploitation of the world market given a cosmopolitan character to production and consumption in every country', how it 'batters down all Chinese walls' and 'compels all nations to adopt the bourgeois mode of production, i.e. to become bourgeois themselves', and so on. 'Globalisation', thus, is nothing new, no new epoch in the history of humankind. It is only another phase in the process of capitalist expansion, of course with its own more or less important specificities.

The most important specificity to be noticed about the current phase of globalisation is its radical departure from the way capitalism existed during the previous period of post-war boom, the 'golden age' of capitalism. Capitalism of this period was marked by Keynesian strategies of moderate macro-economic regulations and the accompanying limits on capital's unending thirst for more profits, collectively known as the 'welfare state', which, incidentally, saved capitalism from its own self-destructive tendencies—as manifested, for example, in the Great Depression—and also helped it acquire a much-needed 'human face', against the internal and external threat of socialism. The onset of a structural crisis of capitalism, which gives every sign of being irreversible, has changed all that. The 1970s saw the world economy going into a downturn that has worsened through every recession since; the gap between business cycles is getting smaller, barely does recovery begin, the growth falters. 'Globalisation', with its neo-liberalism, is essentially a response to this structural crisis of capitalism and signifies a return, as it were, from an atypical to typical capitalism, from the aberration that was the post-war 'golden age', to a period of normal, 'free-market' capitalism. For capital to remain 'competitive' in the global market, Keynesian state interventions in the economy have to go. Nor can capitalism now afford to wear a 'human face'; with the threat of socialism having receded, perhaps, it also does not need to wear it any more. The exceptional circumstances that made it possible for the working classes in the West, especially Western Europe, to fight and curb the exploitative logic of capitalism have passed into history. That these working classes are today fighting to defend their hard won gains should not obscure the fact that even in the advanced capitalist West it is no longer capitalism with a human face but back to the laws of the jungle of a normal capitalism.

'Globalisation' abroad has its own specificity in the new phase. If at home 'globalisation' is capitalism all over again, albeit now showing itself in its nakedness, abroad it is imperialism all over again, albeit in a new shape or form, when, the logic of capitalism now become more or less universal, imperialism achieves its ends not so much by the old forms of military expansion but primarily by unleashing and manipulating the exploitative and destructive impulses of the capitalist market. This however is not to deny the continuing importance of wars or the use of military means for imperialist purposes. We have the most obvious contemporary example of the United States' use of its military power to grab control of the oil resources of the Middle-East and Central Asia and to establish pax-Americana in the world, that is, keep the world 'free' as a freely exploitable area in which giant American corporations can do business on their own terms.

Beyond these two specific features, globalisation in its current phase has an aspect to it which needs to be specifically noted. Post-Soviet collapse, capitalism's impulse to globalise or universalise has so realised itself that capitalism is today a truly global or universal system, such as it has never been before. This has meant universalisation of its polarisations between rich and poor, exploiters and exploited. Its success, so to speak, has carried its failures with it, which however is nothing new or suprising. This is how it has always been with capitalism—

exceptional productivity and most inequitable distribution, production of wealth and poverty at the two poles of society. More significant, however, is the fact of universalisation, and therefore sharpening of its contradictions and self-destructive tendencies, including the inherent tendency to overproduce, to regular crises of overproduction. Historically, capitalism could and was indeed able to resolve or 'displace' these contradictions and escape the consequences of its self-destructive tendencies primarily by deeper penetration within and expansion abroad. To the extent it has become universal, the old escape routes are now that much less available. As Ellen Meiksins Wood has written:

> Now, capitalism has no more escape routes, no more safety valves or corrective mechanisms outside its own internal logic. Even when it's not at war, even when it's not involved in the old forms of inter-imperialist rivalry, it's subject to the constant tensions and contradictions of capitalist competition. Now, having more or less reached its geographic limits and ended the spatial expansion that supported its earlier successes, it can only feed on itself; and the more successful it is on its own terms—in other words, the more it maximizes profit and so-called growth—the more it devours its own human and natural substance.

The ultimate success of capitalism, its universal ascendancy, has also brought it to the brink of its worst failure. This condition is an important component of the structural crisis—a 'depressed continuum', Meszaros has called it—that today grips global capitalism. That some countries are doing well even in the midst of this crisis, or have cyclical upswings, is something that has happened throughout the history of capitalism and does not negate the reality of this crisis, the intractable problems that capitalism as a global system is now faced with. This is not to suggest any imminent collapse of capitalism—systems don't collapse like that and capitalism, supported by the capitalist state, has been exceptionally resilient in the past to survive its crises. But the situation does suggest the need and new opportunities for struggle against capitalism, for that forgotten and forbidden thing called class struggle.

V

In view of the centrality of the question of capitalism and struggle against it for the present and future of our people, I would like to take another look at capitalist triumphalism before turning to a few issues of more specific relevance to India.

Robert Heilbronner's aforementioned *New Yorker* article, 'Triumph of Capitalism', opened with the sentence:

> Less than seventy-five years after it officially began, the contest between capitalism and socialism is over: capitalism has won.

This bland proposition is not as self-evident or unquestionable as it is presented to be. What contest does this capitalist triumphalism has in mind? If the contest was military, the history of our times, from Churchill in 1917 to Reagan in 1987, and Hitler in between, is witness to total failure of capitalism, despite repeated efforts, to destroy socialism as it existed in the Soviet Union or any other socialist state by force of arms. If it was economic, however flawed in planning or deformed otherwise, socialist economy in the Soviet Union had great and in some cases truly astonishing achievements to its credit, without parallel in the history of capitalist development anywhere in the world—all the more significant because of the surrounding circumstances, particularly the starting point of extreme backwardness, made worse by the ruination of the First World War and a civil war, and later, having to begin from the scratch again after the Second World War, and a totally hostile international environment, capitalism's constant pressure of hot and cold war throughout. In terms of quality of life, of how the economy affects the everyday life and well-being of the common man or woman, with its guaranteed employment, cradle-to-grave social security, healthcare, education, housing, transport, etc. within everyone's reach, huge subsidisation of literature, music and arts and the diffusion of classical world culture on a mass scale, the Soviet Union had assured for vast masses of ordinary citizens a life of material security and moral and aesthetic culture far superior to what even the countries of advanced capitalism have to offer to the common people.

Very much more could be said on this subject, but my

concern here is not with this issue but with a logical flaw in Heilbronner's argument which, when taken note of, is suggestive of—beyond the so-called 'triumph of capitalism' or 'failure of socialism' today—the most important feature of the present historical period and the possibilities it holds for our future.

Heilbronner has been more cautious in his later pronouncements. But more to the point is the fact that over a long period of time, since he wrote *The Worldly Philosophers* in 1953, till the mid-1980s and even afterwards, he has been, if anything, a very perceptive critic of capitalism. He did not see capitalism as much of a success and even wrote (in 1985) that 'its eventual demise or supersession by another social order is universally foreseen'. Obviously, it is illogical to conclude from the failure of socialism—the 'actually existing socialism' of the Soviet Union—the success or triumph of capitalism. Rather, the only logically valid proposition Heilbronner is entitled to advance is that both capitalism and the attempt to build 'another social order', namely, socialism, have failed in our time. This is indeed the case today, of course with the important difference that while the failure of socialism was essentially the outcome of contingent human and historical factors—which leaves open the possibility of a successful effort in future—the failure of capitalism, far from being anything contingent, is the inevitable consequences of the basic law of motion, the structural logic of capitalism, its inner accumulative drive and contradictions which even as they are essential to its enormously powerful and creative dynamic of growth, are also the cause of its destructive outcome in the world as a whole.

The failure of both capitalism and the first attempt at building socialism points to the present historical period as a period of an epochal transition—transition from capitalism to socialism—comparable to the transition from feudalism to capitalism. It has all the material, moral and psychological symptoms of a transitional epoch, when the old is, so to speak, played out—the evidence is there all over the capitalist world today—and the new is struggling to be born.

Historians have told us that the first efforts at building

capitalism during the Middle Ages also failed, smothered by the surrounding feudalism, till centuries later, a new conjuncture emerged in which a budding capitalism, benefiting well from its earlier abortive appearances, could take root and grow powerful enough to fend off its enemies and survive, to finally arrive as it did in England and other Atlantic societies, over a period of four or five centuries. Therefore, in a long-term perspective, the failure of history's first socialist effort does not mean that more successful future efforts are impossible. But this 'long-term' is today loaded with a problematic. Once available to capitalism to emerge, consolidate itself, and grow dominant, *time* is no longer available to socialism.

The structural logic of capitalism, its insatiable accumulative appetites, now threaten a universal ecological disaster. J.B. Foster, the eminent eco-sociologist, has written:

> Human society has reached a critical threshold in its relation to the environment. The destruction of the planet, in the sense of making it unusable for human purposes, has grown to such an extent that it now threatens the continuation of much of nature, as well as survival and development of society itself.

Scientists have been warning that we are on the verge of 'the sixth mass extinction'—this time, unlike the previous five, at the hands of humanity. And this is not the only threat looming on our horizon. Another is posed by capitalism's imperialistic militarism, long exemplified by the US and British military policy—'liberal militarism' David Edgerton has called it. Today, the US has the largest stockpile of nuclear and other weapons of mass destruction in the world and it has not hesitated to use them. It is the only country ever to have used the nuclear weapons. As part of its imperialist politics, it has created innumerable 'Ground Zeroes' all over the world. The possibility is real that with its short-run vision, arrogance as well as impotence of power and the Bushite 'make no mistake' 'greatest nationism', the US may well come 'to play Samson in the temple of humanity', as Paul Sweezy once put it.

That socialism may not have time to come up again and be successful has an important implication. Marx always maintained that there are alternatives in history. With capitalism living beyond its historical time, the alternative he foresaw was long ago expressed by Rosa Luxemburg in the formula: 'either socialism or descent into barbarism'. With capitalism now threatening humanity with barbarism, socialism still remains the only alternative. The future of socialism is as bright or bleak as that of humanity itself.

VI

With the country a part of the global capitalist system and our rulers set on globalisation, that is, a new round of capitalist development under cover of 'economic reform', it is important that the forgotten or forbidden question of capitalism, what capitalism this day and age has to offer our people, is put back in the public discourse in our country. Associated with this basic question are several more specific issues that need to be talked of—things which are forgotten but need to be remembered, which are missing or unrecognised in our discussions but need to be recognised and put in country's public discourse, especially in the discourse on the Left.

Most important perhaps is the need to remember that we were very much a globalised country not so long ago. Before 1947, we were part of a global system, well-integrated into a world market economy. We were globalised, but we did not like it. Our globalisation then also had a name, imperialism, and we struggled against it, precisely because it meant—by virtue of its structural logic—accumulation of wealth in England and poverty in India. Like other third world countries we wanted to get out of this globalisation to be able to opt for an independent, self-reliant development in the interest of our common people. Herein lay the essential meaning of our long struggle for freedom. It is significant of our rulers today that those presently in power or their forbears, when not in opposition to this struggle had little to do with it, and those now in Opposition, claiming to be successors of Gandhi and Nehru, have long forgotten what this struggle was about and would like us all to do the same. But our people need to remember. The globalising rulers are promising renewed 'economic growth' and are rather noisy over growth rates, etc.

They are not necessarily wrong and may well prove to be right. But the structural logic of capitalist economic growth remains what it has always been. 'The economy is doing fine, the people are not' is how a President of Brazil once reported it in Washington. So it is and will be with what our rulers are promising. Even the hoped-for 'trickle down', if it occurs, is no better than feeding horses with oats so that some of it passes down to the road for the sparrows, as Galbraith has described it. The consequences of the current globalisation are not likely to be very different from those of the globalisation our people had struggled hard and long to finally escape in 1947. Their peripheralisation this time could well be much worse.

VII

The post-colonial rulers in India, having gained power in the state, went on to set up a 'national project' of self-reliant economic development, promising 'equity and distributive justice', even 'a socialistic pattern of society' to the people. It is important to recognise that what got built as a consequence was not any kind of socialism, as the bourgeois ideologues propagate and people have come to believe, but a state-supported India-specific capitalism. The economy did 'fine', the people did not. There was a significant degree of economic growth, but a third worldist capitalism, there was nothing much in it for the common Indian people.

I cannot here go into the specificities of this capitalism but that things happened this way needs to be clearly understood. In large historical processes there are continuities and there are breaks, at times even revolutionary breaks which involve a change in the *economic basis*, the economic-structural relations, of society. In India, in our times, no revolutionary break has occurred, neither at Independence, nor afterwards. The balance of social forces and ideals in the national movement resulted in the settlement of 1947—its 'transfer of power' involving no basic economic or social or state structural change, but putting new, now *Indian* ruling classes in control of the state power in India. (Nearly two decades later, Gunnar Myrdal was to write of 'the new government's role as the successor to the British raj', of 'the gulf between rulers and ruled' and the lifestyle and conduct of the new rulers which 'encouraged the view that political independence had done little more than displace a foreign with a native privileged group'). The new rulers set about India's economic development even as they maintained, of course, with due modifications, the class (exploitative) structure of the Indian society as a whole. It is the logic of this structure, the new and the old well articulating with each other, which had a determining influence on what eventually came to be built in the country—an India-specific state-supported capitalism, with every aspect of our social life—politics, culture, morality, everything, everywhere—bearing the mark of this somewhat comprador capitalism.

In these matters, the *subjective* concerns of political leaders, of rulers or their political representatives, matter—but only marginally. In the absence of revolutionary politics which changes the *objective*, economic-structural basis of society, not only does the logic of this basis assert itself in the economy, it also decisively conditions developments in other areas of social life, in politics, morals culture, ideology, etc.—all changes, no matter how important otherwise, yet remain essentially superstructural. Thus, for example, we know of Gandhi's love and concern for the Indian people which to him meant, above all, the impoverished peasantry of India—'the semi-starved masses ... slowly sinking to lifelessness' as he once put it—a love and concern (rather paternal in nature, always fearful of people straying from the 'right' path) which was possibly the most distinguishing feature of Gandhi's social philosophy. Metaphorically speaking, he wanted the peasant to inherit this country. Yet it is not Gandhi's peasant but a Birla who inherited India in 1947, along with, of course, communal violence, the partition, and much else that Gandhi did not want. And of decisive importance here is the fact that, besides other limitations, Gandhi's political theory and practice (non-violence, trusteeship, satyagraha, etc.) had no room at all for any genuine economic-structural change, not even for radical land reforms, a necessary though not sufficient condition for any improvement in the life of the vast masses of Indian peasantry. Inevitably he failed, here as also elsewhere in most of his declared purposes. Seeking to ensure 'the rights alike of prince and pauper', Gandhism, in effect, only served as a petty-bourgeois ideology in the service of the big bourgeoisie, in the Indian historical process. It is a mark of the greatness of Gandhi, a truly magnificent human being with all his faults, frailties and foibles, that in sharp contrast to the opportunism or pettiness of his many followers, he recognised his failure when it finally occurred, and confessed it—'I do not understand how all these terrible things are happening in our country... What mistakes have we made, for we must have made mistakes? Otherwise how could all these things happen?'—and died, as he had lived, fighting for his people, a fulfilled yet disillusioned and disconsolate man.

Or, again, we know of Nehru's concern to build socialism in India. He not only argued that 'the only key to the solution of... India's problems lies in socialism', but had insisted: 'and when I use this word I do so not in a vague, humanitarian way, but in a scientific, economic sense'. Aware of the need for 'vast and revolutionary changes', he most perceptively spoke of 'terrible costs of not changing the existing order'. Yet, once in power, Nehru shied away from the cost of even genuine land reforms—'they will present numerous practical problems involving basic social conflicts (and may) give rise to organised forces of disruption', the *Draft Outline* of the First Five-Year Plan warned. What is more, he simply abandoned socialism 'in a scientific, economic sense', that is, as a basic economic-structural change. Apart from the insistence on the state playing 'a vital part in planning and development', the focus is increasingly on the need to ensure 'rapid economic development with continually rising levels of production', 'to exploit natural resources', 'to take sufficient advantage of the advance in science and technology', etc. In fact, in a subtle, perhaps unconscious but politically most convenient shift, he now sought 'the key' not in socialism but in the development of 'science and technology'—'the temples of modern India' and all that. He increasingly opted for what I would describe as 'fetishism of science', that is, investing science with powers it does not in itself have, expecting it to do the job of a social revolution, which it simply cannot. Inevitably, once again, the logic of the economic structure asserted itself. What got built in India was not socialism but capitalism, a state-supported capitalism. The rhetoric of socialism, now redefined as 'a socialistic pattern of society', whatever that meant, served only to deceive and win mass support. And Nehru, even as he gave India the then much-lauded 'vision of socialism', in effect, helped reduce it to only 'a vision' in India. History is indeed a very cruel mistress.

VIII

India's post-freedom 'national project' ended up building *not* socialism but capitalism—it is important to recognise this to make sense of what has happened in our country since Independence. But to understand the recent developments, particularly the turn to 'globalisation' and the rise of '*Hindutva*', it is necessary to recognise what can only be described as the final collapse of India's post-colonial 'national project'.

The Nehru era was, so to speak, the golden age of India's 'national project', such as it was. But mid-1960s onward, all kinds of extraneous factors contributing, it floundered and fast degenerated, its economic crises underpinning and moving in step with the crises of the political system, 'democratic politics' and all that. If India's 'national economy' generated any number of potentially explosive issues, its 'national politics' regularly turned these issues into problems, problems into running sores and these sores into tragedies for the Indian people, in Punjab, Kashmir, almost everywhere. By the end of the 1980s the national project was virtually over. Soon enough a dead-end economic crisis or financial bankruptcy of sorts, produced by the previously pursued policies, coincided with the defeat of the Soviet Union in the Cold War and its eventual disintegration, depriving the Indian ruling classes of whatever little manoeuvrability they still had and leaving them more vulnerable than ever before to the offensive of a recharged global capitalism. Given the strong comprador or lumpen strain inherent in their character, led by their major political formation, the Congress-I, with their other political formations in tow, they succumbed, and hiccups and protests notwithstanding, opted for what is turning out to be a junior partnership within the global capitalist system. As beneficiaries of 'growth' during the Nehru era and afterwards, and now with a substantial economic strength of their own, globalisation also provides them with new avenues of profit-making at home and abroad. Therefore, this 'succumbing' can also be seen as a natural progress for Indian capitalism. India was again globalised, this time through a largely voluntary submission of the Indian rulers. The national project finally and definitively collapsed in 1991.

The evidence of this collapse is there in the disintegration of values and degradation of life all around us, in the continuing poverty of our people and growing consumerism of the elites and a society at once cynical and fearful about the future. It is there in official statistics and pages of the private media and so-called 'national mainstream' which bearing the impress of India's corrupt and corrupting, somewhat lumpen capitalist development, is an increasingly dirty affair—corrupt, communal and criminalised, a repressively homogenising mainstream. Clinching it all perhaps is the evidence provided by the fiftieth anniversary celebrations of Indian independence: the Colgate-sponsored televised selling of *Vande Matarams* by hordes of VIP and VVIP Indians and the supposedly 'stirring' calls made on the occasion—in Parliament for a 'second freedom struggle' and by the Prime Minister to 'begin the struggle for economic freedom', which left one wondering what the past fifty years had been about. A Finance Minister had taken India back into globalisation, asking us not to be afraid of the East India Company, opened up India to the multinationals on the dishonest plea that 'the nation has been living beyond its means' —'nation' indeed, when a good majority of our people have simply no means to live and most others none to indulge in any 'living beyond'! His successor, more honest and ideologically committed, was now publicly pleading with the globalisers in London, the successors of East India Company, to come back to India for another equally long stay: 'You came to India and stayed for 200 years. Now come prepared to invest and stay for another 200 years, and there will be huge rewards.' The post-colonial 'national project' was indeed over and done with.

The post-colonial, Nehruvian national project having finally collapsed, India's ruling classes, through their different political formations, have opted for 'globalisation' as their new strategic alternative—a shift from a state-supported to a wholly privatised, 'free-market' capitalism, from self-reliance in economic development to reliance on FDI and the multinationals. In politics, the shift, at least for the time being, is in some ways an even more dangerous turn for the worse. A somewhat liberal and secular national project having collapsed and the people failing to come up with their own alternative project, immediately it is the utterly reactionary, semi-fascist '*Hindutva* project' that has taken over, spelling its own disasters for the present and future of the Indian people. Here it needs to be understood that '*Hindutva*' has come up because our society today provides a continuing social-material basis for the production and reproduction, the rise, sustenance and spread of such ideas or ideologies and that, therefore, struggle against it has to be waged as part of the struggle to change this basis, that is, to radically transform our society, if it is not to get caught and lost in a 'secular–communal trap' as has indeed happened over the past decade and more. One does not have to be a Marxist to understand or recognise this. A long time ago, suggesting that ideas do not rise and prosper through some inherent power of their own, Herbert Spencer had said: 'Ideas wholly foreign to (a) social state cannot be evolved, and if introduced from without, cannot get accepted, or if accepted die out.' It is the economic, political and moral wreckage left behind by the failure of the Nehruvian project which has provided the 'social state', that is, the necessary social-material basis for the rise and growing acceptance of '*Hindutva*' as religious fundamentalism and a fascistic political ideology. 'Globalisation' or so-called 'economic reform', in its economic, political and moral-cultural consequences is daily piling up more such wreckage, creating more social-material basis for all sorts of religious fundamentalisms, regressive ideologies and disintegrative politics. A decade and a half back, apropos the growing crisis of Nehruvian 'national project', the explosive problems being generated by India's economy and the politics of its ruling classes, I had written: 'it is fashionable these days to speak of India as "a nation-in-the-making". One might add that if you leave it to the ruling classes, India may well be on its way to be "a nation-in-the-unmaking"'. '*Hindutva*' as one form of ruling class politics, like its secular counterparts earlier, is now making its own distinctive contribution to this 'unmaking' and may well be a specific feature of the barbaric situation in India as part of the universal barbarism that capitalism now threatens the world with. That is, if the people do not effectively intervene, and do so in time, with ideology and politics, a strategic alternative, of their own.

IX

This is indeed the key forgotten and forbidden question today. How do people intervene? What should be our people's 'strategic alternative'?

We are here face to face with the most basic question of India's post-colonial existence: what does a late-arriving third world country do in a situation of global domination of capitalism? The question was somewhat obscured in 1947, due largely to the interim successes of the Soviet Union—a poor, backward country which seemed to have successfully broken out of this domination and built a self-reliant economy for the benefit of its people. Now that the Soviet Union has been sucked back into global capitalism—which is not to say it was inevitable—the question is with us, urgent and imperative as never before. Some 'nationalist' hiccups notwithstanding, our rulers and those allied with them have made their choice and in a characteristic act of 'secession of the successful' (the Harvard economist Robert Reich's phrase) 'seceded' from the people and gone over to the joys of junior partnership in the global capitalist economy. But how about the people? What is the people's strategic alternative? It is a real tragedy of the Left in India, and a part of the larger tragedy of the Indian people, that even the question remains unposed. The answer obviously remains unsought, with the consequences I have just pointed out.

X

Regardless of what has happened to socialism in the Soviet Union—there was no structural necessity about its failure, unlike capitalism's continuing failure in different parts of the world—socialism has to be the answer of the Indian people if they would survive and build a better life for themselves. This is an issue which the Left needs to put back in its discourse.

The historical experience in India and elsewhere in the third world makes it abundantly clear that so far as the common people are concerned, there is no answer to their problems in capitalism, national (including the one now, in effect, sought by the RSS and its *Swadeshi Jagaran Manch*) or globalised. The choice for them remains socialism, that is, a planned development and use of resources for people's benefit, or peripheralisation under capitalism.

This is not to posit socialism as achievable today or tomorrow, or even the day after for that matter, but to posit it as an alternative strategic goal, as the principle governing people's politics today, which links together their immediate, ongoing and emerging, struggles in an ultimate project of revolutionary transformation of our society, as the goal of a long transitional process, whose specifics and speed will depend upon the objective material conditions and the nature and balance of the class forces involved at each stage of the struggle for it. Immediately, it means saying 'no' to globalisation. This is not to argue for any kind of 'autarky' in economic development but to pose the issue of whether this development will be governed by *external* imperatives, those issuing from the requirements of the world capitalist market (export-led growth, etc.) and the associated consumerism of the rich, or primarily by *internal* imperatives, those flowing from an assessment of our own resources and the needs of our people.

The issue, in other words, is that of priorities: development for what and whom? Is it to satisfy the basic needs of the people or the consumerism of the elite in our society? The argument is for a pro-people socialism-oriented autonomous development which draws on our own strengths, our domestic resources and capacities, including those of the hardworking poor who still remain the most creative and productive in our society, a development which gives the common people, in both urban and rural areas, a positive stake in the economy and mobilises them for building a better society and, let me add, for the inevitable struggle against global imperialism and its local allies or partners. This has to be the alternative strategic option of the Indian people.

This option has a decisively important implication which needs to be explicitly stated and recognised. A socialism-oriented autonomous development as a strategic option for our people is premised on *people's politics and not 'the market'* commanding the economy (which, however, does not rule out an useful role for the market in the economy). It may be added that if such development is necessary in the interests of our people and they have no choice but to attempt it if they would avoid peripheralisation, with the people *really in power* it is also possible. The failure of the world's first experiment in socialism notwithstanding, there is much in the socialist experience of our times to help guide this attempt and be hopeful about it: for example, in the still unparalleled achievements of the early years of post-revolutionary societies in Russia and elsewhere despite their economic backwardness, in Cuba's heroic struggle to build socialism and save the gains of its socialist revolution, in Lenin's socialist project during the few years that he survived the October Revolution, in the experience of the 'Mao years' in China, and so on. An uncharted territory, we can still enter it with confidence.

XI

The crux of the matter thus is people's power in the state, their 'political supremacy' in society as Marx would put it. Not phoney 'empowerment' from above, but people fighting and winning power for themselves through their own struggles. This demands the Left's recovery of its nearly lost or forgotten tradition of revolutionary politics, its recovery as a politics that knows how to relate to the emergent 'social movements' (including those of the dalits and tribals) and to subordinate parliamentary politics to the ultimately important extra-parliamentary struggles. With the traditional Left politics either exhausted or lost on the terrain of 'mainstream' politics, the problems here are indeed intractable—all the more intractable because of the diversity and the continental dimensions of our country – almost everywhere calling for, if I may put it this way, India-specific versions of Lenin's *What Is To Be Done*? and *Where To Begin*? It is obviously going to be a long haul. Of the issues involved in this recovery of revolutionary politics as an alternative to the politics of the currently dominant classes, immediately I would like to mention only three.

It is a significant achievement of the ruling class politicians in India that, while their 'democratic politics' has failed to deliver so far as the people are concerned, they have managed to give politics itself a dirty name and thus helped themselves and helped better secure their system against revolutionary politics as well. 'Politics is dirty business', the much-mouthed middle class protest is only seemingly radical. It leaves the field all the more open for dirty politics, 'the politicians' politics' (*la politique politicienne*) as Malraux called it, and makes it that more difficult to develop an alternative 'people's politics'.

At the other end, 'civil society' activism—however welcome and admirable in many cases otherwise—has all too often served to rein in and depoliticise people's opposition to the established order of things, even helped the dominant classes to structure and appropriate this opposition for their own interests. Its local or partial focus rules out major struggles over fundamental choices in economy or politics. The rhetoric over 'empowerment of people' conceals the fact that the state as the site of struggle stands abandoned and with it stands abandoned the struggle for political power which, obfuscations of bourgeois political theory or 'civil society' ideologues notwithstanding, remains the pre-eminent form of power in our society. 'Civil society' or 'grass roots' activism has served to de-legitimise people's struggle for power in the state which a revolutionary politics seeks and needs to seek.

As Walter Benjamin pointed out long ago, the ruling classes always seek to take people's history away from them. This is particularly the case with the history of their successful struggles, and heroes from the past. They do so through suppression, misrepresentation or slander, and at times through appropriation for their own purposes. Examples of the former are all too common to be mentioned here; a few can be easily found in the new, saffronised history textbooks of the NCERT. One of the latter, a contemporaneously relevant example is the effort over the years, and again more recently, to so appropriate Bhagat Singh and his struggle by reducing him to a 'great nationalist', when what he stood for was an alternative revolutionary politics, even class struggle, in opposition to the then dominant 'nationalist' politics—a concern most relevant to the present situation. Forget what Bhagat Singh thought or said of Marx or Lenin or the Russian Revolution or socialism. We only need to remember this magnificent statement: charged with 'waging war against the king', he had said:

> Let us declare that the state of war does exist and shall exist so long as the Indian toiling masses are exploited by a handful of exploiters, be they purely British, or British and Indian in alliance, or even purely Indian.

An alternative revolutionary politics has to deny the ruling classes such 'taking away' of our people's history. It has to recover its revolutionary inheritance and combine it with the recovery and use of all other traditional and modern resources for the emancipatory struggles of today—doing this not eclectically, adding up names or ideas, but in a proper theoretical manner, that is, within an adequate, self-consistent framework which, in my opinion, is best provided by Marxism, its basic understanding of society and politics.

XII

Last but not least, we need to talk of 'nationalism', talk of it in a way that the dominant ideological climate in the country virtually forbids but, for that very reason, the situation in the country makes necessary. The viability of an alternative revolutionary politics geared to the strategic goal of socialism-oriented development is crucially dependent on our *critical* understanding of the question of nationalism. It is necessary to recognise the basic class divisions in our society, the divergence of interests between the rulers and the ruled. Beyond the distinctions of religion or caste, we need to recover the distinction between rich and poor, exploiters and exploited, oppressors and oppressed, the distinction between 'them' and 'us' which stands so badly obscured today. The 'we' of the seminars and common parlance is quite deceptive; 'they' have a very real existence in our society which needs to be taken note of. The struggle for a socialism-oriented development cannot be seen as an adjunct of any national aspirations, or as a continuation, as it were, of the Indian people's earlier national struggle for freedom.

Nationalism is undoubtedly a powerful social, political and ideological force in our times. But it needs to be understood that it is yet a historical phenomenon with class and society-specific character, potentialities and limitations, and, therefore, capable of manifesting itself in diverse forms. Located as we are in the third world and with the still alive, though much faded, memories of our long struggle for freedom, we in this country are conventionally inclined to see nationalism as a positive value or ideal, even as a liberationist force or ideology. But this is not always or necessarily the case with nationalism. With the ruling classes in the normal pursuit of their interests, or when faced with situations of crisis, nationalism has often taken all sorts of anti-people, imperialist or statist or racist or fascist forms, providing ideological support to ruling class politics and political domination at home and abroad. In our own country, more particularly in recent decades, nationalism has been used by the post-colonial rulers to cover up or find alibis for their defaults, to conceal the social reality of our much-divided and exploitative society, to divert people away from their real concerns and mobilise them behind ruling class politics. This is what the Congress has traditionally done as part of its 'secular' politics. Defining it as 'cultural nationalism', this is what the BJP is now doing as part of its *'Hindutva politics'*— both doing it for the same purpose, serving the same ruling class interests.

Nationalism in India before 1947 was indeed progressive; under a different, more advanced class leadership and programme, it could have been radical, even revolutionary. It was progressive because it aimed at resolving the basic structural contradictions of Indian society, congealed in imperialism, whose resolution alone could clear the path for Indian people's struggle for a better life. The struggle to resolve them, *against* imperialism, was our national struggle for freedom. But after 1947, with the post-colonial rulers having facilitated a historically specific form of capitalist development in the country, the basic contradictions that now need to be resolved to clear the path for Indian people's continuing struggle for a better life lie *within* the nation, and their resolution is a matter of struggle within, against the Indian ruling classes; therefore, strictly speaking, this struggle cannot be viewed simply as a national struggle. In fact, Indian people's continuing struggle against imperialism, globalisation's neo-colonialism, too is now a part of this new struggle within, and not a continuation of the old pre-1947 anti-imperialist struggle, because the neo-colonialist 'integration', rather reintegration, into the global capitalist economy is now occurring by the grace of, through the opportunities provided by, indeed at the invitation of, the new rulers at Delhi. Nationalism or a national perspective on things only obscures this most basic of all issues facing the Indian people.

(It is worth recalling the justificatory slogan, which soon became a national chorus, with which 'globalisation' or the so-called 'economic reform', was launched: 'the nation has been living beyond its means'—when a good majority of our people had been going to bed hungry and most others had nothing much to indulge in any 'living beyond'. The reference to 'nation' was really a nationalist lie which obscured this reality and provided a cover for those who had indeed been living beyond this country's poor means for long and were now set on continuing to do so under the new dispensation, those whom the Latin Americans have learnt to call 'anti-nation within the nation'.)

That is how the struggle for people's strategic option as against 'globalisation' that the Indian ruling classes have opted for, the struggle for socialism-oriented autonomous development—which alone can also be an ecologically sustainable development as against a globalised Indian capitalism subject to the capital accumulative or profit-making imperatives of the market—is not a national struggle as such, nor a continuation of the earlier national struggle in India, though it can and may be seen as its transcendence in a strictly dialectical sense, that is, a struggle that carries forward the best traditions and hopes of the earlier liberationist struggles of the Indian people. It is in its basic character a class struggle in the proper Marxian sense which eschews its narrow economistic or class-reductionist interpretations. No doubt a great deal of tactical resilience is necessary in relating it, theoretically as well as practically, to the obviously important question of nationalism. But even if this struggle is viewed as a national or 'national-popular' struggle of the Indian people, it cannot but be fighting the 'anti-nation within the nation', as the Latin Americans now call it, or 'rescuing the nation' from its ruling classes, or, as Marx would have put it, the people 'establishing itself as *the* nation', and thus remains, in its essential content, a class struggle. It cannot be seen as a collective struggle of all the people for a common good as, essentially, the struggle for national liberation was; it will be, more than anything else, a struggle for political power, winning it from the ruling classes, for purposes entirely opposite to theirs. That is how the national task, recovering the country for its people, is now, as it were, also a class task of the Indian people, people acting, as it were, as a 'nation class', to borrow a description from the Guinean Marxist revolutionary, Cabral.

XIII

Marx and Marxism? Socialism? People's strategic alternative? Revolutionary politics? Class struggle... all these forgotten or forbidden things? Isn't this asking for the impossible? Answer, the only apt answer for our times, is there, given by the French students in their May-June uprising of 1968. They had said: 'Be practical! Do the impossible!' Three-and-a-half decades later, it may be added: 'If we cannot do the impossible, we better prepare to face the unthinkable!' Some of it is already happening around us.

Chapter 7

A Note on the Current Political Situation in India*

Leaving aside the deeper-lying issues in understanding contemporary Indian politics, and confining myself to the national level, immediately the following facts or considerations are to be noted:

1. The overarching context of Indian politics today is the failure of the post-independence (Nehruvian) national project of state-led self-reliant economic development promising economic growth with 'equity and distributive justice' to the people. For understandable reasons, it did not work out as Nehru had intended. There was a degree of economic growth but not much equity or distributive justice for the people and the project ended up providing an India-specific government-supported third worldist capitalism. The rhetoric of 'socialistic pattern of society' only deceived the people, legitimised the statist capitalism that was coming up and created confusion about it as 'socialism' that has persisted to this day. Passing through a series of economic and political crises mid-1960s onward, the project finally collapsed in 1991. (Incidentally, state-intervention in the economy was deemed necessary by the then

---

* *Mainstream*, September 8-15, 2005. This note was written sometime back as a hurried response to the letter of a friend from abroad who wanted to know how I looked at the current political situation in the country (R.S.).

economically and politically weak, relatively underdeveloped Indian bourgeoisie itself, which, as the major beneficiary of 'economic growth' during the Nehru era and afterwards, soon developed substantial strength of its own and grew hopeful of new avenues of profit-making at home and abroad in partnership with global capitalism).

2. The post-independence national project having collapsed, 1991 onwards, India's ruling classes, through their different political formations, have gone in for 'globalisation' as their new strategic option—a shift from the state-supported capitalism to a wholly privatised 'free market' capitalism and from self-reliance in economic development to reliance on Foreign Direct Investment and the multinationals, a shift euphemistically described as 'economic reform' whose structural logic, as a former President of Brazil once reported it to the masters in Washington, is: 'the economy is doing fine, the people are not', which, therefore, raises contemporary India's most important *unraised* political question: What is the Indian people's alternative strategic option?

3. The economic, political and moral wreackage left behind by the collapse of the Nehruvian national project, to which the neo-liberal 'economic reform' is daily adding its own wreckage, has provided the social-material basis for all sorts of regressive ideologies and politics, including *Hindutva,* which propelled the BJP to power at Delhi. But it is mistaken to see the BJP only as a *Hindutva* or communal party. While its opponents, including the Left, impotently locked themselves up in a 'communalism-secularism' trap, the BJP merrily went on implementing the Congress-initiated 'economic reform' without much notice or objection. As a scholar, Radhika Desai, has recently pointed out:

> The Indian capitalist class may be senior, practically venerable, among the bourgeoisies of the third world, and it may have benefited from liberalising economic policies under practically every administration since the late 1970s. But the NDA governments presided over such a massive dose of the most brazen and unapologetic liberalisation as to constitute a virtual rebirth of the capitalist class, sired by the BJP. Indian capitalists' new filial loyalty cannot be underestimated. The NDA oversaw a vast and

> ungrudging expansion of practically every sector of the urban industrial economy: finance and financial markets, the media, housing and construction, consumer durables and non-durables of every kind. Privatisation was accelerated, giving a great fillip to the stock markets; the foreign exchange regime was further liberalised; FDI and portfolio investments, including by foreign institutional investors, FIIs, flowed in. Consumer credit to finance lifestyles of international standards (indeed, better, thanks to the cheapness of domestic labour) for a small but very visible stratum of those in business and the professions was expanded and liberalised, as was the import regime. The tax burden on the rich was reduced; innumerable small quotas and restrictions on economic activity were lifted; the IT sector boomed, employing thousands of yound professionals and arousing unprecedented hopes of upward mobility among thousands of others; and, not least, the objective of closer ties between India and its wealthy 'diaspora' in the metropoles was pursued by taking the first steps towards granting dual citizenship. All talk of the poor and of larger social goals was dismissed routinely as the leftover cant of yesterday's 'licence-permit raj'. It was truly a dream government for the possessing classes.
>
> Needless to say, the effect of these measures on the whole economy were less than spectacular and, on the poor majority, positively disastrous. More than ever, the NDA governments created two nations in India, already home to some of the starkest divides between poverty and wealth. Every criticism from the Left had its counterpart in appreciation on the part of the rich, and there is no doubt about a feel-good factor among the propertied elite and foreign interests in India: in fact, an overwhelming pro-BJP sentiment.

This, of course, cost the BJP the 2004 Lok Sabha election. But it was no 'rout', as the opponent's wishful thinking tends to view it (the BJP's tally was 136 seats to 145 of the Congress). The corporate world, happy over the BJP's performance in power, is desperately hopeful about its future as a 'modern' political party, alternating with the Congress in the much longed-for two-party system in India's parliamentary democracy. The corporates can well do with its *Hindutva* and the accompanying obscurantism. Capitalism needs science and technology, but, as we know from history, capitalist classes have always needed religion and obscurantism too. The BJP's aggressive nationalist posture could well be an advantage in the harsh competitive world of global economy and politics.

4. It is the Congress which initiated the neo-liberal 'economic reform' in 1991. Compulsions of electrol politics have forced it to take notice of its vicitm, the so-called *aam aadmi* ('the common man') and speak, again of economic growth with economic and social justice, etc. It now seeks 'economic reform with a human face', something which, symbolic gestures apart, is simply not possible for capitalism today, least of all for India's third-worldist capitalism. The current long-term crisis of global capitalism has compelled it to shed its 'human face' even in the advanced capitalist West—dismantling, or struggle over dismantling the welfare state has been a distinct feature of economy and politics in the advanced capitalist countries in recent decades. A return to normal or typical capitalism is in fact a major aspect of capital's current phase of globalisation as against the welfarist capitalism of the earlier period which was really a conjunctual aberration in capitalism's long history as an exploitative system.

(Some muddling along for sometime is always possible. Otherwise, structural nature of things being what it is, 'economic reform' and socio-economic justice don't go together, nor, for that matter, 'economic reform' and democracy).

Having long forgotten what India's struggle for freedom was about, and long forsaken Gandhi and Nehru except for ritualistic purposes, and now hamstrung in its pursuit of 'economic reform' by electoral compulsions and dependence on the Left Front, the Congress does not even have an ideology to speak of, much less one that represents any kind of radical opposition to the BJP. Even in matters of communalism and the accompanying obscurantism, it is not *that* different from the BJP as its leaders would have us believe and some others think, though the difference here can, on occasion, acquire a certain tactical importance. Elsewhere, in political behaviour and economic policies, there is even less to distinguish between the two. 'Lesser evil' is perhaps the only claim to legitimacy the Congress now has. In other words, unless it moves away from 'economic reformism' to recover some of its Nehruvian legacy, the Congress is all set to be *finally* reduced to the status of just another political party of the Indian ruling classes, a Congress tweedledum to the tweedledee BJP in an ideal, albeit coalitional, two-party system of bourgeois democracy that best secures ruling class interests in the economy and politics of India—very much the way it is with the Conservatives and New Labour in Britain where *The Times* has no problem asking people to vote for New Labour, or the Republicans and Democrats in the United States where the only difference between the two, as Ralph Nader had told us, 'is the speed with which their knees hit the floor when Big Capital summons them'.

5. The third important player at the national level politics today is the CPM-led Left Front, the major Left formation in the country today. Its components have been long mired in reformist politics and have gone all the more 'realist' after the collapse of Soviet Union. More than 25 years of uninterrupted power in West Bengal notwithstanding, Indian people have yet to see it as *significantly* different from, or better than, what they see elsewhere in the country. Compromises are not recognised as compromises but celebrated as achievements, with the enemies gleefully advertising them as exemplary implementation of neo-liberal policies. The gap between professions and prctice invites only ridicule in the bourgeois media which once feared and respected the Left, however weak it may have been.

Fortuitously propelled to importance at the national level, the CPM and the Left Front confront an obvious choice: an opportunity to redeem themselves or a tragic denouement of their reformist politics, which will also be a tragedy for the Indian people. They have the opportunity, as they support the Congress-led dispensation at the Centre to keep the BJP out of power and fight for the Common Minimum Programme, to difine and project the Lert's alternative strategic positon or goal in relation to, yet independent of and beyond, these considerations and thereby recover their lost identity as a force for a radical transformation of Indian society. The tragedy will be a further loss of face and legitimacy in the company of the 'economic reformist' Congress and reversion to the infeasible, regionally quarantined, social democratic politics, with the millstones of West Bengal and China round their neck to the cheers and jeers of capitalist roaders everywhere.

With the failure of bourgeois politics, all its post-independence variants, to deliver, the Indian people are looking for an alternative politics. The opportunity is there for a redeeming return to the basics, a consolidation of the *entire* Left—from the CPM-led Left Front to the ML parties and groups to the socialists and militant people's movements—in a shift to politics geared to a people's strategic option *in opposition to* what India's rulers have opted for.

6. A people's alternative strategic option is no longer a matter of some theory or long-term perspective. Socialism as the necessary and possible negation of capitalism is how classical Marxism defined it and with the October Revolution history put it on the agenda for our times. After the initial setback following the collapse of Soviet Union and its socialist experiment, the resumed world revolutionary process is already, again, positing socialism as the necessary and possible future for humankind. As they struggle to forge extra-electoral sanctions to defend their Bolivarian revolution against American imperialism and its local allies, the Venezuelans are speaking of building socialism of the twenty-first century. As they fight their 'People's War', struggle to win the battle of democracy and confront a US-led imperialist intervention in their country, the Maoists in Nepal seek self-reliant economic development oriented towards socialism. As the struggle against globalisation sharpens in Europe, forces are emerging, as for example in Germany, asking for new experiments in socialism. So it has to be in India where, even as they reckon with the complexities and contradictions of their millennia-old history and continent-sized economy and politics, the people face the choice: socialism or peripheralisation in the global capitalist economy. This, as I have argued all along, is not to posit socialism as achievable today or tomorrow, or even the day after for that matter, but to posit it as an alternative strategic goal, as the principle governing people's politics today, which links together their immediate, ongoing and emerging struggles in an ultimate project of

revolutionary transformation of our society, as the goal of a long transitional process, whose specifics and speed will depend upon the objective material conditions and the nature and balance of the class forces involved at each stage of the struggle for it. Immediately, it means saying 'no' to globalisation. This is not to argue for any kind of 'autarky' in economic development but to pose the issue of whether this development will be governed by *external* imperatives, those issuing from the requirements of the world capitalist market (export-led growth, etc.) and the associated consumerism of the rich, or primarily by *internal* imperatives, those flowing from an assessment of our own resources and the needs of our people.

The issue, in other words, is that of priorities: development for what and whom? Is it to satsify the basic needs of the people or the consumerism of the elite in our society? The argument is for a pro-people socialism-oriented endogenous development process which draws on our own strengths, our domestic resources and capacities, including those of the hard working poor who still remain the most creative and productive in our society, a development which gives the common people, in both urban and rural areas, a positive stake in the economy and mobilises them for building a better society and, let me add, for the inevitable struggle against global imperialism and its local allies or partners. This has to be alternative strategic option of the Indian people.

Technological backwardness is often pressed as an argument to counter the plea for such autonomous economic development in a third world country. Here, apart from the fact that in India at least we are not that lacking in either technology or the talent for it, we need to overcome the widely prevalent fetishism of science and technology, which at times (as, for example, with Nehru and his 'temples of modern India', etc.) has even gone to the extent of expecting them to do the job of a social revolution, which they simply cannot. As with the economy so with technology, the question again is one of priorities: technology for what purpose? Once this question is asked, the argument for getting access to the most modern Western technology, via globalisation, loses much of its force. If the purpose is to satisfy the consumerist hunger of the privileged part of our population with the most modern gadgets and designs, and the goodies of the West, then rushing into globalisation indeed makes some sense. But if the purpose or priority is to meet the needs of all the people for decent food, clothing and shelter, clean water, proper sanitation and health protection, education and cultural opportunities, and the like, then devoting scarce resources to the most modern technology is simply wasteful, because there is little in the latest technology of the West that could make a significant contribution. In fact what is most useful and relevant in technology, Western or otherwise, for improving the way of life of the masses, is widely known; moreover, most of it is already available at home and what else is needed, is obtainable in the normal course of magaged trade.

7. A socialism-oriented autonomous economic development as a strategic option for our people is premised on *politics, that is, people's politics and not 'the market'* commanding the economy (which, however, does not rule out an useful role for the market). If such development is necessary in the interest of our people and they have no choice but to attempt it if they would avoid peripheralisation, with the people *really in power* it is also possible. The failure of the world's first experiment in socialism notwithstanding, there is much in the socialist experience of our times to help guide this attempt and be hopeful about it: for example, in the still unparalleled achievements of the early years of the post-revolutionary societies in Russia and elsewhere despite their economic backwardness, in Cuba's heroic struggle to save the gains of its socialist revolution and build socialism, in Lenin's socialist project during the few years that he survived the October Revolution, in the achievement of the 'Mao years' in China, in Venezuela's ongoing struggle for an alternative model of development already marked by a shift from production for the world market to production for the Venezuelan people, channelling of oil revenues away from the pockets of multinationals and the local elite to building houses, hospitals and schools for the people, emphasis on 'made in Venezula' and experiments to develop worker participation,

worker-state co-management, in state-owned enterprises (which, incidentally, rejects not only privatisation but also converting workers into small property owners in co-managed or self-managed enterprises) and so on. Socialism is not that impossible or uncharted a territory as the critics or enemies argue, and even some friends have begun to think. We can well enter it with confidence. Of course, there are no models here. As elsewhere, we have to find our own unique way of entering it, that is, make an India-specific transition to socialism.

8. Perhaps it is too much or too late to hope for the CPM and the Front led by it to make the necessary redeeming shift in their politics. It can be hopefully also argued that the Left Front does not exhaust the radical or revolutionary possibilities in the Indian political situation—and the struggle goes on. Even so, there are no certainties or inevitabilities, and no guarantees of victory here. And, as Engels said long ago, 'History is about the most cruel of all goddesses.' Marx saw capitalism, in its ultimate consequences, capable of destroying humanity. 'Socialism or barbarism' is how Rosa Luxemburg later summed up his prognosis. It is therefore quite possible that India may end up producing an India-specific barbarism of its own as part of the universal barbarism that capitalism now threatens the world with. Perhaps we have already travelled some distance along this road.

Chapter 8

What, then, is the CPM's Strategic Goal?*

An explicitly-stated strategic goal, distinct from and opposed to that of the ruling classes, and the struggle for this goal is what distinguishes revolutionary politics. It is this which gives effective meaning to the struggles of the working people, provides a purposeful direction to their political endeavours, and inspires them to 'attempt the impossible', 'to do something new'. Achieving this goal is invariably a long haul, but this has never deterred Communists from openly proclaiming and fighting for their goal.

What is involved here is our vision of a just and humane society beyond the present-day social orders—which I would still define as 'socialism' as the classical Marxist tradition viewed it. Holding on to this vision, 'Traum' Marx had called it, has been and remains integral to revolutionary politics.

Towards the end of *What Is To Be Done?*—a text which is as relevant today as ever—Lenin, in the midst of the most hard-headed and unsentimental of polemics, quoted the journalist Pisarev:

> if man were completely deprived of the ability to dream... if he could not from time to time run ahead and mentally conceive... the product to which his hands are only just beginning to lend

* *Mainstream*, July 21-27, 2006.

> shape, then I cannot at all imagine what stimulus there would be... (for) art, science, and political endeavour... The rift between reality and dreams causes no harm if only the person dreaming believes seriously in his dream, if he attentively observes life, compares his observations with his castles in the air.... and works conscientiously for the achievement of his fantasies. If there is some connection between dreams and life then all is well.

To which Lenin added:

> Of this kind of dreaming there is unfortunately too little in our movement. And the people most responsible for this are those who boast of their sober senses, their "closeness" to the "concrete".

In the same text, Lenin had insisted: He, who forgets that 'the Communists support every revolutionary movement' and are for that reason obliged 'to expound and emphasise general democratic tasks before the whole people, *without for a moment concealing our socialistic convictions*', is not a Communist.

What, then, is the Leninist 'dreaming' or vision of the CPM, the strategic goal of CPM politics; and how, and how openly or explicitly do they link their current political practices to this vision or the alternative strategic goal?

This question regarding an alternative strategic goal, distinct from and opposed to that of India's major ruling class political formation, the Congress and the BJP, can be legitimately asked of every individual, group or political party in the country that claims to be communist or socialist. I have raised this question—as the Indian people's alternative strategic option in opposition to 'globalisation' or 'economic reform' that India's ruling classes have opted for—on more than one occasion in recent years, even written of it as 'contemporary India's most important *unraised* political question'. Immediately, the provocation to raise this question again the way I am doing now, is the adulation of Buddhadeb Bhatttacharjee and his politics in West Bengal, which has become the daily staple of the bourgeois media and politicians, often in contrast to or 'disconnect' with, what they with unconcealed glee and contempt, describe as 'the rhetoric of comrades in New Delhi'. 'Poster boy of reform', 'the Prime Minister's new poster boy', regular patting on the back and exhortations to 'keep it up'—so the adulation goes on.

There are, however, a couple of other considerations too. For one, the Russian revolutionary Herzen is supposed to have said something to the effect: when the bourgeoisie begins to praise the revolutionaries, it is time for them to stop and take a look at themselves. For, obviously, the borgeoisie could not have changed. And then there is Mr Buddhadeb Bhattacharjee himself: 'We are Communists (but) we are not fools'. 'We have to learn the truth from the facts. We have to change, we have to reform.' So, 'we are practising capitalism.' He is warm about his 'friendship with industrialists' and does not want 'to send wrong signals to investors'. He likes and learns from China and Vietnam, but does not mention Cuba. He proclaims his freedom from 'dogmas', but does not tell us which 'dogmas' he has given up. And all this while: 'I am a Communist and I am proud of it.' Obviously, being a Communist no longer has the meaning it once had.

Our struggle for freedom was a struggle to break out of a globalisation whose structural logic meant wealth in England and poverty in India. This was a necessary, through not suficient, condition to be able to build a better life for our people. Aware of this exploitative logic of the global capitalist market, of centuries of experience of imperialism which provides little evidence of the beneficial effect of roeign investment in countries of the third world so far as the common people are concerned, and in its own way influenced by the interim successes of the Soviet Union, the post-independence (Nehruvian) national project opted for the strategic goal of a state-led self-reliant development promising economic growth with 'equity and distributive justice' to the people. That it did not work out the way it was intended, that there was a significant degree of economic growth but not much equity or distributive justice for the people, that the project ended up building an India-specific government-supported capitalism, and that the rhetoric of 'socialistic pattern of society' only deceived the people, legitimised the statist-capitalism that was coming up, and created confusion about it as 'socialism' that persists to this day—all this, its why and how, is not my concern at the moment. The point to be noted is that passing through a series of economic and political crises, the national project, such as it was, finally and definitvely collapsed in 1991, foregrounding, once again—now in the context of the changed balance of forces in the world following the collapse of the Soviet Union—the question of strategic options for India's future economic and social development.

The post-independence national project having collapsed, 1991 onwards, India's ruling classes, through their different political formations, notably, the Congress and the BJP, have gone in for 'globalisation' as their new strategic option—a shift from the state-supported capitalism to a wholly privatised 'free market' capitalism and from self-relinace in economic development to reliance on Foreign Direct Investment and the multinationals, a shift euphemistically described as 'economic reform' whose structural logic, as a former President of Brazil once reported it to the masters in Washington, is: 'the economy is doing fine, the people are not.' (incidentally, post-independence, state intervention in the economy was deemed necessary by the then economically and politically weak, relatively underdeveloped, Indian bourgeoisie itself, which, as a major beneficiary of 'economic growth' during the Nehru era and afterwards, soon developed substaintial strength of its own and grew hopeful of new avenues of profit-making at home and abroad in partnership with global capitalism. The new strategic option, therefore, can be viewed as a natural progress for the Indian bourgeoisie.)

It is not surprising that its pursuit of the new strategic option, the so-called 'economic reform', had the consequence of the Congress losing its credibility with the people and power to the BJP-led NDA. The NDA Government, now pursued the same 'economic reform' agenda, necessarily producing, in the words of a perceptive scholar, 'a feel good factor among the propertied elite and foreign interests in India' and creating 'more than ever... two nations in India, already home to some of the starkest divides between poverty and wealth'. It was 'India shining', but only for a few at the top, with the many below experiencing its structurally *other* reality. Again, it was not surprising that the BJP lost the 2004 Lok Sabha election and its power at Delhi. Back in power on the *aam aadmi* plank, compulsions of electoral politics forcing it to take note of the victim of 'economic reform', the so-called *aam aadmi* ('the common man'), the Congress now again speaks the Nehruvian language of economic growth with equity and social justice, etc.—a Manmohan-Sonia farce, as it were, to Nehru's tragedy, to paraphrase Marx's famous observation on the caricatured re-appearance of historical phenomenon. The Congress now seeks 'economic reform with a human face', something which, symbolic gestures apart—which are already being forced on it by the supporting Left—is simply not possible for capitalism today, least of all for India's third worldist capitalism. The current long-term crisis of global capitalism has compelled it to shed its 'human face' even in the advanced capitalist West—dismantling, or struggle over dismantling the welfare state has been a distinct feature of economy and politics in the advanced capitalist countries in recent decades. In other words, 'economic reform', the strategic opption of India's ruling establishment, has little to offer to the common Indian people; the much-touted 'growth rates' are no indication of human well-being in a capitalist society. Whatever be the benefits this option brings to a small section at the top, it will further polarise our society, play havoc with the lives of our common people and push them still further into a peripheralised existence within the global capitalist system. This is indeed how it has been over the past decade-and-a-half. And this is where the question of a people's alternative strategic option comes in, which in effect means the question of the CPM's (or the Left Front's) alterntive strategic option or goal.

This is not to overlook the CPM's support to the Congress-led dispensation at the Centre to keep the BJP out of power, which is a fully justified position to take. For, to put it in the simplest possible terms, the BJP in power means 'economic reform' plus a blatantly communal and socially regressive politics. The Congress is equally, if not more, economic reformist and is not above playing a communal and socially regressive politics of its own. But, for good historical reasons, it allows for the possibility, however limited, of intervening and influencing policy in the interest of the people. Hence also the validity of the CPM's fight for the Common Minimum Programme. These are still, essentially, tactical positions. The need to define and project before the people the Left's alternative strategic goal—its 'dream' or vision of a just and humane social order beyond and in opposition to what the ruling class politics offers to the Indian people—and to relate its current politics to that goal remains. And it remains missing in CPM politics, a visible absence even in the CPM's own argument in what little debate the country still has over the present and future of India. The consequent absence of *an independent Left assertion* in contemporary Indian politics is indeed the tragedy of the Indian Left today, a part of the larger tragedy of the Indian people at the end of sixty odd years of independence.

The struggle for an alternative strategic goal, our vision of a just and humane society in India, of course raises a host of extraordinarily complex issues of theory and practice. And achieving this goal is obviously going to be a long haul. But these can never be reasons for Communists and Socialists to abandon the struggle for this goal. This struggle, again, does not rule out mistakes, retreats, at times even departures from principles, but these need to be recognised as mistakes, retreats and departures, to be rectified at the earliest and not rationalised theoretically, least of all celebrated as any kind of success.

What then, is the CPM's strategic goal? We know what the CPM does not want, 'globalisation', 'economic reform' and all that. But what does it want in positive strategic terms, how open or public it is about this strategic goals, 'before the whole people' and 'without for a moment concealing' it, and how does it relate its current political practices at the Centre and in the States to this goal? The question has to be explicitly posed, if ever an answer is to be had. And this answer, rather the adequacy of it, remains crucially important for the future our people will have. Crucially important, because the CPM is today the country's leading Left political formation and its role is central to the independent Left assertion in Indian politics that our people most urgently need.

But, then, perhaps, it is too late, and therefore irrelevant now to raise these issues with the CPM. Maybe the Bhattacharjee turn in CPM politics signals that the old fire gone, happily 'in poer' (rather quarantined) in its three States, the party, 'changed' and 'reformed' by its Bhattacharjees, no longer 'dreams' or thinks in Marxist or Leninist ways. 'One residual consequence of the Soviet collapse', I have noted elsewhere, 'is the sudden inhibition of social imagination'. Maybe, like so many other Coomunists and Socialists, the CPM too has gone 'realist' and finally succumbed to this inhibition. It may even be that the party does not hope of ever being in power at Delhi with its own agenda, and, unable or unwilling 'to do something new' that the situation demands, it sees its future as a pro-people pressure group at the Centre and the best manager of 'economic reform' in the States. There is plenty of room for such social democratic politics in our country today. And, as that 'most ambitious and intransigent theorisation of ultra-capitalism as a global order', Thomas Friedman's *The Lexus and The Olive Tree* has sloganised: "One dare not be a globaliser today without being a social democrat"!

Sad about the situation one hopes that these 'may bes' are not yet a reality with the entire leadership of the CPM, that the party retains enough of Marxism and revolutionary commitment to keep its original promise to the Indian people.

Chapter 9

Future of Socialism*

I have been asked to speak on 'Future of Socialism'. What I am going to say is based on my recently published book, *Crisis of Socialism—Notes in Defence of a Commitment,* which may be referred to for the detailed argument in support of the propositions I am going to advance with the help of passages culled from this book. I am going to deal with the question in four separate but interrelated segments of my addres.

During the heady, rebel days, in the late 1960s, students of Paris used to ask of everyone who would address them to first tell them: 'where do you speak from?' For every speaker, inescapably speaks from a particular philosophical-political standpoint and owes it to his audience to publicity state it. It is only fair to acknowledge that I am going to speak from the standpoint of Marxism, rather Marxism as I understand it. For I have no pretensions to scholarship in Marxism. I picked up some on the way and have found it useful not only in my politics or profession as a teacher, but in living my life as well. This last is not just a formal statement. Knowing Marx does make a difference to what sense you make of life, how you understand, live and act in the world. 'Indeed, I must confess that Karl Marx made a man of me', is how George Bernard Shaw once put it. Marx, therefore, is important to me and, I believe, he is important

---

* An address to the journal *Itihasbodh* at Allahabad on March 8, 2007.

to all of us, today more so than ever before, if for no other reason than this: the world we are living in is a capitalist world, more capitalist than ever before after the Soviet collapse, and Marx more than any other human being, then or now, devoted his life to explaining the reality of this world and his achievement here remains unrivalled. In one sense, this is what I am going to speak about, for socialism, properly understood, is a historically necessary and possible *negation of capitalism.*

I

No discussion of socialism today, least of all its future, can bypass what happened in the erstwhile Soviet Union. What we have here, as I have argued at length in my book, is a failed revolutionary experiement: a grievously deformed socialism that was built and the final crisis and collapse of the *sui generis* class exploitative system it had ultimately degenerated into—all of which is fully amenable to a Marxist explanation in terms of its method of historical materialism and clas analysis. In other words, what failed in the Soviet Union was not socialism but a system that came to be built in its name. I have no time to discuss this subject here. Immediately I would only like to emphasise the need for socialists to understand the why and how, and the implications, of what happened in the erstwhile Soviet Union.

It is indeed imperative for socialists who wish for a future beyond capitalism, to understand what has happened, what was built and what has failure, the collapse of what we have described as 'actually existing socialism', and some others as 'authoritarian communism'—though they must do so fully mindful of the costs and consequences of 'actually existing capitalism' or 'authoritarian capitalism' which has rushed in to pick up the pieces. It was certainly mistaken to see the struggle for socialism in our times as a contest between 'the socialist world' and 'the capitalist world', as official Marxism in the post-1917 period made it out to be. It was, as always, an international class struggle with several more or less important fronts. The countries of 'actually existing socialism', while it lasted, were only one front of this struggle, and while they did condition or influence this struggle, positively as well as negatively, they did not determine or settle the question of its outcome. Nor does the collapse of these countries now, or their return to the capitalist fold, in any way settle the question of the future of socialism—the struggle still goes on and will, so long as capitalism lasts. Nevertheless, these countries constituted what was in many ways a most important front of the ongoing international class struggle and their collapse demands that socialists understand and come to terms with it. If they no more need to carry the burden of a deformed and degenerated socialism or be answerable for its ugliness and cruelities, the burden of a genuine, Marxist explanation of its collapse has still to be carried by them so that our people know the truth and approapriate lessions are drawn for struggles of the future....

We need this explanation not only to learn the right and not wrong lessons from what has happened, but even more because in the absence of *our* explanation, it is *their,* the enemies' explanation which will continue to prevail, and this is: 'socialism has failed'. What is more, we need it to prevent *them* from taking *our* history from us. For the ideologues of capialism, even as they have pronounced the 'end of socialism' and with the post-modernists even deny the ability to learn from history, are busy depicting the October Revolution and what followed, an entire era of people's heroic struggles and achievements, as nothing but a costly aberration in history. Indeed, defending or reclaiming our history is today in itself a revolutionary project for us, as part of our assessment of what has happened in the Soviet Union....

The lessons, often bitter ones, have to be drawn from the past. This is necessary to face reality and rebuild the required politics and culture on the Left. But it is equally ncessary to be properly balanced about it. In other words, it also needs to be recognised that this past is not entirely a bitter heritage. Our assessment or self-accounting must not throw any baby out with the bath water....

An assessment or reassessment of the experience of Soviet Union, culminating in the collapse of history's first great experiment in socialism and of the whole communist movement associated with it, even when not led or dominated by it, is obviously important for socialists everywhere, in the North as well as the South. But those who especially need to master the lessons of this experience are the leaders, and even more the militant cadre of the communist parties for whom Soviet Union was a decisive point of reference and identity, whatever the differences that may have emerged in the later period. In the West, unable or unwilling to find answers to the Soviet collapse and related problems from within Marxism, most of these parties have simply abandoned the socialist project and opted for the social democratic road. Elsewhere, mostly in the third world, though remaining formally communist, they are confused and disoriented by what has happened, and unable to transcend the orthodoxies of official Marxism are content to blame it all on Khrushchevite revisionism, betrayal of a Gorbachev or secret machinations of US imperialism and its CIA. Even the Marxist-Leninist communist formations, or those holding on to the old orthodoxies of Chinese vintage, have, by and large, failed to go beyond this much too simplistic and shallow understanding. Unless the opportunity is now seized to turn to authenitc, creative Marxism to understand the crisis and collapse of Soviet socialism and this understanding made central to a rethinking of the whole question of the long-current reformist or ultra-left practices in the movement, the momentum of the past may keep these communist parties going, but with the old leaders and credibility born of past struggles or gains fading out and the failure of any new radical recruitment, they can only stagnate, or continue to decline down the road of economistic practices, electoralist reforms and even pragmatic adjustments within the ongoing capitalist globalisation; and the Marxist-Leninist or Maoist formations, their avowed revolutionary commitment notwithstanding, will remain the sectarian movements they are, wrangling with each other and quarantined within their limited areas of influence. Though communist in name, these parties and formations will have lost the opportunity to recover and become a politcally effective force on behalf of socialism...

For socialists in the third world, including those who call

themselves communists, the Soviet experience has an added, rather exceptional importance. Classical Marxism, with its perspective of construction of socialism in advanced capitalist countries and on an international scale, had, apart from some general principles, little to say to the Russian Bolsheviks as they set out on their unanticipated journey in an entirely uncharted territory: a struggle for socialism in a single backward country, in the midst of unremitting hostility of internationally dominant capitalism led by its most advanced sectors. Theirs was a pioneering effort. Insofar as the cause of its failure lies, along with the force of objective circumstances in the inadequacies of theory and practice for this unprecedented task, the Soviet experience has invaluable lessons for revolutionaries in the third world as, like Russia, their poor and backward countries, in this period of renewed global capitalist domination, seek a better, necesarily socialist, destiny for themselves...

What has happened in the former Soviet Union does not in any way invalidate Marx's argument for the necessity and possibility of a socialist negation of capitalist social order. Only the struggle for socialism is turning out to be far more complex and difficult than he ever visualised. Socialists of course have no illusions that the struggle for socialism is going to be easy or expeditiously successful. After the first failure it will be far more difficult in many ways than before, it is going to be a long detour to socialism next time. But they have no reason to feel gloomy about the prospects either. The material conditions are more favourable and objective compulsions far stronger than appeared possible a few years ago, and the constituency for the socialist cause can only grow as capitalism shows itself increasingly incapable of coping with the crises it produces....

II

It can be legitimately argued that the reasons which in the first place gave rise to the movement for socialism still hold, more so at the beginning of this century than they did at the beginning of the last or at any time earlier. Capitalism remains a deeply exploitative and ecologically disastrous way of organising social life. Apparently triumphant, capitalism continues to operate under the same structural compulsions, producing the same catastrophic consequences as before. It remains ridden with crises and congenitally unable to subordinate its achievements to the needs of human beings, unable, despite its prodigious productive abilities, to offer even bare survival to vast majorities in the world it dominates. Despite its current apotheosis, capitalism has resolved none of the problems which have for more than a century and a half given sustenance to socialist aspirations and struggles. The logic favouring a worldwide transition to socialism remains as compelling todays as it has ever been.

The collapse in the Soviet Union does not in any way change this logic, except that the economically exploitative, morally repulsive and ecologically unsustainable character of capitalism is now more apparent than at any time in its history....

The objective conditions and more than an embryonic subjectivity at individual and mass organisational levels exist for the reconstruction of a socialist opposition to the currently dominant capitalist system. In the West the euphoria over 'no alternative' is long over. The declaration of 'the end of history', like similar declarations in the past, stands rejected as so much silliness. The long moment people thought typical, the welfarist capitalism, is recognised as not typical, typical is the harsh reality they are now experiencing. People are learning the hard way what capitalism, and about the compradorism or their own ruling elites. The question of an alternative is back on the agenda, and in different shapes and forms, in however confused or muddled a manner, anti-capitalist struggles are being resumed in different parts of the world. These struggles may not produce a remake of the previous century. History certainly has its surprise—and revolutions by the oppressed and exploited are among them....

Revolution is not only armed struggle or insurrection, though it still cannot be ruled out. It does not at all help to see revolution as a punctual moment in history or in terms of iconic images like the taking of the Winter Palace or storming of the Bastille. Revolution is best understood as a complex process—with special complexities of its own in regimes of bourgeois democracy. And however we understand it, we cannot predict the practical and theoretical forms of the revolutions of the future. But we know the surprises that vicissitudes of world history brought us in the twentieth century. And there is no reason to doubt that this one will bring more. The inventiveness of masses in revolt has been and will continue to be beyond the imagination of the most sensitive scholar or philosopher...

Revolution is not over. The basic conflicts between classes, between the oppressed and the oppressors, between a new and the old social order will not cease because the Soviet Union has ceased to be and a Fukuyama has announced the 'end of history'. The dynamics and forces which generated the revolutions of the twentieth century remain as they were in the past. The end of 'historical communism' has not put an end to poverty or to people's thirst for justice. The poor and forsaken of the third world still hope for a better life. Not exactly enthusiastic over revolutions, past or future, Fred Halliday, in his recent study on the subject, has yet pointed to 'the enduring inability of those with power and wealth to comprehend the dept of hostility to them' and 'the ability of history... to surprise', and written: 'the agenda of the revolutions of modern history is still very much with us because the aims they asserted... are far from having been achieved.' This leaves revolution still on the agenda of history. Revolution remains the vital truth, the unifished story of our times—in whatever shape or form and over however long a period the rest of the story may be told....

The story is in fact already being told in the resumed world revolutionary process which, after the intial setback following the failed experiment in the Soviet Union, is again positing socialism as the necessary and possible future for humankind. As they struggle to forge extra-parliamentary sanctions to defend their Bolivarian revolution against American imperialism and its local alliet, the Venezuelans are speaking of building 'socialism of the twenty-first century' and, inspired by Cuba, the pink is threatening to turn red elsewhere in Latin America. Fighting their 'People's War' and now struggling to win the battle of democracy, the Maoists in Nepal seek self-reliant development 'oriented towards socialism'. As the struggle against globalisation sharpens in the West, the *New Yorker* writes of 'The Return of Karl Marx' and in Europe voices are heard asking for new experiments in socialism. Never a narrowly conceived class project, socialism today stands poised, as never before, to be 'the movement of immense majority in the interest of immense majority' as Marx had proclaimed in the *Communist Manifesto.*

III

The collapse in Eastern Europe and the Soviet Union has led any number of scholars, journalists and politicians, ideologues and writers of all sorts, to play zero sum games. If socialism has lost, then its antagonist, capitalism, must have won. If planned socialist economies have broken down, then their binary opposite, free-market capitalism must have triumphed. Apart from its utterly reductionist and adversarial and obviously questionable logic which, equating what was built in the Soviet Union with socialism as such, conflates its failure with a victory for capitalism, such an assessment of the situation is not only logically flawed, it is false on empirical grounds as well. On any objective assessment, at the end of its five centuries old existence, global capitalism is very much a failed system today. The evidence of this failure is starkly visible in every part and aspect of contemporary capitalist world. It is visible in the impoverishment and immiseration on the rise just about everywhere in the world; in the official statistics on rates of unemployment, poverty, homelessness, and hunger, in the sullen slums of major cities of Westerm bourgeois democracies, proliferating urbal ghettos of the gritty capitals of former Soviet block countries and the warrens of teeming tumbledown shanties of the peripheral South; in the gross inequalities of the world, the wretchedness of the impoverished and excluded within the rich Western societies and the huge mass of misery in the poorer countries; in the morally intolerable and cocially unnecessary suffering—what Bourdieu has called *la misere du monde*—produced by capitalism everywhere...

The 'actually existing socialism'—which was not Marx's

socialism whose possibility remains open—has of course, failed. But, surely, the 'actual existing capitalism'—which is the only kind of capitalism possible—has not been the success it is made out to be. In any objective judgement, capitalism too has been a failure in our times. Other considerations apart, capitalism has been a failure in terms of possibly the most legitimate criteria for assessing the performance of a social system: 'fullness of employment' and 'goodness of employment' of the actual and potential resources available in society. Never before in human history has the gap between society's potentiality and society's performance been so immense as it is today in capitalism's current stage of development. Evidence is there in the extraordinary productive capacity that three successive industrial revolutions have put at the disposal of humankind and the poverty and illiteracy, squalid slums and homelessness that are the lot of millions of families in the wealthiest countries of the capitalist world and the hunger and misery of hundreds of millions of people, living out their empty and barren lives in the hovels of the peripheral or semi-peripheral poor countries of the third world. The third world today is indeed a monument to the failure of capitalism in our times....

As hinted above, there is a difference between the two failures that needs to be specifically noted. Socialism may have failed for the time being, but it remains the alternative if humankind would survive and hope for a safe world and life worthy of human beings. It bears repeating that the unacceptable economic, moral and ecological consequences of capitalism, its failure ranging from unemployment, poverty and inequalities to barbarisation, at home and abroad, are not aberrations of the system or 'negative' effects produced by specific circumstances or 'mistaken' policies. They are the product of capitalism's unreformable and uncontrollable systemic or structural logic, the logic of exploitation and polarisation immanent in the system itself. Therefore these 'effects' are permanent, even though they are diminshed in certain phases and increased in others. They are thus essentially irremediable. In other words, the failure of capitalism in our times has a systemic or structural necessity or inevitability about it. In contrast, there was no systemic or structural necessity about the failure of socialism in the Soviet Union. With politics commanding the economy, socialism simply has no structural logic or 'laws' similar to what market-based capitalism has. Socialism failed primarily due to the inadequacies of theory and practice, to the mistaken *choices* that the Communist parties in power made. Apropos the failure of communist regimes (and Social Democracy in Europe), Gabriel Kolko has written: 'Their consistent failure to redeem and significantly (as well as permanently) transform societies when in a position to do so is testimony to their analytic inadequacies and the grave, persistent weaknesses of their leadership and organisations. It is this reality that has marginalised both social democracy and communism in innumerable nations since 1914, providing respite through the century to capitalist classes and their allies that otherwise would never have survived socialist regimes that implemented even a small fraction of the reforms outlined in their program.' While this may be bending the stick too far the other way, the important point is that socialism's was essentially a human failure. It had nothing inevitable about it. The lessons learnt from this failure will help whenever or wherever the attempt is made next time. Socialism therefore is not just the alternative to capitalism, it remains a real choice for humankind....

Socialism as they built it in the Soviet Union has failed. Elsewhere, capitalism too has been a failure. That both socialism as we have known it and capitalism as it has existed have failed in our times suggests that we may well locate the question of 'Future of Socialism' in the problematic of epochal transitions, in this case the transition from capitalism to socialism/communism. In other words, we have a situation where the old has exhausted its positive possibilites and the new is having problems being born. Gramsci had once written, of course of a different historical juncture : 'The old is dying and the new cannot to born; in this interregnum a great variety of morbid symptoms appear'. These 'morbid symptoms' are, to a greater or lesser degree, there all over the advanced and less advanced capitalist countries today, as good an evidence as any of the deep cirsis of the capitalist civilisation, of the ultimate failure of capitalism in our times....

What we are indeed witnessing today is the end of an epoch, the epoch of transition to capitalism. Over these five hundred odd years, as capitalism expanded to structure and restructure an unequal world of core, semi-periphery and periphery regions in terms of economic strength and benefits, at each stage of this expansions, capitalism was able to overcome its permanent contradictions, but not without worsening the situation for itself for their overcoming in future. Now with the possibility of further expansion virtually exhausted, these contradictions are difficult to overcome as in the past. They are manifesting themselves all the more violently with truly disastrous consequences for the people that suggest the passing away of the epoch of capitalism's domination. Even at its best, capitalist development has been a process of 'creative destruction', to use Schumteter's famous phrase. As accumulation takes place, competition forces firms to be creative in order to survive, those firms that are not creative are destroyed. In a world of markets and competition, winners are matched by losers, and creation and destruction become one and the same. Losers, however, have not been simply impersonal firms or abstract inefficient technologies. In the real world, losers have been simply impersonal firms or abstract inefficient technologies. In the real world, losers have been people, sometimes capitalists, but always working people, individually and as communities. 'Creative destruction' has meant the unemployment of real workers, the destitution of real communities, devastation of the environment, and disempowerment of the people. The destructive aspect of capitalism's 'creative destruction' has now reached a point where the historical *raison d'etre* and justification that capitalism, as a mode of production, once had, had disappeared and we can legitimately speak of capitalism living beyond its time, beyond the period of its historical legitimacy.

Capitalism's achievements are now all in the past, its future promises only disasters for humankind. In the *Communist Manifesto*, Marx and Engels had written of class struggle ending 'either in a revolutionary reconstitution of society at large or in the mutual ruin of the contending classes.' The great class struggles of the twentieth century have obviously not resulted in 'a revolutionary reconstitution of society'. What Marx and Engels saw as 'the common ruin of the contending classes' is already on in the world. Economies everywhere in shambles; obscene wealth alongside abject poverty and wanton waste of recources; widespread collapse of law and order; senseless regional and ethnic conflicts; new wars between or within nations almost on a daily basis; spread of weapons of mass destruction and threat of terrorism on a global scale; an all-engulfing ecological crisis—all this in fact points to the common ruin of more than the contending classes as a very realistic prospect in the historically near future. The epoch of capitalism may well end up in 'the total destruction of humanity', the possibility predicted by Marx in 1845 — a perspective that Rosa Luxemburg later summed up in the dictum: 'Socialism or barbarism'. Modifying Rosa Luxemburg's dictum in relation to the dangers we face, Meszaros has suggested adding to 'socialism or barbarism', 'barbarism if we are lucky'—in the sense that the extermination of humankind is the ultimate concomitant of capital's destructive course of development.' Such an outcome, 'the extermination of humankind' is implicit in the uncontrollable accumulative logic of capitalism. It has been rightly pointed out that the truth about capitalism today is not that it is the 'end of history', as the bourgeois ideologues want us to believe, but that its continued existence can really bring on the end of human history....

As suggested above, taking 'the longer view' of things, the present-day defeat and reversal of socialism are best viewed as part of the zigzag that the epochal transition from capitalism to socialism is bound to be....

The twentieth century opened with global capitalism's total domination of the world. Then, as anticipated by Marxian analysis, indeed by Marx himself, came the socialist revolutions of the twentieth century—the European revolutions in the aftermath of the First World War (of which only the Russian Revolution survived), in Eastern Europe after the Second World War, and then in China, Korea, Cuba, Vietnam and elsewhere—

taking approximately a third of the world's population and territory out of the capitalist system. Socialism does not take root and grow withing the confines of capitalist society, as capitalism had done under feudalism. It is a new begining, a society best built on the material basis provided by capitalism. But now these poor and backward countries were called upon to build socialism where this basis hardly existed. It was a task for which they were most ill prepared. Even so, as these countries struggled to build, and other revolutionary regimes and movements profession Marxism and committed to socialism emerged in Africa and elsewhere, for a long time the contest between capitalism and its post-revolutionary rival claiming to be socialist seemed to be close and of uncertain outcome. After the events of the recent past, it may be that the visible future belongs to capitalism. But such a perspective is relatively new. For most of the century, it was far from clear that capitalism would survive into the third millennium. Now it is the post-revolutionary rival claimed to be socialism that has failed even to last till the end of the second millennium. This, however, is not any end of the earlier perspective. The Soviet experiment in socialism has failed because the conditions, both objective and subjective, were most unfavourable for it. There was the initial economic backwardness, then internal class war and armed and unarmed for foreign intervention, global capitalism's continuous effort to prevent any successful construction of socialism. Decisive in its own way were the factors of inadequate and often erroneous theory that guided, or misguided, this experiment and poor political leadership. But it is important to recognise that what has been tried and failed is not socialism but history's first serious effort to build socialism. The reasons that produced the cause of socialism as well as the revolutions aimed at its achievement are still very much there. There is no reason to presume that new revolutions aimed at its achievement are still very much there. There is no reason to presume that new revolutions, surprising as ever for the dominant capitalism, will no longer take place and new efforts to build socialism will not be made. And even less reason to presume that given favourable circumstances, more adequate theory and better political leadership, such efforts will not succeed...

Here a look at capitalism's emergence and spread can be quite instructive. Scholars have pointed out that the late Middle Ages witnessed not one but several promising yet false starts for capitalism. But weak and divided, they lacked the stamina to survive in the hostile, predominantly feudal environment of the period. Smothered by surrounding feudalism, the emerging capitalism simply failed to catch on. It was not until centuries later that a new conjucture emerged in which a budding capitalism, benefiting well from its earlier abortive appearances, could take root and grow powerful enough to fend off its enemies and survive, to finally arrive as it did in England and other Atlantic societies. Once arrived, the struggle with feudalism still continued, a struggle between two actually existing social formations for supremacy, i.e. for state power (monopoly over the means of coercion) and the right to organise society in accordance with their respective interests and ideas. Moreover, the process was a prolonged one in which the 'new' social formation had ample time to prepare itself, both economically and ideologically, for the role of undisputed dominance. It is thus that capitalism grew and developed into the globally dominant system of our times, till socialism made its first efforts to make a breach into it, an effort which has now failed...

But the failure of history's first socialist effort does not mean that more successful future efforts are impossbile. The evidence of history suggests otherwise. As we have just noticed, it was only after many centuries of turmoil, though a long process of advances and retreats, that capitalism established itself as the dominant world economic system. In the centuries-long struggle between feudalism and capitalism, there were many triumphs of feudalism', but in the long run, capitalism finally prevailed. So in the case of the transition from capitalism to socialism, the struggle may continue for centuries. There have been, and undoubtedly will be, other 'triumphs of capitalism', but in the end socialism may yet prevail. By historical standards, a few centuries is not a long time and socialism has existed for only a very short time. It is certainly mistaken and premature to superficially extrapolate from the developments of the recent, historically limited, past and speak of the ultimate failure of socialsim, to take an entirely bleak view of its future prospects. It is certainly not justified to regard the Soviet effort as only a 'heroic but tragic experience', 'an abortive serarch for an impossible short cut', a 'parenthesis' or 'interlude' in the history of capitalism, or, as in Stefan Heym's phrase, merely a 'footnote in history', and so on. Rather dismissive in nature, such assessments tend to suggest a failure of socialism as such. On the contrary, it is far more legitimate to argue that in view of the epochal nature of the transition involved, the Soviet collapse does not mean the end of socialism but only the end of world's first large-scale attempt to transcend capitalism and build a socialist society. In the larger perspective of next century or two, the developments since the 1920s can be better understood as a disastrous but still educative false start and the current crisis of socialism as a period of temporary retreat in the epochal transition to socialism. Therefore, if we believe that capitalism needs to be negated in socialism, that the underlyig ideas and ideals of socialism as a period of temporary retreat in the epochal transition to socialism. Therefore, if we believe that capitalism needs to be negated in socialism, that the underlying ideas and ideals of socialism provide the only possible framework for a decent human society, we certainly don't have to abandon hope simply because the first attempts to realise them in practice — under very difficult and unfavourable conditions, it should be noted—proved unsuccessful. We can and must still hopefully struggle for socialism and refuse to accept capitalism as the inescapable destiny for humankind. It is thus that the contest between these two approaches to human social development is still unsettled. Its outcome remains open. In a long-term historical perspective, 1917, as Goethe said of 1789, may yet mark the beginning of a new epoch in the history of humankind....

But this 'long-term' is today loaded with a problematic. Once available to capitalism to emerge, consolidate itself, and grow dominant, *time* is no longer so avlailable to socialism—which, incidentaly, also has most serious implications for the future of humanity. The reason lies in the growing ecological crisis in the world, where the accumulative logic of capitalism now threatens the very existence of humankind on the planet, earth....

Capitalism has indeed shown remarkable resilience and survived beyond what can be described as its historical time. But its survival has now put a question mark over the future of humankind. Hobsbawm has written: 'If humanity is to have a recognisable future, it cannot be by prolonging the past or the present. If we try to buillld the third miennium on that basis, we shall fail. And the price of failure, that is to say, the alternative to a changeed society, is darkness.' 'Darkness' yet does not capture the ful gravity of what lies ahead. Caught in a global structural crisis, capitalism has become more creative than ever in unleashing its destructive potential. Its accumulative logic and America-led global politics are threatening humanity with unheard-of ecological disasters and nuclear exterminism. With capitalism, humanity is indeed headed for a colective suicide and destruction of the earth itself. Socialism, therefore, is not just 'a changed society', a superior social order, it is today the necessary defence of humanity and our planet earth. This in its own way makes socialism all the more possible as an alternative to capitalism. Alternatives are discovered or invented, or even recovered when it becomes clear that we cannot survive without them. So it is now with socialism. Pointing to the human tragedy that capitalism's continued existence now portends for humankind, this is how Chomsky has put it is his characteristically simple manner: 'At this stage of history, either one of two things is possible. Either the general population will take control of its own destiny and will concern itself with community interests, guided by values of solidarity, sympathy, and concern for others, or, alternatively, there wil be no destiny for anyone to control.' ....

Years ago, the French students in their May-June uprising of 1968 expressed this sharp contrst of alternatives magnificently in their slogan: 'Be practical! Do the impossible!' Marcuse had suggested that the new generation that faces the next (that is, twenty-first) century needs to add to this demand 'the more solemn injunction: If we don't do the impossible, we shall be faced with the unthinkable!' The 'unthinkable' today is more than mere 'deccent into barbarism'. What is at stake is the actual existence of the world, and with it of the human species. And the task, as ecos-feminist Francoise d'Eaubonne, paraphrasing Marx has said, is 'to change the world.... so that there can still be a world'. Socialism is precisely the changed world we need. Once a promise of liberation, socialism has now become a question of survival too. The human species needs socialism not only to reaslise its potentials but even to survive. That is how the chances of survival and realisation of the potentials of both human species and socialism have come to be interlinked today. Which also means that the future of socialism is as bleak or bright as that of humankind....

IV

It was Engels' adjuration to followers to 'not pick quotations from Marx or from him as if from sacred texts, but think as Marx would have thought in their place.' He had insisted that 'it was only in that sense that the word Marxist had any raison d'etre'.....

Accordingly, I would make a few concluding observations on the question of socialism today, again with the help of passages culled from my *Crisis of Socialism — Notes in Defence of a Commitment,* which carrries a detailed discussion of the issues now being touched upon.

❖

Socialism arose in opposition to capitalism with the rise of modern capitalism itself. Marx's many-sided critique of capitalism soon provide it with a scientific theoretical basis, establishing it as socialism of our times, distiguishing it from its various other forms—some of which (Revolutionary Socialsim, Petty Bourgeois Socialism, German or 'True' Socialism, Conservative or Bourgeois Socialism, Critical Utopian Socialism, etc.) Marx himself noted in the *Communist Manifesto*—forms in which it keeps reappearing from time to time. In other words, socialism came up long before the Soviet Union did, and we are socialist because of capitalism and not because of the Soviet Union. Some of us were in fact socialist despite the Soviet Union. And socialism remains on the agenda of history so long as capitalism lasts.

❖

For Marx socialism is essentially a negation of capitalism, a negation of its economy, politics and ethical-aesthetic values, its multiple alienations and commodification of life. These are no blueprints of socialist society of the future in Marx's social theory. His scientific method forbidding any such speculation, Marx simply refused to 'compose the music of the future'. He visualised the construction of socialism, or communist society proper, as constituting a long period of transition. But the problems of this transition were never seriously discussed or theorised by Marx.

There are only scattered references to it in different writings of Marx and Engels, concerned primarily with characteristics of socialism as a transitional society between capitalism and communism (which they regarded as the goal towards which history was moving). The most important single document of classical Marxism here, that is, on the subject of construction of a new socialist society, is Marx's *Critique of the Gotha Programme*—really Marx's marginal notes to the programme of the German Workers Party, published by Engels after Marx's death, sixteen years after Marx wrote them. The very title is significant. The only time Marx is drawn into making a somewhat detailed, yet all to brief, comment on the subject, it is as a critique of his own party or followers in Germany for their confused and shoddy thinking over several issues, which also included that concerning the socialist society of the future—a critique distinguished for 'the ruthless severity' and 'mercilessness' typical of Marx in matters of theory. To be specifically noted here is that Marx never saw socialism, 'advanced', 'developed', or any other, as a social formation existing in its own right (as Soviet Marxism did); that would be plainly violative of its essential character as Marx defined it, that is a transition between capitalism and communism. As was common in his times, there is a certain loose usage of the term 'socialism' in Karl Marx. Quite often, he used 'socialism' and 'communism' as synonymous terms, both referring to the same kind of society, that is, a 'cooperative society' or 'association' based on 'free associated labour'. More specifically, it is what Marx called 'the first phase of communist society' which later Marxists, including Lenin, came to describe as 'socialism' (as opposed to 'communism' proper). Marx, therefore, nowhere speaks of 'socialism' as a distinct stage or social formation or of 'transition between socialim and communism'. For Marx, as the new society emerges from the capitalist society itself, the former is obviously an integral part of the same new society, being its 'first phase' only chronologically, with the specific kind of developments corresponding to it. For him, between capitalism and communism lies no stage or stages, only a transition, more or less prolonged according to circumstances, possibly a whole epoch or perhaps even more than one historical epoch. Lenin, though sharing the loose usage often equated socialism with communism, was equally explicit in speaking of 'transition period between capitalism and communism'....

I would suggest that Marx's view here is theoretically correct and politically more fruitful as against positing the transition in terms of stages such as 'new democracy', 'people's democracy', a 'revolutionary democracy', 'socialist society', etc.

That there is no fore-ordained model or blueprint of socialism or socialist transition, certainly none suitable for all countries and all times, does not mean absence of general principles that flow from the Marxist tradition, the experience gained in national liberation and social revolutionary struggles and the efforts at socialist construction so far. For this reason, a critical understanding of Marxist tradition and revolutionary struggles of the past, and an equally critical analysis of and drawing of lessons from the past experiments in socialism, even when they have failed, is more than an intellectual game; it is an urgent and practical necessity for socialists everywhere, including those in the third world, seeking a proper perspective on possible socialist transition in their countries....

❖

Socialism, for Marx, is not merely a set of humane economic arrangements; it is *an emancipatory project.* Marx saw socialism in its transition to communism as humankind's transition to 'the realm of freedom' which according to him lies beyond material pursuits, beyond all activity geared to economic needs. He wrote:

> .... The realm of freedom actually begins only where labour which is determined by necessity and mundane considerations ceases; thus *in the very nature of things* it lies beyond the sphere of actual material production. Just as the savage must wrestle with nature to satisfy his wants, to maintain and reproduce life, so must civilised man, and he must do so in all social formations and under all modes of production.... Freedom in this field can only consist in socialised man, the associated producers, rationally regulating their interchange with nature, bringing it under their common control, instead of being ruled by it as by a blind power; and achieving this with the least expenditure of energy and under conditions most favourable to, and worthy of, their human rature. But it nonetheless still remains a realm of necessity. Beyond it begins that development of human power which is an end in itself, the true realm of freedom, which, however, can blossom forth only with this realm of necessity as its basis.

The aspirations of vision that Marx here sets forth is in fact as old as civilisation; it is there, for instance, in Plato and Aristotle, though its realisation, then and afterwards, was seen possible only for a few. Marx put more substance into this aspiration and sought its realisation for all human beings. In other words, economic activity was, throughout, deemed to have meaning only it it serves something other than itself. For Marx this is activities 'valued as an end in theselves' (as he phrased it in the *Grundrisse)*, which for him is indeed 'the true measure of wealth'.....

Marx, in line with his mode of thinking, took a historical view of the growth of needs and desires of human beings as one aspect of the general development of human nature, which is also the subjective aspect of the growth of human powers and capacities. His argument is suggestive of an infinite future of creation and cultivation of 'the wealth of subjective human sensitivity', of specifically human senses, which is really the same as human nature all the time *becoming more human*. And the important point is that, for Marx, the exercise of these naturally and historically produced specifically human senses—the sense for music and poetry, art, science and history, love, justice and compassions, and so on—constituted the very essence of a truly human appropriation of life and nature, a genuinely rich human life. That is how, in pointing out the alienating, depersonalising and dehumanising consequences of capitalism, Marx particularly focused attention of the fact that for all the glorious human senses, whose active and concrete exercise alone constitutes the true content of a genuinely rich human life, capitalism substitutes a single abstract sense, the sense for property, a particular, historically transient, substitute sense which plays havoc with human personality and plunges man, in the words of Ladislav Stoll, 'into the terrible inner sickness of a dehumanised world', Marx wrote: 'In place of all these physical and mental senses there has .... come the sheer estrangement of all these senses—the sense of having. The human being had to be reduced to this absolute poverty in order that he might yield his inner wealth to the outer world'. 'The more you have', said Marx, 'the less you are'. Hence his insistence that 'the transcendence of private property is therefore the complete *emancipation* of all human senses and attributes'. He spoke of communism, 'the actual phase necessary for the next stage of historical development in the process of human emancipation and recovery', 'as the positive transcendence of *private property* as *human self-estrangement*, and therefore as the real *appropriation of the human* essence by and for man; communism therefore as the complete return of man to himself as a social (i.e. human) being—a return become conscious, and accomplished within the entire wealth of previous development'. Marx added: 'What is to be avoided above all is the re-establishing of 'Society' as an abstraction *vis-a-vis* the individual. The individual is the social being. His life.... is therefore an expression and confirmation of *social life*'. Marx is an individualist in the basic sense that his ultimate vision was a society where every individual could be a fully *human* being, where, as Marx himself put it, 'the free development of each is the condition for the free development of all'......

Such is the fulfilment Marx's socialism/communism seeks for humankind. As Engels expressed it, 'it is humanity's leap from the realm of necessity into the realm of freedom', the end of its' pre-history' and beginning of 'truly human history'.

❖

For Marx, socialism is nothing inevitable, it is something to be struggled for.

Marx was no determinist, ever. Whatever determinism there is in his Marxism, is a most conditional one, which accords primacy to human praxis, to revolutionary politics. If attention was drawn to the economic-structural necessities underlying the historical processes, it was for enhancing the freedom for *praxis,* for not foreclosing but liberating human practice, for freer choices by humans, free not in some abstract or metaphysical sense, but in the only possible *human* sense of men and women choosing and acting with the fullest possible knowledge and consideration of the necessities of the objective material situation or circumstances. Such is the dialectics of freedom and necessity in Marx.....

Thus there are no inevitablities in Marx and no guarantees of victory either; only alternatives. Even as he insisted in the *Communist Manifesto* that 'the history of all hitherto existing society is the history of class struggle'. Marx had immediately added that this struggle 'each time ended, either in a revolutionary reconstitution of society at large, or in the common ruin of the contending classes'. Again, he had hailed the productive achievements of capitalism—'it has been the first to show what man's activity can bring about', creating 'more massive and more colossal productive forces than have all preceding generations together' (*Communist Manifesto*). But he had also pointed out not only the damage that capitalism regularly inflicts upon humans and nature but also its long-term destructive potential—'its accumulation process', Marx wrote in *Grundrisse,* can have 'the consequences even for the total destruction of humanity'—a prognosis which Rosa Luxemburg later summed up as the alternative: 'socialism or barbarism'.

Incidentally, these alternatives to socialism—the threat of 'common ruin of the contending classes', and 'the total destruction of humanity' are already a part of the reality of our world today.

❖

For whatever reasons, which certainly included an underestimation of capitalism's productive potential and resilience, Marx gave capitalism a short lease of life, which allowed for the possibility of realising socialism as an emancipatory project, that is initiating the epochal transition this project implied. In his main theory on the subject, based on his view of the historical tendencies of advanced capitalist development in Europe, Marx visualised the necessity as well as the possibility of a transition from capitalism to socialism/ communism in the countries of advanced industrial development, with their mature productive basis and proletatian presence—'Empirically, communism is only possible as the act of the dominant peoples "all at once" and simultaneously, which presupposes the universal development of productive forces and the world intercourse bound up with them', is how Marx put it in *The German Ideology*. Accordingly, Marx looked forward to an early revolution in Europe—though he also recognised (in a letter to Engels in 1858): 'For us the difficult question is this: the revolution on the Continent is imminent and its character will be at once socialist; will it not be necessarily crushed in this little corner of the world, since on a much larger terrain the development of bourgeois society is still in the ascendant'. The hoped-for European revolution finally arrived in the aftermath of the first world war but it survived only in Russia, confronting Lenin and his Bolsheviks with a totally unanticipated task: attempt a socialist transition in a single backward country, a situation or possibility that was never theorised by Marx. And now, though not inevitable, the attempt has failed. History seems to have played a trick on the doctrine of Karl Marx. This trick including the failure in the Soviet Union is eminently amendable to explanation in terms of this very doctrine but more important is to note the consequent reality of the contemporary world in relation to Marx's own perspective on socialism and the struggle for socialism in our times.

Of this reality, three features need to be particularly noticed.

First, as a capitalist world, it is a world of 'overdeveloped', 'underdeveloped' or so-called 'developing' countries. The latter two categories are generally well understood but we need to take a closer look at the 'overdeveloped' countries of advanced capitalism. For one, capitalism survives and is indeed dominant today, but as noticed earlier, it remains a failed system. Other considerations apart, capitalism has been a failure in terms of possibly the most legitimate criteria for assessing the performance of a social system: 'fullness of employment' and 'goodness of employment' of the actual and potential resources available in society. Never before in human history has the gap between society's potentiality and society's performance been so immense as it is today is capitalism's current stage of development. Evidence is there, as we have already noticed, in the extraordinary productive capacity that three successive industrial revolutions have put at the disposal of humankind and the poverty and illiteracy, squalid slums and homelessness that are the lot of millions of families in the wealthiest countries of the capitalist world and the hunger and misery of hundreds of millions of people, living out their empty and barren lives in the hovels of the peripheral or semi-peripheral poor countries of the third world....

Capitalism continues to survive but this by itself, cannot be seen as an argument for the desirability, or a sign of the progressiveness of the capitalist order, much less as any sort of 'triumph' of capitalism. 'That position', says Paul Baran, 'is no more defensible than would be the view that an inability of the human body to resist tuberculosis, however caused, furnishes a proof of the harmlessness or even usefulness of that illness'....

He adds: 'The failure of an irrationally organised society to generate internal forces pressing towards and resulting in its abolition and replacement by more rational, more humane social relations results necessarily in economic stagnation, cultural decay, and a widespread sense of despondency. Such a society—even if once the most advanced in the world—loses its position of leadership, slides into the backwaters of historical development, and turns into a breeding ground of reaction inhumanity, and obscurantism.' This is indeed the case today, not only in the United States but increasingly in the other so-called advanced societies of late capitalism....

The US leading, these societies are, in a profound sense, to a greater or lesser degree, sick societies. Concerned scholars have written of the phenomenon of 'alienation' in these societies, their citizens' growing sense of anomie and estrangement, of isolation, hostility and frustration. They are sick with these and a hundred other social and psychic ailments born of prolonged living under an essentially irational system, sick with apathy and boredom, with 'other-directedness' and conformism, with fears, insecurities and neuroses of all kinds. Their sustained social regression is reflected as much in the reaction and obscurantism they breed, their frivolous consumption and culture of drugs, and even guns, as in the debilitating barrage of fraudulent politics, barren culture and stupefying entertainment, inspirational rackets and demoralising press, and comic books, to which their people, even otherwise ill-educated, are exposed all the time. Societies in the grip of crises which they cannot resolve, they are inevitably producing deep pathological deformations which manifest themselves variously in different places as racism, sexism, anti-Semitism, xenophobia, ethnic or national hatred, fundamentalism and intolerance, even as plain cruelty and aggression. Poverty, unemployment and insecurity-related crimes and associated phenomena—ill health and suicides, alcoholism and drug addiction, racist discrimination and criminal violence, violence against women and child abuse, etc.—are on the rise everywhere. In many of these 'advanced' societies, marginal indigenous populations are rapidly being wiped out for one reason or another. By their very nature, profoundly immoral societies, based as they are on domination and exploitation of man by man, along with humanistic values and culture and all human relationships, even their professed moralities and principles now stand devastated by the morality and values of 'the market'. And, most significantly, there is the near-absence of ideals in these societies, of any concern for a better future to strive for, that has been the motive force of all human progress in the past. The instruments of communication and discovery invented by their technological genius have become the means of debasing people's understanding and preventing them from looking beyond the capitalist horizon....

Indeed, the sickness of these so-called advanced societies, the spiritual disarray of the capitalist civilisation they represent, is nowhere more evident than in their cynical idealisation of capitalism as it exists and utter lack of any vision of a s secure and more satisfying life beyond their 'consumerist heaven of instant gratification', a life which would be satisfactory of basic human needs—decent livelihood, knowledge, solidarity, cooperation with fellow human beings, gratification in work and freedom from toil—and provide the possibility of men and women appropriating the world with all their glorious *human* senses. It needs to be added that these societies are all the more sick societies because they need to change the existing state of affairs but are unable to generate the necessary social forces for carrying out the revolutionary change they so badly need.....

The continuance of capitalism as 'sick' societies of advanced capitalist West has an important implication. In a sense socialism arrived a little before its time, attempted as it was first in Russia, a society that was not prepared to build it. The Bolsheviks had to contend with the problems of a backward, underdeveloped capitalist-feudal social order, problems which caused grave distortions and contributed to the ultimate failure of their attempt to build socialism. Those who may be called upon to build a late-arrived socialism in advanced capitalist countries will have to contend with equally difficult but *different* problems of an 'overdeveloped' capitalism—a capitalism living beyond its time as it were, beyond the period of its historical legitimacy. In other words, as with 'underdevelopment', 'overdevelopment' too poses its own unanticipated problems for the realisationof Marx's project of socialism.

Socialism, of course, remains on the agenda wherever capitalism exists, be it 'overdeveloped', 'underdeveloped', 'developing' or any other. And there is always the overarching question as to what kind of society we, as human beings, want to have. Surely it is people and not 'economic growth' or productivity that must come first in such a society. It has to be a humane society that fosters cooperation, solidarity and respect for universal ethical values, and makes for a non-alienated, 'truly rich human life' that Marx spoke of. Of course, such a society is impossible without basic material security and need satisfaction. But to believe that you can assure need satisfaction through greed, private acquisitive drives, universal competition and strife—the values of capitalism—and yet hope for a humane society of cooperation and solidarity is utopianism of the worst kind. Subordinating humanity to economics, to imperatives of the market, capitalism commodifies life and undermines and rots away the relations between human beings which constitute societies. Its ethos of the marketplace—competition, egoism, aggression, alienation, universal venality, in short the rat race—creates a moral vacuum in which nothing counts except what the individual wants and can grab, here and now. At the end of it all, even when wants are satisfied, the people are ever more subordinated, ever less free, ever more flattened and made passive by the dictatorship of consumerism, that arbitratily shapes values, imposing on them the heavy burden of uniformity. The values of difference, individualisation (not individualism), all-sided development of man, of human freedom itself, disappear in the marketplace which is proclaimed to the free. As human beings, people simply don't fit into capitalism, which is a quintessential market society. For a truly humane society to come into existence, capitalism has to go....

But, in view of their 'overdeveloped', 'underdeveloped' or 'developing' character, to speak of socialism in relation to these capitalist societies is not to posit socialism as achievable today or tomorrow, or even the day after, but to posit it as people's alternative strategic goal, as the principle governing people's politics which links together their immediate, ongoing and emerging struggles in an ultimate specifics and speed will depend on the objective material conditions and the nature and balance of class forces involved at each stage of the struggle......

In other words, while expressions like 'building socialism' or 'building socialism of the 21st century' have a certain historical and political legitimacy, what is on the agenda is a *socialism-oriented development*, such that, no matter how slow or halting or contradictions-laden, it is a development away from capitalism and the imperatives of its market and *towards* Marx's emancipatory vision of socialism, which, in any case, was visualised as a transition spanning an entire epoch even more than one epoch.

This, again, is not to suggest any 'model' of socialist politics. Just as there is no single or foreordained model of socialism, one that is suitable for all climes and all times, there is none of socialist politics either. The specific conditions or demands and the forms of struggle they generated will vary from country to country. Which however, does not mean the absence of general principles to guide it that flow from the Marxist tradition and the experience gained in social revolutionary and national liberation struggles. The recovery of these principles is in fact a must for any successful pursuit of socialist politics today....

Second, since global capitalism is nationally organised and immediately dependent on national states, national economies and national states remain the primary terrain of anit-capitalist organisation and struggle. Of course, an international perspective, working people's solidarity across national frontiers, remains vital to any socialist movement. And today there exists a focus for such solidarity as has, perhaps, never before existed in the history of capitalism. The universalisation of capitalism has not brought about the cessation but instead the universalisation of struggle against capitalism. When, with globalisation, just about every state is following the same destructive logic, domestic struggles against that common logic can be the basis—in fact the strongest possible basis—of a new internationalism. But looking for that internationalism must not be an excuse for giving up on local national struggles. The main arenas of struggle against global capitalism still remain local and national. 'Workers of all countries, unite' remains the motto but this 'unity' obviously begins at home. There is a growing space for common transnational struggles, but the established order has still to be primarily fought on our own home pitch. As the *Manifesto* put it a long time ago: 'the proletariat of each country must, of course, first of all settle matters with its own bourgeoisie.' If the historical experience of more than a century since the Paris Commune is any guide this is exactly how it has been. The world revolutionary process has turned out to be extremely uneven and has moved from country to country.....

In other words, the nation state is indeed the concrete terrain on which the struggle for the radical transformation of society must begin and may have to be carried forward. It may be added that to argue that a nation state—and this includes states of the size and resources of Britain, France or Italy, or for that matter, India, China or Russia—cannot provide the ground on which the radical transformation of society can be attempted is to rule out such a transition for the forthcoming historical period. It is to abdicate the struggle for socialism in our time......

Third, it was Marx's prognosis that capitalism in its ultimate consequences could spell even 'the total destruction of humanity'. But, giving capitalism a short lease of life, Marx never explored this distant possibility. The distant possibility is now an imminent threat hanging over the future of humankind. As noted earlier, Rosa Luxemburg had summed up Marx's prognosis in her famous poser 'socialism or barbarism'. Capitalism living beyond its historical time indeed spells a future of barbarism for humankind. It could be a nuclear holocaust that its politics has threatened for more than half a century of the almost certain ecological disaster which—noise over so-called 'sustainable development' notwithstanding—capitalism's accumulative logic now portends. This makes the struggle for socialism all the more imperative and urgent today.

❖

It can be legitimately argued, without any underestimation of the prospects of socialist renewal in the advanced capitalist West or the erstwhile 'socialist world', that it is the countries of the third world which are likely to be the storm centres of such struggle, keeping socialism still on the agenda for the future of humankind. For the simple reason that they have no other choice, the common people there have no future otherwise. For the same reasons as in the past, the world revolutionary process is more likely to proceed through the backward, 'less developed' or 'developing' countries of the periphery and semi-periphery of the world capitalist system....

Therefore, a couple of additional observations on the question of struggle for socialism in these countries will not be out of place.

As a result of the unequal development in capitalist expansion, for causes that are neither local nor conjunctural but systemic and structural to capitalism as a world system, socialist revolutions or revolutionary movements of our time have appeared most often not at the centre but at the periphery of world capitalism—in Russia, China, Cuba, Indo-China, or in the name of socialism, Asia, Africa, and Latin America. For this is indeed where the worst victims of global capitalism's irrationality and exploitation are to be found, and therefore from where the challenge to capitalism emanated. The collapse of the Soviet Union does not end or modify the structural logic of global capitalism as manifested in poverty, underdevelopment, deindustrialisation and exploitation in Asia, Africa, and Latin America. It has only made global capitalism all the more powerful and given a new edge to its predatory logic. Any social system built on inequality in the command of human and natural resources works in many ways to reproduce itself and to increase the extent of the in-built inequality. So does capitalism. But as a market-governed system, capitalism carries this process to the extremes. The law of accumultion of capital inexorably produces, reproduces, and enhances inequality—wealth at one end and poverty at the other, not only within countries but on a world scale. And this is precisely what *globalisation*—another of the currently fashionable, reality-obscuring buzzwords—does. It has only sharpened the global capitalism's contradiction between its developed centre and exploited periphery. But this, if the past is any guide, also makes this periphery, the third world of the worst victims of contemporary capitalism, the site of revolts, of new countrywide challenges to the global capitalist order, of the resumed struggle for socialism.....

This, as mentioned earlier, is not to posit socialism as achievable today or tomorrow, or even the day after, but to posit it as people's alternative strategic goal, as the principle governing people's politics which links together their immediate, ongoing and emerging struggles in an ultimate project of revolutionary transformation of society, as the goal of a long transitional process whose specifics and speed will depend on the objective material conditions and the nature and balance of class forces involved at each stage of the struggle for the socialist goal. Immediately it means saying 'no' to globalisation, a 'delinking' from the global capitalist market—which however does not mean any kind of 'autarky'—and opting for a pro-people socialism-oriented autonomous development, one governed not by external imperatives, those flowing from the requirements of the world capitalist market (export-led growth, etc.) and the associated consumerism of the rich, but primarily by *internal* imperatives, those flowing from an assessment of country's own resources and the needs of its people. Development which can meet the material needs of the people in the third world is impossible within the framework of capitalism, national or globalised. Socialism has to be the strategic goal, whatever be the long or short transitional route to it. Historical experience allows no other choice....

Any attempt at saying 'no' to globalisation or 'delinking' is likely to exact a heavy price in many ways, including an unavoidable trade-off between the requirements of productivity and those of minimising the polarising impact of global capitalism's enourmous economic power. But once 'productivism' is abandoned and human welfare has the priority, this need not be a deterrent to adopting the strategy that 'delinking' involves. The details of economic policies in pursuit of this strategy will obviously vary from country to country. Here only a few broadly suggestive observations can be made.....

This strategy postulates a revolutionary state, representative of a popular front of workers and peasants, undertaking at the very outset a comprehensive programme of eradication of mass poverty, universal primary education, healthcare, housing, and provision of basic necessities for all. Initiating steps towards redistribution of incomes and development of backward areas will be a priority for state's active intervention in the economy which, even as it covers such areas as foreign relations, production and social distribution, research and training, and the like, will need to secure an effective transitional combination of planning and market forces without letting the market or its values take over. Agrarian revolution benefiting the rural proletariat and small farmers, thereby improving the productive capacity in the rural areas, and laying the basis of cooperative effort and voluntary collectivisation of agriculture should be high on its agenda of economic reconstruction, as should be the transformation of the informal sector into a popularly managed transitional economy. A building up or restructuring of industry is obviously necessary. But it can neither be one based on 'international competitiveness' (that is promoting exports through low costs of local labour) nor on 'import substitution' (promoting production for the consumption of the privileged local classes). Not that all effort in these directions is ruled out; some of it may even be necessary. Only priorities, for years to come, lie elsewhere. The important thing is to develop and organise productive forces in a manner that helps the rural sector leap forward, carries industrialisation to the countryside and in general ensures a pattern of growth which, refusing the wasteful production to satisfy elite consumerism, immediately benefits the popular masses, satisfying their basic needs, needs created and satisfiable by the redistribution of income. It should be obvious that the overall development of a third world country today cannot support the first world consumption levels of its elites. What is needed is a diversification and development of internal markets for domestic goods and services governed by the overall priciple that, beyond a certain necessary priority charges of an unequal nature, private needs and wants should be satisfied (and this goes for their increasing satisfaction) only at a level at which they can be satisfied for all, and beyond this all increase in the production of consumer goods should be for collective consumption....

Such a socialism oriented pro-people endogenous development process will draw on its own strengths and domestic resources and capacities, including those of the hardworking poor who yet remain the most creative ane productive force in society. It will give the common people, an overwhelming mass of workers and peasants, a positive stake in the economy and mobilise them for building a better society as well as for the inevitable struggle against global imperialism and its local allies or partners—an awakened and aroused people are indeed the best defence even against armed aggression. Needless to add, such popular mobilisation and struggle will be all the time necessary to carry through the strategic option that socialism-oriented delinking involves....

What the above strategy in effect demands is that not economics but politics, that is class politics, is put in command of the economy. 'Politics in command' means posing such questions as: growth? but which growth? for what purpose? for whose sake, whose benefit or profit? for what kind of society and within which environment? These are questions which are central to any search for a real alternative to capitalism, vital for the very survival of socialist movement today. They are all the more vital to pose in the third world suffering the worst ravages of capitalism. We must ask: is our goal meeting 'the needs of the economy', its 'anonymous masters' as they have been called—'abstractions such as financial markets, interest rates, exchange rates, commodity prices, indexes and statistical artefacts of all kinds'—or satisfaction of the needs of the people, allowing citizens the possibility of living as human beings? Is the starting point of our economic exercises to be calculation of deficits in order to cut them at the cost of the people or a determination of resources needed to satisfy people's needs in order to find or raise them? And our language? Do we practise the obscurantism of GDP, fiscal and revenue deficits, balance or payments, growth rates, etc., or speak more humanely in terms of such things as food and clean drinking water, health care and sanitation, housing and education, etc. so that economy becomes a transparent and accountable means of integrating these basic human needs of the people with a planned use of domestic resources, an use which also takes care of questions of equality, social justice including gender justice, employment, ecologically sustainable development, etc.?...

Economic and technological backwardness is often presssed as an argument to counter the plea for such autonomous economic development. (Getting access to the most modern technology is another usual argument for the need to actively participate in world trade). This calls for two very brief observations. In the first place it is useful to recognise that if, despite economic backwardness, the priority is given to the needs of the poorest and most deprived sections of the people, there is much that can be done at the outset even in absence of growth of productive forces. The redistribution of wealth and the use of idle or under-utilised human and material resources, their more productive deployment, can bring quick improvement in health, education and general living conditions of large masses of people. Early years of post-revolutionary societies in the Soviet Union and elsewhere provide ample evidence of this achievement which could be the basis for further development along socialist lines.

In the second place, once we overcome the fetishism of science and technology—which attributes to them properties or power they do not possess, and at times even expects them to do the job of a social revolution which they simply cannot—and, as with economic development so with technology, ask the basic question: 'technology for what purpose?', the argument for getting access to the most modern Western technology via globalisation—even if that was certain which it most certainly is not—loses much of its force. If the purpose is to satisfy the consumerist hunger of the privileged part of the population and therefore supply it with the most modern gadgets, designs, and goodies of the West, then rushing into globalisation is indeed understandable. But if the purpose or priority is to meet the needs of all the people for decent food, clothing and shelter, clean water, proper sanitation and health protection, education and cultural opportunities and the like, then devoting scarce resources to the most modern technology will be only wasteful because there is little in the latest technology of the West that would make a significant contribution. Infact what is most useful and relevant in technology, western or otherwise, for improving the way of life of the masses is widely known. Most of this technology is already available at home and what else is needed is obtainable in the normal course of managed trade....

❖

My observations so far are directly or indirectly relevant to the struggle for socialism in India. But, exemplified by the crises of CPM politics in West Bengal, the issue of this struggle has also come up, in a *sui generis* form, at the level of state politics in India which calles for a brief discussion in its own right.

Our struggle for freedom was a struggle to break out of a globalisation whose structural logic meant wealth in England and poverty in India. This was a necessary, though not sufficient, condition to be able to build a better life for our people. Aware of this exploitative logic of the global capitalist market, of centuries of experience of imperialism which provides little evidence of the beneficial effect of foreign investment in countries of the third world so far as the common people are concerned, and in its own way influenced by the interim successes of the Soviet Union, the post-independence (Nehruvian) national project opted for the strategic goal of a state-led self-reliant development promising economic growth with 'equity and distributive justice' to the people. For understandable reasons, it did not work out as Nehru had intended. There was a degree of economic growth but not much equity or distributive justice for the people and the project ended up building an India-specific government-supported third worldist capitalism. The rhetoric of 'socialistic pattern of society' only deceived the people, legitimised the statist capitalism that was coming up and created confusion about it as 'socialism' so that when, passing through a series of economic and political crises mid-1960s onward, the project finally collapsed in 1991, it was, and continues to be, misinterpreted as the failure of socialism in India.

The post-independence national project having collapse, 1991 onwards, India's ruling classes, through their different political formations, notably, the Congress and the BJP, have gone in for 'globalisation' as their new strategic option—a shift from the state-supported capitalism to a wholly privatised 'free market' capitalism and from self-reliance in economic development to reliance on Foreign Direct Investment and the multinationals, a shift euphemistically described as 'economic reforms' which has little to offer to the common Indian people.

The much-touted 'growth rates' are no indication of general well-being in a capitalist society and the so-called 'trickle down', if and when it occurs, is no better than feeding horses with oats so that something passes down to the road for the sparrows, as Galbraith once described it. Over the past decade-and-a-half or so, whatever be the benefits 'economic reforms' has brought to a small section at the top, it has further polarised our society, played havoc with the lives of our common people and pushed them still further into a peripheralised existence within the global capitalist system.

This is nothing surprising. 'Economic reforms' is only a euphemism for capitalist development whose structural logic, as a former President of Brazil once reported it to the masters in Washington, is : 'the economy is doing fine, the people are not.' A market-governed economic growth simply cannot deliver 'inclusive growth', to use another of the proliferating buzz words of our time. Instead, it is by its vary nature exculusionary, and the logic of the market, with its inevitable winners and losers, only makes for 'the secession of the successful', as the economist Robert Reich once phrased it. One look at their economic policies or concerns, their lifestyles and values will reveal how far 'the successful' of India's marketplace have already 'seceded' from the vast majority of their supposedly 'unsuccessful' follow countryman.

Pointing out that 'the unprecedented high economic growth on which privileged India prides itself is a measure of the high speed at which India of privilege is distancing itself from the India of crushing poverty (and that) the higher the rate of economic growth along this pattern becomes, the greater would be the underdevelopment of India', Amit Bhaduri has written: 'Destruction of livelihoods and displacement of the poor in the name of industrialization, big dams of power generation and irrigation, corporatisation of agriculture despite farmers' sucides, modernization and beautification of our cities by demolishing slums are showing everyday how development can turn perverse.... The devil in angel's guise would soon appear when large populations in rural India would be rendered landless, jobless, homeless, incomeless, rootless and displaced making way for gragantuan SEZs, the so-called epitomes of economic development.'

This raises what I have elsewhere described as 'contemporary India's most important *unraised* political question', the question of a people's strategic option, an alternative path of development distinct from and in opposition to that of India's ruling classes. The absence of this option, an alternative path of development, which can only be a socialism-oriented autonomous development, is the tragedy of the Left in India, part of the larger tragedy of the Indian people today.

And this is where lie the roots of the current crisis or tragedy of the CPM politics in West Bengal. That is how, despite its 30 odd years of uninterrupted power in the state, the CPM has not been able to project the image of doing something *significantly* different from or better than what is happening in other states; instead, operating on the terrain of bourgeois politics, responding to issues it presents and accepting the choice it offers, has entailed a corruption of consciousness and loss of revolutionary commitment. Criticism of bourgeois parties for failing by their own standards and programmes—a staple of parliamentary politics—has led to the CPM endorsing these standards and programmes itself so that its own original concerns have come to be given a go-by. And now, to the adulation of the corporate world and ridicule of the bourgeois media, West Bengal, like the other states, often in competition with them, has chosen to tread the centre-decreed neo-liberal, that is capitalist path of development. Left rhetoric apart, the only difference is that, possibly because the communists, unlike others, take theory—no matter what it is—seriously, their government alone, in its pursuit of this path (its corporate-led industrialisation and Special Economic Zones) has gone in for a shooting spree against the people!

The best of official defence is in terms of 'the role of a Left-ruled state government in a situation when the Centre has embraced neo-liberal polities'; 'The state governments', we are told, 'function within severe constraints. The simplistic notion that the West Bengal, Kerala and Tripura governments can adopt an alternative model to the Centre's policies has to be dispelled.'

At its worst there is unqualified justification and advocacy of neo-liberal policies, the corporate-ed industrialisation and Special Economic Zones. As this 'defence' is repeated by one Party leader or ideologue after another, one is reminded of the 'secondary illiterates' that poet Hans Magnus Enzensberger has spoken of—those who had the benefit of literacy once and come to know a few things, know them to be true, but now, gone illiterate, have forgotten whatever they once knew. (The tribe of 'secondary illiterates', in a truly rich variety, is growing and prospering outside the CPM too, if the media, especially TV, its talk shows, 'debates' and 'big fights' are any indication).

Capitalism is today so powerful and pervasive as to have become invisible, and it is all the more powerful for being invisible. You no longer see or recognise it, even refer to by its proper name. Thus it is 'globalisation', 'neo-liberalism' or 'liberalisation', 'structural adjustment', 'new economic policy', 'economic reforms' (and now with the CPM joining in) 'industrialisation', 'development and progress', even 'civilisation'—that is anything but capitalism. If you cannot even *see or think* capitalism you obviously cannot argue or act against it. And it capitalism is not recognised, its negation, socialism too disappears from your theory and practice. CPM leaders no longer speak in the language of socialism or class politics, not in public at least, not even when bourgeois ideologues of TV anchores get provocatively aggressive. And on the rare occasions they refer to Marxism, only vulgarise it. Here is a gem of a vulgarisation from Budhadeb Bhattacharjee, Chief Minister of West Bengal: 'From agriculture to industry, from villages to cities, this is civilisation. We Marxists never deny this aim. We too want this to happen'. One again recalls Hans Magnus Enzensberger. This time his moving short peom, *Karl Heinrich Marx*:

> I see you betrayed
> by your disciples
> only your enemies
> remained what they were.

Let me cut this dismal story short and speak of what the situation demands and what needs to be done. The situation demands that we return to calling things by their proper names and that right questions be asked if right answers are to be had. In other words, 'economic reforms' has a proper name, capitalist development, which, therefore, has to be rejected by communists or socialists at both national and state or local levels; and the question to be asked is: what can be done and what should not be done in West Bengal in the light of socialist principles? The need is to mobilise all the available resources within and without the Left parties to work out an answer to this question, that is, a programme of possible alternative socialism-oriented policies for the state. The resources are there, among them the Left's own mass base and organisations, the state's revolutionary traditions, a significant section of supportive intelligentsia and what Victor G. Kiernan has called 'mankind's moral reserves, its accumulation of moral capital', which socialism as an ideal can legitimately claim for itself and bank on. Socialism today, more than ever before has the potential to be 'a movement of immense majority in the interest of immense majority' as *Communist Manifesto* had proclaimed. Whole areas—education, healthcare, people's empowerment, ethical governance, environment, the closed down or locked out factories in urban areas, the stalled land reforms in rural areas and poverty and hunger in both places—are crying out for possible socialism-oriented initiatives in the state. The question is really of priorities, of putting politics, that is class politics in command and making socialism-inspired choices. The CPM itself could do with some socialism-inspired rectification.

It is not for me to suggest any concrete policies. This is best done by the people of West Bengal, its workers, peasants and the allied intelligentsia. I will only share a few general considrations. Primarily relevant at the national level, these considerations are not without their relevance for policies at the state or local levels.

The concept of 'development' is by nature ideological, suggestive of something desirable, involving 'the overarching question' I have raised and answered earlier, as to what kind of society we as human beings want to have. And the answer holds even for our poor and backward people. With its subordination of humanity to economy, and the consequent commodification of life, its ethos of greed, private acquisitive drives, egoism and aggression, competition and strife, in short rat race, its 'pseudo-moral principles', as Keynes once put it, 'which have hag-ridden us for 200 years (and) by which we have exalted some of the most distasteful of human qualities into the position of the highest virtues', and its production process which, as Marx said, turns worker into 'an automatic motor of a fractional operation' and 'cripples his body and mind', capitalist society is not the society we want to have. However poor or backward today, we need to *move away* from capitalism-oriented development and, however slowly or falteringly, *move towards* building a humane, socialist society, that fosters equality, cooperation, solidarity and respect for universal ethical values.

Again, 'development' is not synonymous with capitalist development, nor industrialisation ipso facto industrialisation sponsored by the private sector, corporate or any ohter. Nor is it that industrial activities are a natural monopoly of private entities, domestic or foreign. These are all ideology-determined positions, bearing witness to the hegemonic control of boureois ideology in our society these days. Historical experience makes it abundantly clear that paths of development other than the capitalist path are possible and there can be varieties of ways of industrialisation. For example, under the aegis of public or cooperative sectors, or as 'a programme of decentralised, employment intensive rural industrialisation through participatory democracy at the local level'.

The public sector *by itself* has no socialist implications. But it remains a serious industrialisation and employment option. Leave aside it successes elesewhere, even in India, the public sector has not been the kind of failure bourgeois ideologues make it out to be. There are, 'the stunning achievements of the National Thermal Power Corporation, Bharate Heavy Electricals, Nalco, the Oil and Natural Gas Commission, the Gas Authority of India or the Indian Oil Corporation' as a knowledgeable scholar has recently pointed out. And even the failure of public sector in India, such as it has been, is better understood as the failure of Indian democracy whence alone correctives to its malfunctioning or failure could have come, unlike the private sector where correctives come from the market, though often needing to be backed by the state. Therefore, the answer to this failure is a differently working democracy, an effective exercise of people's power in the state, and not a market-based private sector with its record of now well established worse failures.

As for corporate-led industrialisation being an answer to the problem of unemployment, such industrialisation generally does not generate much employment. Even as it simultaneously destroys employment in activities supplanted by it and its offshoots, its primary concern with profit-making involves cutting costs including labour costs. It is indeed an illusion that corporate industrialisation with its labour-saving automated technologies can ever generate net employment opportunities. As to the promise of 'indirect' employment created in the wake of industry, it has been well-described as 'a pie in the sky for the peasants'. Above and beyond all this is the overarching issue of the *quantity and even more quality of employment* in this age of globalisation, with its 'jobless growth', ruthless competition in the markets at home and abroad, and vast masses of our people reduced to be 'the reserve army of labour' for national and global capitalism.

Yet again: that the initial modern economic and industrial development, that in the west, occurred in the capitalist form is no reason to believe that this is the only way it can take place. Marx, who studied and theorised this development, certainly did not think so. In his now well-known letter to the editorial board of the Russian periodical, *Otechestvenniye Zapiski,* in response to a critic, 'honouring me too much' as he said, Marx specifically disowned any claims of having provided a 'master key' or 'universal passport' of 'a general historico-philosophical theory, the supreme virtue of which consists in being super-historical'. Rejecting the very notion of such a theory, he insisted that Capital contained 'my historical sketch of the genesis of capitalism in Western-Europe' and it must not be metamorphosed into 'an historic-philosophic theory of the general path every people is fated to tread, whatever the historical circumstances in which it finds itself.'......

Later, apropos of the possible historical options for Russia, Marx wrote of 'the finest chance ever offered by history to a people' to pass directly from a feudal to a communist phase of development. Marx believed that it could, provided there was an early revolution in Russia, early enough to save the peasant commune from being destroyed. Marx specifically distanced himself from his 'disciples' in Russia, Plekhanov and others, whose strictly evolutionist Marxism saw history as constituted by necessary stages and postulated the necessity of a capitalist stage in Russia's advance to socialism. Marx found their doctrines 'boring' and referred to them deriseively as 'Russian capitalism admirers'. Marx's position also involved a new recognition of the great revolutionary potential of the peasantry.......

I may add that historical experience of construction of socialism in the Soviet Union, during the Mao years in China and now in Cuba, more than validates the view that economic development including industrialisation along other than the capitalist path is possible.

I would here also like to reproduce a couple of passages from Marx and Engels which are in their own way relevant to the context of the issue under discussion. The passages from Marx relate to the Marxist concept of 'primitive accumulation of capital.'

> The capitalist system presupposes the complete separation of the labourers from all property in the means by which they can realise their labour... a process that transforms, on the one hand, the social means of subsistence and of production into capital, on the other, the immediate producers into wage labourers. This historical process... appears as primitive, because it form the pre-historic stage of capital....

Most basic in this process are

> those moments when great masses of men are suddenly and forcibly torn from their means of subsistence, and hurled as free and 'unattached' proletarians on the labour market... law itself becomes... the instrument of the theft of the people's land... The history of this expropriation, in different countries, assumes different aspects, and runs through its various phases in different orders of succession, and at different periods.

The passage from Engels deals with the question of 'small peasantry':

> What, then, is our attitude towards the small peasantry? How shall we have to deal with it on the day of our accession to power?... we foresee the inevitable doom of the small peasant, but .... it is not our mission to hasten it by any interference on our part.
>
> Secondly, it is just as evident that when we are in possession of state power, we shall not even think of forcibly expropriating the small peasants (regardless of whether with or without compensation), as we shall have to do in the case of the big landowners. Our task relative to the small peasant consists, in the first place, in effecting a transition of his private enterprise and private possession to cooperative ones, not forcibly but by dint of example and the proffer of social assistance for this purpose...
>
> We, of course, are decidedly on the side of the small peasant; we shall do everything at all permissible to make his lot more bearable, to facilitate his transition to the cooperative should he decide to do so, and even to make it possible for him to remain on his small holding for a protracted length of time to think the matter over, should he still be unable to bring himself to this decision.
>
> We do this not only because we consider the small peasant living by his own labour as virtually belonging to us, but also in the direct interest of the Party. The greater the number of peasants whom we can save from being actually hurled down into the proletariat, whom we can win to our side while they are still peasants, the more quickly and easily the social transformation will be accomplished.

Worker-peasant alliance was always at the core of revolutionary politics in Marx and Lenin.

Finally, there is the consideration that backwardness, such as there is, is not without its advantages. To put it most briefly, we can learn from the past experience with economic development, avoid its negative consequences, for example, the damage that capitalist development regularly inflicts upon human beings and natural environment. We can avoid the supposedly Marxist fascination with 'development of productive forces' that characterised the erstwhile 'socialist' economies and the obsession with 'economic growth' that plagues a capitalist economy. We can better negotiate the necessary trade-offs between economic development and social justice, between requirements of productivity or efficiency and environmental sustainability or quality life which is not entirely a matter of material progress or economic growth. In other words, our backwardness gives us the opportunity 'to do something new', the all-important option of a path of development which, subordinating economy to humanity, plans and develops it in a way that is, in Marx's word, 'worthy of our human nature.'

To conclude: it is simply inconceivable that there can ever be a situation where socialist principles do not indicate what can be done and what should not be done in the light of these principles. With politics, that is class politics in command, socialism-oriented initiatives are indeed possible at the state and local levels in the Left-ruled states. The need is for the CPM to mobilise all the resources within and without the Left parties to work out an alternative path of development geared to the strategic goal of socialism, implement whatever part of it is implementable at the state and local levels in the states where the Left is in power, and mobilise the people elsewhere for it with primacy given to extra-parliamentary struggles. This will make the Left-ruled states an example for the rest of the country and help the Party and the Left to rally all the radical forces in the country—NAPM, ultra-Left formations, militant NGOs, etc.—to emerge as a genuine and effective alternative to the ruling class class politics at the centre, with its own agenda of pro-people, self-realiant socialism-oriented development for the country. Of course, it is going to be a long haul and we don't have to mix up our own mortality with a time-table for the achievement of socialist goals.

But then, perhaps, it is too much or too late for the CPM to make a principled Marxist response to the situation it faces.

Some time back, in a critical comment on CPM's lack of a strategic goal, distinct from and opposed to that of the ruling classes, and its pursuit or neo-liberal policies in West Bengal, I had written:

> May be the Bhattacharjee turn in CPM politics signals that the old fire gone, happily 'in power' (rather quarantined) in its three States,

> the party, 'changes' and 'reformed' by its Bhattacharjees, no longer 'dreams' or thinks in Marxist or Leninst ways. 'One residual consequence of the Soviet collapse', I have noted elsewher, 'is the sudden inhibition of social imagination.' May be, like so many other Communists and Socialists, the CPM too has gone 'ralist' and finally succembed to this inhibition. It may even be that the party does not hope of ever being in power at Delhi with its own agenda, and, unable or unwilling 'to do something new' that the situation demands, it ses its future as a pro-people pressure group at the Centre and the best manager of 'economic reforms' in the States. There is plenty of room for such social democratic politics in our country today. And, as that 'most ambitious and intransigent theorisation of ultra-capitalism as a global order', Thomas Friedman's *The Lexus and the Olive Tree* has sloganised: 'one dare not be a globaliser today without being a social democrat'!

But I had then added:

> Sad about the situation one hopes that these 'may bes' are not yet a reality with the entire leadership of the CPM, that the party retains enough of Marxism and revolutionary commitment to keep its original promise to the India people.

Today, while sadness persists and hope has continued to dwindle, a possibility threatens which critics on the Left, including the ultra-Left, themselves unable to develop a genuine alternative to ruling class economics and politics, need to take serious note of. The policies and politics currently pursued by the CPM in West Bengal may well lead to its disintegration and decline as any kind of Left force in Indian politics. And this will be yet another tragedy for our long-suffering people.

Chapter 10

On Violence and the Question of Means and Ends*

I must confess that I have nothing much to say about 'Emerging Trends of Violence in North-West India'. I simply lack the requisite knowledge. As I see it, developments in recent years, particularly the economic policies and politics pursued by the ruling classes in India, have sharpened all the divides and fissures, failures and faultlines of Indian society, leading to new or increased violence in the country as a whole, which is often subsumed under what America's imperialist politics has come to describe as 'terrorism'—an omnibus concept that ruling establishments everywhere are lapping up as an ideological device that helps them escape responsibility for the diversely specific forms of violence engendered by their policies and politics. However, the organizers have, very rightly in my opinion, posited a very wide framework of discussion, with sub-themes and symposia touching on issues ranging from 'theoretical perspectives' to 'Gandhi and Non-Violence'. This allows me to make a few very general observations, including a brief comment on Gandhian non-violence and the question of means and ends.

Among the excitingly significant slogans and practices of the

---

* Inaugural Address to the Conference on 'Emerging Trends of Violence in North-West India' at Punjabi University, Patiala, on November 5, 2007

rebel students of Paris in the late 1960s was one where they used to ask of everyone who would address them to first tell them: 'Where do you speak from?' For every speaker inescapably speaks from a particular philosophical-political standpoint and owes it to his audience to publicly state it. It is only fair to acknowledge that I am going to speak from the standpoint of Marxism, rather Marxism as I understand it. For I have no pretensions to scholarship in Marxism. I picked up some on the way and have found it useful not only in my politics, or profession as a teacher, but in living my life as well. This last is not just a formal statement. Knowing Marx does make a difference to what sense you make of life, how you understand, live and act in the world. 'Indeed, I must confess that Karl Marx made a man of me', is how George Bernard Shaw once put it.

I shall be making my observations occasionally with the help of what I have said or written elsewhere.

Violence in our society, for that matter anywhere else in the world, is a social, conjuncturally produced phenomenon. It is not something inherent in human nature, as conservative thinking generally has it. Violence is far more repugnant to human nature than consistent with it. Human beings in fact have a natural aversion to violence, natural not in any transcendental sense, validated by the charms of abstract ideals or some superhuman source or authority, but in the same sense in which our moral principles or ideals are natural to human beings, produced and ordained by them in response to social needs, above all their need for a humane social existence. Human nature, a product of our interacting biological and sociological inheritances, is essentially modifiable and has been changing from one epoch to another. And this changing, reflected in the growth of our moral principles, ideals or values, has also meant human nature all the time becoming more *human*. That is how human beings' aversion to violence is a moral principle that needs to be respected, above all by revolutionary politics, though, it must be added, this does not exhaust the question of violence for it.

As a social scientific enterprise, the study of violence in modern societies posits a host of difficult problems. Immediately I would like to share two very general considerations in this regard.

The covering note for this conference speaks of 'violence in modern democratic societies'. This is an ideologically-loaded misdescription of things, which is quite common in contemporary social science literature. For what we have here is, at best, more or less democratic political systems and not democratic societies—a fact that was well noted for America's 'modern society' by the American Supreme Court Justice Louis Brandies a long time back. He had said: 'We can have a democratic society or we can have the concentration of great wealth in the hands of the few. We cannot have both'. In other words, 'democratic politics' notwithstanding, what we are dealing with are essentially undemocratic societies—class divided, unequal and exploitative, more or less iniquitous and oppressive. It is an important aspect of the undemocratic nature of these societies that some of the worst forms of violence in the world today is generated by their very structure and by the interests, policies and politics of those who are dominant in these societies. Hence there is a strong social pressure of the established dominant elites, the beneficiaries of the present organisation of society, to prevent a truthful understanding of violence in their societies. The problem here was well-stated by the English philosopher, Thomas Hobbes, way back in the 17th century. Pointing to the risky nature of the search for truth in the kind of societies we have, he had written:

> I doubt not, but if it had been a thing contrary to any man's right of dominion, or to the interest of men that have dominion, *that the three angles of a triangle, should be equal to two angles of a square*, that doctrine should have been, if not disputed, yet by the burning of all books of geometry, suppressed, as far as he whom it concerned was able.

More recently, Barrows Dunham has made the same point. Referring to the 'hierarchy of sciences' in the learned world—with mathematics and physics at the top and psychology and sociology at the bottom—and the reasons conventionally cited for the general backwardness and lack of prestige of the social sciences, he has written: 'The real reason is that the physical sciences are fairly neutral politically, while the social sciences are full of dynamite'. Barrows Dunham points out that 'generally speaking truth has been suffered to exist in the world just to the extent that it profited the rulers of society,' adding, 'there was a time—and not so very long ago—when these rulers could not afford the knowledge that the earth is round'.

Again, arguing that the backwardness of social sciences derives 'not so much from the intrinsic differences or the mere complexity of subject-matter, but from the strong social pressure of established ruling groups to prevent serious discussion of the foundations of society', J.D. Bernal in his classic *Science in History*, has pointed out that it has always been 'a very dangerous thing to look too closely into the workings of one's own society'.

It is indeed dangerous to be truthful about the way things are in 'modern' societies. Hence the *apologetic* character of most mainstream social science—'a secular priesthood' is how Chomsky once described its practitioners. Hence also the relevance of J.D. Bernal's adjuration:

> What social science needs is less use of elaborate techniques and more courage to tackle, rather than dodge, the central issues.

Given the importance of the issues involved, this adjuration is all the more relevant to the study of violence in our society.

My other consideration relates to techniques and methods of research which have, in their own way, facilitated, even reinforced the apologetic character of mainstream social science, pushing research away from a truthful understanding of things. As 'Methodology' what has dominated the field has been, in the main, a modernised version of 'the metaphysical mode of thought' which Engels had found wanting as 'one-sided, limited, abstract' because it studies things 'in their isolation, detached from the whole vast interconnection of things and, therefore, not in their motion, but in their repose; not in their life, but in their death....in considering individual things it loses sight of their connections; in contemplating their existence it forgets their coming into being and passing away; in looking at them at rest it leaves their motion out of account....it cannot see the woods for the trees.' An 'abstracted empiricism' has been abroad wherein 'the immediately observable, measurable fact' has been 'the moloch', as Paul Baran called it, 'which is always seeking to devour analytic thought in contemporary social science'; 'a social science of the narrow focus, the trivial detail, the abstracted almighty unimportant fact' is how C. Wright Mills described it. David McLellan has observed:

> ...the huge development of the social sciences in the century since Marx's death has often brought with it results that are thin in two respects: first in the vertical sense of being produced inside a narrow specialization by scholars who know more and more about less and less, and secondly in the horizontal sense that they spring from a preoccupation with the surface phenomena of society, so easily available for observation and quantification.

What I want to suggest is that along with courage, we need to have the requisite methodological sophistication that helps us search for interconnections—'the truth is the whole', Hegel has said—so that our study of violence takes us behind 'the appearance' to 'the nature of things' (Marx), that is, goes beyond descriptive or classificatory exercises to produce explanations. For that is, after all, what scientific understanding is about.

Way back in 1991, in my inaugural address to the Seventh State Conference of the Andhra Pradesh Civil Liberties Committee in Karimnagar—'Terrorism, State Terrorism and Democratic Rights'—I had briefly digressed to refer to violence in our society. Admittedly non-comprehensive and dated—particularly noticeable is absence of reference to gender dimension of violence where recent years have seen even the emergence of 'a political culture of sexual violence' as a mode of establishing the domination of one group over another or of stifling popular protest—the argument is not without its relevance today. I had said:

> (We don't have to) ignore or in any way underestimate the problem that private violence has come to be in our society today—its ever-

growing level, scale and diversity are indeed frightening. More and more of the conflicts and tensions generated in this society, above all, by its economy and politics, are seeking to express themselves outside the constitutionally ordained institutional frameworks, including the electoral process which has witnessed a steady decline in popular interest or participation in recent years. If there is widespread socio-political turbulence in society, there is also the widespread, not unjustified, impression that peaceful ways seldom work and issues arrest political attention only through recourse to violence. But any adequate response to the problem of this spreading violence in our society demands, at the very least, the recognition that while any form of violence in due course acquires a certain autonomous dimension, it always arises on and is sustained by a given socio-material basis, and that its various forms, various because of differences of causation, context and conjuncture, need to be carefully distinguished from each other before we decide and act in the matter.

There is, for example, the ordinary personal-motivated violence of different kinds in our society; a most common occurrence, for so long as we have money-and-profit dominated economy and society, all forms of crime and violence which promise to pay will continue to be committed. Any effective response to this violence, obviously, must begin by questioning this domination. Or, again, given the fact that this society is full of glaring injustice and iniquities, oppression and exploitation, it will always have its victims, frustrated and desperate men and women, ready to avenge themselves or their fellow victims, violently or otherwise. The need here is not to pass moral judgements or condemn their motives and actions, but to do whatever we possibly can to change their conditions which make such frustration and desperation, and the accompanying violence, inevitable.

Yet again, along with this 'normal' violence, we have a great deal of specific anti-people violence in our society. There is the recurring violence among the people, on one issue or another, often generated, even actively promoted, by unscrupulous politics at the top. Communal or caste violence is an obvious example; its condemnation, or opposition to such violence does not pose any problems at all. But we need to take particular notice of a more pervasive kind of private anti-people violence, which has finally arrived. The crisis of our poor possessive-market society, its manifold conflicts, its lumpen rapacity and crumbling structures of authority, with the people desperately struggling to survive, has given rise to a great deal of private violence of the rich and powerful against the people below—landlord armies, armed gangs or vigilante groups of the dominant classes, a rich variety of mafias, all sorts of 'goon squads', often linked with the police, politicians and businessmen, and always available for hire, and so on.

This violence, which, given its overall class character is generally backed, condoned or connived at by the state, deserves to be condemned without reservation. But this private violence, or for that matter lawless violence of the state itself, may provoke counter-violence on the part of the people. The people may be compelled to resist and even retaliate. They may find it necessary to turn to violence in sheer self-defence, or in defence of their democratic right to organise and struggle peacefully. They may need to resort to violence to defend the gains of their past struggles or to exercise the rights they still have including the right to vote, and so on. Such private violence by or on behalf of the people is well-justified; it certainly cannot be treated or condemned in the usual manner.

Our society has also given rise to certain specific forms of private violence, armed protests or struggles by individuals and groups, which are, despite their differences of causation, character and possible futures, generally lumped together as 'terrorism', the country's foremost political problem today. It is not my concern to analyse this problem beyond the general observations I have already made. But one aspect of it does interest us here. We don't have to lump together the various historically specific expressions of this private violence to recognise that even as this 'terrorism' fights the Indian state, it is known to turn, to a greater or lesser degree, against the people too. And this calls for a brief comment.

In any armed protest, resistance or struggle, the quality of its politics, politics commanding the gun, is of decisive importance. If the quality of this politics is poor, the gun becomes increasingly more important, it tends to itself become politics, just as state terrorism tends to do at the other end. In other words, if an armed resistance or struggle lacks a coherent liberationist ideology and programme, the requisite revolutionary theory and practice, which may help it gain the willing support of the people and mobilise them in a popular movement, it will, sooner rather than later, seek to use force to gain this support—really the people's acquiescence or compliance through fear and terror-hardened sensibilities. The policies and actions of the 'terrorists' become increasingly self-defeating, harming the very people whose cause they otherwise claim to espouse in taking up arms against the state. Just as at the other end, seeking to gain their acquiescence or compliance the same way, state terrorism too harms the people, alienating them from 'India' it claims to be defending for them against the terrorists. In this situation, dependence on foreign aid, aids only the process of moral and political degeneration of the original armed protest or struggle. The consequences are the dead-end game of killing and getting killed, a vicious circle of competitive atrocities and reprisals, intermittent internecine warfare among the various groups and a brutalisation of everyday life of the common people, all of which provides an excellent cover to all sorts of anti-social elements, and every kind of criminal activity. May be Punjab is very much on my mind, but the argument certainly has its general relevance.

Needless to add, terrorist violence against the people has no moral or political justification at all. It can only be condemned. Though, for obvious reasons, detailed knowledge and careful analysis is necessary before we pass judgment in each case. We need to know the truth and not its official version only.

In a society like ours which is structurally saturated with violence, with exploitation and oppression, injustice and inequality, there is always room for revolutionary violence. To reject such violence and uphold non-violence on principle has no justification, rational or moral, in the light of the historical experience of the struggles of the oppressed the world over. As the French philosopher Maurice Merleau-Ponty once put it, 'to teach non-violence is to strengthen established violence, that is to say, a system of production which makes misery and war inevitable.' Revolutionary violence aims at destroying this established violence and creating a new system of production and society in which 'misery and war' are no longer inevitable. It is a violence, as he put it, 'which transcends itself on the way to the human future'. Thus, for example, the problem that the "Naxalites', as they are called, present to our society is not one of private violence to be condemned, but of an exploitative and oppressive social order crying out for revolutionary change.

Revolutionary violence may indeed be criticised, even rejected, but not on abstract moral grounds. The grounds have to be specific such as a negative assessment about its 'appropriateness' in a given situation, a lack of 'proportionality' between means and ends, and so on. On the basis of historical experience, it is also possible to argue against the general efficacy and appropriateness of individual or group acts of revolutionary violence. Even when deemed necessary, one needs to be aware of the dangerous possibility of getting sidetracked or lost in a vicious circle of violence and counter-violence. It is thus absolutely imperative for those so involved to be constantly self-critical of their theory and practice in this regard, as elsewhere, in the interests of the revolutionary movement as a whole. It seems to me, however, that the real issue of revolutionary violence is not so much its rights or wrongs as the taking of sides in the ongoing class war between the people and their oppressors and exploiters.

Looming large over all these forms of violence in our society is the violence that Indian state has come to represent today. The issue here is not its inherently violent nature *as a state*, or the violence implicit in the socio-economic structures this state normally defends, violently or otherwise. What needs to be noticed is its emergence as the single large perpetrator of violence on the people today. Such is the explicit material expression of this violence in recent years that scholars and laymen alike have been compelled to speak of 'state terrorism' or 'the terrorist state' in contemporary India. There is the ever-growing draconian legislation and the ever-expanding apparatus of repression, and the ruthless use of both everywhere in this vast land of ours. The old, extended or new laws are there—ESMA, MISA, NSA, different Armed Forces Special Powers Acts, many kinds of Disturbed or Terrorist Affected Areas Acts, amendments to the Constitution and the Criminal Procedure Code... and so on—which provide for new structures of authority, a new hierarchy of courts, new legal procedures, new ranges of offences, new and stiffer penalties, new detentions without trial and new and harsher powers for the police, para-military forces and the army. New restrictions have come to be imposed on the life and liberties of the people in violation of old and established Constitutional safeguards and new authorisation provided for the lawlessness of the state, including extra-judicial kidnappings and killings known as 'encounters'; and along with 'custodial deaths' even the phenomenon of 'missing', long associated with the dictatorial regimes of Latin America, has arrived.

To execute these laws and this lawlessness, along with the old we now have any number of new police and paramilitary formations, new security set-ups, armed wings, guards and protection groups and the rest, well-supported by the army on the one hand and the well-rewarded state or politician-sponsored terrorist or vigilante groups on the other. The much-touted 'financial crunch' notwithstanding, financing all this has been no problem at all. In large 'terrorist-affected' parts of the country, it is a situation of massive power, without any checks or accountability, but with an irresistible temptation to confuse every expression of popular protest, dissent or even recalcitrance with terrorism and therefore meant to be handled with ruthless brutality. Unchecked power has its own logic; corruption rampant in the system has taken care of the rest. Whatever its other problems, or problematic success in fighting 'terrorism', the state's terrorism has been remarkably successful in alienating the people and pushing them out of its own 'mainstream', leaving the 'national press' free to deceive itself and mislead the rest of 'the Indian nation'.

Only the nationalistically blind will fail to see that it is this mindless violence of the state, growing ever more mindless in its failure or impotence and the accompanying loss of legitimacy, which spawns anew and fuels the terrorist violence in the country. The two in fact regularly feed, justify and legitimise each other—all the while adding to the misery and suffering of the common people everywhere.

❖

The above discussion of violence in Indian society of course requires to be updated. Perhaps I also need to take specific note of violence that America's foreign policy describes as 'terrorism' and the kinds of violence in our society now sought to be subsumed under this concept; though, as already suggested, most of this violence, including the *jihadist* version is the result of policies and practices of the concerned ruling elites[1]; the associated religious fundamentalism, in all its rich variety, too has come up the same way on the social-material basis provided

---

1. The *jihadist* violence in its international dimension is in fact understandable only in relation to America's imperialist policies and politics in the Middle-East which have, particularly with the issue of Palestine, made it the site of possibly the most outrageous violence of our times.
2. As I have suggested elsewhere, contemporary religious fundamentalism is significant, partly at least, for its opposition to 'consumerism of the West' or 'the American way of life', the

by the kind of society and politics we have.[2] But immediately I want to focus on 'structural violence', not only because, though the most basic form of violence in our society, it remains least understood and recognised, but even more because, equating revolution with violence, the votaries of non-violence are evading the key question of revolutionary transformation of our society that elimination of this violence calls for. They continue to advocate non-violence or 'the Gandhian way', dialogue, debate, democracy, etc., to achieve ends which these methods regularly fail to achieve because what is involved here is a structural transformation of society which the theory of these votaries of non-violence, in its abstract and exclusive concern with non-violence (or violence), cannot accommodate and their practice, therefore, cannot accomplish.

❖

Marx's historical materialism, his discovery of 'the law of development of human history', indeed opened up the continent of social sciences, as Althusser stated it years ago. One signal achievement here was a structural mapping of society and social change. Marx's analysis of the modern capitalist society postulates a structural dynamics for its mode of production—an interchange with nature to satisfy human wants, to maintain and reproduce life, which is necessary in all social formations and under all modes of production—which for all its productive achievements is structurally saturated with violence, so degrading and damaging to human beings that Marx saw it as not 'worthy of their human nature' and argued for its negation in a socialist mode of production.

The structural violence inhering in capitalism is today starkly visible in every part and aspect of contemporary capitalist world. It is visible in the impoverishment and immiseration on the rise just about everywhere in the world; in

---

imperialist cultural domination it is resourceless to understand or overcome. And it has acquired this significance because the traditional Left alternative, in particular the great revolutionary traditions of Marxism and communism seem to have become, for the time being at least, unavailable.

the statistics on rates of unemployment, poverty, homelessness and hunger; in the sullen slums of major cities of Western bourgeois democracies, proliferating urban ghettoes of the gritty capitals of former Soviet bloc countries and the warrens of teeming tumbledown shanties of the peripheral South; in the gross inequalities of the world, the wretchedness of the impoverished and excluded within the rich Western societies and the huge mass of misery in the poorer countries; in the morally intolerable and socially unnecessary suffering—what Bourdieu has called *la misere du monde*—produced by capitalism everywhere.

It is no different with India as a 'developing' capitalist society. The evidence is there, scattered all around us if only we are willing to see: a little reason and ability to interconnect is all that is needed. Violence is not only the blood you see flowing.[1] It is violence also when blood dries up in the veins of the poor in our country. It is violence also when 'the market' lords it over life and millions go to bed hungry, when children die at childbirth or if they survive the first year, die a few years later down the line of hunger, malnutrition or disease, when debt-ridden farmers commit suicides, when the young suffer the indignity of unemployment, kids drop out of school to pick rags or labour at *dhabas*, and women walk miles for water, when whole populations are rendered landless and homeless to make

1. Though, even here, the bloodshed by the ruling classes and their counter-revolutions has been far more and worse than the bloodshed attributed, to revolution or revolutionaries by the ideologues and historians of the ruling classes. The October Revolution of 1917 is as good an example here as any other. Bourgeois propaganda's violence in the Russian Revolution did not accompany but *followed* a most peaceful revolution, and was the result of the foreign-backed armed counter-revolution by the former ruling classes. It was a General Kornilov, a major leader of the White Terror unleashed by the counter-revolution, who said: 'The greater the terror, the greater our victories'. 'We must save Russia', he declared, 'even if we have to set fire to half of it and shed the blood of three-fourth of all the Russians'.

way for Special Economic Zones or livelihoods are destroyed in the name of development. There is violence also in the 'terrible costs of not changing the existing order' that Nehru once spoke of....

Incidentally, this 'changing the existing order', a structural transformation, is what Gandhian non-violence is resourceless to carry out and equating revolution with violence, its present-day advocates regularly evade.

❖

For socialists or communists revolution, a socialist transformation of society, is a matter, not of violence or non-violence, but of fundamental structural change in society. As I have written elsewhere: it is not a matter of resorting to violence or picking up arms, which are purely tactical questions, though not to be dismissed on abstract moral grounds. Socialism is about a fundamental change in social production relations which a real, not merely juridical or formal, social ownership of the means of production makes possible. And here, properly interpreted, Marx still remains the guide: 'peaceful if possible, with arms if necessary'. That is, it all depends on historical conditions and possibilities of the objective situation. A peaceful transition is of course the desirable thing. But the issue involved—peaceful or otherwise, or how peaceful—is really one for the ruling classes to respond to: are they willing to accept the people's peaceful, democratic verdict for socialism? As it is, these ruling classes have not even remotely shown this willingness so far. Instead they have invariably used their enormous economic and political power, often across countries, to thwart changes far, far less radical in nature than socialism. One has only to recall the overthrow of Mohammed Massadegh in Iran in 1953, of Arbenz in Guatemala in 1954, of Joao Goulart in Brazil in 1964, of Juan Bosch in the Dominican Republic in 1965, of Salvador Allande in Chile in 1973, and so on right up to the current efforts to overthrow Hugo Chavez in Venezuela — all of them constitutional democratic regimes...

The world over any effort to seek radical or revolutionary change through democratic processes has been seen by the ruling classes as a challenge to capitalism or the established order and therefore too dangerous to be allowed to proceed. It has been regularly thwarted or destroyed. Defending America-backed armed intervention against democracy in Chile, Henry Kissinger declared: 'I don't see why we have to let a country go Marxist just because its people are irresponsible'. I will readily concede that democracy, bourgeois democracy to be precise, has often checked or corrected particular abuses of capitalism, made the struggle against its exploitation less painful, sometimes ratified victories that occurred elsewhere. But it has never yet led to the liberation of the oppressed classes.

Our experience with democracy in India has been no different. More than a decade back, in 1992, I had written:

> Obviously, democracy has not meant effective political power for the Indian people. Within almost two decades of Indian freedom and democracy, even so sympathetic a scholar as Gunnar Myrdal, a personal friend of Nehru, wrote of 'the new government's role as the successor to the British raj', of 'the gulf between rulers and ruled', and the life-style and conduct of the new rulers which 'encouraged the view that political independence had done little more than displace a foreign with a native privileged group'. Pointing out that 'India is ruled by a select group of upper class citizens who use their political power to secure their privileged positions' and that 'the power struggle has mainly remained one between individuals and groups in the upper class in the broader sense', he concluded: 'Democracy has not enabled the majority of poor people to grasp, and organise themselves for utilising political power to advance their own interests'. In 1973, V.K.R.V. Rao spoke of 'a political alliance of the intermediate classes with the upper classes, resorting to socialist ideology only to win mass support but using all levers of power to facilitate a type of capitalist development in the interest of a narrow section of Indian society'; and fifteen years later he most emphatically stated that so far as 'the poor and deprived sections of the people' are concerned, 'parliamentary democracy has not been able to meet the challenge'.

The assessment still holds.

This however is not to reject whatever, or whatever kind of, democracy we still have. As I stated above, a peaceful socialist transformation, a transformation through democratic processes remains desirable. But a most important qualification has to be added. Again, as I have argued elsewhere:

> For the people, therefore, if or when they decide to travel the peaceful road, the principle is clear. This is how, in his times, Cromwell, forced to make a revolution, put it: 'Trust in God, and keep your powder dry!' How people 'keep their powder dry' is not my concern at the moment. Only do it they must. What is involved is forging adequate extra-parliamentary sanctions to defend and enforce their democratic verdict, which includes preparedness to counter the inevitable 'slave-holders rebellion', as Marx had called it. Failure to do so will cost them dear, as it did the Chilean people in 1973. They failed to develop their own armed counterweight to defend their democratic verdict against the military coup which soon defied and overturned it, and eventuated in a most brutal counter-revolution, massacre of virtually the entire Chilean left, including the democratically elected President Allende himself and the setting up of the notorious Pinochet dictatorship, all aided and abetted by the forces of international capital headed by the well-known defender of democracy in the world, the United States. I don't have to detail the lessons.

Socialists or communists, I may add, do not *advocate* violence. For them it is a tragic necessity to defend the revolution with violence when the ruling classes violate the victories and rights of the people. People have a natural aversion to violence and revolutionaries respect it—a respect, as Trotsky has underlined in his account of the Russian Revolution, the Bolsheviks demonstrated remarkably in 1917.

Gandhi remains central to any discussion of violence, and therefore non-violence in the world today. Presently his 'non-violence' is a matter of celebrations the world over. If his birth and death anniversaries are occasions for elaborate official and non-official functions in India and the University Grants Commission (UGC) has gone into an overdrive with seminars on 'Gandhi's Satyagraha', etc., the United Nations has declared October 2 as the World Non-violence Day and for the Nobel Foundation it is 'a big regret' that he could not be awarded the Peace Prize. Obviously, Gandhi has been well sanitised and tamed, and accommodated in the system; his 'non-violence' is no threat to the established order or ruling class hegemony anywhere.

This however is too much or too problematic to concede for the present-day votaries of non-violence. As the argument over the efficacy of non-violence proceeds, it is customary for them to refer to 'the two apostles of peace', Martin Luther King Jr. and Nelson Mandela. They are supposed to exemplify the successful use of Gandhi's doctrine of non-violence. King is lauded as 'an apostle of social harmony' along with a rather loud advocacy of 'Gandhi-King' style of politics, and Mandela is hailed 'as the most outstanding Gandhian leader of modern times'. There is no critical assessment of either King's civil rights movement in the US or Mandela's Gandhianism in South Africa, of what is gained or even lost in the latter case, no awareness at all of how the issue of structural transformation of society still remains central to the situation in each case.

One does not have to deny the gains of the black civil rights movement to note that the Voting Rights Act was described by Ronald Reagan as 'humiliating to the South' and that 'white backlash' and 'racial polarisation' are still facts of life and politics in the United States. Ramsey Clark, former US Attorney General has even suggested a reason here why Islam 'has touched the lives of African Americans'—'they find peace, dignity and a faith they can believe in'. As a recent comment has it:

> The civil rights movement's challenge to Jim Crow in the south had secured major advances, but had also exposed the intractability of American racism. Legal segregation had been destroyed, but economic inequality loomed larger than ever.

No wonder King was himself soon moving to a more radical understanding of the situation. Mike Marqusee has noted:

> After the first flush of fame, leading the Montgomery Bus Boycott in 1956-57, and winning a Nobel Peace Prize in 1963, it would have been easy for him to rise above the fray and enjoy his prestige. He chose to do the opposite. He chose to take the hardest course, confronting the realities of power, the scale of change necessary and the obstacles to that change....The real Dr. King was an altogether more demanding and inspiring figure than the emollient angel being celebrated.

Assessing the overall situation, this is what I wrote sometime back:

> The majority of blacks constitute a distinct underclass in the US economy that has been reproduced over and over again since the time of slavery. And despite all the hype over the achievements of the 'Gandhian' civil rights movement, the black youth have remained the underclass they were. The issue of justice to this vast majority of women and men goes to the very heart of the *totality* of US life and cannot be really resolved without structural, that is revolutionary transformation.
>
> It is significant and worth pointing out that the main lesson that grew out of the later phase of the black civil rights movement was that a poor people's movement which is to continue to advance must eventually evolve from a question of rights to a question of power, from civil or political to human emancipation. And this requires a shift in the nature of the organised struggle towards class politics, that is, collective resistance to capitalism. It is not surprising that by 1968, shortly before his assassination, Martin Luther King Jr. was publicly speaking of what he called 'radical redistribution of economic and political power' and 'a radical reconstruction of American society', of 'self-transforming and structure-transforming direct action'. 'We are engaged in the class struggle', he publicly stated, and pointed out: 'We have been in a reform movement... But after Selma and the voting rights bill (in 1965) we moved into a new era which must be an era of revolution. I think we must see the great distinction here between a reform movement and a revolutionary movement'.

Again, one does not need to be an expert on the history of struggle against apartheid in South Africa to note that Nelson Mandela's African National Congress, during its decades-long struggle, was never a votary of non-violence, Gandhian or any other. It had an effectively functioning military wing. And it had an economic programme which is best described as socialism-oriented. Two weeks before he was freed, in January 1990, in a note to his supporters from prison, Nelson Mandela had said: 'The nationalisation of the mines, banks and monopoly industries is the policy of the African National Congress (ANC) (and changing) our views... is inconceivable. Black economic empowerment is a goal we fully support and encourage, but in our situation state control of certain sectors of the economy is unavoidable.' Such indeed was the policy of ANC spelled out in 1955 in its Freedom Charter. Now turned Gandhian and reconciliationist, 'an apostle of peace' and a votary of non-violence, Mandela, along with Mbeki and others has also turned away from ANC's programme of a revolutionary restructuring of South African society and opted for neo-liberal, admittedly Thatcherite policies, with disastrous consequences for the common people of South Africa. After over a decade of this new agenda (1994–2006), Naomi Klein in her book *The Shock Doctrine* has thus highlighted the toll, showing conditions today much worse than under apartheid: the number of people living on less than $1 a day doubled from two to four million; the unemployment rate more than doubled to 48% from 1991 to 2002; only 5,000 of 35 million black South Africans earn over $60,000 a year; the ANC government built 1.8 million homes while two million South Africans lost theirs; nearly one million South Africans were evicted from farms in the first decade of democracy; as a result, the shack-dweller population grew by 50%, and in 2006, 25% of South Africans lived in them with no running water or electricity. And there's more: the HIV/AIDS infection rate is about 20%, and the Mbeki government shamefully denied the severity of the crisis and did little to alleviate it; it's been a major reason why average life expectancy in the country declined by 13 years since 1990; 40% of schools have no electricity; 25% of people have no access to clean water and most who do can't afford the cost; and 60% of people have inadequate sanitation, and 40% no telephones....

I will only add that, unlike in India where poverty and wretchedness of the poor is more visible, in South Africa it remains tucked away in the poor townships, 17-18 kilometres away from the city, as was the case under apartheid.

With Nelson Mandela's Gandhian turn, South Africa today is a classic example of a revolutionary resistance movement's betrayal of its people.

❖

Even in India, Gandhi's non-violence has not been the success it is made out to be, not unoften simply assumed to be. Apropos this, way back in 1990, I had written:

> ...In large historical processes there are continuities and there are breaks, at times even revolutionary breaks which involve a change in the *economic basis*, the economic-structural relations, of society. In India, in our times, no revolutionary break has occurred, neither at independence, nor afterwards. The balance of social forces and ideals in the national movement resulted in the settlement of 1947 —its 'transfer of power' involving no basic economic or social or state structural change, but putting new, now *Indian* ruling classes in control of the state power in India. (Nearly two decades later, Gunnar Myrdal was to write of 'the new government's role as the successor to the British raj', of 'the gulf between rulers and ruled' and the life-style and conduct of the new rulers which 'encouraged the view that political independence had done little more than displace a foreign with a native privileged group'). The new rulers set about India's economic development even as they maintained, of course, with due modifications, the class (exploitative) structure of the Indian society as a whole. It is the logic of this structure, the new and the old well articulating with each other, which had a determining influence on what eventually came to be built in the country—an India-specific state-supported capitalism, with every aspect of our social life—politics, culture, morality, everything, everywhere—bearing the mark of this somewhat comprador capitalism.
>
> In these matters, the *subjective* concerns of political leaders, of rulers or their political representatives, matter—but only marginally. In the absence of revolutionary politics which changes the *objective*, economic-structural basis of society, not only does the logic of this basis assert itself in the economy, it also decisively conditions developments in other areas of social life, in politics, morals, culture, ideology, etc.—all changes, no matter how important otherwise, yet remain essentially superstructural. Thus, for example, we know of Gandhi's love and concern for the Indian people which to him meant, above all, the impoverished peasantry of India—'the semi-starved masses... slowly sinking to lifelessness' as he once put it—a love and concern (rather paternal in nature, always fearful of people straying from the 'right' path) which was possibly the most distinguishing feature of Gandhi's social philosophy. Metaphorically speaking, he wanted the peasant to

> inherit this country. Yet it is not Gandhi's peasant but a Birla who inherited India in 1947, along with, of course, communal violence, the partition, and much else that Gandhi did not want. And of decisive importance here is the fact that, besides other limitations, Gandhi's political theory and practice (non-violence, trusteeship, satyagraha, etc.) had no room at all for any genuine economic-structural change, not even for radical land reforms, a necessary though not sufficient condition for any improvement in the life of the vast masses of Indian peasantry. Inevitably he failed, here as also elsewhere in most of his declared purposes. Seeking to ensure 'the rights alike of prince and pauper', Gandhism, in effect, only served as a petty-bourgeois ideology in the service of the big bourgeoisie, in the Indian historical process. It is a mark of the greatness of Gandhi, a truly magnificent human being with all his faults, frailties and foibles, that in sharp contrast to the opportunism or pettiness of his many followers, he recognised his failure when it finally occurred, and confessed it—'I do not understand how all these terrible things are happening in our country… What mistakes have we made, for we must have made mistakes? Otherwise how could all these things happen?'—and died, as he had lived, fighting for his people, a fulfilled yet disillusioned and disconsolate man.

I had gone on to refer to Nehru also, whose social theory came to exhibit the same inadequacy, a lack of structural mapping of society and social change.

> Or, again, we know of Nehru's concern to build socialism in India. He not only argued that 'the only key to the solution of… India's problems lies in socialism', but had insisted: 'and when I use this word I do so not in a vague, humanitarian way, but in a scientific, economic sense'. Aware of the need for 'vast and revolutionary changes', he most perceptively spoke of 'terrible costs of not changing the existing order'. Yet, once in power, Nehru shied away from the cost of even genuine land reforms—'they will present numerous practical problems involving basic social conflicts (and may) give rise to organised forces of disruption', the *Draft Outline* of the First Five-Year Plan warned. What is more, he simply abandoned socialism 'in a scientific, economic sense', that is, as a basic economic-structural change. Apart from the insistence on the state playing 'a vital part in planning and development', the focus is increasingly on the need to ensure 'rapid economic development with continually rising levels of production', 'to

exploit natural resources', 'to take sufficient advantage of the advance in science and technology', etc. In fact, in a subtle, perhaps unconscious but politically most convenient shift, he now sought 'the key' not in socialism but in the development of 'science and technology'—'the temples of modern India' and all that. He increasingly opted for what I would describe as 'fetishism of science', that is, investing science with powers it does not in itself have, expecting it to do the job of a social revolution, which it simply cannot. Inevitably, once again, the logic of the economic structure asserted itself. What got built in India was not socialism but capitalism, a state-supported capitalism. The rhetoric of socialism, now redefined as 'a socialistic pattern of society', whatever that meant, served only to deceive and win mass support. And Nehru, even as he gave India the then much-lauded 'vision of socialism', in effect, helped reduce it to only 'a vision' in India. History is indeed a very cruel mistress.

Indian today is indeed a monument to the failure of Gandhi and his non-violence. He himself stands reduced to a symbol frozen in monuments, statues, road names and occasionally the politicians' Khadi, and his non-violence to a subject for Bollywoodian *gandhigiri*. Not a single one of his ideas and ideals, his hopes and dreams for the Indian people, the ends his politics of non-violence sought, has been realised. Instead, India, in its post-Independence capitalist development, has steadily moved away from them, leaving the country more riddled with conflict, disharmony and violence than ever before in its history.

Even so, through all this, all his faults, frailties and failures, all the inadequacies of his theory and practice, peeps a Gandhi who needs to be distinguished from the motley crowd of 'pious do-gooders' and putative 'statesmen' at home and abroad, including not a few Gandhi Peace Prize winners, who today invoke him and preach non-violence to the world. They simply lack Gandhi's greatness of spirit, his honesty and courage, his humanity and, above all, his passionate love and concern for the common man which is indeed *the* distinguishing and redeeming feature of his social theory. They have little in common with a Gandhi who recognised *himsa* in 'the wanton humiliation and oppression of the weak and the killing of their self respect', in 'the starvation and exploitation to which they are subjected', a Gandhi to whom freedom had no meaning until 'we have wiped every tear from every eye', who offered this 'talisman' for choosing the right course of action: 'Recall the face of the poorest and the weakest human being you may have seen and ask yourself if the step you are contemplating was going to be of any use to him? Will he gain anything by it? Will it restore him a control over his own life and destiny?' Gandhi sought a pro-people transformation of Indian society, even though he had no clear theory of how to go about it. He denounced the shackles of a false civilisation and inspired hatred against it, even though his theory provided no solution here, no way to overcome and go beyond it. This Gandhi's legacy is indeed 'political dynamite'. Hence the need to rescue Gandhi from the assorted lot of present-day Gandhians and make him part of Indian people's emancipatory project today—doing this not eclectically, adding up his name or ideas, but in a proper theoretical manner, within an adequate, self-consistent framework which, in my opinion, is best provided by Marxism, its basic understanding of society and social transformation.

Even with the best of the present-day Gandhians, given the essential inadequacy of their theory—which, incidentally, they share with Gandhi—their advocacy of non-violence is only so much moralising politics, a form of utopianism which in its ultimate outcome only serves conservative ends.

Apropos this, I have commented:

> A most important aspect of Marxism is its rejection of utopianism in politics. Criticism of utopian thinking by Marx and Engels, regarding socialism or elsewhere, is common knowledge. In a general way Marxism enjoys a theoretical advantage in that its analysis or understanding of society and therefore its politics is a structural and a non-moralising one. In 'Marxism of Karl Marx' moral passion as part of revolutionary ethics is of course central to revolutionary politics, but by itself it generates only a most ephemeral kind of politics which is quickly reabsorbed and recontained by the system it seeks to question and transform. In fact, as historical experience reveals, a moralising politics tends to develop where a structural cognition and mapping of society is blocked. Or, as a scholar has well put it: 'voluntaristic wishful

> thinking—often wedded to a direct appeal to the authority of claimed moral imperatives—tends to predominate in politics precisely at times when the advocated political objectives are poorly grounded, due to the inherent weakness of those who promote them. Direct appeal to morality in such political discourse is used as an imaginary substitute for identifiable material and political forces which would secure the realisation of the desired objectives.'

❖

Advocacy of non-violence is almost invariably accompanied by a confused and confusing discussion of the question of means and ends. I would like to make a brief clarificatory comment on the controversy[1] and then relate it to the issue of the often cited or acclaimed success of Gandhi's non-violence in winning India's freedom.

It is axiomatic that the means are justified by the end they achieve; there is simply no other way to justify them. As Professor G.C. Field, a scholar of impeccable orthodoxy has argued in his book *Moral Theory*:

> Of course the end justifies the means; if we will the end we will the means to it. As for doing evil that good may come, it is really a meaningless phrase: because if good comes of it, and it was done with that intention, it cannot be evil.

Put a bit strongly, the argument essentially holds. Against this we have the conventional view. As formulated by one of its leading advocates:

> I suppose that of the many lessons that Gandhiji taught, perhaps the most important was that means are more important than ends. If in the process of achieving the ends, the means are bad or twisted, we will not reach the ends. If our aim in life is a good life, how can we reach it by unworthy means?

Though well-meaning, this is a confused view and the confusion here is caused by three interrelated reasons.

The first reason concerns the origin and nature of the morality or 'goodness' of the means. In the conventional view

1. The argument here is reproduced from John Lewis' two contributions to *The Modern Quarterly*, in 1946 and 1950.

they are assumed to be or treated as 'good' in themselves, which is simply not the case. Our morals, ideals or ethical principles do not exist in themselves, in their own right, independently of nature and history, rooted in God, gods or scriptures or in some way possessing an eternal, absolute, authoritative reality of their own. According to a naturalistic view of man and his world, now accepted by most scholars of ethics and by anthropologists, psychologists and scientists in general, all mental, moral or spiritual phenomena are genuine functions of living organisms at the human level of development (just as life itself is a mode of behaviour of matter at a particular level). It is thus argued that the evolutionary process has risen higher than its source, nature has evolved humans with their morals, ideals or ethical principles. These emerge from the requirement of social life and derive their validity from their usefulness. Hence they are also subject to modification according to circumstances and may, under certain conditions, be suspended.

The conventional view, in effect, postulates that we must confine ourselves to *means that are in themselves good*, judging the morality of our actions by reference to some absolute rule and not by the consequences. But this is not a moral proceeding. Sound ethics requires us always to judge the action by the results, good and bad, and not by its conformity to a rule, regardless of results. The validity of moral rules does not lie in themselves as though strict conformity to them were good regardless of what happened. That a moral rule has come to be established means of course that it is generally to the interests of people that it should be followed and that when it is broken evil results, but that does not mean that it must never be broken. It may be necessary, though if that is the case it will be exceptional and regrettable, and evil will follow.

This immediately suggests the second reason for confusion in the conventional view: the failure to draw a distinction between what is evil and what is morally wrong. It is a good rule, for instance, not to inflict pain, but serious operations involving suffering are sometimes necessary, and if we avoid them even more pain will result. The evil in such cases has to be accepted. Again, lying is generally wrong and always an evil, but we resort to deception of the enemy in war, and sometimes conceal the truth from sick persons. There are certainly occasions when not to lie would be a most immoral course of conduct, as when we might have to misdirect an intending murderer to save his victim's life. There is an ethical principle involved here: *There is no moral rule that duty may not compel us to break in exceptional cases.*[1]

Every morally serious person finds himself from time to time in a situation where he must break a moral rule to achieve a greater good; and he believes that he is *right* to do so. The principle that it is never right to depart from moral principles, even to achieve some good end, no matter how many people would suffer if the rule were not broken, far from reflecting a superior ethical standpoint, is supremely unethical and is generally regarded as such.

When moral rules are broken we become responsible for evil and although at the same time we may be achieving good, that good is diminished by reason of the evil we do. We must never console ourselves by saying that the evil is really good because it attains good ends. It would be quite incorrect to say that any means that produce a good end are themselves *ipso facto* good. That would indeed be an expression of the thoroughly unethical doctrine that the end justifies the means, and so would any decision which considered *only* the end and its value and did not balance against it the evil involved in the means. An ethical approach will acknowledge that the means are evil and will weigh that evil against the good that it achieves; if the decision is to adopt those means, they are still recognised as evil, but because the good outweighs that evil it is morally right to adopt them. The means are evil—but it may nevertheless be immoral not to use them.

The person who sticks to the rule regardless of the fact that by doing so he is responsible for more evil that if he broke it, is

---

1. Gandhi, incidentally, allowed such breaking of moral rules and did not rule out even adoption of violence under certain circumstances.

not the highly moral person that he claims to be, but morally irresponsible.

The third reason for confusion in the conventional view is implicit in the two reasons discussed above. As Professor Field has stated it:

> From the point of view of practical decision, the end does always justify the means in the sense that the course of action which will produce a balance of good results in the circumstances should be adopted. [But] the particular course of action which may be the best means to a particular end, may also produce other results which are not desirable; and if on striking a balance we find that this course of action will produce more evil than good, it should, of course, not be adopted.

In other words, when considering the end likely to be achieved by the means we are contemplating, one must take into consideration *all* the consequences of the means adopted—not merely the direct consequence, the main end, but the indirect consequences, those perhaps undesirable results flowing from the means but not part of the result aimed at. A good deal of misunderstanding is obviously due to the critics entirely ignoring this generally admitted qualification. They invariably assume, and on no grounds at all except their own determination to put their opponents in the wrong, that those who select the means appropriate to a certain end deliberately ignore the evil flowing from those means. Why in the world should they? The means are chosen because they are suitable; they are suitable because their results are good, and these results include *all* and not merely *some* of the results.

The real issue in the controversy over means and ends is not therefore as to whether we may or may not adopt means involving evil to attain a good which outbalances that evil or to avoid a still greater evil, but as to *whether the good attained is really worth the cost, or whether there is another route to that good involving less evil*. We may also disagree not only as to worth of the good to be achieved but as to the extent of the evil involved in attaining it, and here the point of view and the social position of the contestants affects considerably their decisions. No class will ever resent the injustice done to others as much as it resents the injustice from which it suffers. Those who do not themselves suffer from the evils of unemployment will never regard it as an evil greater than the evil to them of social remedies for unemployment which touch their privileges. It is factors like these that underlie the ethical struggles in matters of willed social change or transformation.

I will only add that adoption of means involving evil, however necessary, needs to be done in full awareness of the insidiously corrupting power of evil. It is not a matter of 'a little water clears us of this deed'. Evil, and for that matter good, is not something that you can switch off and on at will, as Machiavelli says his Prince can and should. Far more relevant and insightful here is Shakespeare when King Macbeth desperately asks: Will these hands never be clean again? ('Will all great Neptune's ocean wash this blood clean from my hand? No; this my hand will rather the multitudinous seas incarnadine, making green one red.')

The above discussion puts the issue of 'India winning freedom through Gandhian non-violence' in proper light. I am not going to discuss the validity of this claim or attempt any exhaustive assessment of Gandhian politics in our freedom struggle, much less his role as an astute politician as, for example, in the Subhas Bose episode or as an idealist as, for example, in the Bhagat Singh episode where, there is always the consideration that those truly passionate about an ideal tend to justify any means to achieve it. I will only draw attention to a few considerations to argue for a more honest or balanced view of the success of Gandhian non-violence in winning India's freedom in 1947.

We may again note Gandhi's own view in this regard, as expressed in the wake of the Mountbatten settlement and the accompanying horrors of communal conflict and massacres spread over wide areas of India:

> I do not understand how all these terrible things are happening in our country. For many years the Congress has struggled and grown, and it has grown stronger and stronger, and advanced higher and higher; but now, after we have reached the pinnacle, somehow these horrible things are happening, and the Congress

> is not able to do anything effective to stop them. What mistakes have we made, for we must have made mistakes? Otherwise how could all these things happen? It seems that while we were building the Congress, at the same time it was decaying; and today it is obvious that it has decayed, because it is not able to fight all the bad things that are going on in India today.

Again:

> Everything looks dark to me, very dark, and I see very little hope. Some people say that after the dark night comes the bright dawn; but I only see the darkness of the night. I do not know when the dawn will come.

Yet again, when Gandhi proclaimed his last fast (on January 12, 1948) against the spreading horror:

> Death for me would be a glorious deliverance rather than I should be a helpless witness to the destruction of India.

We have also noted that India today is a monument to the failure of Gandhi's politics of non-violence. Not only his larger ideas and ideals stand abandoned, even his particular hopes or promises remain unrealised. For example, communal peace and harmony he sought remains as distant as ever and those whom he anointed *'harijans'* continue to suffer as they have done all along.

(Perhaps Gandhi had some presentiment of this failure. His fast of January 12, 1948 was not only for communal peace but also against corruption in the Congress—'factionalism and money-making activities' of its legislators and ministers. 'Let us beware' he had warned and advised even disbanding of the Congress—an advice which was simply ignored by power-hungry Congress leaders).

Surely it is not denying Gandhi's greatness, or his pioneering role in mobilising millions in the cause of India's freedom, to suggest that all this and much else that is wrong with India today, has something to do with Gandhi's politics of non-violence in India's freedom struggle.

Votaries of non-violence at home or abroad, however, continue to cite India's freedom as a success story of Gandhian non-violence. As I have said above, my concern here is not with the merits of this claim, only with pointing out that in terms of means-ends controversy, this a confused, if not dishonest, claim in the sense that focusing on *the* end in view, India's freedom, it overlooks other ends or consequences resulting from the Gandhian means.

The first and foremost consideration here is the partition of the country, the hideous orgy of violence, of mass murders and destruction which accompanied it, and the long-term cost of it all that we are still paying and the future generations will continue to pay.

It is true that when the peaceful settlement he sought arrived in the shape of the Mountbatten Award and was revealed to bring about the partition of India and communal riots, Gandhi was the first to sound the alarm and oppose it. 'Vivisection of India can only take place over my dead body' he declared and jumped into the fray. Gandhi indeed died, battling in the cause of communal peace and unity of India. Even so, Gandhi's politics cannot escape the responsibility for the partition of India and what accompanied or followed it. The parts of India which ultimately went into the making of Pakistan were predominantly feudal areas with vast masses of impoverished Muslim peasantry. Gandhi's policy prescriptions for India's national movement had little or nothing to offer this peasantry to draw it into India's freedom struggle. Gandhi's social theory simply could not accommodate a programme of radical land reforms. The absence of any such programme, together with Gandhi's combination of nationalism with Hindu revivalism and his use of Hindu symbols in the national movement, left this Muslim peasantry eminently vulnerable to the appeal of Muslim League's communal politics as also to the imperialist policies of playing on religious divisions—all of which helped to sow the seeds of the terrible harvest that was the partition of India. This denouement was also, in part at least, the nemesis of a quarter century's preaching of non-violence frustrating the revolutionary energy of the masses.

Again, Gandhi's search for a peaceful, negotiated settlement with the British allowed them to continue with their imperialist policies and intrigues, foment divisive communalism, play the Congress and Muslim League against each other and ultimately succeed in partitioning India and salvaging as much of their imperialist interests as possible. Peaceful settlement also meant that there was no revolutionary overthrow of the imperialist rule, no *breaking away* from the old order of things. The freedom that was won involved no economic, social or political revolution in the country, only a transfer of power from the foreign rulers to Indian rulers—'the political independence has done little more than displace a foreign with a native privileged group' is how Gunnar Mydral saw it a couple of decades later.

It was typical of Gandhi's politics of non-violence that when the greatest national upsurge swept India after the second world war—popular support for the Indian National Army (INA) soldiers on trial, strike in the Royal Indian Navy, peasant struggles (for example, Tebhaga in Bengal and Telangana in Hyderabad) working-class actions (for example, the countrywide postal strike), people's movements and revolts in the Princely states, etc.—which also witnessed unprecedented Hindu-Muslim fraternisation in the streets, Gandhi saw in this upsurge only the threat of 'delivering India over to the rabble' and hastened to welcome the Cabinet Mission and advocate a compromise settlement with the British. If, for Viceroy Wavell, as he noted in his journal, India was 'on the edge of a volcano', which soon led the British to abandon any hopes of holding out longer, particularly since even the loyalty of Indians in the army was now suspect, for Gandhi, this revolt from below with its revolutionary possibilities was the menace of 'red ruin and anarchy', which had to be countered or averted with a compromise settlement with the British.

Yet again, implicit in the peaceful settlement noted above was another long-term consequence that needs to be considered. It was the old socio-economic and state-bureaucratic structures left behind by the freedom of 1947, which, with all their structural compulsions, became the basis for the post-Independence Nehruvian national project of self-reliant economic development promising 'growth with equity and distributive justice', but which, given the structural logic of its basis, almost inevitably ended up as 'a type of capitalist development in the interests of a narrow section of Indian society', as V.K.R.V. Rao described it. Passing through a series of crises mid-1960s onwards, the Nehruvian project finally collapsed in 1991, with the ruling classes going for 'globalisation' as their new strategic option—a shift from the state-supported capitalism to a wholly privatised 'free market' capitalism and from self-reliance in economic development to reliance on Foreign Direct Investment and the multinationals, a shift euphemistically described as 'economic reform', whose structural logic, as a former President of Brazil once reported it to the masters in Washington, is: 'the economy is doing fine, the people are not'. Whatever be the benefits that 'economic reform' has brought to a small section at the top, it has further polarised our society, played havoc with the lives and livelihoods of the common people and pushed our poor still further into a peripheralised existence within the global capitalist system.

Apropos India's 'development' during the Nehru era, I had written:

> To borrow from Tom Paine's metaphoric rejoinder to Burke's attack on the French revolution, admiration for the 'plumage' of India's 'national development' should not prevent us from seeing its failure in 'the dying bird'. The world indeed looks very different from below, when the poor and oppressed of 'our nation' look at it.

This is even more true of 'development' during the current era of neo-liberal economic reform, when we not only continue to move away from everything Gandhi held dear or wanted for his people, but our society remains structurally saturated with violence and our people continue to bear the 'terrible costs of not changing the existing order'.

This too is, in its own way, a consequence of Gandhi's politics of non-violence, the means which, it is claimed, won us our freedom.

There is much else in Gandhi's politics or in India today which can be considered as the consequences other than freedom of India which the votaries of non-violence almost invariably ignore. For example, Gandhi's love and concern for the common man notwithstanding, his 'non-violence' continues to be useful to the ruling classes in various ways. Or, Gandhi's involvement with Hinduism (including his effort to purify it), his combination of nationalism with Hindu revivalism or mixing of religion with politics, his openly avowed and expressed religiosity may not have much to do with the present day *Hindutva*, 'cultural nationalism', religiosity or revivalism, but all this has certainly served as an obstacle to the much-needed secularisation of Indian polity. Or the obscurantist elements in Gandhi's world outlook, which have obviously reactionary, anti-people implications and which, incidentally, have allowed today's post-modernist obscurantism to line up Gandhi in support of its attack on what is described as 'imperious enlightenment vision'; and so on.

One can concede these other consequences—other than India's freedom—flowing from or associated with Gandhi's politics of non-violence and still argue that freedom as won in 1947 was worth the cost or that it was the only suitable route to India's freedom. But the argument has to be more honest or balanced than it normally is or has been. It should, at the very least, allow for a different assessment of the cost and suitability of both this route and a possibly better and less costly *revolutionary* route to India's freedom espoused, among others, by Bhagat Singh later in his life. As Indian people's struggle for freedom continues, the issue in any case remains open and relevant today.

❖

I will conclude this address by returning to the point I had made at the beginning. Violence is a social, conjuncturally produced phenomenon. Most violence today arises from the way 'the modern society' is organised and from the politics and practices of the dominant classes or elites. To borrow Macpherson's analogy, complaining about the bread (violence in this case) we must not forget the bakery (that is the society) which produces it. Therefore, even as we seek specific remedies for specific forms of violence in our society—which, however arisen, often tend to become an autonomous factor in society—we need to move towards organising a just and humane, genuinely democratic society. It is going to be a long haul. But there is no alternative.

Chapter 11

Of Parliamentary Politics*

I

Socialists' loss of their vision of the future has, as we have seen, many negative consequences for their politics. The most important such consequence, to be specifically noted, is that socialists seem to have lost the capacity to think in terms of a different, alternative project in oppositon to the currently dominant capitalist project. People are being driven by their conditions to protest and rebel, movements with distinct anti-systemic thrust are coming up everywhere. The absence of a socialist vision of the future and, therefore, of a gadical alternative geared to it, cripples and frustrates these emerging struggles of the people, even helps the enemy to divert popular discontent and grustration in dangerous directions. Again, it is idle to expect people to engage in sustained political action for an alternative social order unless they know something about the ends and the means, about where we are going and how we intend to get there. After the broken hopes and shattered dreams of the recent past, it is all the more clear that no movement will now embark on a long, historical journey without knowing what it is aiming at and what is the route to it. Socialists therefore need to recover the capacity to think and

* Excerpts from the author's *Crisis of Socialism—Notes in Defence of a Commitment*.

act in terms of an alternative sociality project. That this project has to be formulated for each different country is obvious enough—the nation-state remains the main arena of struggle in each country has to find its own answers to its problems. But while such diversity is both necessary and desirable, there is still one overriding consideration. The current success of capitalism rendering reformist gradualism irrelevant and its adherents themselves abandoning their socialism altogether, revolutionary socialism is the sole realistic agenda today. More than ever before, a socialist project today has to be a project of revolutionary socialism and its politics, diversity notwithstanding, has to be revolutionary politics. But here at least one clarifiction is in order.

Revolutionary politics does not mean thinking and acting in terms of storming the Bastille or seizing the Winter Palace, or launching an immediate armed struggle. There are socialists for whom revolutionary politics is unthinkable except in association with a revolutionary upheaval. For them the task is to set about organising this upheaval, 'to make a revolution'—anything else is dangerous and discredited reformism. This is a wholly mistaken view in that it misses out on the necessarily long period of preparatory ideological and political struggles that go into the making of a socialist revoution, even if it is viewed as an upheaval. At its worst, this view even ends up as so much posturing, an alibi for doing nothing. This is not to deny or foreclose the issue that situations may be there in some parts of the world where the main task is to concentrate on organising a revolution, though even here success is most likely only if the task is undertaken with due care and preparation, which does not necessarily rule out all 'reformist' activity. But the situation generally, and certainly in most parts of the world today, is one of long haul. The main task here is to reach out to the people, organise their class and mass struggles, constantly raise these struggles to the level of political struggles, and relate them to the overall objective of revolutionary transformation of society, the socialist revolution we seek. It is only through such struggles that people will learn to need and make this revolution, whatever eventual shape or form it takes.

This is not an easy task to carry out. Here we are indeed face with a problem that is as old as socialism itself. The movement for socialism has an inevitable duality within it. A socialist movement has to fight within the framework of existing capitalist society but must inevitably offer solutions which ultimately lie beyond that framework; it has to struggle for a socialist future from within a capitalist present. If it concentrates too much on that future it runs the risk of sectarian isolation. Yet if it limits itself to struggle within the system, it loses its original *raison d'etre,* the search for a radically different society. The task for the socialist movement thus is to preserve a permanent link between its current partial or defensive struggles and its vision of a future socialist society which is at once distant and crucial. As the *Communist Manifesto* has it:

> The Communists fight for the attainment of the immediate aims, for the enforcement of the momentary interests of the working class; but in the movement of the present, they also represent and take care of the future of that movement.

At the tactical level we have the Leninist insistence that socialists must constantly relate specific grievances to a criticism of the system *as a whole,* constantly showing how they are linked together and therefore how people's specific struggles are also linked to the struggle for a revolutionary transformation of society. In other words, the key task is to establish linkages between theory and practice which would lead everyday resistance beyond short-term demands towards socialism. As Lenin, among many others including Gramisci,understood, these linkages did not spontaneously emerge from ordinary working class life or struggle. It was up to socialists to perceive them theoretically and then forge them into practices or actions which made sense to the working people and linked their ongoing struggles to the coming of a socialist future.

Though easy to formulate in theory, what is involved here is possibly the most difficult yet vital practical task in the struggle for socialism: to link the *immediate* (necessarily reformist) activity with the *ultimate* (essentially revolutionary) objectives; or to phrase it differently, to preserve the integrity of the *ultimate* perspective without losing contact with the *immediate* demands, determinations and potentialties of the historically given condition. Struggle for the immediate or limited aims and objectives is how people, necessarily, begin their struggle against the system and for a better life. Important as a way of saying '*No*' to capitalism in a concrete manner or winning gains for the people, given *socialist* leadership, this struggle can also be a means of enhancing people's consciousness and organisation for the ultimate socialist transformation. Reform and revolution thus must not be seen as mutually exclusive oppsites. The task rather is to subordinae reform to revolution.

This is how Marx had argued in his controversy with Bakunin and anarchists. As a revolutionary, Marx rejected voluntarism. As against his opponents who tended to rely on 'spontaneity' and 'instinctive conscience of the popular masses', Marx viewed the development of a *socialist mass consciousness* as necessary for a socialist revolutionary reconstruction of society. For him this was possible only through struggles over a long period.

To conclude, even as we recongnise that struggle for socialism, as always, is a *revolutionary* struggle and that socialist politics is nothing if it is not *revolutionary* politics, it does not mean any kind of rejection of reforms. What is demanded is that socialists struggle for reforms as revolutionaries, that is, they remain faithful to socialist principles, imbue the necessarily partial popular struggles with socialist consciousness, put *socialist meaning* into people's experience as they struggle for, win or lose, reforms, and thus help them become more effective subjects or makers of the socialist revolution, in whatever shape or form it has to be eventually made....

II

Our view of the struggle in defence of democracy also points to the right perspective for the revolutionary Left's participation in electoral or parliamentary politics—an issue to which, given its importance, I shall be returning later in these notes. There is no denying that this politics has built-in pressures towards reformism. But this by itself is not and cannot be an argument against participation in such politics, against the use of electoral or parliamentary politics as part of the revolutionary struggle against capitalism. What is important here is the meaning you put into it, the ideology or political consciousness that informs such use, or for that matter the struggle against capitalism as a whole. Every form of political activity or struggle is potentially 'reformist' if it is conducted in ideological and organisational isolation from the broader struggle where the capitalist system is the enemy to confront, if the immediate struggle is not linked to the ultimate or strategic object or a socialist transformation of society. Reform, a contest with the ruling class where you are, or within the existing institutions, is where you begin the revolution,—and you cannot begin it otherwise, elsewhere. But it is a beginning, a part of the revolutionary process only if it is suffused with the revolutionary consciousness of a socialist. What is really involved here is the relation between reform and revolution where its mistaken understanding has often seen it as an either or question and thus counterposed one against the other. A proper understanding, as Marx, the active revolutionary, himself emphasised, says 'yes' to both but insists that in revolutionary politcs reform needs to be subordinated to revolution. A revolutionary struggle agaisnt capitalism, therefore, does not in any way rule out the exercise of the rights of bourgeois democracy or the use of its institutions as futile. On the contrary, and very rightly too, revolutionary socialist poltics enjoins such exercise and use whenever, wherever and to the degree possible. And this, in principle, includes participation in electoral or parliamentary politics. To argue for such participation is not to deny or overlook either the ultimately violent nature of the bourgeois democaratic state or the subordination of the electrol-parliamentary regimes to the rules established by this state. It is to suggest that notwithstanding its problems and pitfalls, or 'civilising' influence on the revolutionaries, electoral or parliamentary politics can be and need to be treated as another arena of class struggle, where openings are available for ideological-political struggle against the capitalist social order, where we can carry our own agenda to a vast potential constituency of ours, where we can educate and organise people for non-electoral, extra-parliamentary revolutionary socialist politics. What is ruled out is primary reliance on electoral strategies or anything else that would encourage the illusion of a primarily electoral or parliamentary route to socialism.

Participation in electoral or parliamentary politics is essentially a tactical and not a strategic question which, therefore, always admits of exceptions. But wherever possible or opted for, it has to be subordinated to extra-parliamentary class and mass politics, including the larger counter-hegemonic struggle against capitalism. People's power grows primarily out of such politics, out of their own activity, organisation and struggle, as these come to be suffused with revolutionary consciousness. Following Lenin, Gramsci is a good guide here. For him, participation in electoral or parliamentary poltics is a tactical issue contingent on the strategic struggles centred on the class and mass organisations challenging the ruling class state. This relationship between strategic extra-parliamentary and tactical electoral politics must not be inverted. Nor is the notion of revolutionary praxis to be divorced from the self-organised and autonomous class struggle of the working masses in the name of 'flexible tactics', 'realism' and 'possiblilism', or by raising the bogey of 'sectarianism', 'adventurism' or 'political immaturity'—formulas and phrases which social-democratic reformism has used over the years, all over the world, to rationalise class collaboration and justify or condone any and every kind of pragmatism, even opportunism on the terrain of bourgeois democratic politics.

It is necessary to recognise the decisive importance of extra-parliamentary class and mass politics for any renewed struggle for socialism, or, for that matter, any significantly radical pro-people change in society today. This is particularly necessary in view of the dismal failure of parliamentary politics in recent decades and globalisation's continued undermining of parliamentary-democratic intitutions. It is not only that capital, which is 'by definition, and very effectively in its mode of acting and function, an extra-parliamentary force', is powerful over society by virute of its dominance in the economy; its power is further reinforced by the capitalist classes' ideology and personnel-wise domination of the various apparatuses of the state. This truly massive extra-parliamentary power of capitalism can only be matched by the working people's extra-parliamentary force and modes of action, their articulation in forms which are capable of offensive action against capitalism. It is significant that important economic or political 'gains' of the working people have almost invariably been the result of their reliance on 'extra-parliamentary' forms of struggle and organisation, whether in unions, protest movements, militant actions, or elsewhere, through the extra-electoral pressure they exercised on different institutions of the state. Indeed, to be at all effective, parliamentary politics itself has needed and today even more badly needs the radicalising pressure and support of extra-parliametary politics. Beyond that, if the aim be socialism, it is unthinkable that the struggle for socialism can today at all advance without a radical reconstitution of the socialist movement as a strategically oriented and sustained extra-parliamentary mass movement capable of mounting an effective challenge to the capitalist powers that be.

Our emphasis on the importance of active extra-parliamentary politics does not imply any kind of lawlessness, nor, as we have already clarified, an aprioristic rejection of electoral or parliamentary politics. But it does demand freeing of the working people's movement from the crippling constraints which the parliamentary 'rules of the game' one-sidedly impose on it in the name of 'democratic politics'. It certainly rejects delusions of successful struggle against capitalism through parliamentary means. But it does not in any way pre-empt the issure of peaceful transition to socialism. Socialism, as we had insisted earlier, is not a matter of resorting to violence or picking up arms, which are purely tactical questions, though not to be dismissed on abstract moral grounds. Socialism is about a fundamental change in social production relations which a real, not merely juridical or formal, social ownership of the means of production maeks possible. And here, properly interprted, Marx still remains the guide:

'peaceful if possible, with arms if necessary'. That is, it all depends on historical conditions and possibilities of the objective situation. A peaceful transition is of course the desirable thing. But the issue involved—peaceful or otherwise, or how peaceful—is really one for the ruling classes to respond to: are they willing to accept the people's peaceful, democratic verdict for socialism? As it is, these ruling classes have not even remotely shown this willingness so far. Instead, they have invariably used their enormous economic and political power, often across countries, to thwart changes far, far less radical in nature than socialism. For the people, therefore, if or when they decide to travel the peaceful road, the principle is clear. This is how, in his times, Cromwel, forced to make a revolution, put it: 'Trust in God, and keep your powder dry!' How people 'keep their powder dry' is not my concern at the moment. Only do it they must. What is involved is forging adequate extra-parliamentary sanctions to defend and enforce their democratic verdict, which includes preparedness to counter the inevitable 'slave-holders' rebellion', as Marx had called it. Failure to do so will cost them dear, as it did the Chilean people in 1973. They failed to develop their own armed counterweight to defend their democratic verdict against the military coup which soon defied and overturned it, and eventuated in a most brutal counter-revolution, massacre of virtually the entire Chilean Left including the democratically elected President Allende himself and the setting up of the notorious Pincochet dictatorship, all aided and abetted by the forces of international capital headed by the well-known defender of democracy in the world, the United States. I don't have to detail the lessons....

III

The question of people's power in the state, their struggle for 'political supremacy' or state power is absolutely central to any struggle for a better life for the common people. There is no way a serious people's movement can avoid the question of political power. The real issue here is the concrete forms of struggle for it. This, obviously, cannot be settled beforehand; the objectives and the forms of struggle to be adopted or combined depend on the specific and ever-changing historical circumstances. While the revolutionary tradition has a great deal to offer here, the formula remains that of the great tactician Napoleon Bonaparte which Lenin was fond of reiterating; *'On e'engage et puis on voil'* (we join the battle and then we'll see). But there is one issue here which, though noted earlier, deserves a more specific reference, namely, the pursuit of revolutionary politics in regimes of more or less developed bourgeois democracy, where participation in parliamentary politics has posed so many intractable, still unresolved problems for the revolutionaries.

Problems here are far too many to be listed. The critics have pointed their accusing finger at the Socialist and Communist Parties which, opting for parliamentary politcs, have steadily slid into reformism. Such participation breeds 'parliamentary cretinism', a naive equation of electoral victory with winning of power, even with radical change itself, so that there is no need for or interest any longer in developing a militant revolutionary movement. Whatever movements exist or are built outside are subordinated to the 'struggle' inside the parliament. The electoral success is bought at the cost of an ideological backslide which has lasting deleterious effect. Operating on the terrain of bourgeois politics, responding to issues it presents and accepting the choices it offers, entails a corruption of political consciousness and loss of revolutionary commitment. Criticism of bourgeois parties for failing by their own standards—a staple of parliamentary politics—almost invariably leads to endorsing these standards yourself so that your original concerns come to be given a go-by. The process of making yourself electable on the terms set by the establishment leads to mirroring the establishment's view of the revolutionary Left who are now seen as an embarrassment, when not treated with plain hostility. Parliamentary politics, even as it corrupts in so many ways, exercises a most 'civilising' influence on revolutionaries, as Laski was fond of pointing out. It is no coincidence that the ruling classes looking for 'the most outstanding parliamentarians', or models of 'parliamentary rectitude', for their awards and honours have not unoften found them among leaders of Socialist or Communist Parties. They are hailed by the mainstream media as 'statesmen' for their role as the best custodians of bourgeois politics. And so on.

That the ruling classes have been eminently successful in using democracy, its rights and institutions against the people and for promoting their own class interests and that the greatest enemy of democratisation in the world today, the US, can hawk 'democracy' around the world in support of its imperialist politics makes parliamentary politics all the more suspect in the eyes of its critics.

The critics are fully justified in what they say, but their criticism does not add up to a justification for any kind of 'anti-parliamentary cretinism', the in-principle rejection of parliamentary politics by certain ultra-Left sections of the revolutionary movement. What we have here are problems that have to be confronted and resolved in terms of revolutionary vigilance in theory and practice and not evaded in a cretinous rejection of 'bourgeois democracy'. Parliamentary politics and electoral struggles are not to be rejected, or even treated as mere defensive tactics for the working people. They are today an integral part of any long revolutionary. They do not necessarily prevent a revolutionary movement or party from establishing and functioning on its own terrain, the terrain of independent class-based people's politics, which even as it confronts bourgeois politics on the latter's terrain, in parliament or outside, uses it to pose its own issues and choices, in its own way, before the people—not just for some electoral gains but real political advance. In other words, there is nothing in bourgeois democracy or parliamentary politics that in itself prevents its being subordinated to the extra-parliametary politics of a revolutionary party or movement. Parties or movements are indeed coming up today, notably in Latin America, which are thus combining parliamentary and extra-parliamentary methods in pursuit of their revolutionary objectives.

The issue here is not commitment to democracy which has always been a vital part of the socialist agenda—and it is people who have fought for and won whatever democracy we have; and they need and value it most. Nor is it 'bourgeois democracy'—apropos which Miliband, with the bitter Soviet experience in mind, has written:

> Regimes which do, either by necessity or choice, depend on the suppression of all opposition and the stifling of all civic freedoms must be taken to represent a disastrous regression, in political terms, from bourgeois democracy, whatever the economic and social achievements of which they must be capable... The civic freedoms which, however inadequately, form part of bourgeois democracy are the product of centuries of unremitting popular struggles. The task of Marxist politics is to defend these freedoms and to make possible their enlargement by the removal of their class boundaries.

It is not even that parliamentary politics, as a form of politics, has its possibilities in the struggle for socialism and cannot be rejected so long as these possibilities remain unexhausted, not in your theory but in people's own practical experience, and, therefore, as a general principle, participation in parliamentary politics is necessary whenever and wherever possible—though exceptions to this principle are admissible in specific historical situations when people's interests, interests of their revolutionary movement so demand. The real issue here is an approach distant both from ultra-Leftism on the one hand and from social democratic politics of accommadation on the other. It is the principle, but without any exception this time, that parliamentary politics needs always to be subordinated to extra-partliamentary class and mass politics. It can never be over-emphasised that people's power grows only out of such politics, out of their own activity, organisation and struggles as these come to be suffused with revolutionary socialist consciousness.

It may be added that participation in parliamentary politics does not by itself or necessarily mean accepting the prevalent social order. Engels had categorically stated :

> the political freedoms, the right of assembly and association and the freedom of the press—these are our weapons. Are we to sit back and abstain when somebody tries to rob us of them? It is said that a political act on our part implies that we accept the existing state of affairs. On the contrary, so long as this state of affairs offers us the means of protesting against it, our use of these means does not signify that we recognise the prevailing order.

These means, including participation in parliamentary politics, can in fact be used to redefine and extend the democratic parameters of the prevailing order in favour of the revolutionary movement, its extra-parliamentary struggles.

A Marxist perspective on the revolutionary process does not pose the issue of struggle for socialism, as its simplistic or ignorant critics think, in terms of violence or non-violence or insurrectionist versus non-insurrectionist strategy. For it the real issue is an articulation and relationship between two terrains of struggle, that waged *within* the existing institutions of bourgeois democracy, and that waged *outside* them, in which the latter is always and ultimately the *decisive* terrain. Such was the perspective of Lenin, the principle underlying his notion of 'dual power'. Conceptualised by him in relation to the revolutionary process in Russia, 'dual power' has generally been taken to mean an adversary relation between a revolutionary movement operating in a revolutionary situation, and a bourgeois government under challenge from that movement. But it is suggestive of a more basic principle in relation to the two terrains of struggle mentioned above, in which the latter is always and ultimately the decisive terrain. This Leninist position still holds. (Such also was the perspective of Gramsci, though he has not been spared a reformist reading to locate the decisive terrain of struggle within existing institutions)....

And here, while struggle within existing institutions remains a very important complement to the overall struggle, historical experience is, in its own way, quite instructive and needs to be taken note of. The presence of Soviets as effective organs of *dual power*, a power outside of existing institutions, was an important factor in the success of the October Revolution. Similar organs of potential or actual dual power emerged later in several other revolutionary processes too—in the Finnish Revolution and Bela Kun's Hungary in 1918, in 19191-23 Germany, in Italy in 1920, in Spain in 1936, in Chile in 1972-73, in Portugal in 1974-75 and so on. Their lack of effective power was a contributory factor in the ultimate dismal outcomes. Details apart, what historical experience the world over points to is the paramount need to build up people's organised strength, a social power, on the terrain outside the established institutions of bourgeois democracy as necessary sanctions for the success of the revolutionary process. This will also be an important factor in determining how peaceful or 'non-violent' this revolutionary process is going to be.....

As we have noted earlier, Marx himself had warned that even in countries with the possibility of a relatively peaceful socialist revolution, the ruling classes will not give in without staging 'a slave-holders' revolt'. Engels had written:

> the time for surprise attacks, of revolutions carried out by small conscious minorities at the head of unconscious masses in past. When it is a question of complete transformation of the social organisation, the masses themselves must also be in it, must themselves already have grasped what is at stake, what they are going in for with body and soul.

He had urged the socialists to 'first win the great mass of the people'. Even so, he did not rule out a violent capitalist reaction to any peaceful bid for power—'a blood-letting like that of 1871 in Paris'. The obvious implication is that extra-parliamentary struggles, the essential basis of any serious preparation to meet such a contingency, cannot and must not be subordinated to parliamentary politics. Mass extra-parliamentary socio-political movements and struggles indeed remain the cental axis, the decisive terrain of the struggle for a socialist revolution. In fact capitalism is itself, by definition, and very effectively in its mode of acting and functioning, an extra-parliamentary force, and the capitalist state holds within itself any number of forces not amenable to the conventional democractic or parliamentary control. 'The "dominant class" is not a figure of speech', Miliband has pointed out, 'it denotes a very real and formidable concentration of power, a close partnership of capital and the capitalist state, a combined force of class power and state power, armed with vast resources, and determined to use them to the full, in conjunction with its allies abroad, to prevent an effective challenge to its power.' There will be no advance whatsoever until the working people's movement is activated in the form of becoming capable of *offensive* action—as against the usual defensive action through conventional trade unionism, party politics in parliament or outside, etc.—against capital and the dominant classes through its own appropriate institutions and through its extra-parliamentary force, its organised and conscious social power in society.

Here indeed also lies the answer to the question of how violent or peaceful, armed insurrectionary or otherwise, the revolutionary process will be. Violence is not the essence of the matter and there is nothing un-Marxist or irrational in seeking to carry through a revolutionary process without violence or force of arms. But its possibility depends, above all, upon whether the ruling classes will allow it to be non-violent or peaceful. Historical experience, October Revolution included, bears witness that they will not. (Chile is a classic example in more recent times.) Even so, the greater the strength of the extra-parliamentary force or social power the revolutionaries have, the more evident their ability and willingness to meet counter-revolutionary violence with overwhelming revolutionary violence, the greater the chance that violence can be avoided and the revolutionary process be relatively peaceful.

The amount of violence that will be involved in a given revolutionary process is indeed impossible to predict in advance. It depends on the one hand on the nature and amount of ruling class resistance but in a large part, also, on how successfully the socialists have built people's social power from below and how hegemonic or influential they are in society as a whole. As Wilhelm Reich has argued,

> the larger the mass base of the revolutionary movement, the less violence will be required and the more, also, will the masses lose their fear of revolution. The increasing degree of influence of the revolutionary movement inside the army and the state apparatus has the same effect. For this reason the Russian revolution had only a minimum of casualties.

(Bourgeois propagnada's violence in the Russian revolution did not accompany but *followed* the revolution, thanks to the foreign-backed armed counter-revolution by the former ruling classes.)

For Socialists or Communists, revolution is a matter, not of violence or non-violence, but of fundamental structural change in society. As revolutionaries they do no *advocate* violence. For them it is a tragic necessity to defend the revolution with violence when the ruling classes violate the victories and rights of the people. People have a natural aversion to violence and revolutionaries respect it—a respect, as Trotsky has underlined in his account of the Russian Revolution, the Bolsheviks remarkably demonstrated in 1917....

Chapter 12

Of Globalisation*

I

In his dominant way of thinking, Marx analysed the capitalist mode of production as it came up in Western Europe, and even as he visualised a rapid worldwide universalising mission for it, he focused on the fundamental class struggle between the proletariat and the bourgeoisie in the advanced capitalist countries. Recognising the proletariat as the worst victims of the irrationality and exploitation of capitalism, as they indeed then were, and optimistic about their 'winning the theoretic awareness of their loss', Marx postulated 'workers' revolutions', which would open up, on the basis of advanced productive forces, a successful transition to socialism/communism, the higher form of society he visualised as a transcending successor to the capitalist social order. But the further development of capitalism (which, incidentally also witnessed the rise of reformism in the socialist movement) falsified these assumptions and history took a different course. This however was not entirely unanticipated by Marx.

At the very outset, in the *Communist Manifesto*, this is how Marx characterised the ever-expanding capitalist world market:

> the need for a constantly expanding market for its products chases the bourgeoisie over the whole surface of the globe. It must nestle

---

* Excerpts from the author's *Crisis of Socialism—Notes in Defence of a Commitment*.

> everywhere, settle everywhere, establish connections everywhere. The bourgeoisie has through its exploitation of the world-market given a cosmopolitan character to production and consumption in every country. The bourgeoisie by the rapid improvement of all instruments of production, by the immensely facilitated means of communication, draws all, even the most barbarian, nations into civilisation. It compels all nations, on pain of extinction, to adopt the bourgeois mode of production...

But even as Marx underlined this globalising nature of capitalism, he saw it making 'nations of peasants (dependent) on nations of bourgeois, the East on the West'; and the *Manifesto* unambiguously suggested that the capitalist world market cannot rescue these backward (peasant) nations from their misery. Later he wrote of the devastation, the misery and suffering British rule caused in India, and noticed, in *Capital,* the emergence of a new, an international division of labour suited to the requirements of the chief centres of modern industry, which 'converts one part of the globe into a chiefly agricultural field of production for supplying the other part', etc. The point to notice here is that as part of this other understanding of capitalist development, its uneven, unequal or combined character, which he never lived long enough to develop, he had all along postulated another theory of revolution, this time in the underdeveloped parts of the capitalist world.

This we have discussed earlier in some detail. The important fact is that, as a result of the unequal development in capitalist expansion, for causes that are neither local nor conjunctural but systemic and structural to capitalism as a world system, socialist revolutions or revolutionary movements of our time have appeared most often not at the centre but at the periphery of world capitalism—in Russia, China, Cuba, Indo-China, or in the name of socialism, in Asia, Africa, and Latin America. For this is indeed where the worst victims of global capitalism's irrationality and exploitation are to be found, and therefore from where the challenge to capitalism emanated. The collapse of the Soviet Union does not end or modify the structural logic of global capitalism as manifested in poverty, underdevelopment, deindustrialisation and exploitation in Asia, Africa, and Latin America. It has only made global capitalism all the more powerful and given a new edge to its predatory logic. Any social system built on inequality in the command of human and natural resources works in many ways to reproduce itself and to increase the extent of the in-built inequality. So does capitalism. But as a market-governed system, capitalism carries this process to the extremes. The law of accumulation of capital inexorably produces, reproduces, and enhances inequality—wealth at one end and poverty at the other, not only within countries but on a world scale. And this is precisely what *globalisation*—another of the currently fashionable, reality-obscuring buzzwords—does. It has only sharpened the global capitalism's contradiction between its developed centre and exploited periphery. But this, if the past is any guide, also makes this periphery, the third world of the worst victims of contemporary capitalism, the site of revolts, of new countrywise challenges to the global capitalist order.

❖

'Globalisation' so called is a subject I shall be specifically returning to later in these notes. In the immediate context it needs to be recognised that it is no sudden new condition or phenomenon it is often made out to be. On the contrary, it is a process that has been going on for a long time, in fact ever since capitalism came into the world as a viable form of society four or five centuries ago. Capitalism was indeed born in the process of creating a world market through its centuries long spread by conquest and exploitation of Asia, Africa and Latin America and economic penetration and plunder everywhere. Thus born, capitalism in its innermost essence is an expanding system both internally and externally, its different units constantly compete among themselves for control of the weaker including remaining non-capitalist areas. The classic analysis of emergence, evolution and expansion of capitalism is of course Marx's *Capital*. And he showed that the logic of the always expansive and often explosive capital accumulation necessarily generates inequality in society, wealth and affluence at one end, poverty and deprivation at the other. In other words, capitalism cannot and does not make for universal success and prosperity. It can only universalise its contradictions, its polarisation between rich and poor, exploiters and exploited. In fact, insofar as it is successful, its successes are also its failures. The more successful it is on its own terms, that is, the more it maximises profit and so-called growth, the more it devours its own human and natural resources. In doing so, one may add, capitalism also makes for new opportunities for that unfashionable thing called class struggle.

The general law of capitalist accumulation, as Marx called it, which governs the dynamic of capitalism, and generates increasing wealth and affluence at one pole of society and growing poverty and degradation at the opposite pole, does so not only within nations but, as a global or world system, among nations as well, leading necessarily to the polarisation of the world into centre and periphery nations, nations rich and poor. This double process of polarisation is immanent in capitalism, its permanent and basic feature, a product of the structural logic of actually existing capitalism. This predatory logic has been, now and then, somewhat curbed, but never irreversibly, within the countries of advanced capitalism—a curbing made possible by the successful struggles of the working classes and an expanding capitalism which could accommodate the success of these struggles, and facilitated by the threat of socialism, through Soviet existence or otherwise, which exercised its own *civilising* influence on metropolitan capitalism. But the accumulation process has operated all the more effectively and ruthlessly on the world scale, all the time shaping and reshaping the peripheral economies in line with the needs of capitalism at the centre and thus all the time widening the overall gap between the countries of the centre and those of the periphery or semi-periphery in the third world. By its very nature, global capitalism tends to perpetuate and deepen this structural inequality and disparity, regardless of the intentions of individual capitalists or state managers. This is a characteristic of capitalism in all its stages of development that was explicitly noticed by Marx and further theorised by Lenin and later Marxists. Throughout it has been in the interest of the first world of advanced capitalist countries to have colonies or semi-colonial areas as preserves to make profit in whatever way it could be made. Contemporary 'globalisation' is no exception. In relation to the third world, it is imperialism all over again, albeit in a new shape or form, when, the logic of capitalism now become more or less universal, imperialism achieves its ends not so much by the old forms of military expansion or political control—not that these have become unimportant—but primarily by unleashing and manipulating the exploitative and destructive impulses of the capitalist market. As against the conventional liberal wisdom, it has to be clearly understood that the increasing disparity observed at the periphery of the system, the all too visible underdevelopment and its consequences, is not a vestige of a pre-capitalist past (the fashionable neo-Weberian thesis), but the inevitable product of their capitalist present, not a condition of inadequate capitalist development (the developmentalist thesis) but in reality an inevitable outcome of the accumulation process of the global capitalist system to which countries of the periphery, that is the third world, belong as much as those of the first world.

The post-Second World War period, a period of rapid and generally sustained capitalist expansion also saw new worldwide awareness of the deep-rooted disparities between the rich countries and those of the third world, an awareness which in the West was certainly compelled by the attraction the alternative Soviet model of development exerted in the post-colonial third world. But despite all the noise made about bridging the gap between the North and the South, the promises based on the supposedly scientific discoveries of a new discipline called 'development economics', UN resolutions and foreign aid programmes, all the talk about the New International Economic Order etc., the gap between the rich and poor countries kept widening. As Harry Magdoff has put it: 'Despite the striking transformations in the world capitalist system since the end of the Second World War, two major distinguishing features of the third world did not change: in general, and in a fundamental sense, the chains of dependency binding the periphery to the centre remain, (and) the gap between the periphery and the centre, as throughout the history of capitalism, keeps on widening'. It is important to recognise in this connection that this North–South gap and the conflict resulting from it, which is one of the basic contradictions of actually existing capitalism, has never been the product of East-West, that is, US-USSR conflict or its projection outside Europe, though a reciprocal interaction was always there and the support of USSR for certain third world nationalist forces helped sustain this impression. The North-South conflict is anterior and primordial, it has defined, for five centuries, capitalism as a polarising world system, bringing only misery and suffering to the peoples of the third world, and for this very reason intolerable to the vast majority of people on this planet, earth.

'Globalisation', today's watchword was thus a reality yesterday too—a capitalist world economy characterised by centre-periphery relations of domination and exploitation—though this reality was somewhat distorted and obscured by the post-war retreat of the all too visible colonial empires. But, part of an ongoing process with a five centuries-old history, the current splurge of globalisation, as with all such phenomena, has its historical specificity which in its own way reinforces the subordination of the periphery to the more self-driven productive accumulation pattern of the centre: it is simultaneously propelled by a new accumulation crisis of capitalism and a renewed ascendancy of rightwing politics the world over.

The economic context of today's globalisation has been the current recession of capitalism beginning in the 1970s, marked by the interrelated processes of retarded growth, ever increasing monopolisation and transnationalisation of the economy and the financialisation of the accumulation process, with all their contradictions. There is a swelling flow of profits but a reduced demand for additional investment in increasingly controlled markets and thus a shift away from capitalism's productive moorings accompanied inevitably by exceedingly high levels of unemployment in the advanced capitalist world as a whole.

There is the growing tendency for profits, unable to find profitable outlets in real capital formation, to be diverted into purely financial, and mostly speculative channels. An increasingly intense double process of faltering real investment and burgeoning financialisation has been on, the ongoing technological, especially information revolution facilitating literally worldwide fluidity of highly volatile finance capital ('hot money' economists call it), with all its contagious uncertainties and exploitative-cum-explosive consequences. Central to the current economic recession has been a slowing down of capital accumulation and with it of economic growth which under capitalism is powered by capital accumulation. This crisis within capitalism as a profit-driven system, a crisis made all the more intractable by growing class conflict, has underlined the insufficiencies of the limited globalisation of the earlier period associated with the welfare state. Therefore even as the welfare state is dismantled (and with it disappear the remaining illusions of Keynesianism), a new overseas expansion, an absolute breaching of the national barriers, becomes more urgent than ever before. It is this compulsion, and not the much too abstractly treated 'technological changes' or 'world market imperatives', which underlies the current thrust of global capitalism, its need, even as it 'restructures' economy at home for intensified exploitation of working classes, to prise open the third world economies for penetration not only of metropolitan goods and capital, but even more important of metropolitan finance with all its speculative proclivities. From the other end, economic instability or breakdowns in the countries of the third world, often facing a crisis if not a failure of their projects of national development, together with the collapse of economies of Eastern Europe and the Soviet Union, have made for both a need and an opportunity for global capitalism to intervene in order to protect and secure its worldwide old and new imperial interests.

The political context of this new globalising thrust of capitalism was provided, along with a general failure of social-democratic left in the advanced capitalist countries, by a worldwide retreat of radicalism, and more particularly defeats of revolutionary left in Latin America, Africa and Asia during this period, notably the destruction of the guerrilla campaigns in Latin America followed by the rise of military dictatorships, exhaustion of socialist hopes in Ethiopia, Mozambique and Angola in repression and civil wars and, buttressing the earlier destruction of Indonesian communism, the consolidation of the capitalist turn in China in the late 1970s and 1980s. This collapse or destruction of the left in the third world which was, as is now well-documented, actively engineered, supported or abetted by the capitalist powers led by the United States, simply 'disorganised' any real opposition to global capitalism. To cap it all came the collapse in Eastern Europe and the disintegration of the Soviet Union leading to a capitalist triumphalism where 'the market' comes to be so celebrated as to question and run down all forms of real or perceived intervention against it, not only traditional socialism but even Keynesianism, any kind of welfarism by conventional social democracy, third world nationalism, the statist dirigisme developmental model, everything. The new agenda must reflect the all-encompassing sovereignty of 'the market': rapid and comprehensive liberalisation of trade, capital flows and foreign direct investment, the cutting down of state budgets and subsidies or social welfare, privatisation of public sectors and security for now more than ever sacred private property rights of both local and foreign investors, and, of course, a starkly diminished role of the state so far as economy is concerned. Given its historically specific economic and political context, the ongoing globalisation has, in recent years, literally acquired the form of a worldwide offensive of global capitalism, carried out with its economic instrumentalities of foreign investment, money-lending and international trade, organised institutional structures like the World Bank and the International Monetary Fund, and buttressed by the neo-liberal ideology with its reductionist remedy for all ills—the market.

Globalisation, in its current neo-liberal version, has presented itself as a benign process that brings multiple benefits to those who participate in it, all inhabitants of capitalist countries, at the centre as well as the periphery. Academic experts, public officials and the mass media alike have gone to town interpreting it as something fundamentally different from what we have known, indeed as a new era in human affairs where national economies, functioning as units of a world market, undergo, and share in the advantages of, a mutually beneficent integration and recomposition. But this is only so much bourgeois ideology purveying the conventional wisdom of capitalism. The process of globalisation has indeed produced much that is new in the world's economy and politics but it has *not* changed the basic ways capitalism operates. And unequal access to natural resources, control over international financial institutions, scientific and technological monopolies, extra-economic mechanisms of political and military coercion, together with the cultural domination of lifestyles that the powerful reach of modern media ensures, have only served to intensify exploitation and increase in every dimension the polarisation between the rich and poor countries produced by the structural logic of capitalism. That some third world countries have managed to make at times—often only for a time—notable progress with their industrialisation and trade, or that third world elites have conspicuously benefited from globalisation, does not alter this basic fact, the overall gap between core and periphery nations has kept widening. Within the globalised capitalist world, the poor, polarised third world as a whole remains what it has been throughout the history of capitalism, the locus for capital accumulation and profit-making by giant corporations and financial institutions of the advanced capitalist nations. And it must so remain. With four-fifth of the world's population as a vital reserve army of labour and indispensable natural resources, the periphery must be preserved—it is not marginal as many economists believe, the two Gulf Wars are a good recent illustration—and subordinated to the expansion of capital however polarising this may be—to the extent that even as this permits a certain peripheral industrialisation in one part, it makes for the 'fourth-worldisation' of another, as, for example, in parts of Africa, creating nations like Haiti which were formerly integrated into the capitalist system but have been since marginalised, even abandoned, by the resulting exhaustion of their natural resources. This 'fourth world' is sometimes spoken of as something new but we know of areas destroyed by capitalism in its earlier forms. Such destruction in fact has been a constant feature of capitalist expansion.

The current globalisation has been pre-eminently propelled by global capital's macro-economic 'structural adjustment programme' (SAP), a powerful instrument of economic restructuring which bears a direct relationship to the above-mentioned process of global impoverishment; it further deepens the centre-periphery polarisation. The development of the periphery has in fact been the history of a never-ending 'adjustment' to the demands and constraints of the dominant global capitalism. The centres 'restructure' themselves and the peripheries are 'adjusted' to these restructurings. And International Monetary Fund and World Bank have been the two most important institutions involved in sponsoring the current programmes of 'economic stabilisation' and 'structural adjustment' in the third world. This is what Harry Magdoff has to say on the significance of these transnational institutions' rise to world dominance in recent years:

> I don't think that there has been a significant change in the role of the IMF and the World Bank. From their inception at the time the Second World War was winding down to this day, their main function has not varied. Their job has been, and continues to be, the strengthening and enlargement of the imperialist network of trade and investment. There have been three key components to this strategy. The first was to reconstruct and stabilize the international financial system which had been wrecked by the Great Depression and the war. The second was to tie the colonial, and subsequently decolonized, nations firmly to the economies of the great powers, and thereby widen investment opportunities and enlarge markets in the periphery. The third was to sabotage the efforts of those nations that wanted to break out of the imperialist network by shifting to policies of self-reliance and/or developing close relations with non-capitalist countries.

> The increasing level of activity of these agencies in recent years reflects not a new role but the spread of a general crisis in the last quarter century. As the so-called golden years of the 1950s and 1960s turned into a long-run stagnation, these agencies intervened more often because breakdowns in the periphery threatened the stability of financial institutions and markets of the leading capitalist powers. In addition, these agencies have become more brazen and open in imposing conditions for granting loans. Before 1972 these conditions were by and large kept secret as long as possible. They became overt when the axe fell on the masses, who were expected to pay directly and indirectly the debt service charges to international banks. The more recent openness in disclosing the conditions imposed by the IMF and the World Bank no doubt reflects the increasing hegemony of bourgeois ideology, according to which the removal of subsidies that give some protection to the poor, so-called free markets and free international trade, privatization, and unrestricted foreign investment are supposed to be principal ways to obtain economic recovery and growth.
>
> Increasing intervention by the IMF and the World Bank? Yes, but it is intervention for the sake of capital and its financial markets. Why put the finger on the servants instead of the masters? There has been no significant change in the thrust by the imperial powers to control and influence the periphery. What is new is the inability of capital to creep out of the morass of a long-lasting stagnation, accompanied by increasing fragility of financial institutions. In such times, the squeeze on the weaker nations is bound to get tougher.

The Fund-Bank-sponsored SAP has been, with a few variations to account for the inescapable local conditions, offering almost identical answers to problems in diverse places—be it Russia and other countries of ex-Soviet Union, the transition economies of East Europe, the Sub-Saharan Africa and the poor countries of Latin America, East and South-East Asia, including India, and so on. The formulas being advanced are the same everywhere: a rolling back of the state from the economic arena so that private enterprise and free markets can get on with the job of 'growth' (really profit making) unencumbered by any controls or regulations, disinvestment or wholesale privatisation of public sector enterprises, free and friendly entry for foreign capital, liberalisation of international trade with elimination of tariff and other barriers, drastic cutting of government expenditure on social services and subsidies for mass consumption and, above all, dependence on loans from international financial institutions and reliance on export-led growth even at the cost of domestic needs, etc.—the essence of it all being a development governed by external imperatives, those flowing from the world capitalist market. The outcome, naturally, has been more or less the same everywhere: stagflation and recession, crisis and virtual collapse of domestic economy and of course an ultimate fall into the debt trap. All this is accompanied by rising unemployment, a drastic fall in basic consumption, deterioration of education, health and social welfare, aggravating the sufferings of the poor millions in the periphery of global capitalism who indeed bear the brunt of the Fund-Bank-sponsored 'structural adjustment', all the more so when it comes imposed in its draconian form known as 'shock therapy'.

This should be no cause for surprise. After all, the International Monetary Fund and World Bank are not in the business of philanthropy, or in the development and growth business either as they claim or are claimed to be. They are in the business of lending and making money on it for, or otherwise securing the interests of, their global masters. Surely it is not their business to help develop new rivals to them in the ever-shrinking world market. As instruments of global capitalism, they are committed, through 'conditionalities' they impose, to promote the interests of major capitalist powers who, especially the United States, have clout in them and exercise it to enforce neoclassical policies of stabilisation and structural adjustment in the borrowing countries. The IMF is now widely, and very rightly, perceived as a 'gendarme of international rentier interests', and together the Fund-Bank duo has been well described as 'watchdogs of global capitalism'. It is not at all surprising that Fund-Bank-sponsored structural adjustment has been a systemic mechanism which cannot but distort economies, reproduce unequal development and perpetuate capitalism's ancient polarisations within and across countries on a global scale.

That this is indeed the case is now widely recognised. The United Nations Human Development Report (1996), for example, identified five types of distortions or 'imbalances' that can come to afflict the process of economic growth anywhere: jobless growth (growth without new employment), ruthless growth (inequalising growth with rich becoming richer and poor not any better off), voiceless growth (rapid growth under an authoritarian regime, where economic prosperity is not accompanied by political freedom), rootless growth (where material prosperity is achieved at the cost of cultural, social and ethnic identity), and, finally, futureless growth (growth which is environment-unfriendly, where the present generation squanders resources needed by future generations)—these distortions or imbalances are today a more or less conspicuous feature of the economic development in Fund-Bank loan or aid recipient countries of the third world, accompanied by the reality of a world further divided into two unequal worlds, each unequal within itself with growing inequalities of its own. Systemic inequality engendered by a turn to free market apart, even as the rolling back of the state from economic sphere (deregulation, privatisation, etc.) has directly benefited the dominant classes within and the foreign investors, its retreat from the social sphere (cutting of state welfare expenditure and consumption subsidies, etc.) has only added to the misery and suffering of the common people living in the periphery and semi-periphery of global capitalism. Speaking of the 'fiscal stabilisation' and 'structural adjustment' programmes of the IMF and World Bank, the Human Development Report has wryly quipped: 'they often balanced budgets by unbalancing people's lives'.

Capital is now globally mobile, more so than ever before, the amount of Foreign Direct Investment involved varying from country to country, depending as it does on the local economic and still more political climate, and producing for the investors maximum and needfully resilient profits. With rising labour costs and the shift to higher value-added products at home, multinational corporations have moved an increasing part of their production elsewhere. Products now produced in countries abroad by their foreign affiliates are then sold there as well as exported across the globe including to the home countries of the multinationals. The important point is that, even when entering into partnership with local capital, rarely do these multinational corporations relinquish control over either advanced technology or their production-sales chains, thus ensuring a steady stream of profits for stockholders back home. But far more important than such foreign investment is the fact that what has become generally mobile across countries is not so much productive capital as short-term finance in the form of foreign currency deposits, portfolio investment, etc., which are essentially indistinguishable from 'hot money' (a most important aspect of today's 'actually existing capitalism') which moves around from country to country in search of quick profits, especially in the form of speculative gains. In other words, what has really happened in world capitalism is not so much a tendency towards globalisation of production as a tendency towards globalisation of finance. And this form of capital does not generate economic growth in the recipient country. The foreign creditors are not interested in undertaking any productive venture, speculation in the market is their preferred interest; though the 'hot money' inflow can be and has been as well used for stimulating imports of consumption goods for the local elite. Needless to add, the inevitably sudden outflow of such capital plunges the recipient country into a new financial crisis. The imperative to generate the requisite surplus for financing the outflow compels a drastic squeeze on the living standards of the poor, sharp cutbacks in whatever productive investment was occurring and the transfer of national assets to foreign creditors 'for a song', as has indeed happened in recent years in Mexico and elsewhere. Lenin had pointed out that finance capital is associated with swindling, bribery and corruption—what European 'professors' of his time condescendingly called 'the American ethics'. The third world is today witness to a wholesale resurgence of this 'ethics of the market', the emergence of an entire new breed of buccaneers in business or sharks on the stock exchanges, international racketeers, fixers, upstart middlemen, often with non-resident origins or links or linked to smuggling and arms trade, parasitic intermediaries—all without any real production base and all of them in pursuit of their 'holy grail' in a 'free' and 'open' economy.

It is advocated that 'free trade' is the very *basis* of economic development and that all attempts to regulate trade are therefore responsible for slowing down growth and perpetuating underdevelopment. Bourgeois ideologue Thomas Friedman has even contended that the anti-globalisation protesters 'by inhibiting global trade expansion are choking the only route out of poverty for the world's poor'. There could not be a more phoney argument. As Arthur MacEwan has pointed out: 'There is no substance to the neo-liberal claim that "free trade" has been the foundation, historically and in the current era, of successful economic growth.' It is a historical fact that England did not become a vigorous advocate of free trade until it had a marked advantage as the leader of the industrial revolution and found the tariff walls standing in the way of its road to global hegemony in industry, finance, and empire building. From the other end, the rising rival empire builders and industrialisers—Germany, the United States, and Japan—thumbed their noses at the ideology of free trade. They built high tariff walls to protect their infant industries. Today's enormous pressure by the rich nations to impose free trade on the poor has a clear aim, consistent with history: to increase the wealth of the rich and impose chains on those countries that hope to develop and protect their own industries and thus find the way for economic independence from the imperial powers. That the ruling classes or elites of the poor third world countries are, by and large, succumbing to the pressure of the rich nations does not alter the fact that the effect, in practice, of 'trade liberalisation', as it is called, will be to re-institute the colonial pattern of international division of labour.

The neo-liberal dispensation ordains 'free trade' to supplement capital's freedom to flow, in or out, across state frontiers, though labour's freedom to do so, to so migrate, is no part of this dispensation. The overall interests of capitalist centres would not countenance this. The same reason explains why, in this age of 'globalisation' and 'free markets', so much importance is being given to monopolising trade and transit routes. While constant and relentless pressure is brought to bear by the World Bank and the World Trade Organisation regime (with its trade-related aspects of International Property Rights, etc.) on the third world countries to open up their economies more and more, the latter's access to the American and European markets faces all kinds of obstacles including those arising from matters unrelated to trade, for example, the so-called 'social clauses'. Legitimate concerns such as environmental protection, human rights, labour standards, the protection of children from exploitation, health and safety norms, etc. are sought to be misused as protectionist measures by the advanced capitalist countries. The rules of the game being fashioned and implemented by the World Trade Organisation (WTO) regime are and continue to remain loaded against the countries of the third world.

In an earlier era of imperialism, (before the first world war), when trade was an important feature of the economy and free trade a proclaimed principle—'Jesus Christ is free trade. Free trade is Jesus Christ', John Cobden had pronounced in the middle of the nineteenth century—it was even then not such an era of trade liberalisation as it has been often made out to be. Even at its victorian high noon, economic liberalism was never *that* free as its protagonists then claimed. On the contrary, trade policy in the developed centres was a picture of 'islands of liberalism surrounded by a sea of protectionism', while the periphery was characterised by 'an ocean of liberalism with islands of protection'. This openness in the periphery—free access to products of the colonial powers—was a most important aspect of colonial rule. Since then, as monopolisation and transnationalisation of capital has grown apace, genuinely free or competitive 'market forces' is a dogma long dead in global capitalism. And as in the past, so now, in the new type of 'imperialism' that is globalisation, 'free trade' is turning out to be a selective mixture of liberalisation and protectionism designed to expand the power and profits of transnational corporations.

Capitalism's 'global treadmill' as it has been called, is indeed so designed that the poor countries of the world often end up help financing the rich ones—a recent study has found the third world a 'net *exporter* of hard currency to the developed countries, on average 30 billion dollars per year' during the period from 1982 to 1990. Indebtedness via Fund-Bank loans and grants with their conditionalities has only facilitated this capital transfer from the poor South to the rich North.

During the eightees and ninetees of the last century, the third world debtors were calculated to have remitted to their creditors in the wealthy nations an average of almost 12.5 billion dollars per month in payments on debt alone. In one specific case, Africa from 1990–93, 57 per cent of gross bilateral loans and grants were reported to have been diverted to debt services which often went straight back into the coffers of rich creditors. 'Every man, women and child in Sub-Saharan Africa now owes $400 to rich creditors,' the report said. 'That is less than one week's wages for many people in Britain, but more than many Africans earn in a whole year.' These loans and grants have certainly benefited—apart from Fund-Bank bureaucrats and 'many heads of government, especially those who rule without the support of their populace, (who) have relied on the Bank to supply the cash they could not otherwise obtain' as one commentator has put it—a whole army of contractors and consultants, besides the multinational corporations and international banks whose activities have primarily helped the richest citizens of the rich countries. But in the third world, whatever needs of 'the economy' or the locally dominant rich they may have served, they have served no needs of the poor. Instead, as the ghastly effects of debt-trapping—which have surfaced in many third world countries 1980s onward—have demonstrated the poor have paid dearly for these financial tie-ups between ruling classes at home and abroad and, unless a major reversal of policy at home takes place, their descendants will continue to pay dearly in future. As Harry Magdoff has summed up: 'With debt as with foreign investment by the multinationals, while the foreign funds might be used for developing productive resources, the net result, in the short as in the long run, is (i) a transfer of economic surplus from the underdeveloped countries to the centres of capital, and (ii) an entrenchment of dependent ties from the weaker to the stronger nations'. Herein indeed lies the real importance of the foreign debt of the third world: it gives the First World a means or an instrument by which it can circumscribe the economy, and even politics, of the indebted third world and dictate 'structural adjustments' which make any pro-people industrialisation or economic development impossible. The instrument is ideal for it secures this objective in ways that apparently have nothing to do with it. The objective is obscured; what is visible is the debt of the third world countries and their inability to pay it, not the determination of the First World to perpetuate the peripheral or semi-peripheral character of development in these third world countries.

The overall outcome of the 'globalised' economic growth in the third world is now well documented, not the least in Reports coming from the United Nations itself: the benefits have mainly flowed to a small number of countries at the top and to the rich of the world, they have simply failed to trickle down. Thus, as some recent reports have it (and figures here always admit of a certain give and take), 89 countries and a quarter of the world's population, overwhelmingly in the third world, are now worse off economically than they were ten or more years ago. A small group of billionaires—358 of them—control assets greater than the combined income of countries with 45 per cent of the world's people. Between 1960 and 1991 the share of the richest 20 per cent rose from 70 per cent of global income to 85 per cent, while that of the poorest 20 per cent declined from 2.3 to 1.4 per cent. The income gap between the richest and poorest of the world's population escalated from a ratio of 30 to 1 in 1960 to 74 to 1 in 1997. More than three-fourth of the world's people live in the so-called 'developing countries' but they enjoy only 16 per cent of the world's income while the richest 20 per cent have 85 per cent of global income. The number of poor on this globe continues to grow relentlessly. A third of the global population of around 6 billion lives below the poverty line. Over a billion people are hungry every day. Pointing out that 'as the social effects of adjustment processes become more obvious it can also be seen that the heaviest burden is falling on the children', UNICEF has reported that 12 million children under the age of five die every year from preventable illnesses including malnutrition. That is 33,000 children dying every day, an overwhelmingly large number of them in the third world. A more recent (1997) United Nations report on 'world social situation', has yet again confirmed that poverty and deprivation is on the rise in Asia, especially South Asia (which includes India), Africa and Latin America. According to the data and definitions presented in this report, the number of people below the poverty line rose from 480 million to 550 million in South Asia, from 180 million to 219 million in Sub-Saharan Africa, and from 91 million to 110 million in Latin America, between 1987 and 1991. Currently more than 1.3 billion people live on below one dollar a day. UNDP administrator, James Gustave Speth, in his preface to one such report has concluded: 'The world has become more economically polarised, both between countries and within countries (and) if present trends continue, economic disparities between industrial and developing nations will move from inequitable to inhuman'. The World Bank and IMF themselves have been finding it difficult to gloss over the evidence of deepening poverty and inequality in different countries as a result of their prescriptions of 'economic reforms'. Several of World Bank's own reports apart, its ex-chief economist, Joseph Stiglitz, has recently told us how Fund-Bank policies—policies, in effect, tailored to benefit financial conglomerates in the West—have aggravated the situation in many places (Southeast Asia, Russia, Brazil, Argentina, etc.), and no less a person than Michel Camdessus, former chief of the International Monetary Fund has described as 'morally outrageous' the gap between the rich and the poor today.

There is no doubt that polarisation characteristic of global capitalism has today given rise to a wide and ever-widening gap between the living standards of the core capitalist countries and those of the dependent or underdeveloped countries of the periphery or semi periphery. Long range study of global economic patterns by Giovanni Arrighi and others have shown the extraordinary rigidity of this unequal relationship. Despite the post-war decolonisation and after more than thirty years of developmental efforts of all kinds, this overall hierarchy of wealth remains, the gaps that separate the incomes of the South from those of the North are today wider than ever before. It would suffice to notice here what the Canadian economist Michel Chossudovski has to say on this. Describing the 1980s as 'the decade of global impoverishment', Chossudovski has written:

> The disparities in income and life-styles between the 'rich' and the 'poor' have reached unprecedented proportions: an average middle class family in a Paris suburb has an income more than one hundred times higher than a rural household in south-east Asia; a Filipino peasant has to work for two years to earn what a New York lawyer earns in an hour. The amount spent by Americans (30 billion dollars a year) on Pepsi and Coca Cola at fast food outlets and super-markets across the United States is nearly twice the gross national product of Bangladesh... The per capita income of a middle class household in an industrialised western country (17,470 dollars) is approximately 100 times higher than the per capita income of an average rural household in south-east Asia.

Even as he explores 'the nature of this unfolding world economic system, on what structure of global poverty and income inequality is it based?' and points out that 'by the turn of the century, the world population will be six billion of which five billion will be living in poor countries'. Chossudovski adds:

> While the rich countries with some 15 per cent of the world population—including the rich oil producers of the Persian Gulf—control close to 80 per cent of total world income, some 56 per cent of the world population constituting the group of 'low income countries' (including India and China) and a population of nearly three billion receive 5.4 per cent of world income, less than the GDP of France and its overseas territories.

This system of global inequality reinforces not only overpopulation (since poverty spurs population growth) but also rapacious economic development associated with the destruction of tropical rain forests in the third world. Summing up the work of several scholars pointing to the new dimensions that world inequality has now reached, James Petras and Chronis Polychroniou have written:

> At the same time, the principle of profit maximisation, which nowadays goes completely unchecked under the pretext of operating in a 'global market', threatens the world with an ecological disaster. The tropical forests, already eliminated by more than 40 per cent, are disappearing 'at a rate of 30,000 to 37,000 sq miles every year'...as multinational timber companies are having a field day under free trade, free market legislation.
>
> Indeed, the ecological effects of globalisation are strikingly catastrophic. Under the fiscal pressures imposed by capital movements, the third world state in particular sells off more and more of its public resources—forests, mining regions, natural reserves, maritime resources. In this context, the greater the external integration, the greater the exploitation of domestic resources to fuel overseas expansion. External linkages between third world capitalists and the multinationals require vast amounts of capital and, in a dependent capitalist setting, cheap labour and pillage of the natural resources are the only means available for the necessary accumulation of capital. For the economic elite, the price of 'integration' into the world economy is expensive and the quickest road is via unlimited exploitation of non-renewable resources. This is the lesson of Brazil, Chile, Mexico, Guyana, Nigeria and so many other third world nations.

The evidence, now available in UN reports and studies by concerned scholars makes it abundantly clear that the 'structural adjustment'-governed and 'market'-driven policies pursued in the third world countries have not helped them overcome their poverty and underdevelopment. Instead they have left an overwhelming majority of their citizens worse off. Large parts of Africa, exposed to more than two decades of so-called 'economic reforms' are today disintegrating before our eyes, still trapped in the colonial-age international division of labour and populated by swelling masses of pauperised and marginalised people. Globalisation in Latin America has been equally 'a very destructive and painful process', as a scholar, Arthur MacEwan, has put it, especially for the peasantry who now face a prospect of precarious survival at ever deeper levels of pauperisation and misery. Neo-liberal economic policies have forced many to become part of a genuine rural proletariat, working on plantations and other large estates. Others have migrated to the cities and into the slums and joined the informal sector of the economy. 'Free trade' only accentuates this break-up of peasantries, just as the rest of 'reforms' (involving austerity programmes, cuts in social spending and consumption subsides, lowering of wages and rising unemployment, etc.) continue to further depress the living conditions of the working people in the industrial and urban sectors. 'Reforms' have worked no differently in Africa or Asia. Of India, among the more developed countries in the third world, surveying six years of its open and active pursuit of the new economic policies, a discerning critic had written: 'Two Indias are emerging: a desperately poor two-thirds backwater, and a not-so-poor but unbalanced and sleazy one-third. Urban–rural disparities have increased too. Ill-managed cities are imploding under the impact of rural migrants unable to subsist on land. They are super-polluted cesspools of anomie, crime, social unrest and deep resentment.' Since then the situation in India, as elsewhere, has only worsened. Globalisation of poverty is emerging as *the* distinctive feature of capitalism's new international economic order.

Recently we have had the warning that unless the countries of the South woke up, 'those managing the international economic system will continue to pay inadequate attention to the concerns of three-fourths of humanity living in the developing world'. It came from no less a person than the economist who, as India's finance minister definitively pushed India into 'globalisation', opening up its economy to the Fund-Bank and the multinationals. Maybe it was a momentary lapse into lucidity—for he even spoke up for 'the vision of a people-centred self-reliant development'—induced by the occasion, a meeting at the South Centre in Geneva where he had once penned his *South Report*, for—maybe as part of his newfound political career—he still finds it necessary to press for 'reforms' at home; though the possibility cannot be ruled out of political career in whatever kind of democratic politics India still has forcing some, genuine or spurious, 'rethink'—for democracy and neo-liberal policies simply do not go together in the third world. Be that as it may, there is no discounting the harsh truth implicit in the economist's rather mildly worded warning. For the now abundantly documented fact is that the Fund-Bank sponsored, big stick liberalisation policies are, more than anything else, the instruments for the mass impoverishment of the third world, and this now includes quite a bit of East Europe and the whole of Yeltsin's and now Putin's Russia that on their own now stand reduced to be a part of the third world.

That economic growth or progress of a kind has occurred in many of the third world countries is not to be denied; growth rates and certain macro-economic statistics can be cited in its favour. But such growth or progress has primarily benefited foreign investors and multinationals and the domestic elites, including 'the national bourgeoisie' and a class of the new rich and affluent middle classes. For the bulk of population, it has only meant further impoverishment which finds its worst victims in women and children, an absolute deterioration in living conditions even as 'the new poor' appear alongside the old ones and all of them bear the grim consequences of the debt-trap into which the ruling classes have led their countries. That this is indeed the case was endorsed by the International People's Tribunal to Judge the G7 in their Tokyo verdict of 1993. As one report summed it up: 'According to the Tribunal, the general consequences of SAPs have been: a sharp increase in unemployment, a fall in the remuneration of work, an increase in food dependency, a grave deterioration of the environment, a deterioration in healthcare systems, a fall in admissions to educational institutions, a decline in the productive capacity of many nations, the sabotage of democratic systems and the continued growth of external debt.' An important explicitly stated conclusion was that the policies instituted by international institutions in obedience to strategies adopted by the G7 are the cause of the brutal and massive impoverishment of popular majorities, particularly in the South and East. In a sharper comment, recognising globalisation as world capitalism's offensive against the third world, leader of Brazil's Workers' Party, Luis Ignacio da Silva (Lula)—whatever be his later compromises with this situation—has said (at the Havana Debt Conference in 1985):

> Without being radical or overly bold, I will tell you that the third world War has already started—a silent war, not for that reason any the less sinister. This war is tearing down Brazil, Latin America and practically all the third world. Instead of soldiers dying, there are children; instead of millions of wounded there are millions of unemployed; instead of destruction of bridges there is the tearing down of factories, schools, hospitals and entire economies.... It is a war by the US against the Latin American continent and the third world. It is a war over the foreign debt, one which has as its main weapon, interest, a weapon more deadly than the atom bomb, more shattering than a laser beam....

(That come to power as President of Brazil, Lula has, to the dismay and disillusionment of his people and many in his party, deserted this understanding is a common experience with social democratic leadership of even professedly socialist parties).

Decades of austerity, deregulation and structural adjustment in Latin America has swelled the ranks of the rural and urban poor and squeezed the livelihood of most employees and small producers, and with the US backed ruling classes embracing neo-liberal economics, set the scene for a social rebellion in the continent's backlands and in the *barrios* where the impoverished people struggle to make ends meet. This is how Argentina's communist leader, Luis Zamora has recently put it:

> Neo-liberalism and globalisation is nothing more than imperialism in a sweet-smelling fancy dress. It is this killer force that has pushed us into the ground. Over 60 per cent of our people are living below the poverty line and there's no sign that we have reached the bottom of the trough. Our country is ruled not by a bunch of Mafiosi but by a Mafia state buttressed by the US.... We simply cannot continue in the old ways, which means that the diseased political scum that has misruled us for decades must be discarded. It goes without saying that in this blueprint of ours the IMF and the World Bank and their masters will have no place.

In his speech at the opening session of the Group of 77 (G77) South Summit in April 2000 in Havana, Cuba, Fidel Castro thus noticed 'the mucky social results of this neoliberal race to catastrophe': 'in over one hundred countries, the per capita income is lower than fifteen years ago; at the moment, 1.6 billion people are faring worse than at the beginning of the 1980s; over 820 million people are undernourished and 790 million of them live in the third world; it is estimated that 507 million people living in the South today will not live to see their fortieth birthday; in the third-world countries represented here, two out of every five children suffer from growth retardation and one out of every three is underweight; thirty thousand who could be saved are dying every day; two million girls are forced into prostitution; 130 million children do not have access to elementary education; and 250 million minors under fifteen are bound to work for a living; the world economic order works for 20 per cent of the population but it leaves out, demeans, and degrades the remaining 80 per cent.'

He also pointed out: 'If Cuba has successfully carried out education, healthcare, culture, science, sports, and other programs, which nobody in the world would question—despite four decades of economic blockade—and revalued its currency seven times in the last five years in relation to the U.S. dollar, it has been thanks to its privileged position as a non-member of the International Monetary Fund (IMF).'

Castro posed the issue facing humankind today and warned of the catastrophic future that globalisation portends:

> Never before did humankind have such formidable scientific and technological potential, such extraordinary capacity to produce riches and well-being but never before were disparity and inequity so profound in the world.
>
> Technological wonders that have been shrinking the planet in terms of communications and distances coexist today with the increasingly wider gap separating wealth and poverty, development and underdevelopment.
>
> Globalisation is an objective reality underlining the fact that we are all passengers on the same vessel, that is, this planet where we all live. But, passengers on this vessel are travelling in very different conditions.

> Trifling minorities are travelling in luxurious cabins furnished with Internet, cell phones, and access to global communication networks. They enjoy a nutritious, abundant, and balanced diet as well as clean water supplies. They have access to sophisticated medical care and to culture.
>
> Overwhelming and herded majorities are travelling in conditions that resemble the terrible slave trade from Africa to America in our colonial past. That is, 85 percent of the passengers on this ship are crowded together in its dirty hold, suffering hunger, diseases and helplessness.
>
> Obviously, this vessel is carrying too much injustice to remain afloat and it pursues such an irrational and senseless route that it cannot call on a safe port. This vessel seems destined to clash with an iceberg. If that happened, we would all sink with it.

Samir Amin has written:

> It is commonly believed that Marxism in general and Maoism in particular belong to the past. This is certainly nonsense. On the contrary, it is the neo-liberal reactionary utopia which constitutes the dominant fashion today that has no future. It does not provide any answer to the social problems with which the vast majority of peoples are confronted everywhere, in the South as well as in the former East and even the West. In fact, the liberal recipe and all the so-called structural adjustment policies are generating only growing mass poverty, unemployment, marginalisation and dislocation of whole societies. It does not even create a 'sound ground' for relaunching a new wave of capitalist expansion. It generates only chaos: social, economic and political; and cannot therefore last….

The 'structural adjustment' or 'economic reform' of course began with and continues professing different, benevolent aims, promising stabilisation and growth of third world economies including eradication of poverty in countries willing to so adjust or reform. The evident failure of the Fund-Bank-sponsored programme to deliver on its promises is explained away as 'the price we have to pay for a period of transition' that will eventually lead to a new, allegedly healthier and more dynamic economy from which all will benefit. Often, amidst a chorus of 'irreversibility of reforms' among the ruling circles on both sides, the failure so far is attributed to the ill effects of slow or inadequate integration into global economy and more of such reforming integration is recommended, which however has the same disastrous consequences as before—mounting unemployment, inflation, degraded environment and the debt-trap. One witness to it all is Latin America where the debt-crises of the early 1980s led to Fund-Bank successfully pushing for yet more 'reforms' and now the same eighties are being described as the 'lost decade'! Faced with the rather dismal outcome of its efforts, World Bank has, in recent years, gone in for 'self-criticism', shedding tears over the plight of 'the poor' and, in tandem with that interesting phenomenon of recent decades, 'summit-led humanitarianism', spoken of humanising its programmes, of giving adjustment a 'human face'. A Tony Blair has even been advocating 'globalisation with a conscience' or 'compassionate globalisation'. This is a tacit acknowledgement that the earlier 'liberalisation' or 'reforms' or 'globalisation' have been indeed inhuman, without 'conscience' or 'compassion', that is, iniquitous and harsh on the poor. But then 'the poor' were never on the agenda of policies carried out earlier, before the 1980s, and even now it is hard to see this 'human face' anywhere, least of all in the African and Latin American countries which have received multiple-doses of 'adjustment'.

The harsh fact is that there is no such thing as 'liberalisation with a human face'. By definition the poor are the residual in its market processes since they simply lack purchasing power or financial muscle; 'marketisation' only marginalises them still more. 'Free market' is by definition free of morality, equity, justice or concern for the poor, market-commanded growth naturally tends to flood up and not trickle down, which even in the best of circumstances means, as Galbraith's 'less than-elegant metaphor' puts it: 'if you feed the horse enough oats, some will pass through to the road, for the sparrows'. Humanism in the prevailing economic order, based on cut-throat competition for control of the market, would ensure no return in terms of profit. 'Free market' simply cannot be on friendly terms with any genuine notion of human development. One may add, not friendly to the poor or any *humane* development, free market is more than friendly to drug-trafficking, arms and flesh trades, gambling and speculation, and similar other profit-yielding enterprises—all of which today stand well and truly globalised.

Amply documented in the literature on the subject, the failure —in terms of the publicly professed aims—of structural adjustment programmes is tacitly acknowledged by the IMF and World Bank themselves whose own evaluative studies over the past decades 'cannot say with certainty whether programmes have "worked" or not.' In taking note of this, we may here as well notice a similarly admitted important aspect of the politics involved in the 'working' of these economic programmes—a subject to which I will return for a slightly detailed comment later in these notes.

Viewed as a failure or otherwise, the outcome of 'structural adjustment' clearly establishes its character as a form of economic repression, which has inevitably given rise to a parallel political repression to support it, of course with the collusion of the third world elites. The social unrest and political instability flowing from this programme, including the popular resistance often evoked by it, has led to a strengthening of the internal repressive apparatuses in the concerned states. Despite the neo-liberal rhetoric about 'democracy' and 'free market' going together, the implementation of the 'economic reforms' has invariably required the firm backing of the military and of the authoritarian state. It is only a seeming paradox that a liberalised market-oriented economy needs its obverse in politics, an autocratic regime, to sustain it. This in fact confronts the existing democracy in the third world, which is already falling short of addressing fundamental social problems within or challenging the relations of dependence and subjugation to global capitalism without, with an insoluble problem. Its surrender to the demands of the 'structural adjustment programme' in opting for a market-based industrial take-off will compel it to give up even more on any substantial social reforms and thus lose whatever legitimacy it still has. Popular resistance will only drive the political system into one or the other form of authoritarianism. A stable democracy accompanying a 'structural adjustment' governed capitalist path of economic development will turn out to be an illusion in the third world countries. The World Bank has itself admitted that authoritarianism often has been 'a useful, if regrettable, expedient for effective policy-making' in pursuit of its programme, while democracies have been 'unable so far to make a rapid progress'.

We have already noticed the true nature of this 'progress'. It has meant surrender to world unification through the market on the part of the countries of the periphery which transforms them into open economic territories and their 'national economies' into reserves of cheap labour and natural resources, establishing a new form of 'market colonialism' which subordinates peoples and governments to itself through the impersonal interplay as well as deliberate manipulation of market forces. The structural adjustment programme applied in over 70 countries simultaneously has already exacted devastatingly high economic, social and cultural costs from the peoples there, particularly from the urban and rural poor, the vast masses in the third world, the outsiders to the market. This official economic medicine has really been itself a disease, all the more ravaging for the moral and cultural sickness that inevitably comes with it. That it is best administered through authoritarian means is therefore no cause for surprise.

Apropos the just-mentioned politics of structural adjustment, let me digress a little to discuss a theme in the mythology of globalisation which has interpreted it as 'retreat of the state'. It is in many ways an old theme, which acquired new dimensions in the Reagan-Thatcher era as the two went about dismantling the welfare state at home. The structural adjustment programme in the third world too set out demanding that the state cut down its social welfare spending and consumption subsidies, etc. to balance budgets and stabilise the economy. The theme gathered momentum with the collapse of the so-called 'statist socialism' of the Soviet Union, and charged with a certain triumphalism, the discourse of economic liberalisation, the supporting theory of globalisation, has rather aggressively, and successfully, insisted that state withdraw from ownership as well as control of operations in the economy, which is best left to private enterprise and the market. Equally if not more significant in this connection is the argument of international finance capital—as represented by the IMF, the World Bank, the WTO, etc.—that the concept of 'nation state' is now *passe*, the world is at last truly 'global', and the third world states should open up to an all barriers-free flow of metropolitan goods and capital. The state in the periphery and semi-periphery is sought to be ideologically delegitimised to not only facilitate this process but also undermine its capacity to defend national interests against the onslaught of global capitalism—though, rhetoric over 'global village' notwithstanding, no country at the centre is willing to give up its own status as a nation state to be able to defend its own economic interests, primarily the interests of its still nation-based multinationals. Again, as it is, facing a crisis of their own post-colonial development, a crisis now made worse by the impact of globalisation, third world nations, or 'nations-in-the-making', are facing the prospect of being 'nations-in-the-unmaking', torn within by all sorts of disruptive developments, often around genuine grievances, just as they are also being unravelled by the legitimate and not so legitimate demands of other or alternative identities which in turn is giving rise to movements for alternative life styles, traditional ways of managing things (environment etc.) and a certain kind of localism that looks askance at the centre—all of which has been, quite expectedly, taken positive note of by theorists of 'civil society' in their criticism of the state. Of particular interest here is that the World Bank too has not been unwilling to nod its post-modernist approval of such developments. This may not seem very consistent with its policies that seek to globalise the power of the market, that is the power of a handful of transnational corporations. But an ideologically delegitimised and enfeebled state or power at the centre, incapable of standing up to or challenging the controllers of global governance, is surely not unwelcome to this foremost financial institution of the globalisers. The supposed 'retreat of the state' has also been seen, in some Left or progressive circles, as a welcome trend towards 'internationalism' or the much hoped for 'one world'.

Developments such as these do lend substance of one sort or the other to the argument in favour of 'retreat of the state'. But to accept it would be most misleading, for, as we shall be arguing, whatever be the extent or nature of its retreat, the state remains central to the economy and politics of our globalised world. Briefly put, and looked at from opposite ends, the state is central not only to the world capital's ability to push through globalisation but even more to people's ability in the third world to effectively resist it and secure conditions for an autonomous economic development in their own interest.

In the 'state versus market' part of the ideology of globalisation, 'the state' is supposed to have retreated before 'the market' and the latter is then treated almost as a mythical identity. Now, to speak of 'the market' or 'market forces', 'power', 'imperatives' or 'demands' of the market, is certainly meaningful in making sense of what happens. But the use of such language must not involve an anthropomorphism which obscures the objective reality of things. Strictly speaking, the market 'enforces' or 'demands' nothing. Only specific people (based in class-like corporate executives) or organised in economic institutions (like directors of the IMF and the World Bank) demand (and enforce)—in the name of the market—economic policies favourable to their interests. The 'market' is a symbol or code word for capitalists, and the 'world market' for capitalists linked to multinational corporations and banks. This apart, the basic questions relating to the behaviour or functioning of the market—for example, how open or closed an economy will be in relation to the market—are essentially political questions which are ultimately resolved by state policy, that is, by political decision makers. That is how the globalisation of production and exchange is not the outcome of any 'world market imperatives'; a particular decision emanating from a set of classes (big capitalists, exporters, financiers, etc.) it is yet a product of state policies linked to international economic institutions. Again, it is mistaken to think that these inter- or supra-national agencies directly reflecting the interests of world capital—like the International Monetary Fund or the Group of Seven—have supplanted territorial state sovereignty, directly imposing the concrete terms of national economic interventions. Far from constituting themselves independently as new sources of autonomous political and economic power to which states are forced to submit, these agencies reflect state-sponsored processes of globalisation. I may add that, like market or supra-national agencies, 'technology' too is not an autonomous social force at work in globalisation, as it is sometimes made out to be. The new computer-driven technologies do make for better information flows, increase the velocity of transfers and movements of capital, provide the communication networks that ease plant relocations, etc., but it is the rates of profit which determine how and where these technologies will be utilised and this utilisation is, ultimately, a matter of socio-political decisions; the new technologies only facilitate and provide resources for such decision-making by class or classes currently dominant in the economy and the state. As Nicos Poulantzas has pointed out, the internationalisation of capital 'neither suppresses nor bypasses nation state, either in the direction of a peaceful integration of capital "above" the state level (since every process of internationalisation is effected under the dominance of the capital of a definite country), or in the direction of their extinction by the American super-state'. On the contrary, national states provide the necessary mechanisms and 'take charge of the interest of the dominant imperialist capital in its development within the "national" social formation'. Arguing the point with his characteristic lucidity and forcefulness, Harry Magdoff has stressed: 'it is important to keep in mind that almost all the multinationals are in fact national organizations operating on a global scale. We are in no way denying that capitalism is, and has from its very beginning been, a world system, or that this system has been further integrated by the multinationals. But just as it is essential to understand, and analyze, capitalism as a world system, it is equally necessary to recognize that each capitalist firm relates to the world system through, and must eventually rely on, the nation state.' Multinationals may operate across national boundaries but this does not mean that they are not based in a nation. It is the nation state on which they depend for protection and promotion of their interests both at home and abroad. 'The term "multinational"', Meszaros has suggested, 'is frequently used as a complete misnomer, hiding the real issue of domination of the local economies—in tune with the innermost determinations and antagonisms of the global capital system—by the capitalist enterprises of a more powerful nation. As a rule the dominant capitalist nations enforce their interests with all means at their disposal, peacefully for as long as they can, but resorting to war if there is no other way of doing so.... The representatives of the most powerful sections of capital understand that they are not in a position to dispense with the protection afforded to their vital interests by their national states.'

This is how the modern state, at the centres of global capitalism, has been throughout active in helping capitalism along, creating conditions conducive for its development and, when necessary, through direct intervention in the economy. Therefore it has also been throughout an imperial state, promoting (through economic policies, military alliances and wars) capitalist expansion abroad, intervening to retain old and secure new regions for imperialist exploitation, and, in recent years, brokering 'transitions' from colonies to political independence that guaranteed access and opportunities to its multinationals in the post-colonial states. In still more recent years the state has played a most important role in formulating and executing the strategies of globalisation, allocating economic resources to 'global actors' (that is, its multinationals), bailing out elite losers and reinforcing the policing of victims and opponents of globalisation. The multinationals and their state-backed exploitation at home and abroad is thus not a new phenomenon in the history of capitalism. But a certain shift in the situation has certainly occurred. Earlier, often still national firms in terms of who owned their capital, for their deployment and activity abroad they needed and sought the active, positive support of their government. Today, as multi-or transnationals, they have become powerful enough to not only develop their own strategies of overseas expansion but, in pursuit of their private interests, subordinate the state policies to these strategies. At home the imperative is a more effective extraction of domestic resources to finance overseas expansion, and abroad the securing of more effective conditions for the reproduction of global capital accumulation. An important aspect of the former imperative, especially in a situation of economic stagnation, is the dismantling of the welfare state, which had in a way meant subordinating 'the market' to serve social interests, at least to a limited degree and in the short run. Here a very real retreat of the state has indeed occurred but accompanied by, as it were, a compensating advance for it as a coercive state (breaking the power of the trade unions, etc). Abroad the state has played the principal role in opening the world economy through the creation of supposedly international economic institutions such as the World Bank, International Monetary Fund, World Trade Organisation, etc. Controlled by the appointees of the respective states, and backed by their political and military power, their function—especially with the globalising thrust and the intensive 'adjustments' of the 1980s —has been to break down all barriers, displace national markets and local producers and undermine popular social legislation in order to facilitate the entry of multinationals and help secure the primacy of domestic export elites producing for the markets of the countries at the centre. That the United States has led in all this and its officials and spokespersons have publicly acknowledged these international economic institutions as 'long standing furtherers of American influence' which 'support our values and policy goals', 'our foreign policy objectives', and 'provide a powerful way for us to leverage our resources', underlines not only the importance of state in the process of globalisation, but, more specifically, also the United States' long standing role of what Isaac Deutscher described as 'world's gendarme of counter revolution', seeking to preserve the 'free world' as a freely exploitable area in which not only American corporations but global capitalism as well can do business on their own terms.

Arguing that globalisation emanates from no imperatives of either 'a world market' or 'new technologies', but is rather the result of the superior politico-military organisation of social classes linked to 'global markets', James Petras and Chronis Polychronion have written:

> In a word, the imperial state played a fundamental role in the economic reconstruction of the major corporate dominated economies, provided a military-political shell for its expansion, intervened to preserve and deepen its presence while it financed at the same time 'international' lending agencies that were established for the sole purpose of opening new markets and creating new investment sites. Far from being anti-statist, multinational capital demands an 'activist state', but one that dismantles the welfare state in favour of globalisation. Under the impetus of export/multinational capital, the imperial state subsidises and finances global expansion while facilitating internal exploitation to accumulate capital for export.

It hardly makes any sense to speak of a retreat of the state at the centres of global capitalism.

That the imperial state has been more than active in the periphery, backing up particular multinationals and global capitalism as a whole, with all its economic, political and, when and wherever necessary, military might is too well known to need any elaboration. But the third world state itself has been no less active in the interests of the globlising multinationals and the collaborating local elites, a 'conditionalities'-laden dialectical relation obtaining between the state's role in the domestic economy and its integration into the world market on the one hand, and the state ceasing to be an active agent of control in the economy to become a facilitator in the process of globalisation on the other.

Disturbed by the consequences of its early policies—when, obsessed with trimming the fiscal deficits of countries which approached them for 'structural assistance', IMF and WB had compelled them to restructure and cut down expenditure on social welfare, leaving little if any scope for public transfers for health and education or alleviation of poverty and unemployment—in a significant reversal of its policy position, the World Bank has been asking the state to be active with 'social safety net' and 'investing in people'. And why not? One might ask. After all the citizenry needs to be reasonably healthy and educated enough for extraction of surplus value and piling up of profits. The World Bank's concern, however, has been different. It is the long-term social unrest and conflicts in society generated by structural adjustment which have been and continue to be more worrisome for the powers that be, especially when the much-touted 'social safety net' has turned out to be only a euphemism used for maintaining the facade of the welfare state—whatever of it there has been in the third world—while it continues to be dismantled. Still more alarming have been the economic crises and financial breakdowns among countries undergoing 'adjustment', and the new phenomenon of the 'failed states', as they are called. Naturally enough, the World Bank's thoughts have of late turned to the question of 'governance', the need for 'good governance' in the 'interests of society'. A departure from neo-liberal orthodoxy, it is however a far cry from a similar departure earlier, the philosophy of the Keynesian state, when the Great Depression had led to state intervention against depredations of the market which threatened capitalism itself. The purpose now is stability to secure better implementation of the policies of liberalisation and globalisation. Terms like democracy, responsive government, transparency, social protection for the vulnerable, concern for environment and human rights, etc.—in any case unavoidable these days—now abound in its literature, but what is really sought by the World Bank is a 'politics-free' techno-economic state with a decisive role for bureaucracy whose decision-making is supposed to be impersonal and governed only by considerations of expertise. Needless to say, if this state does materialise, which is least likely, as facilitator of globalisation it will need to be as active and effective as any other. Only with its 'politics-free' pretensions and throwing of a mantle of technocratic legitimacy over the adjustment measures, it will also serve to shift attention away from the other more substantial shift in class power and privilege which the typical adjustment programme invariably involves. Such shift, however, has been difficult, if not impossible to conceal, and this also explains why in the real world, structural adjustment has generally found its best desirable political counterpart in the authoritarian state. This is how Barton Biggs (Director of Global Strategy, Morgan Stanley), speaking about South Korea, has put it:

> It's very helpful to have a dictatorship in the bootstrap stage of an emerging market and an emerging economy. Dictators make the tough decisions and demand the sacrifices that have to be made to turn a poor country into a wealthy one...

Fund-Bank's heightened concern with governance is understandable. Given the lender-borrower nexus involved, the due has a legitimate stake in the capacity of its borrower governments to pay and, in order to do so, to effectively implement (or 'govern') the projects and programmes assisted by it. But this concern does not mean any abandonment of their earlier belief. This is clear from the way bad management or governance of society is defined, namely, the refusal by the old state to take the intrinsic wisdom of the market as the beginning and end for all action, for that is where the 'interests of society' ultimately lie. Good governance is precisely a reversal of this folly or sin which ensures that market-serving technocratic imperatives prevail. In other words, rhetoric apart, Bank's view of good governance has little to do with popular participation in politics and policies, with democratic governance, which can only be a hindrance to the smooth introduction and execution of structural adjustment; given democracy, people would be simply unwilling, and will refuse, to pay the price of adjustment. It is not surprising that, as suggested above, adjusting countries have invariably experienced atrophy of their democratic institutions and growth of authoritarianism. The World Bank has itself reported that, though it is regrettable, adjustment has worked more effectively under authoritarian auspices. If some of the more committed ideologues have favoured deceit and camouflage to manipulate people and push adjustment through —'Losses and benefits to various constituents should not be made clear. The higher the potential political and economic costs of adjustment, the greater the premium on obfuscation', as one of them has urged—others have suggested 'deliberately provoking a crisis' or conceiving a 'pseudo crisis' to smoothen the authoritarian path to adjustment.

So much for the neo-liberal discourse on 'retreat of the state'. The state at the centre and in the periphery, that is in the third world, remains on essential element in the ongoing globalisation, elaborating and executing 'structural adjustment' that facilitates it, benefiting the rich and powerful in both places while shifting at the same time the burdens and costs of it all on to the shoulders of the common people everywhere. Insofar as the state has indeed retreated from its welfare functions, this, together with the resistance that adjustment provokes from the people, has necessarily enhanced its role as the most formidable instrument of coercion in society.

It only needs to be added that this centrality of the state to the economy and politics of our globalised world, also makes it, everywhere, the most important site of struggle against globalisation.

That the state is the most important site of struggle against globalisation has an aspect to it in the third world that needs to be specifically underlined. 'Anti-statism' has been a distinctive, almost defining feature of the neo-liberal project. For its purposes in the third world, it has aimed directly at discrediting and dismantling the state. But to discredit the state is to discredit the one agency best capable of organising and articulating people's collective aspirations and of developing effective resistance to neo-liberal depredations. Hence the overriding reason for people in the third world needing the state for their own purposes. That the third world bourgeoisie or ruling elites in control of the state have failed to deliver so far as common people's interests are concerned and far from providing leadership in the struggle against its intrusions have now opted for collaboration with global capitalism, takes nothing away from the decisive importance of the state, the nation state, in the third world people's struggle against neo-liberal policies, the new imperialism that is globalisation, and for securing autonomous economic development that serves their interests.

Of course, this implies not phoney 'empowerment' being dished out by ruling establishments, but real people's power in the state, it has to be *their* state. Fashionable academic talk of 'failure of the third world state', must not be allowed to obscure this fact. It has not been a failure of state *per se*. William Graf has rightly observed:

> 'The real state in the third world thus remains the major, and perhaps only, framework within which the important social and political issues can be dealt with in the context of a world system permanently stacked against peripheral societies and economies, while the theoretical state is probably the only conceptual framework capable of developing a counter-hegemonic project sufficiently comprehensive to challenge neo-liberal globalisation. Without the state, therefore, there can be no large-scale, long-term emancipatory project for the South. After all, 'insofar as there is any effective democracy at all in relation to the power of capitalists and bureaucrats, it is still embedded in political structures which are national or subnational in scope'.
>
> Only the state can offer a feasible *agency* capable of aggregating the multifarious counter-hegemonic forces in the peripheral state. Only state-economic power in the South has any prospects of standing up to, negotiating with or countering the pervasive economic power of international capital... only the state.. can forge collective emancipatory projects directed against the hegemonic powers. And certainly any strategy for democratic or radical change, in a globalized world of states, must start from the state.
>
> Without a real state, and a real state theory, then, the South would appear to have no way forward, out, or back. The question that needs to be posed, therefore, is not: state or market? but: what kind of state, and whose state?....

In the context of contemporary globalisation, two facts particularly need to be recognised. In the first place the world capitalist system is not to be considered a neutral or ambiguous, or even remotely a benevolent factor in the world which, giving it the buzz-name 'globalisation', its ideologues are making it out to be. Capitalism today is so pervasive and powerful as to have become invisible, and is all the more powerful for this invisibility, leading, even among many on the left, to a failure to see it or a refusal to name it properly. Invisible as globalisation, it masquerades, without a proper name—it is 'liberalisation', 'structural adjustment', 'new economic policy', 'economic reform', 'reform process', 'industrialisation', even 'democracy', anything but 'capitalism'. But globalisation has its proper name, capitalism, and in the third world it is the continued reality of imperialism. It is customary in polite academic and political circles these days to deny the existence of imperialism. The concept itself is often dismissed with scorn as 'unscientific' in the West or 'outdated' by the ruling classes in the third world. Professors, journalists and government officials use euphemisms or weave fancy theories to disguise what is going on. That some third world countries manage, with whatever ultimate outcome or denouement, to advance beyond the typical third world lot, or that forms of exploitation in Africa, Latin America or Asia have diversified beyond simple extraction of minerals and agricultural produce, does not mean the end of imperialism. The major segments of third world countries (as indeed their counterparts in industrial capitalist and erstwhile 'socialist' countries) continue to experience the aggressive encroachments of imperialism under the aegis of policies of 'free market economics' and 'liberalisation' that globalisation stands for. That globalisation has found it increasingly necessary to speak in the language of 'integration'—it helps create the illusion of inclusion or sharing in a worldwide economic development —does not alter the fact that it is imperialism in a new form, that globalisation is really a code word—an obscuring or misleading one at that—for a system in which the logic of capitalism has become more or less universalised and where imperialism achieves its ends not so much by the older 'extra-economic' and military ways but by unleashing and manipulating the exploitative and destructive impulses of the capitalist market. Globalisation is thus the reality of imperialism whose intervention, economic, political, cultural or military, in the affairs of the third world has always been essentially negative. It has never brought with it economic prosperity, or for that matter democracy, to the peoples of Asia, Africa or Latin America. Today as in the past or in the future, the thoroughly integrated global capitalist system, dominated by the double-dialectic of centre-periphery and development-underdevelopment, often backed by its armies, can only bring to these peoples further servitude, the exploitation of their labour, the expropriation of their riches and the denial of their rights. Given its structural logic, the model of productive growth and consumption of the West, even if deemed desirable—and this is surely questionable—cannot be extended as such to the rest of the world. Countries of the periphery or semi-periphery of global capitalism can never hope to reach the levels of its dominant centre. They can only be the sites of misery and inequality, social desperation and hopelessness of peoples impoverished by the interplay of global market forces backed by the economic and armed might of the dominant centre.

The other fact that needs to be particularly recognised is that today this dominant centre, itself in deep crisis in the capitalist heartlands, in an effort to cope with the inherent problems of late capitalism, is opting for a harsher selection in its attitude to the countries of the periphery and semi-periphery (which now includes the former 'socialist' countries). In doing so, it seeks to co-opt a certain fringe of countries and classes, and hasten the marginalisation of the rest, almost the whole African continent and huge masses of people in Asia and Latin America, all the while tackling the ensuing conflicts, opposition or resistance, by means of an armed-to-the-teeth international police, the global gendarme that America has become today. The economic order produced by the world market and presided over by the North is turning out to be a grand disorder needing to be capped with a military order that ensures effective repression of recalcitrant states or popular revolts in the South, selectively permitting festering situations and suppressing those become threatening to capitalism, and secures unquestioned domination for global capitalism. All these trends have been apparent in the Gulf Wars, the war on Afghanistan, the strangling of Nicaragua and similar plans for Cuba, and the conversion of NATO into a rapid-deployment force on behalf of global capitalism led by the United States. We are becoming familiar with the affluent capitalist West's supercilious reference to the rest of the world as 'residual countries' oftentimes fit only to provide markets for arms and obsolete technologies and sites for still profitable but polluting industries!

Herein lies the real or ultimate meaning of contemporary globalisation. In a clever if not cynical political manoeuvre, it has borrowed its terminology from the language and politics of the radical 1960s, but what has been conducted as 'liberalisation', 'structural adjustment' or 'economic reforms', etc. is essentially a class struggle under another name which has everywhere organised a drastic shift in class power to the benefit of the rich and the privileged. In the third world, as argued above, it is only a new form of imperialism, with consequences that imperialism always had in the third world. As 'structural adjustment' or 'economic reform' are universalised so is peripheralisation of the people in the third world. Alongside, its 'global interdependence or unification' has involved a worldwide cultural penetration of global capitalism. Imperialism or global capitalism has always sought to buttress its economic and political domination with ideological, and equally with its cultural domination. This is how during the last three or four decades, it has forged a new mould of global culture, shaping and turning it variously in accordance with the requirements of the late capitalist market. Western economics, capitalist production and technological advances have so combined that cultural life has been homogenised through uniformities and standardisations or regimentations which now determine fashion, musical tastes (for example, pop culture), food consumption (for example, fast foods), leisure activities and numerous other material and non-material spheres of life. What is on is an attempt to steal and standardise the imagination of the world, a massive corruption of consciousness and culture in behalf of capitalism which at times is nothing less than 'culturecide' by capitalism. It is this new-fangled global culture—which in its American version, with its overriding consumerist thrust, has earned the name of 'McDonaldisation'—that is invariably accompanying the process of globalisation, finding eager adherents or converts among the elites of the third world (as well as the politically powerful and economically affluent sections of the former 'socialist' countries), who, dazzled by the high lifestyles and high-tech culture of the West, the fads and fashions of upper-class Western consumerism, see the accumulation of computers, automobiles and gadgets of all kinds as the purpose of life and elevate quantity and style of personal possessions over the quality of life for society as a whole. This for them is the criterion for development and progress. What is indeed underway is a cultural assault which threatens erosion, corruption and 'McDonaldisation' of local life and cultures, even as it successfully co-opts the local elites and reaches out to the middle class and petty bourgeoisie of the third world countries, thus extending the social base for globalisation in both urban and rural sectors, by integrating 10, 15 or even 20 per cent of the country's population into the socio-political and cultural system of global capitalism.

This cooption, the emerging divergence of values, attitudes, culture and life-styles between the elites and the common people —a cultural 'secession of the successful', counterpart of what is happening in the economic sphere—does not exhaust the phenomenon underway. Culture penetration is not just an extension but integral part of globalisation as imperialist domination. Imperialism has never been merely an economic-military system of control and exploitation. Cultural domination, an effort to penetrate and dominate the cultural life of the popular classes in order to reorder the values, behaviour, institutions and identity of the oppressed peoples to conform with the interests of the imperial classes, was always an integral part of it. So it is now with globalisation as a new, latest form of imperialism. Besides, there are now direct material benefits to be had, as never before. Recognising American economic and cultural domination in the ongoing globalisation, James Petras has written:

> US cultural imperialism has two goals—one economic and the other political—to capture markets for its cultural commodities and to establish hegemony by shaping popular consciousness. The export of entertainment commodities is one of the most important sources of capital accumulation and global profits displacing

> manufacturing exports. In the political sphere, cultural imperialism plays a major role in dissociating people from their cultural roots and traditions of solidarity, replacing them with media created 'needs', which change with every publicity campaign. The political effect is to alienate people from traditional class and community bonds, atomising and separating individuals from each other.

It may be mentioned that religious fundamentalism (especially Islamic or Hindu) so rampant today, is significant, partly at least, for its opposition to 'consumerism of the west' or 'the American way of life', the imperialist cultural domination it is resourceless to understand or overcome. But it has acquired this significance primarily because the traditional Left alternatives, in particular the great revolutionary traditions of Marxism and communism seem to have become, for the time being at least, unavailable.

II

The collapse of the Soviet Union has been a historic gain for global capitalism. The challenge that communist regimes and movements born of the October Revolution had posed to its hegemony over 70 odd years has been eliminated, making for its almost unquestioned sway over economy and politics of the contemporary world. The 'communist threat' has receded globally, at least for the time being. The radical change in the relationship of forces and geography of power in international politics resulting from the dissolution of a great power and its system of alliances has led to the near complete supremacy of a group of major capitalist powers, centred on the United States of America. Of the reinforced capitalist hegemony, at least two aspects need to be immediately noted. The conflict of interests among these capitalist powers notwithstanding, they are firmly united in their economic structure. Transnational integration among the capitalist classes has still to reckon with the fact of the national locus of the owners and the boards of directors of the leading transnational corporations. But the transnational corporations have managed to bring a 'new class consciousness' to the world, consolidating it around themselves. The differences and contradictions remain and can be really sharp and explosive at times, but as in any class project, the part is subordinate to the whole, the particular to the general. Therefore, if there is one class in the contemporary world which could be said to be 'class for itself' in the Marxian sense, it is the monopoly bourgeoisie, more particularly of the United States, Germany and Japan. They are enormously powerful, very well aware of their interests and have the means, economic, political and military, to defend and pursue them the world over. The 'new world order', being promulgated only heralds the demolition of the barriers to the global domination of this bourgeoisie, so that the much celebrated 'free world', now more 'free' than ever before, remains a freely exploitable area in which giant multinational corporations can do business on their own terms. This class, feeling more safe and powerful that at any time since at least the first decade of the twentieth century, if not since the Paris Commune, is today determined to rule the world by its own lights, using its economic and cultural supremacy, and if needs be by the exercise of brute military force. *And* presiding over this system of global capitalist domination and oppression is the United States, the world's only remaining superpower. It is the most important single fact of world politics in our times that since the world war two, the US has been at the centre of world reaction. It has used its enormous resources to crush, curb and contain democratic movements and progressive or left-wing regimes in all continents. In the post-Soviet 'new world order', the US has arrogated to itself the natural right of international policing, continuing even more freely with its role of 'world's gendarme of counter revolution', as Isaac Deutscher once called it, even as it also uses its military power to secure American capitalism's economic interests and imperialist domination abroad.

The emerging reality of the 'new world order', the reborn unilateralism of global capitalism or *pax-Americana*, the military might, technological prowess and economic clout as well as moral self-righteousness and cultural arrogance of the triumphalist capitalist West was early and fully displayed in the mounting and conduct of the First Gulf War, when, even as the Soviet Union was collapsing, Western powers played fast and loose with the provisions of the United Nations Charter and, in the words of Canada's former Ambassador to the United Nations, Stephen Lewis, 'conscripted (the UN) into the role of providing cover for US foreign policy', in the process shredding to bits whatever remained of either 'non-alignment' or 'North-South dialogue', reducing the rest of the world to an impotent, mute witness to the orgy of mass destruction visited on Iraq that brought alive the nightmarish memories of Hiroshima and Nagasaki. Thus was unquestioned Western hegemony established in the oil-rich Arab world and a warning issued that only severe punishment awaits the governments which for one reason or another ran counter to the wishes or interests of American or global capitalism—a warning later brutally reissued by America's equally unilateral and indiscriminatory bombing of Yugoslavia, and more recently, by war on Afghanistan and then again on Iraq.

A more or less peaceful counterpart of this armed assertion abroad have been the recent policies of the American, indeed of global capitalism, whereby all economic and political means have been used, more particularly through international institutions like the IMF, World Bank and WTO and so-called aid and structural adjustment programmes, to thrust the Western agenda down the throats of the rest of the world—in the areas of international economic development and monetary management, cutting-edge technology, informatics, audio-visual production and services, trade and intellectual property rights, sports and culture, and so on. Leave alone any radical or socialist change, even the search for a 'third way' as it is sometimes called—any kind of relatively autonomous or self-reliant development that does not slavishly seek to follow the Western approved capitalist model—is denied to countries of the third or former second world. Needless to add, global capitalism's renewed assertion abroad is not without its counterpart at home. All sorts of old or new right-wing agendas have come alive in the domestic domain of the countries of advanced capitalism, including the US. The keyword here has been 'roll back' and the welfare state continues to be dismantled. As Chomsky has put it, 'now they feel they can move on to roll back and unravel the entire social contract which developed through large-scale popular struggle over a century and a half, which did sort of soften the edges of predatory private tyranny, and softened them a lot.' This rollback is accompanied by a new offensive against the working classes and a 'restructuring' of capitalist economy to allow for their intensified exploitation.

More important than its current economic, political or military power is the ideological hegemony that global capitalism, with US at its head, has come to acquire today. The collapse of the Soviet and East European communist regimes and their ignorantly accepted or cleverly imputed identification with socialism, has enabled the capitalist propaganda at its most triumphant to proclaim the failure or defeat of socialism itself and the success or inevitability of capitalism. With the means provided by the contemporary communications revolution, a veritable carpet bombing of public consciousness has occurred producing an ideological consensus on behalf of capitalism, from one country to another, and from liberals and conservatives to any number of ex-socialists. The Left as a whole has succumbed, singularly failing to play its time-honoured role, precisely when it was most needed, as critics of capitalism, of combating the consensus of the right (which, incidentally, makes nonsense of the much-vaunted pluralism of bourgeois democracy, gaining for it a spurious credibility only by a bizarre blowing up of minor differences among competitors in the politics of 'actually existing capitalism'). Once again, as in the 1950s and 1960s, 'the end of ideology' is proclaimed. 'An intellectual celebration of apathy', 'a consensus of a few provincials about their own immediate and provincial position (that helped them) to acquiesce in and to justify the status quo', as C. Wright Mills had then put it, 'the end of ideology' today is an equally myopic and status quoist celebration of the consensus around 'the triumph of capitalism', the near-exclusive dominance of its ideological discourse. Now it is not only the end of socialism, but the 'end of history' itself, its culmination in an eternal and inevitable capitalism. Once, these very bourgeois ideologues, theorising about 'Soviet totalitarianism' had claimed that the 'empire of evil' and its satellites were immutable, that it was a hell from which there was no exit. With their persistent myopia about historical change, instead of self-criticism, they have only produced a transfer: it is now capitalism which is a system from which there is no exit. Margaret Thatcher's 'There is no alternative' (TINA)—duly echoed by all and sundry including a Gorbachev once—has become the new chorus in defence of capitalism. What is more, in its omnipresence and newly acquired immunity to criticism, capitalism has become virtually invisible, its invisibility well secured by another of the proliferating buzzwords of our time, 'globalisation', and the accompanying clutch of concepts like 'liberalisation', 'structural adjustment', 'economic reform', 'new economic policy', etc.

I have touched upon this subject earlier. Another, more focused look at it, particularly in relation to the First World of capitalism, will not be out of place.

'Globalisation' is far from being an unambiguous or conceptually-clear theoretical construct. Given the fuzziness of language over it, Peter Marcuse has even called it a 'non-concept': 'a simple catalogue of everything that seems different since, say, 1970, whether advances in information technology, widespread use of air freight, speculation in currencies, increased capital flows across borders, Disneyfication of culture, mass marketing, global warming, genetic engineering, multinational corporate power, new international division of labour, international mobility of labour, reduced power of nation-states, post-modernism, or post-Fordism'. But this is not all. As Peter Marcuse adds: 'The issue is more than one of careless use of words: intellectually, such muddy use of the term fogs any effort to separate cause from effect, to analyse what is being done, by whom, to whom, for what, and with what effect. Politically, leaving the term vague and ghostly permits its conversion to something with a life of its own, making it a force, fetishising it as something that has an existence independent of the will of human beings, inevitable and irresistible.'

Thus, for its ardent ideologue Thomas Friedman—a big time columnist of the *New York Times*—globalisation is a new technological-economic system based in the microchip and ruled by an 'electronic herd' of financial investors and multinational corporations, sweeping away everything that came before—capitalism and socialism, the nation-state, imperialism, class struggle, everything. And we have even well-meaning mainstream scholars coming up with what can at best be described as deceptively confusing interpretations. For John Harriss, for example, 'globalisation' is a recent phenomena. He views the use of the term 'in the last 10 years or so' as 'an indication that something has been happening out there', and goes on to describe it in conventional fuzzy terms: '...the world is more inter-connected and supposedly more interdependent than it was formerly, as a result of changes in the global economy—notably rapid movements of large volumes of money and the increased volume of trade—as well as of changes in communications and in information technology. These trends are related in turn and more controversially, with a variety of political and cultural changes, including perhaps especially the ideas of 'deterritorialisation', of the decline of the nation state and of a shift to politics of presence.' For Amartya Sen globalistion is almost as old as civilisation itself: 'Over thousands of years, globalisation has progressed through travel, trade, migration, spread of cultural influences and dissemination of knowledge (including of science and technology)'. Sen recognises 'the dual presence of abject misery and unprecedented prosperity in the world in which we live'—'incomparably richer than ever before, ours is also a world of extraordinary deprivation and staggering inequality'—to end up urging support for globalisation 'in the best sense of that idea', and pleading: 'what is needed is a fairer distribution of the fruits of globalisation'. Globalisation's historically specific reality today is evaded through an appeal to its so-called 'idea in the best sense', which only adds to the prevailing fuzziness and confusion in the use of this term or concept.

Be that as it may, there are many reasons to doubt that 'globalisation' represents an accurate account of the phenomena it purports to describe. On the other hand, there are good reasons to treat it, in its current usage, as an ideological mystification.

As a theoretical concept, globalisation came up in the late 1960s and early 1970s to account for a recent complex of developments in global economy, particularly the major expansion and conquest of markets by the multinationals, seeking to present this international capitalist expansion in a favourable light, an alternative to Marxist vocabulary with its concepts of imperialism, capitalism, etc. In its current widely accepted usage, acquiring new credibility with the collapse of 'Soviet socialism', the concept is characterised by two distinct emphases. In the first place, linked to what has been called the third technological revolution, this internationalisation of capital has come to be viewed as a tide sweeping over borders in which technology and irresistible market forces transform the global system in ways beyond the power of everyone to do much to change. The view is often buttressed by a kind of technological determinism where the new electronic technologies make globalisation not only possible or necessary, but inevitable. Globalisation is viewed as an entity in itself, an inevitable, irreversible natural process, which independently of any human will or politics is now taking over and transforming the world. In its second distinctive emphasis, globalisation is seen as a historical rupture of a qualitative kind from the changes that have been occurring in capitalism since its inception. The changes now taking place represent a distinctive and unique kind of 'epochal shift'—a notion which these days runs as a kind of *leitmotif* through a wide spectrum of intellectual currents, where 'post' is the presiding buzzword. We are told that we are now, since the early 1970s to be precise, living through an epochal shift, the birth of a new era, a major qualitative leap so different from the earlier changes in the process of capitalist development that the very logic of capitalism stands superseded. In the globalised world of today there is no capitalism with its exploitation and oppressions, its classes and class struggles, its structural defects and explosive antagonisms, its chronic problems or crises. Imperialism too is now a thing of the past.

Around this notion of a technology-driven 'globalisation' has grown a new orthodoxy—that of 'a dematerialised world', which yet again suggests supersession of capitalism as an economic system and therefore obsolescence of the associated categories of analysis. In a recent article, speaking of 'the Myth of Weightless Economy', Ursula Huws has written:

> 'The Death of Distance', 'Weightless World', the 'Connected Economy', the 'Digital Economy', the 'Knowledge-Based Economy', the 'Virtual Organization'. All these phrases were culled from the titles of books published in the six months prior to writing this essay, in spring, 1998. They could have been multiplied many times: 'virtual', 'cyber', 'tele-', 'networked' or even just 'e-' can, it seems, be prefixed interchangeably to an almost infinite range of abstract nouns. Without even straying from the field of economics, you can try 'enterprise', 'work', 'banking', 'trade', 'commerce', or 'business' (although the device works equally well in other areas: for instance 'culture', 'politics', 'sex', 'democracy', 'relationship', 'drama', 'community', 'art', 'society', 'shopping' or 'crime').
>
> A consensus seems to be emerging—in economics as in other fields —that something entirely new is happening: that the world as we know it is becoming quite dematerialised (or, as Marx put it, 'all that is solid melts into air') and that this somehow throws into question all the conceptual models which have been developed to make sense of the old material world. We are offered a paradoxical universe: geography without distance, history without time, value without weight, transactions without cash. This is an economics which sits comfortably in a Baudrillardian philosophical framework, in which all reality has become a simulacrum and human agency, to the extent that it can be said to exist at all, is reduced to the manipulation of abstractions...

The ideological-political implications are obvious. As in the current conventional conception of 'globalisation', capitalism, the historically specific capitalist processes, the capitalist exploitation of human beings and natural resources, simply disappear. The frenetic and feverish manner in which the information revolution is hyped, makes it appear that the entire system of organised capitalism dating back to Industrial Revolution (and even earlier) is being displaced by a new age of 'the electronic republic' and 'digital futurologies' where information or 'knowledge' is the only source of value and work is something contingent and delocalisable if not dispensable, where the demand or need to produce material means of living, indeed any assertion of the physical claims of the human body in the here-and-now is an old-fashioned concern, where 'the computer', lord and master of it all, refashions economy and society, human beings themselves, in its own image...

As capitalism goes out of sight, 'globalisation' as a universal category of analysis displaces the critical socialist concepts of 'capitalism', or imperialism, and together with its technological determinism undercuts any notion of radical or systemic transformative politics. Any kind of anti-capitalist project is ruled out. A natural, inevitable process, any resistance to 'globalisation' is futile. There is no alternative but accept its dictates. 'Globalisation' thus disarms any opposition to almighty capital, becomes an ideological tool instilling a certain fatalism in the working people, nations and states to induce them to follow policies of adjustment to the demands of global capitalism, at home and abroad.

The conventional theorising over 'globalisation'—'globaloney' it has been called—mystifies the reality of our world. Postulating an utterly fictitious world of superseded capitalism, it makes capitalism safe against criticism and opposition and using the argument of 'inevitability', it wants us to believe that in this globalised world there is no alternative to the meek acceptance of the conditions necessary for its trouble-free functioning, which in effect means trouble-free functioning of the global capitalist system.

It only needs to be added that today quite a few on the left, indeed a painfully large majority, too has succumbed to the infashion 'globloney' of the right. This left has presently joined the right in accepting that 'There Is No Alternative'—not just no alternative to capitalism but, as we shall see, to a more or less (the right goes for more, the left somewhat less) ruthlessly 'flexible' capitalism.

Globalisation is argued for as an almost automatic solution to all the encountered problems and contradictions of our economy, if not our society as a whole—its promise of universal benevolence reminding us of the once similarly hailed and revered notion of 'invisible hand', Adam Smith's assurance that went so grievously sour as soon as the logic of *capitalist* market asserted itself. This solution, as noticed above, is presented as a complete novelty as if the issue of globalisation appeared on the historical horizon only in the last couple of decades, marking an entirely new, qualitatively different phase in the development of capitalism. This, however, is only so much 'globaloney'. Globalisation is nothing qualitatively new in the history of bourgeois society, it is a process that has been going on for a long time, in fact ever since capitalism came into the world as a viable form of society four or five centuries ago. An ever-changing system, capitalism was born and grew, and grew to maturity only as a world system. In other words capitalism has always been a global or globalising system, one moving inexorably towards 'globalisation' from its very inception. The most significant elements of what is called globalisation have always been part of capitalist development, even if the specific forms and features of this development including globalisation —that is, the global process of capital expansion and accumulation— have been different in different periods (including our own). That capitalism is in its innermost essence an expanding system both internally and externally was pointed out by Marx a long time ago. Once rooted, propelled by the law of accumulation of capital, it both grows and spreads. The classic analysis of this double movement is of course Marx's *Capital*. But the *globalising* nature of capitalism was diagnosed and emphasised by him more than 150 years ago in the *Communist Manifesto* itself. Marx has been proved uncannily right about many things but perhaps nowhere has he been vindicated more completely than in his account of capitalist expansion or globalisation. Here, for example, are a couple of passages from the *Manifesto*: 'The bourgeoisie has through its exploitation of the world market given a cosmopolitan character to production and consumption in every country ... All old-established national industries have been destroyed or are being destroyed. They are dislodged by new industries, whose introduction becomes a life and death question for all nations, by industries that no longer work up indigenous raw material, but raw material drawn from the remotest zones; industries whose products are consumed not only at home, but in every quarter of the globe. In place of the old wants, satisfied by the productions of the country, we find new wants, requiring for their satisfaction the products of distant lands and climes... in place of the old local and national seclusion and self-sufficiency, we have intercourse in every direction, universal interdependence of nations...'. Again: 'The need of a constantly expanding market for its productions chases the bourgeoisie over the whole surface of the globe. It must nestle everywhere, settle everywhere, establish connections everywhere...'. Yet again: the bourgeoisie 'batters down all Chinese walls' and 'compels all nations, on pain of extinction, to adopt the bourgeois mode of production; it compels them to introduce what it calls civilisation into their midst, i.e., to become bourgeois themselves. In one word, it creates a world after its own image.' Of course, these passages from the *Communist Manifesto* (1848) are not a simple description of contemporary reality. A statement of general and long-term processes that have been part of capitalist development from the beginning, they are more an anticipation of the future that is ours today. They represent an analysis which is much truer today than when the *Manifesto* was composed. It is true, as we have pointed out before, that Marx underestimated the durability of capitalism and how long it could keep on expanding. But for all today's fashionable talk about 'globalisation', it would be hard to find a more effective description of what is happening today than what he wrote 150 odd years ago.

It needs to be noted that what is involved here is not merely expansion of capitalism but also its *domination* abroad. In the *Manifesto* as elsewhere, Marx's treatment of the exploitation process, which is the backbone of capital accumulation, is mostly focused on the relationship between labour and owners of capital in Western Europe. But he was not unaware of the fact that while capitalism by its very nature lives by accumulation and geographic expansion, it does so in a most unequal fashion. 'The historic task of bourgeois society'. Marx had said, 'is the establishment of the world market'. But inequality, for him, was already a feature of the relationship between the advanced nations and the rest in the world market. The language is obviously Eurocentric and is but poorly qualified by the phrase 'what it calls civilisation' in its reference to the Western bourgeois world. Nevertheless, suggestive of the process of unequal relationship or colonisation immanent in capitalist expansion abroad, the *Manifesto* noted that the bourgeoisie 'has made barbarian and semi-barbarian countries dependent on the civilised ones, nations of peasants on nations of bourgeois, the East on the West.' As we have noticed on an earlier occasion, there are firmer statements of this colonising dimension in *Capital* and late Marx, and Marx has in more than one place written of the havoc wrought by capitalism in its 'progress' abroad—for example, in India—likening it, in a telling metaphor to 'the pagan god, who would not drink nectar except in skulls of the slain'. This dimension of capitalist globalisation was, however, never subjected to a comprehensive critical analysis by Marx, for the simple reason that it came to maturity much after him. This task was carried out by Marxists who followed, notably Lenin whose study of *Imperialism*, among other things noted the dominating presence of monopolies in every field of economy and society and traced the growth of capitalism into a world system of not just colonial oppression but also 'the financial strangulation of the overwhelming majority of the population of the world by a handful of "advanced" countries'. Lenin drew specific attention to such phenomena as 'the predominance of finance capital', 'the rise of an all-powerful financial oligarchy', of 'a small number of financially "powerful" states.' He wrote of the usurer state and usuary imperialism, of the division of the world into a handful of usurer states and creditor countries and 'the rest of the world (which) is more or less the debtor to and tributary of these international banker countries'. He pointed out 'that the development of capitalism has arrived at a stage when, although commodity production still "reigns" and continues to be regarded as the basis of economic life, it has in reality been undermined and the bulk of the profits go to the "geniuses" of financial manipulation.' Lenin located finance capital in a non-industrial or speculative setting, noticed the 'extraordinary growth of a class, or rather, of a stratum of rentiers, i.e., people who live by "clipping coupons", ... whose profession is idleness', and showed how 'the export of capital, one of most essential economic bases of imperialism, still more completely isolates the rentiers from production and sets the seal of parasitism on the whole country that lives by exploiting the labour of several overseas countries and colonies.' These are issues, it may be noted, which are at the centre of the current phase of globalisation.

Marx's is analytically the most sophisticated recognition of capitalism as a system that is uniquely expansionary and international, one tangentially 'global' since the very beginning, but a more than working recognition of this dimension of capitalism was common to classical thinkers such as Adam Smith, and later to most mainstream economists before the first world war. Multinational manufacturing firms appeared in the middle of the nineteenth century and were well established by the beginning of the twentieth century to make internationalisation of capital a common preoccupation not only of Marxist theorists like Luxemburg, Lenin or Bukharin. Analysts have pointed out that foreign trade and overseas income was a greater percentage of GNP in Europe during the late nineteenth century than at the end of the twentieth century, that world financial markets in the late nineteenth and early twentieth centuries were more fully integrated than they were before or have been since. As a commentator for the *Financial Times* of London has recently put it, 'Before 1914 the world economy was in many respects as integrated as it is today and in certain respects more so'. This integration, with capital and commodities freely traversing the globe, had also made for internationalisation of social and economic life. This is how John Maynard Keynes saw it: 'The inhabitant of London could order by telephone, sipping his morning tea in bed, the various products of the whole earth, in such quantity as he might see fit, and reasonably expect their early delivery upon his doorstep; he could at the same moment and by the same means adventure his wealth in the natural resources and new enterprises in any quarter of the world, and share, without exertion or even trouble, in their prospective fruits and advantages; or he could decide to couple the security of his fortunes with the good faith of the townspeople of any substantial municipality in any continent that fancy or information might recommend. He could secure forthwith, if he wished it, cheap and comfortable means of transit to any country or climate without passport or other formality....But, most important of all, he regarded this state of affairs as normal, certain, and permanent, except in the direction of improvement... The internationalization of (social and economic life) was nearly complete...' Thus, if 'globalisation' is no novelty in the history of capitalist development, the associated notion of 'a borderless world' too is no recent invention.

Writing of 'the short twentieth century' (1914 to the end of Soviet era), E.H. Hobsbawm has demarcated three distinct periods: an 'Age of Catastrophe' from 1914 to the aftermath of the Second World War, marked by two world wars, two waves of revolution, the crumbling of colonial empires, an unprecedented crisis of capitalism followed by a crisis of liberal democracy; a 'Golden Age' from 1950 until 1970, marked by extraordinary productive achievements of capitalism, the rise of welfare state and Keynesian economics, the promise of 'developmentalism' in the third world; and finally a period of 'Landslide', 1970 to 1991, marked by a global crisis, mass unemployment and growing inequality, severe cyclical swings of national economies, crisis of third world developmentalism, erosion of the welfare state, rise of economic liberalism, and ending up with the general chaos resulting from the collapse of 'Soviet socialism'. These roughly defined three periods, eventually reflecting three phases of development of capitalism in our time are indicative of the essential nature of capitalist development which, given the contradictions inherent in capitalism, has always been a crisis-ridden, bumpy and uneven affair. It is no different with globalisation as a capitalist process. Its progress too has been essentially bumpy and uneven, and shot through with local, regional and more than regional crises. There have been periods of 'high' globalisation and periods in which economic flows have, to a greater or lesser degree, turned inward in response to changed economic and political conditions. Thus, the second half of the nineteenth century witnessed an escalating thrust of 'globalisation' as a part of capitalism's normal existence. It continued in the twentieth century and globalisation was really intense until 1914. Two world wars, a great depression, revolution in Russia and working class struggles somewhat interrupted this trend, creating what Hobsbawn has described as an interlude of national economics between eras of international economics. This interlude saw the domestic economies turn in on themselves and there was a prolonged shift to a period of 'national development', of 'largely delinked, managed national economies', as one description has it—the so-called Keynesian era which was the unique product of a catastrophic period for capitalism in the first half of the twentieth century. Once a certain degree of economic and political recovery was achieved, there was an increasing and uneven effort from the 1950s onwards to return to active globalisation. The effort picked up with the onset of the crisis in the 1970s, when together with a return to its normal functioning at home, capitalism resumed its path towards internationalisation with a vengeance, to be soon provided a new specific thrust by the collapse in the East. The erosion and disintegration of Keynesianism (with its regulated capitalism and welfare state) and the onset of so-called 'globalisation' not only reflected the depth of the new crisis but also demonstrated capital's inherent, and now increasingly desperate, drive to create a world economy 'in its own image'. Such has been the changing trajectory of globalisation in our time.

Viewed in this perspective, the increasing integration of national economies and the globalisation of trade and investment are not new phenomena, only a new phase in the normal existence of capitalism as a global system. What has taken place, far from being some new departure, is rather a return, a turning back to trends that marked the 'high' globalisation of the nineteenth century, a resumption of the drive that had temporarily slowed down during the intervening period of 'low' globalisation. And with this resumed globalisation, given the depth of the current economic crisis, we are also back—with a new vengeance this time—to pre-Keynesian economics and ideological hegemony of *laissez faire*.

The talk about 'globalisation' as 'a new era' or 'an epochal shift' therefore represents more an ideological-political phenomenon than a serious analysis of the new situation. But the phenomenon nevertheless has a certain basis—in the lived memory of a happy Keynesian past and in the significant fact of the end of the post-war boom in the 1970s, which sharpened the contrast between the new present and *that* past. The state-regulated and welfare-statist monopoly capitalism of the Keynesian era (roughly 1945–1975), really an aberration in the history of capitalism, was assumed to be the normal and natural form of capitalism. The globalisation over the past 25 years, when capitalism has come to resemble that of the late nineteenth century more than it does that of the 1950s and 1960s, could therefore be seen or interpreted as a dramatic break, a rupture, in the history of capitalism, one that effectively constitutes an epochal shift. Capitalism's global ascendancy following the Soviet collapse has made for both a worldwide acceptance of this shift and its positive interpretation. The resumed hegemony of bourgeois ideology has even persuaded people to see in it the promise of universal benevolence! That many on the left have succumbed to 'globalisation' and its TINA chorus only reflects the disarray in the political and intellectual life of the left and the pervasive power of bourgeois ideology.

It is of course mistaken, a case of ahistorical thinking, to interpret the era of 'globalisation' of the past thirty years or so as an epochal rupture with the essential logic of capitalism. But to argue that it represents a reversion to form for capitalism after the anomaly of the so-called 'Keynesian era', is not to even remotely suggest that it is simply that, that no new phenomena are at work. Capitalism *is* undergoing unique and important transformations, as it has throughout its history. Major changes *have* occurred in the capitalist economy since the end of the post-war boom, with global capitalism acquiring quite a few significantly new features. This phase of 'globalisation' has its own historical specificities, its own specific contradictions and dynamics, as has been the case with other specific phases in the history of ever-changing capitalism.

The specificities of context or conjuncture of the current phase of globalisation lie in a new crisis of capital accumulation, the long drawn-out downturn and stagnation which brought the post-war 'golden age' to an end—something different from, or at least more protracted than, the classic episodic crises of capitalism—and led to dismantling of the welfare state at home and capital's furious thrust abroad in search of a new world of profits. This search has of course been greatly facilitated by the technological revolution of our time but the new scope and scale of movement of capital and commodities across the globe has been less due to technological than to political changes or conjunctures. Most noticeable here is the extension of capitalism directly associated with the collapse of the Soviet Union and communist regimes of Eastern Europe, as well as with the turn to capitalism in China and Vietnam. The demise of 'socialism' in the former communist countries of Europe and Asia, together with the crisis or collapse of Third-World developmentalism—though not without leaving behind such sections of society as 'the great Asian middle class' as *The Economist* has rather courteously called it—and the consequent subjection of national-populist third world regimes to the rule of unregulated capitalism, has opened up vast new markets for sales and investment and thus accumulation of profits. The political victories of capitalism are thus central to the advance of the contemporary process of globalisation as compared to the historical period immediately following the second world war or the mid-1970s and certainly in relation to the inter-war period.

Today the capitalist world system has for the first time in history become really global. The scale, scope and speed of the circulation of capital and commodities, particularly financial flows between deregulated economies, is something unprecedented. Technological changes are a distinctive feature of the current phase of globalisation and those in the sphere of information and communications (computer, fax, e-mail, etc.) have lent a rare velocity to movements of capital and goods across the globe. All sorts of new supra national institutions promoting the needs of transnational finance, production and trade (NAFTA, EU, WTO, MAI, multilateral trade agreements, etc.) have come up, which, together with changes in technology and politics have greatly increased the ability of capital to do what it has always wanted to do—turn the world into one 'free market' for finance, production, and wage labour. The whole planet has been opened up to capitalist penetration, making it possible for capital to extract and realise *relative* surplus value on a global scale—if not exactly everywhere at least somewhere in many parts of every continent and subcontinent—in a way that earlier forms of globalisation had not achieved. Globalisation today thus marks a qualitatively new stage of capital accumulation on a world scale.

The increasing strategic importance of multinationals or transnationals in capitalist economy is a significant feature of the new stage of globalisation. It was not till after 1945 that the multinational corporations, developed in the inter-war years, became generalised. In this, it is the vigorous expansion of the US multinationals in the 1950s, part and parcel of United States' hegemonic role at the time, that led the way. They created an environment in which giant corporations of all nations, driven by motives of self-defence as well as by their eagerness for new accumulation opportunities, had to turn multinational and widen their international base. But it was not until the 1980s that, with the aid of computerisation, the multinational corporations realised their full potential for worldwide control of production and finance. Today some 40,000 multinational corporations—fifty of them now receiving more revenue than two-third of world's states, and, with their subsidiaries around the world, owning one-third of the world's productive capacity —determine trade, investment and employment patterns across the globe. No nation, poor or rich is immune to their globalising pressure.

Associated with the increased strategic importance of multinationals in the global economy is the rising tide of foreign direct investment (FDI). Another key measure of globalisation, the speeded-up flow of direct investment from one country to another is also a response to the post-boom stagnation mentioned above. Capital needs no extra-special stimulus to seek out project opportunities, and the export of capital has been a tool for economic growth over the ages. Foreign direct investment—that is, multinational business—has always existed and many of the world's largest firms have been transnational from birth. Capital, therefore, was bound to take advantage of the current opening up of the planet to capitalist penetration. Still, any slowing down of economic growth intensifies the competitive drive in foreign as well as domestic markets. It is not surprising therefore that we witnessed an unusually great leap in foreign investment in the 1980s and then onwards. It is equally important to notice the changing composition of this new phase of direct foreign investment. Global operations of the multinationals in manufacturing and marketing have now undergone vital changes in many ways. One of these is a growing shift of investment at home from the manufacturing to the services—finance and insurance, communications, advertising and sales, the media, etc. About 60 per cent of the total employment in developed countries is now provided by the services sector. As for manufacturing capital, it has been migrating in search of low wages and taxes and compliant governments wherever it can find them around the globe. In the 1990s almost one-half of the FDI stock of transnational corporations (TNCs) in the developed countries was in the services sector, while manufacturing accounted for the largest sector in the developing countries. In other words, cheap labour and natural resources, along with unconcern for environmental pollution in the developing countries have persuaded the TNCs to shift a large share of their investment allocation to the latter. The first wave of foreign investment after the Second World War concentrated on raw materials and other primary products. Apart from investments of this kind, capital flowed to the third world for manufacturing enterprises to profit from the exceptionally low wages and to take advantage of the demand generated by the local rich and middle classes. The capital absorption capacity of these enterprises was, however, always limited and capital surplus in search of outlets was growing all the time. The new opportunities and the shift in the investment policies of the TNCs has meant a radical change in the situation. In the 'new international division of labour' as it is called—and which, dating from about 1970, is another significant development in the history of ongoing globalisation – no longer is the third world relegated to only production and export of primary products and importation of manufactured goods from the first world. With technology increasing the global reach of capitalist production processes and allowing easier, cheaper and faster communication and transportation as well as breaking up of production processes into segments that can be parcelled all over the globe, we now have a more truly global manufacturing system with multinational or transnational firms investing abroad and producing key components of fully manufactured goods in countries ranging from Mexico to Malaysia. It may be added that this has had negative consequences for the wages and working conditions of workers in the advanced capitalist countries. The 'social power' of western labour has declined and impoverishment—or the threat of it—has returned.

The internationalisation of finance capital is another notably distinguishing attribute of the current globalisation process. The dramatic developments in the system of international finance, in the concentration of capital on an international plane that we are witnessing today, are even seen by some to constitute, in some ways, the real *differentia specifica* of contemporary capitalism. Over the last two decades or so, the world has seen a phenomenal growth of financial capital, accompanied by unprecedented forms of international credit and currency flows, including the utterly new role of bank lending across national borders. On a national as well as on an international scale, the financial sectors of the advanced capitalist countries seem to have taken on a life of their own. The sheer volume and the tremendous speed with which financial transactions occur in today's digital markets is evident in the fact that every day more than one trillion dollars turn over in foreign exchange markets, only about 15 per cent of which represents actual capital flows and trade in commodities. This ballooning of international finance, together with the new ability to transfer money worldwide instantaneously has spawned a host of new methods of financial speculation and manipulation. The significant autonomy that these financial flows have developed from the actions of governments and central banks has meant not only a heightened volatility in world financial markets but also that these flows are engaged largely in pure speculation: more than 80 per cent of the capital in national exchanges is speculative and the primary form of international finance capital today is 'hot money' flows in search of quick profits.

Finally, we need to take notice of the ideological and cultural sweep of capitalist ideas and values that, in its own way, defines the current phase of globalisation, its neo-liberalism whereby the bourgeoisie today 'makes the world in its own image' with an impunity almost unparalleled since Marx wrote these words 150 odd years ago. With capitalism become all but universal, it has also become ideologically hegemonic as never before. It is not only that capitalist laws of motion, the logic of capitalism has penetrated ever deeper into the societies of advanced capitalism and spatially throughout the world. Today every human practice, every social relationship, virtually everything under the sun including the natural environment is subject to the requirements of profit-maximisation. Capitalism's technological ingenuity has made it possible for its principles to find their way into social, institutional and cultural spaces that even a few decades ago were beyond their reach. Commodity relations and moralities of the market are penetrating into every aspect of our lives, producing profit of course, but also ravaging morals and culture everywhere. Michael Lowy has written:

> Indeed, never until this end of the 20th century has capital succeeded in exerting such a complete, absolute, undivided, universal, and unlimited sway over the whole world. Never in the past has it had its current ability to impose its rules, its policies, its dogmas, and its interests upon all the nations of the globe. Never have international finance capital and multinational corporations been so out of control by states and peoples. Never before now has their existed such a dense network of international institutions —International Monetary Fund, World Bank, World Trade Organisation—devoted to controlling, governing, and

> administering human life according to the strict rules of the capitalist free market and unrestricted pursuit of capitalist profitability. Finally, never in any preceding epoch have all spheres of human life—social relationships, culture, art, politics, sexuality, health, education, sports, recreation—been so completely dominated by capital, so deeply submerged in 'the icy water of egotistical calculation.'

Capitalism with its globalising thrust is a constantly changing system. It is not the same capitalism as it was, say, in the mid-19th century when Karl Marx wrote his *Capital*. Its development has been marked by slow or rapid changes, qualitative shifts or 'discontinuities', throughout its centuries old history. We have noticed some of these changes or shifts, specific new features in the current phase of its development. But it is wrong and ahistorical to focus on these real or apparent changes or discontinuities to argue, as theories of 'globalisation' (or 'post-modernity') do, that we have now moved into a type of post-capitalist economic system which is basically different from what we have known. In recognising the discontinuities, we must not lose sight of the fact that, at the level of the system, continuities within capitalism are more significant than the discontinuities. We need to be clear not only about what has changed but even more about what has stayed the same: the unique systemic logic of capitalism, the specific 'laws of motion' or 'logic of process' common to capitalism in all its forms and phases—the logic which indeed generates or governs the constantly occurring changes in capitalism. Massive changes have indeed occurred in capitalism in recent decades, but this has been part of a process in capitalism since its inception—a process which is a manifestation of capitalism's logic of expansion and integration both vertically and horizontally. 'Globalisation' today represents only a new phase of this historical process, no departure, only capitalism's logic extended across a much greater horizon. It is the logic of capitalism universalising itself and reaching a level of maturity never realised before.

Thus viewed, 'globalisation' is not what it is often made out to be, itself a driving force of world economy. It remains what it has been throughout the history of capitalism: the always expansive and often explosive capital accumulation process. It is a myth that the market now has as its principal purpose the service of human needs. It remains subject to capitalist imperatives of accumulation and profit-maximisation, an arena of aggrandisement for capitalists and their corporations. That is why it makes sense to speak of 'the capitalist system' rather than 'the global market'. The issue here is not just this or that phase of capitalism or just globalisation, but of a world economy still subject to capitalism's laws of motion. The more globalised economy of today remains one driven by classic patterns of capitalist investment and accumulation—and thus characterised by tendencies towards over accumulation and crisis. It features its classical correlates too: capital-capital competition in the market, capital-labour contradiction at home and imperialist exploitation abroad.

The universalisation of capital does not mean the universalisation of capitalist prosperity, success, industrialisation or development, as promised by the globalisers. On the contrary, it can only mean the universalisation of capitalist polarisation, for such is the structural logic of capitalist development. And this is precisely what has been happening. Capitalism's tendency to generate wealth for the relatively few and poverty for the many is as much in evidence today in both the developed North and the developing South as it was in the nineteenth century England of 'dark satanic mills' that Marx and Engels so perceptively analysed. Now, as then, the poor grow poorer as the rich grow richer. Polarisation abroad has meant the marginalisation and increasing impoverishment of whole regions outside the advanced capitalist countries. The class polarisations of capitalism are as much evident in the North–South divide as in the growing impoverishment of so-called 'underclasses' within advanced capitalist countries.

We may here specifically notice a key feature of contemporary globalisation that it retains from its earlier phases: its driving forces are centred in the imperial states and the dominant classes within these states who own or control and run the multinational corporations and banks duly backed by the international financial institutions. Thus we have, as in the past, 'globalising' nations and classes and the 'globalised', a hierarchical system of power, exchange and benefits: there are wealthy creditors and bankrupt debtors, super-rich speculators and impoverished peasants and unemployed workers, imperial states that direct international financial institutions and subordinate states that submit to their dictates, and so on. There has been much 'globaloney' over 'interdependence of nations' and its 'globally shared benefits'. Surely 'imperialism' is a more useful concept to comprehend this aspect of the reality of our globalised world.

Skewed distribution of benefits is however only one issue. 'Globalisation' is really the globalisation of capitalism's basic dynamics, including the contradictions inherent in its relentless drive to maximise profit and accumulate. As a consequence we not only have a ravaging of humanity, mass unemployment and underemployment and active impoverishment of large populations at the centre and in the periphery of global capitalism and a destruction of natural environment all over the globe but also a global economy characterised by over-accumulation, enormous excess capacity and crisis of profitability, an ever-growing structure of debt, speculative volatility and financial turmoils and, typically, by recurring economic crises and prolonged downturns like the current one. By virtue of its inherent contradictions, though globally dominant, capitalism yet remains fraught with instabilities, beset as it is by economic breakdowns even in its most dynamic centres of investment and trade and by a succession of national and regional crises—in Mexico, East and South-East Asia, Russia, Brazil, Argentina, etc.—produced by the globalist restructuring of recent decades.

There is an unending hype, 'infobabble' really, over information technology which, together with globalisation it has so remarkably facilitated, is supposed to usher in the epochal shift that takes us into a world beyond and better than capitalism, indeed makes the very notion of capitalism historically irrelevant. Involving two closely linked technological departure points, the computer and instantaneous communication system, a fusion as it were of computing and communications (*networks*) that has developed in an explosive trajectory in recent years, this technological development has been not unjustifiably described as a revolution, 'information revolution', that is. The importance, however ambiguous, of this revolution for our economy and social life is not to be denied. For good or ill, it has enormously significant implications for the present and future of humankind—implications that socialists need to take serious note of. As Reg Whitaker, in a most perceptive essay on the subject, has insisted, 'this revolution cannot be ignored by those seeking real alternatives. Cyberspace is a new reality, a spectre haunting the world. As some of the old terrains of struggle shrink, cyberspace expands as a new terrain to be studied, and to be acted upon.' But this revolution itself does not either change the structural logic of capitalism or offer, or make for, any alternatives to the present social order.

New information technology, as with technological innovations in the past, certainly makes people better at doing things they have always done. But even here we don't need to be breathless about it. It is difficult to see how, as claimed, the nature of manufacturing has been 'fundamentally altered' by it. The evidence so far shows only very small impact on productivity from the large investment made in information technology in the United States or for that matter elsewhere. Production has indeed been globalised, but it remains doubtful if the telecommunications revolution has really had a major impact. It has been suggested that 'the invention of relatively simple things, like steamship transport, did more for world trade than digitalised data transmission through fiber optic cables.' In other words, its truly remarkable technological innovations and the hype over them notwithstanding, in the ultimate analysis, 'information revolution' is only another case of incremental change in the way we do things.

'Information revolution' is emphatically *not* itself an answer to the problems we face—problems primarily born of capitalism and its structural logic. These are problems we ourselves have to solve, with or without the aid of technology. 'Information is power', or the computer as 'empowerment' do have a certain, though ambiguous, validity. But 'infobabble' over such propositions has little to do with any notion of redistribution of wealth and power in our society. A computer in every office or home will not somehow solve the problem of unemployment or economic crisis or regional economic decline and imbalances. The poor cannot 'unload' from the NET food and shelter or equitable economic development they are denied by the capitalist market. Information technology does not and cannot in any way alter capital's drive to accumulate or its quest for higher profits and stock prices. Instead it has only served to make this quest more penetrating and effective. As with other technologies under capitalism, information technology too is today subservient to capitalist imperatives of accumulation and profit maximisation. Command over information and its transmission has already become the key to success in the capitalist market place. A wholesale commodification of information by capital is on and the much celebrated 'cyberspace' is taking on the appearance of a 'vast mysterious collections of data looming like mega-fortresses fiercely guarded by giant corporations—while the "real world" wallows in urban squalor, petty criminality, violence and tawdry escapism.' This is how Reg Whitaker has posed and answered the key question: 'Does the Information Revolution offer *an alternative*? Yes and no. It does offer an alternative capitalist future, but it is unlikely, under present circumstances, to offer an alternative *to* capitalism'.

'Globalisation is only another word for U.S. domination', Henry Kissinger has arrogantly claimed. Posing the issue equally bluntly, Fredric Jameson has asked: '...when we talk about the spreading power and influence of globalization, aren't we really referring to the spreading economic and military might of the US? And in speaking of the weakening of the nation-state, are we not actually describing the subordination of the other nation-states to American power, either through consent and collaboration, or by the use of brute force and economic threat?' He adds: 'Looming behind the anxieties expressed here is a new version of what used to be called imperialism, which we can now trace through a whole dynasty of forms. An earlier version was that of the pre-First World War colonialist order, practised by a number of European countries, the US and Japan; this was replaced after the Second World War and the subsequent wave of decolonisation by a Cold War form, less obvious but no less insidious in its use of economic pressure and blackmail ('advisers'; covert putsches such as those in Guatemala and Iran), now led predominantly by the US but still involving a few Western European powers. Now perhaps we have a third stage, in which the United States pursues what Samuel Huntington has defined as a three-pronged strategy: nuclear weapons for the US alone; human rights and American-style electoral democracy; and (less obviously) limits to immigration and the free flow of labour. One might add a fourth crucial policy here: the propagation of the free market across the globe....' Jameson sees 'the US (and such utterly subordinated satellites as the UK)' as playing 'the role of the world's policemen' and enforcing 'their rule through selected interventions (mostly bombings, from a great height) in various alleged danger zones.'

These two views from opposite ends draw our attention to a most important aspect of the current phase of globalisation—America's hegemony over the global economy and politics. Its victory in the Cold War, just as it confirmed America's leadership of global capitalism, also settled the question of what kind of capitalism it was going to be. Scholars have written of different, indeed 'rival variants' of capitalism, notably the 'Anglo American' (now really 'American') deregulated, 'free market', Chicago School version and 'the Rhine model of capitalism', based on a high level of state intervention, corporate bargaining and welfare spending—'social market economy' as it has been sometimes called—predominant in continental Europe. It is the former, essentially American model today, which is being imposed worldwide in the name of globalisation. A mood of triumphalism, induced by the relatively better performance of American capitalism, when the continuing crisis of global capitalist economy has been manifesting itself in one crash after another in countries across the globe, has led even Alan Greenspan, the normally cautious chairman of the US Federal Reserve to pronounce 'market capitalism as practiced in the U.S.' to be 'the superior model' that other countries have to follow. If this has been the message from the IMF, WB and WTO to the third and the former second world countries, recent concern with 'safety nets' to stave off popular discontent notwithstanding, the message being sent to the European governments, and accepted, is no different: the US is the example to be followed. What is being offered, it may be noted, is no 'magic vision of America', that staple of establishment ideology, 'the American dream'. It is the reality of America today, the US model of capitalism with its huge and growing gap between the haves and the have-nots, its ridiculous minimum wage, 'working poor' and 'labour flexibility', its millions without health insurance and its terribly deficient welfare services now under constant attack. Europe is told that in the world of deregulated, 'free market' capitalism, it can no longer afford a bearable minimum wage, some degree of security of tenure, fairly decent unemployment benefits or old-age pensions, or for that matter, a national health scheme. Henceforth, it has to rely on private insurance and private schools, on two-tier health and two-tier education. To cut a long message short, Europe must dismantle its welfare state. And capitalists and their governments in Europe have been only too willing to come along.

(It may be noted that since this welfare state was social democracy's main claim to gratitude and success, this dismantling marks its deepest ever crisis. This crisis however must not be seen as the result of betrayal by ambitious politicians and union bosses. It is really a question of the scope for meeting popular demands within the existing capitalist society. During the thirty post-war years of unprecedented prosperity, the climate was particularly propitious for social democracy to prosper. During the last thirty years, on the contrary, conditions have become more and more unfavourable. If the collapse of 'Soviet socialism' has left capitalism free to let fall its mask, and to abandon any pretence of wearing a 'human face', its renewed and continuing crisis leaves it unable to wear one any longer).

In pursuit of its hegemony over global economy, the US has led in imposing an unequal economic order on the world. It is using its enormous power and dominance over institutions like the IMF and WB to thrust extraneous agendas on other countries and distort the global market relations in its own favour. A pioneer in practising protectionism while employing the shibbolethus of 'free market' and 'free trade' to systematically prise open foreign markets, the United States today pursues the same policy in the name of 'positive economic nationalism', as Robert Reich, Clinton's former Labour Secretary has phrased it. But above and beyond its hegemony over global economy or pursuit of particular 'national' interests, America has, more evidently than ever before, emerged and self-identified itself, as the country with the power and responsibility to police the world in defence of capitalism. A leading diplomatic historian, Gerald Haines (who is also the senior historian of the CIA) has observed that after World War II, the United State 'assumed, out of self-interest, responsibility for the welfare of the world capitalist system.' President Clinton and his Secretary of State Madeleine Albright saw the US as the world's only 'indispensable nation', and Anthony Lake, his National Security Advisor, in line with a former such Advisor Brezhenski's public defence of the 'necessity' of American leadership in the world, even announced a so-called 'Clinton Doctrine': 'Throughout the Cold War, we contained a global threat to market democracies', now we can 'consolidate the victory of democracy and open markets'—the formula however is redundant since the latter adequately captures what is really meant by 'democracy'. More recently (1999), in his much noticed 'Manifesto for the Fast World' in the *New York Times Magazine*, the well-known columnist Thomas Friedman has argued that since the United States is the country that benefits most from globalisation, it is also the one that has to take the main responsibility for sustaining it. 'Sustaining globalization is our overarching national interest ... Globalization-is-U.S.' This, he clarifies, is different from 'old-fashioned imperialism, when one country physically occupies another.' Now, it's a matter of maintaining 'an abstract globalization system'. And this 'requires a stable geopolitical power structure, which simply cannot be maintained without the active involvement of the United States.' Bush Junior has since, in his own way, made abundantly clear what this means.

An important aspect of this 'active involvement' has been the bullying of the United Nations into becoming a body which ratifies and legitimises American decisions taken in America's interest, including its naked and lawless exercise of economic, political and military power. A Kofi Annan is imposed as Secretary General and the UN is sought to be reduced to an extension of the US State Department. The United States bullies or manipulates the UN when it can and bypasses it when it cannot. It threatens to withdraw from agencies like WHO and UNESCO when they offer as much as a hint of disapproval towards the US policies and makes the payment of even defaulted dues contingent upon the reform of the UN system according to its wishes. American policies inside the UN, as outside, are fraudulently claimed to be 'the will of the international community' and the UN summits—ranging from Environment and Human Rights to Population, Social Development and Women—invariably fail to breach the parameters of the currently dominant discourse of globalisation and generally end up rationalising the America-led domination of global capitalism.

This domination has an interesting ideological dimension in that America has sought a 'noble' or 'saintly' guise for its policies abroad. It pursues them in the name of 'human rights' and 'democracy', which only reveals how cynical or hypocritical the sole superpower's global politics can be. Take the UN Declaration of Human Rights, Half of it concerns social and economic rights. The West largely rejects them, the US totally. They limit themselves primarily to what they call civil and political rights. This apart, if the record of the UN on human rights is painfully bad, it is understandably so because it has been, and still is, dominated by the United States: the country with innumerable violations of human rights all over the world, from the Philippines at the turn of the last century to installing Marcos there after the war; from the invasion of Guatemala, the Dominican Republic and Grenada to the Vietnam war; from installing Suharto in Indonesia (and more than one million murdered in the course of Suharto's US-backed counter-revolution) to imposing and sustaining dictatorial regimes in Latin America (including Pinochet in Chile) and Africa; not to mention the authoritarian regimes in the Middle East, the Colonel's Dictatorship in Greece and the death of one million children in Iraq as a result of sanctions continued to be imposed by the United States and rubber stamped by the UN, with the total subservience of its allies, before it again attacked Iraq in a blatant violation of international law. America's interpretation of human rights, replacing the common interests of humanity with the particular interests and arbitrary actions of the United States, violates any meaningful conception of human rights. Even otherwise, America's extremely selective concern with human rights in pursuit of its interests abroad has been justifiably regarded as a new form of imperialism, 'Human Rights Imperialism'.

It is no different with America's concern for democracy. The essential criterion once again is what best serves American interests. American policy makers have had no hesitation in lining up on their side some of the most corrupt dictatorial regimes that there were, often hailing them as members of their 'free world'. These have included the apartheid regime of South Africa, Syngman Rhee and the military rulers of South Korea, Ferdinand Marcos of the Philippines, Lon Nol and other dictators of South Vietnam, Ayub Khan and Yahya Khan of Pakistan, the Shah of Iran, the Duvaliers of Haiti, Pinochet of Chile, Suharto of Indonesia and any number of other tyrants or authoritarian rulers in Africa, Central and South America and the Middle East, including, once upon a time, Saddam Hussein in Iraq. It is to them that American aid and armaments have overwhelmingly gone. 'He may be a son of a bitch, but he is *our-son-of-a-bitch*'. This has been Washington's refreshingly honest view of the Somozas, Batistas and Duvaliers of the world. Obviously, the absence of democracy is alright so long as a country is supportive of the United States. 'Democracy', like 'human rights' is only an ideological cover for the pursuit of

America's more mundane material, that is, imperialist interests abroad.

Now that, having conquered the country through an illegal war, the United States is on its mission to bring 'democracy' to Iraq, here is one comment on it (by Naomi Klein in *The Nation*):

> The streets of Baghdad are a swamp of crime and uncollected garbage. Battered local businesses are going bankrupt, unable to compete with cheap imports. Unemployment is soaring and thousands of laid-off state workers are protesting in the streets. In other words, Iraq looks like every other country that has undergone rapid-fire 'structural adjustments' prescribed by Washington, from Russia's infamous 'shock therapy' in the early 1990s to Argentina's disastrous 'surgery without anaesthetic'. Except that Iraq's 'reconstruction' makes those wrenching reforms look like spa treatments.
>
> Paul Bremer, the US-appointed governor of Iraq, has already proved something of a flop in the democracy department in the few weeks there, nixing plans for Iraqis to select their own interim government in favour of his own handpicked team of advisers. But Bremer has proved to have something of a gift when it comes to rolling out the red carpet for US multinationals. For a few weeks Bremer has been hacking away at Iraq's public sector....
>
> As the Bush Administration becomes increasingly open about its plan to privatise Iraq's state industries and parts of the government, Bremer's de-Baathification takes on new meaning. Is he working only to get rid of Baath Party members, or is he also working to shrink the public sector as a whole so that hospitals, schools and even the army are primed for privatisation by US firms? Just as reconstruction is the guise for privatisation, de-Baathification looks a lot like disguised downsizing....

Ideological deception has its uses, no doubt, but there is nothing like exercise of naked military power to secure and sustain particular imperialist interests and overall global hegemony. With the collapse of the Soviet Union, the United States has acquired a global dominance as the one remaining military super power, indeed the dominant imperialist power in the world. Contrary to the notion that globalisation and the establishment of the world market have made military power redundant, the US maintains, by a very wide margin, the world's largest military. Empires throughout human history have relied on foreign military bases to enforce their rule and protect their interests, and in this respect Pax Americana is no different from Pax Romana or Pax Britannica. The United States has military bases in sixty-nine countries, with this number on the increase with the wars against Afghanistan and Iraq. The United States totally dominates NATO—recently redefined as a self-legitimating aggressive force—as well as the far eastern military alliances, especially the 'US-Japan security treaty'. Despite the publicly proclaimed end of the Cold War, the US military budget remains very large, accounting for fully a third of world spending on arms. For the US ruling class, in view of what it sees as its responsibilities in the global capitalist order—which one scholar has summarised as: 'to keep the system functioning; to control the underlying populations; to safeguard the United States as the centre of the international financial system; to maintain the United States (and, specially, US capitalists/corporations) in the top perch in the imperialist pecking order; and to prevent countries from breaking away from the system of global controls'—it is not enough to have a military bigger than that of any other power; it must be bigger than that of any plausible combination of other powers, and this applies of course not only to immediate situation but to what might be the situation five or ten years from now, when the potential challenges of today might become real. It is pushing ahead with plans for a capability to fight two major regional conflicts at the same time.

The United States has the world's largest stockpile of weapons of mass destruction, chemical, biological and nuclear, and is the only state ever to have used the nuclear weapons. It is an arch votary of the unequal Nuclear Non-Proliferation Treaty and, even as it regularly armtwists the minor nuclear nations, has refused to ratify the Comprehensive Nuclear Test Ban Treaty (CTBT). It has unilaterally withdrawn from the Anti-Ballistic Missile (ABM) Treaty and is busy developing weapons like the nuclear bunker-busting bombs. According to a classified Pentagon report, the Bush administration has directed the military to prepare contingency plans to use nuclear weapons against countries it sees as America's immediate or potential enemies, and to build new smaller nuclear weapons for use in certain battlefield situations. Despite objections from its European allies that it is unnecessary and will most likely trigger a new arms race, despite opposition of Russia and China, despite a protest by as many as 50 Nobel Laureates headed by Hans A. Bethe, one of the architects of the atom bomb, who have called it a 'wasteful' and 'dangerous' system, the National Missile Defence System remains a priority on the agenda of the United States. Its National Security Strategy, with its policy of military supremacy over the entire earth and the doctrine of pre-emption, is nothing less than the declaration of a new imperial order, to be backed up not only by the threat but also the aggressive, pre-emptive employment of overwhelming power against any country not to its liking. Most recently, following upon its yesterday's 'Star Wars Project' or the current 'Missile Defence System'—argued for as 'defensive shields', though nothing of the kind—the United States has gone in for their heavily updated, blatantly offensive successor, codenamed 'Falcon' (Force Application and Launch from the Continental US), to be completed by mid-2006—its unmanned delivery vehicles, carrying a payload of 12,000 pounds and flying at speeds of up to 10 times the speed of sound, will be able to strike targets 9,000 nautical miles distant in less than two hours. As John Pike, head of the Washington think tank, Global Security.Org. has commented: 'It is about blowing people up on the other side of the planet even if no country on earth will allow us to use their territory'. The purpose, obviously, is to enable the US to *go it alone* against whichever country they please to subdue or destroy in their design to achieve world domination.

The global expansion of military power on the part of the hegemonic state of world capitalism is an integral part of economic globalisation. (The other advanced capitalist countries, tied into the system, are also reliant on the US as the main enforcer of the rules of the game). The American ruling class knows that economics are ultimately a matter of politics, that it is relations of power, above all military power, that command the market, that there will be no 'global market' without an American military empire. 'The hidden hand of the market will never work without the hidden fist—McDonald's cannot flourish without McDonnell Douglas, the designer of the F-15. And the hidden fist that keeps the world safe for Silicon Valley's technologies is called the United States Army, Air Force, Navy and Marine Corps.'—this is how Thomas Friedman, who incidentally was also an adviser to Madeleine Albright, has put it in his article we have noticed earlier. Friedman goes on to quote approvingly from foreign policy historian Robert Kagan: 'Good ideas and technologies need a strong power that promotes those ideas by example and protects those ideas by winning on the battlefield. If a lesser power were promoting our ideas and technologies, they would not have the global currency that they have.'

Naturally, the hidden fist has to come out of hiding from time to time if it is going to make its point. And here the United has a long history. Monroe doctrine onwards it is a history of armed interventions or wars along with coercive diplomacy, bloody coups and covert actions against other sovereign states to make the world 'safe' for American business. In the half century since the World War II alone, on one pretext or another —'containing communism' 'protecting American lives', 'punishing "rogue" states', 'war on terrorism' or even 'promoting democracy', etc.—America has thus aggressed against countries as far afield as Greece and Cuba, Chile and Vietnam, Brazil, Guatemala and Dominican Republic, Grenada, Nicaragua, EL Salvador and Panama, Angola and Mozambique, Iran, Iraq, Libya and Afghanistan. And the list is far from complete.

There has been a great deal of noise over the end of the Cold War. It surely ended for the Soviet Union when it threw in the towel in 1989-90. But it has continued for the United States. When the Soviet Union collapsed, there was much talk in the US of a large and growing 'peace dividend' that would be available for all kinds of good works. But this 'peace dividend' never materialised. Instead, National Defence outlays have continued to grow. An independent research study in the mid-

1990s calculated US defence expenditures to have exceeded the combined total of 13 nations behind it on the list of big weapons spenders. (Incidentally, the United States is also the world's largest exporter of arms and about 75 per cent of these sales go to countries where the citizens have no right to choose their own governments).

America's growing military expenditure is not difficult to understand. The declared objective of the Cold War was to defeat an imaginary threat of Soviet expansionism. The real objective was to rid the world of 'communism', meaning any and all forms of society organised on any but 'free market', that is, capitalist lines. The imaginary threat is no longer there. But what about the real objectives? Way back in 1989, a distinguished American scholar of history, Professor Edward Pessen in a letter to the *The New York Times*, under the heading 'Cold War Isn't Over While the U.S. Can Help It', thus summed up the Cold War policies of the US administration from Truman to Reagan: 'We have formed worldwide military alliances against the "Soviet threat"; we ringed the Soviets with bases; we initiated what may turn out to be an irreversible nuclear arms race; we've toppled governments the world over that we found insufficiently anti-communist or uncongenial; in Arnold Toynbee's phrase, we became the new Roman Empire, everywhere opposing revolutions of the poor against the rich; we've waged massive unconstitutional wars against distant nations that had not lifted a finger against us; and we've stigmatized as possible subversives domestic critics of these policies and actions.' Obviously the real objectives are still very much there. 'Communism' is not entirely finished off, capitalism continues to have its enemies, 'the new Roman Empire', now vastly expanded, has still to be made and kept safe for the American multinationals.

Many of the interests that generated the first Cold War have been reasserting themselves, as in the dismemberment of Yugoslavia and the expansion of NATO in Eastern Europe right upto the borders of Russia. Galbraith has written of the autonomous character of military power in the US which in itself and as part of 'military-industrial complex' has not only prevented any reduction in military expenditure even after the Soviet power collapsed but also pushed for continuance of the old foreign policies. There is the politics of 'national security' at home common to both Republican and Democratic parties which well serves the interests of the American ruling class. US capitalism, it seems, cannot do without a permanent war economy, or for that matter, without wars abroad. The Cold War may be over, but according to the U.S. Commission on National Security, reporting in 1999, 'since the end of the Cold War, the United States has embarked upon nearly four dozen military interventions... as opposed to only 16 during the entire period of the Cold War'. As a corollary, we have regular generation of, often tacitly complicit, demonised 'necessary enemies' to justify the globally repressive apparatus of the American national security state. ('Terrorism', a product of America's foreign policies and the depredations of global capitalism it presides over, is another recent excuse.) In other words, there is an enormously powerful, and in the present circumstances quite possibly decisive, domestic and foreign dependence of US capitalism on the continuation of the Cold War.

Hence also NATO's ability to survive the collapse of the adversary that was its *raison d'etre*. NATO's rationale as a counterweight to Soviet military power implied that it should have been wound up after the Soviet capitulation in the Cold War (1989-90). But by the late 1990s its role had been extended to such tasks as military intervention in the Balkans, to be followed later by NATO's expansion eastwards to the border of the former Soviet Union which has served both to incorporate Moscow's former east European clients within the Western bloc and to reassert US primacy within that bloc. Today, redefined as a 'self-legitimating aggressive force', NATO is the principal tool in the service of Washington's global strategy. Military expenditures by the US and other NATO countries are now more than 10 times the level of former Warsaw Pact nations. NATO speaks in the name of 'international community', thereby expressing its contempt for the democratic principle that is supposed to govern this community through the United Nations. In fact, with the decision makers in Washington establishing, through NATO or otherwise, 'force' as the supreme principle in international politics to the complete detriment of international law, the UN seems set to succumb to the fate of the League of Nations. NATO's claim to an odd 'right of intervention' is disturbingly reminiscent of the 'mission civilisatrice' of nineteenth century imperialism and well jells with its contemporary version, the Huntingtonian thesis of 'clash of civilisations' and its appeal to preserve and defend the higher aspects of Western civilisation in the world!

As the world's sole super power over the past decade and more, the US has shown a growing disregard for international legal norms. Whether on economic or political issues, the US has increasingly talked the language of sanctions and coercion. It has not hesitated to act unilaterally—of course mostly with the consultation of its allies in tow—whenever and wherever it has deemed fit. A decade back Iraq was one early example, the war over Kosovo that followed was another; and between them, the two also showed the extent and nature of US' growing domination of the world. Perry Anderson has written: 'the Balkan War has rounded off the decade with the military-diplomatic demonstration of the ascendancy of this constellation. Comparison with the Gulf War suggests how much stronger the New World Order has become since the early nineties. Bush had to mobilise a vast army to reverse the Iraqi invasion in Kuwait, in the name of protecting Western oil supplies and a feudal dynasty; without succeeding in either overthrowing the regime in Baghdad, or drawing Russia—still unpredictable—into the alliance against it. Clinton has bombed Serbia into submission without so much as a soldier having to fire a shot, in the name of a moral imperative to stop ethnic cleansing...; and brigaded Russia effortlessly into the occupation force as a token auxiliary. Meanwhile China, after the destruction of its embassy—on the heels of a respectful visit by its Premier to the US—has cooperated meekly in setting up a UN screen for the NATO protectorate in Kosovo, and made clear that nothing will be allowed to disturb good relations with Washington. For its part, the European Union is basking in a new comradeship-in-arms with the United States, and joint purpose in generous reconstruction of the Balkans. Victory in Kosovo has in this sense not been just military and political. It is also an ideological triumph, that sets a new standard for interventions on behalf of human rights—as construed in Washington: Chechens or Palestinians need not apply—around the world. The society created by the capitalist free-for-all of the past twenty years was in need of a good conscience. Operation Allied Force has provided it.' As for 'human rights' and 'a good conscience', here is Bill Clinton who presided over it all: 'If we're going to have a strong economic relationship that includes our ability to sell around the world, Europe has got to be a key ... That's what this Kosovo thing is all about.'

Away from Europe, essentially, this is what the recent wars against Afghanistan and Iraq have been about. The terrorist attack on the World Trade Centre and the Pentagon was a new godsend for a Wall Street suffering from economic stagnation and growing uncertainties and for the hegemonic state of global capitalism presently on a course of imperial expansion in pursuit of its political and imperial interests. The war against 'terrorism', which is in many ways a direct or indirect product of the projection of US hegemonic power is now being used to justify the further projection of that power. A 'new imperialism' which is necessary to discipline and reorder the world, is how a subservient Tony Blair has seen it. From the other end, Chomsky has seen it as establishing that the US, the hegemonic power of global capitalism, is the world's 'leading terrorist state'. That some allies—'Old Europe', for example—have not always or fully gone along with it only indicates that inter-imperialist conflict of interests remains a reality in capital's globalised world.

Militarism has been integral to America's imperialist expansion abroad. Described as 'imperialist militarism', it has never been devoid of mundane materialist objectives. Even in the Vietnam war, as historians have pointed out, 'tin, rubber, rice, copra, iron ore, tungsten and oil were integral to American policy considerations from the inception'. Oil in the Middle East was obviously a key consideration in the two Gulf wars and the war in Afghanistan. But apart from specific economic objectives or military gains, a most significant aspect of America's use of military force since the end of the Second World War—its important wars from Korea to the Balkans, the Gulf and Afghanistan—has been its political objectives: the 'containment' of external enemies or of internal opposition, diverting attention from tricky domestic problems or even the narrower political objectives of electoral advantage through displays of 'toughness' or tough 'nationalism'. That is how it needs to be noted that as a globalising power America's militarism does not generally have territorial ambitions, it does not seek direct physical control or hegemony over specific colonies. It is, typically, the use of massive displays of force to assert the dominance of global capital so that this capital, particularly the American segment of it, can freely navigate the global economy without hindrance. If at times it has the appearance of a naked display of imperial power for its own sake, without any specific or immediate objectives—and an outright military victory is neither an issue nor even a possible outcome—it is just to show who is boss, that is, to make a general point about US domination of the world, its hegemony over global economy. As one comment has it, 'such display of imperial power only shows that US imperial hegemony can't now rely, if it ever could, on economic superiority alone, and that it depends on periodic display of sheer force. It hardly matters where or for what ostensible purpose, though it helps if the target is non-European or non-white.' ....

Clarity about the role of the state, more specifically the nation state, is central to understanding of both 'globalisation' and the struggle against 'globalisation' today. We have earlier touched upon this subject in different contexts. It is worth our while however to take another look at it, in view of the 'anti-state' hoopla of the globalisers.

The basic assumption underlying this hoopla, the key idea of neo-liberalism in recent times, against a background of the downfall of other ideologies, is variously the 'retreat', 'death' or 'impotence of the state' under contemporary global capitalism. On this view governments are regarded as powerless in relation to transnational corporations, to international financial institutions, and finally to inter-state formations in different parts of the world. The power is supposed to have passed to a transnational capitalist class united in a variety of international organisations. The more 'global' capital is, the less the state can do. Even otherwise, because the process of globalisation has initially taken place on the basis of neo-classical economics, it has presented itself in terms of reducing the role of the state in relation to both domestic economy and international markets. With 'private-property' enthroned and a 'free-market fetishism' taking over, any and every kind of state control is frowned upon as a departure from the received economic wisdom. The state is best done away with. And this is precisely what is now supposed to have happened under 'globalisation'. More specifically, the nation state is perceived to have been replaced by a 'transnational global economy'. The conventional view of 'globalisation' suggests a submergence of the nation-state by contemporary internationalisation of capitalist development, even if the process is admittedly still far from over. In any case, the internationalisation of capital and the development of the nation-state stand in inverse relation to each other so that the more internationalisation, the less nation-state. In other words, 'globalisation' involves a shift of sovereignty away from the nation-state to international agencies of capital, it is making the nation-state increasingly irrelevant. All this, however, like much else about 'globalisation', is only so much ideological mythmaking, 'globaloney' as it has been called, which has nothing to do with the reality of global capitalism and the nation-state today.

Looked at historically, the emergence of capitalism was closely tied to the rise of the nation-state and this linkage has shaped the development and expansion of capitalism throughout its history. Though its origins can be traced back to centuries past, it was only towards the end of the eighteenth century that modern capitalism finally came up, rooted in the social structures of particular western countries. This 'national capitalism', like modern nations themselves, was of course not a precondition for but a product of the development of capitalism as a world system. There is vital truth in Wallerstein's argument that 'modern states are not the primordial frameworks within which historical development has occurred,' and that 'they may be more usefully conceived as one set of social institutions within the capitalist world-economy, this latter being the framework with which, and of which, we can analyse the structures, conjunctures, and events.' Certainly, the systemic weaknesses of capitalism, its contradictions and endemic crises, are not strictly national in origin. They are global, and they are inherent in the system, rooted in capitalism's basic laws of motion. In the final analysis, they are not caused by any specific national policy, nor are they answerable to resolution by any specific national strategy. Nevertheless, modern capitalism grew up and has remained a nationally organised global system, and throughout its history, capitalists have needed and used the state to advance the interests of capital, subject of course to the influence of changes in the economic conditions and the strength of pressures from below. States have maintained order in society guaranteeing the continued existence and expansion of capitalism. State's role has been central to capital's monopolistic growth at home and imperialist expansion abroad. As capitalism has developed across the world, the role of the state has only increased (which incidentally creates real empirical difficulties for the currently fashionable idea that state regulation or control is somehow non- or even anti-capitalist). The state has throughout accommodated and accelerated the process of global integration and, in war or peace, served as an important adjustment mechanism of global capitalism. It is no different with the current phase of capitalist globalisation.

That capitalism has now again become directly, and more universally, global does not put an end to national societies or states. To say that capitalism is now universal as never before is not to say that all, or even most capital is transnational. We still have national economies, national states, nationally-based capital, even nationally-based transnationals. The production still takes place in largely nationally-based companies and the capitalists can still successfully invoke 'national interests' to justify measures dictated by their selfish class interests. As global economic changes combined with domestic challenges have compelled capitalists to seek freedom from the class compromises of the immediate post-war period, to be able to chart their new course, it is through the state that they have carried out their class agenda which has included the removal of fetters on international trade and investment, smashing domestic unions and lowering wages, rolling back environmental regulation, and dismantling welfare-state protections. The state remains as important as ever for the capitalist system, domesticating the system-threatening aspects of neo-liberal policies and facilitating their profit-enhancing aspects in all their fury. It is the direct interventions by the US government, for example, that have underpinned the national economy in recent decades. Despite all the talk about the 'death' of the state, it is state institutions, ranging from national ones like the US Treasury and the Federal Reserve to international ones like the World Bank and the IMF that have managed to prevent a replay of the 1920s' collapse, despite the recurrent financial crises of recent decades. They have kept the third world crisis or 'melodrama' from metasising into a global implosion. Instead they have used the crisis to great advantage in forcing a variety of 'reforms' on the debtor countries for the benefit of the creditors in the advanced capitalist world. The neo-colonial thrust of 'globalisation' is impossible to conceive without the support given to national capitals of advanced capitalist countries by their own nation-states.

It has been pointed out that 'globalisation', with all its neo-liberal policies, has almost nowhere led to a reduction in the size of the government apparatus or state expenditure. Indeed, so powerful are the pressures in advanced capitalism to maintain a high profile for the state that in the 1980s and 1990s—the decades of supposed privatisation and globalisation —average state expenditure as a percentage of output actually rose in leading West-European countries. It is not only that while some government services have shrunk, others have grown—the most obvious here is the case of cuts in spending on social needs being accompanied by increases in spending on the repressive apparatus of the state—it is far more because of the sheer range of functions that the state is now called on to perform in this 'new epoch' of globalisation. Even a cursory look will reveal that the importance of state action in enabling the global capitalist system to function has, if anything, increased, not reduced as that system has spread internationally as never before.

The 'globalisation' theory postulates decline of the nation state and national capitalist classes, the transfer of sovereignty from the state to the organs of some kind of unified transnational capital. However, nothing like this has happened and seems unlikely to ever happen. Instead, the transnationalisation of capital has been throughout accompanied by the proliferation of modern capital's original political form, the nation state, and this state is more universal today than ever before. Again, as globaloney has it there is an inverse relation between the internationalisation of the economy and the power of the state: the more globalisation, the smaller the role of the state. Instead, 'globalisation' *presupposes* the state and while state may have lost some of its traditional functions, it has gained many more new ones, especially as the main conduit through which national (or indeed multinational) capital is inserted into the global market. Far from being rendered irrelevant, state is today the main agent of 'globalisation', its penetration of the capitalist logic deeper into the societies of advanced capitalism and spatially throughout the world.

State plays a central role as capital's channel into the global market, as the creator of the right environment for capital's accumulation, and as capital's main line of defence against internal disorder. Globalisation is so much a phenomenon of national economies and national states that it is impossible to make sense of it without taking account of competition among national economies, and national states carrying out policies to promote international 'competitiveness'. This quest for competitiveness demands a state that will keep social costs to a minimum, while keeping in check the social conflict and disorder generated by the policies to ensure this. Each state is the main agent forcing on its citizens the austerities and hardships needed to maintain or restore profitability to domestic capital. State promotes the free movement of capital while confining labour within national boundaries and subjecting it to necessary disciplines in the interests of capital. In addition to the usual policing and repression of labour and protesting social movements, the state continues to establish the essential infrastructural and juridical conditions relating to markets, private property, and contract within its territorial domain. It is mainly through the instrumentality of the state that the necessary policy choices for globalisation are made and executed and each state, again, is the main instrument for containing the conflicts engendered by these policies. A 'hands off government' is alright as a back-up ideology when social justice is at stake. But state is all over the place when protection or rescue of capitalist interets is involved.

As the main agent of globalisation, states are becoming more and more attuned to accommodating and fostering capital accumulation on a world scale. They do so by creating and sustaining global markets. It is they who are making the necessary changes in the rules governing capital movements, investment, currency exchange, trade and migration flows that permit a new stage of global accumulation to come about. It is through inter-state relations, as these are formalised in international agreements, treaties, and the rules governing international agencies, that the necessary international juridical and infrastructural conditions for global capital accumulation are established and maintained. The importance attached by the international business interests to the WTO, tariff agreements, the governmental enforcement of contractual rights and the protection of intellectual property interests attest to the continuing, and growing, importance of the state, which in effect means the nation state. Even as the nation state protects and promotes capitalist interests at home, it provides every possible material, diplomatic and military support for the country's capitalists as they go gallavanting through international markets. One may add that even when policies deliberately designed to forfeit national sovereignty for the sake of globalisation are made, they are the result of policy choices made by the national state itself.

The powers of the nation state at the centre have not been in any way weakened by the spiralling internationalisation of finance, or the growing importance of multinational institutions. As sponsors of globalisation, providing ever-greater opportunities for foreign investment and markets for the multinationals, especially in the decolonised periphery and semi-periphery of global capitalism, international agencies of capital like the IMF and the World Bank have indeed acquired enormous influence. But they cannot pursue their policies except through the agency of the state. They are above all agents of specific national capitals and derive whatever powers of enforcement they have from nation-states, both the imperial states that command them and the subordinate states that carry out their orders. Commenting on the policy-making process of multinational institutions like the IMF, WB and WTO, William K. Tabb has written: 'Before any of these organizations meet, the United States makes proposals which are discussed within the QUAD—a group composed of the United States, the European Union (EU), Japan, and Canada—which convenes separately, and, in secrecy, makes key decisions without the participation of the other members of the world community. The QUAD is not recognized in any of their charters, but it acts as an executive committee that determines their direction. In Seattle, the vast majority of WTO members waited outside the exclusive Green Room meetings, as they were called, for the QUAD to reach decisions that would then be discussed by the body. It was clear to the other delegates that they were essentially excluded from real decision-making.' That is how the multinational institutions that have emerged or grown functionally important with 'globalisation', do not so much bypass or displace the nation state as restructure and give it new roles—and in case of major capitalist powers, provide them with new instruments and power to pursue the interests of their respective national capitals. That these major powers do not always have their way, as they want it, in these institutions does not affect the point being made.

'Globalisation', the ongoing universalisation of capitalism, as we have noted, is taking place in a world of nation states. In a way, the whole point of 'globalisation' is competition as much between individual multinationals or transnationals, as between whole national economies. Behind every multinational or transnational is a national base, which depends on its local state to sustain its viability and other states to give it access to other markets and other labour forces. As a consequence, the nation state has acquired new functions as an instrument of competition in the global market. This apart, today transnational capital may be more effective than was the old-style military imperialism in penetrating every corner of the world, but this penetration is still taking place in a world of developed and less developed capitalist countries, and is often accomplished through the medium of local capitals as well as the national states of the latter which are required to maintain the conditions of economic stability and labour discipline that are the essential conditions of profitable investment. The less developed states serve as transmission belts for other, more powerful capitalist states. This is also a situation in which every new opportunity for transnational cooperation between major national capitals is matched by opportunities for new kinds of inter-imperilaist rivalry—in which the nation state is again the principal agent. The logic of this rivalry does not rule out state-supported military adventures. Beyond it all, there is the more likely use of the military power of a single nation state, the last remaining 'superpower', to sustain 'the sovereignty of the market'. In other words, the effort, peaceful or otherwise, to establish sovereignty over global markets, no less than the sovereignty over specific colonial countries in the past, is today a project pursued by state powers, and by one state above all.

The state remains central to the existence and functioning of global capitalism. It is impossible to think of today's globalisation without the complex of national policies implemented by national states. Pointing out that globalisation implies, among other things, those ruthless state actions we associate with neo-liberalism, that is, policies designed to enhance 'competitiveness' and 'flexibility', not just for individual firms but for whole national economies in the global market, policies which are adopted not just because capital *wants* them but because it *needs* them to generate maximum profitability in an integrated and competitive global economy, Ellen M. Wood has written:

> Contrary to much conventional wisdom today, 'globalization' has made the state not less but more important to capital. Capital needs the state to maintain the conditions of accumulation and 'competitiveness' in various ways, including direct subsidies at tax-payers' expense; to preserve labor discipline and social order in the face of austerity and 'flexibility'; to enhance the mobility of capital while blocking the mobility of labour; to administer huge rescue operations for capitalist economies in crisis... operations often organized by international agencies but always paid for by national taxes and enforced by national governments. Even the imperialism of the major capitalist states requires the collaboration of subordinate states to act as transmission belts and agents of enforcement. 'Neoliberalism' is not just a withdrawal of the state from social provision. It is a set of active policies, a new form of state intervention designed to enhance capitalist profitability in an integrated global market.

It is worth noticing that the globalisers are themselves, in different contexts, coming to recognise the important role of the state in globalisation. The fragility of the global financial system because of the speculation and extensive risk-taking that have accompanied financial transnationalisation, has inevitably led to calls for a *more* active, interventionist state to protect the banks and the money markets. In the face of recurring financial crises, globalising capitalists have been retreating to national bunkers and their ideologues discovering the virtues of capital controls. The growing contradictions of globalisation have compelled even the World Bank to argue in one of its recent reports that 'development without an effective state is impossible.' In an explicit departure from its former thesis about 'overloaded governments' and advocacy of a 'minimalist state', the World Bank, with its advocacy of 'safety nets', 'good governance', etc. now sees the state as a necessary 'partner, catalyst, facilitator' of globalisation. The Bank now insists on the importance of 'an effective state', which 'harnessing the energy of private business and individuals...acts as their partner and catalyst, instead of restricting their partnership.'

Of course, we know all too well what Bank's 'effective state' or 'partnership' means. The World Bank is primarily concerned with the development of those state capacities which facilitate more effective integration into globalisation. 'Good governance' it advocates is obviously important for this purpose. Its advocacy of state action for social protection or 'safety nets'—well described as 'social democratisation' of globalisation—is to secure both stability in society and legitimacy for state as the agent of globalisation. But the nature of World Bank's concerns does not take anything away from the substantive point being made, namely, the World Bank's recognition that 'the state' is not an outsider to globalisation but an integral part of it. The state involved is, of course, the nation state and a state acting in the interests of the dominant classes. Globalisation's neo-liberal state remains a capitalist class state.

There is an aspect to the centrality of the state in the globalisation process which needs to be specifically noted. Capitalist globalisation and therefore its oppressions are everywhere being experienced by people locally, and are everywhere mediated by their national states. It is no accident that people's protests and demonstrations that we have been seeing in so many countries across the world are directed against the actions of their respective states in pursuit of 'globalisation'. This draws our attention to the important question of state and the struggle against globalisation. Immediately, I would like to make only two very brief points in this regard.

As a historically specific phase of capitalist expansion, globalisation is capitalist exploitation of human beings and natural resources, aided and abetted by a direct collaboration between the state and capital. With its policies of 'flexibility', 'competitiveness' and 'globalisation', state has been active in restructuring the economy and worldwide promotion of the interest of capitalists to the detriment of everyone else. In many ways, the collusion or symbiosis between capital and state is today closer and more apparent than ever. The state is seen to be more visibly implicated in class exploitation than it has been for a long time. It is not surprising, therefore, that it is the actions of the state that have driven people into the streets, in opposition to the policies of the 'globalising' state. This not only suggests the centrality of state in the struggle against globalisation but also the key task facing this struggle today: people's opposition, their experience of globalisation in general, needs to be critically interpreted and theorised, and people's consciousness deepened, to recover state as *the* target of struggle against globalisation. This is important because the question of state power, of people's power in the state, their 'political supremacy' in society, is central to the success of struggle against globalisation.

There is good reason for me to stress this point. It is the ideological need of capitalism today to disguise and mystify the increasingly direct and obvious collusion between capital and state. The concept of globalisation well serves this need. Its 'anti-state' hoopla, the argument that the integration of world capitalism, the existence of transnational corporations, etc. somehow makes the nation state irrelevant, that the state has ceased to be a major player in the economy as a result of globalisation, not only directly denies or obscures this collusion, but has many other allied implications. The most important implication is that the question of state power, of people's power in the state, is no longer relevant, least of all central to any alternative, presumably, radical politics. And, aided of course by the recent collapse of socialist-communist politics and the general disorientation on the Left, 'globalisation's' ideological obfuscation has not been entirely unsuccessful: state as the classic target for political struggle against capitalism has virtually disappeared from the scene, giving way to all kinds of fragmented politics—of social movements, 'civil society', voluntary organisations or NGOs, identities, etc. The positive role or significance of much of this politics is not to be denied but no struggle for people's interest, including struggle against globalisation, can bypass the struggle for political power and state as *the* terrain and target of this struggle and still hope to be effective or successful.

The state in advanced capitalist countries is today the principal agent of globalisation. By the same token, state alone can be the effective means of blocking globalisation. At the other end, the imperialist states cannot just penetrate all borders without working through other local states which are often in direct and deliberate collusion with imperial powers and transnational corporations. In both cases, it is the state which has to be the focus or target in the struggle against globalisation. This in effect means that the struggle against globalisation has to be a struggle for people's power in the state, for political power in the right hands, a truly *democratic* political power. It means a state which does not simply 'intervene' in the capitalist economy or provide a 'safety net' against the ravages of capitalism, or practise some other kind of paternalism, but is willing and capable of seeking an alternative to capitalism, of subjecting the economy—above all its allocation of resources and disposition of economic surpluses—to people's needs in accordance with a social logic different from the logic of capitalist competition and profitability, of capital accumulation and market imperatives. This logic today can only be the logic of socialism as visualised by classical Marxism.

The second point—already made in another context but important enough to be reiterated—is that since global capitalism is nationally organised and immediately dependent on national states, national economies and national states remain the primary terrain of anti-capitalist organisation and struggle. Of course an international perspective, working people's solidarity across national frontiers, remains vital to any socialist movement. And today there exists a focus for such solidarity as has, perhaps, never before existed in the history of capitalism. The universalisation of capitalism has not brought about the cessation but instead the universalisation of struggle against capitalism. When, with globalisation, just about every state is following the same destructive logic, domestic struggles against that common logic can be the basis—in fact the strongest possible basis—of a new internationalism. But looking for that internationalism must not be an excuse for giving up on local national struggles. The main arenas of struggle against global capitalism still remain local and national. 'Workers of all countries unite' remains the motto but this 'unity' obviously begins at home. There is a growing space for common transnational struggles, but the established order has still to be primarily fought on our own home pitch. As the *Manifesto* put it a long time ago: 'The proletariat of each country must, of course, first of all settle matters with its own bourgeoisie.'

Socialism, like capitalism, tends to be universal and internationalism is indeed the only genuine reply to globalisation. But this internationalism will come up mediated by local and national struggles. In fact, they will be the main channel into the ultimately necessary international struggles. 'The final confrontation,' it has been metaphorically suggested, 'will take place throughout the planet, from Paris to Peking and from Seoul to Seattle.' But this 'confrontation' will grow on the basis of mutual support among various local and national movements in their respective struggles against their own domestic capitalists and states.

The nation state is indeed the concrete terrain on which the struggle for the radical transformation of society must begin and may have to be carried forward. It may be added that to argue that a nation state—and this includes states of the size and resources of Britain, France or Italy, or for that matter, India, China or Russia—cannot provide the ground on which the radical transformation of society can be attempted is to rule out such a transition for the forthcoming historical period. It is to abdicate the struggle for socialism in our time.....

Chapter 13

Crisis of Socialism Today*

The crisis of socialism today is really a crisis of the social revolution of our times—a revolution which remains necessary if humanity is to survive and make further progress. Even in the failure of its first efforts, it has left the world significantly changed for the better, and though in crisis, it has enough resources left for a resumed struggle for socialism. The proper socialist response to the crisis is neither to mourn the passing of 'actually existing socialism', nor to seek answers in the so-called 'socialism of the market' which can only produce new versions of capitalism. Lessons of course have to be learnt from what went wrong in the past. The proper response, however, is to set about building the socialist movement of the future.

The reasons which in the first place gave rise to the movement for socialism still hold, more so at the beginning of this century than they did at the beginning of the last or at any time earlier. Capitalism remains a deeply exploitative and ecologically disatrous way of organising social life. Apparently triumphant, capitalism continues to operate under the same structural compulsions, producing the same catastrophic consequences as before. It remains ridden with crises and congenitally unable to subordinate its achievements to the needs of human beings, unable, despite its prodigious productive

---

* The concluding chapter of the author's *Crisis of Socialism—Notes in Defence of a Commitment.*

abilities, to offer even bare survival to vast majorities in the world it dominates. Despite its current apotheosis, capitalism has resolved none of the problems which have for more than a century-and-a-half given sustenance to socialist aspirations and struggles. The logic favouring a worldwide transition to socialism remains as compelling today as it has ever been.

The collapse of the Soviet Union does not in any way change this logic, except that the economically exploitative, morally repulsive and ecologically unsustainable character of capitalism is now more aggparent than at any time in its history. The Cuban writer, Pablo Armando, when asked about how the collapse in the East was being interpreted by the United States, wrote:

> They are happy now. They are celebrating. For them the world had ended. History has ended. How very silly to think that! Communism has not diappeared. The Utopias of socialism and communism are not going to disappear as long as there are exploiters and exploited. You have to be very happy having one piece of bread to eat while others throw meat to their dogs. I didn't have to read Marx to know the difference.

Even as the enemies were, once again, declaring socialism dead, Eduardo Galeano had warned against claiming too much for what had happened. 'In their rush to the funeral, they are burying the wrong corpse', he had commented. Socialism was not born with the Soviet Union, but a long time before it, with capitalism—as a response to, indeed the negation of capitalism. Socialism cannot be dead as long as capitalism lives. Given its ineradicable contradictions and limitations, capitalism guarantees that men and women everywhere will continue to search for alternatives to it; and socialism continues to represent the only rational and humane alternative to capitalism. Our business as socialists, now more than ever, is to defend and advance that alternative, to resume the 'journey of hope', a 'shared search' for human emancipation, as Raymond Williams called it.

II

The objective conditions and more than an embryonic subjectivity at individual and mass organisational levels exist for the reconstruction of a socialist opposition to the currently dominant capitalist system. In the West, the euphoria over 'no alternative' is long over. The declaration of 'the end of history', like similar declarations in the past, stands rejected as so much silliness. The long moment people thought typical, the welfarist capitalism is recognised as not typical; typical is the harsh reality they are now experiencing. People are learning the hard way what capitalism is really about. Just as in the hinterlands of global capitalism, ravaged by 'globalisation' and subjected to the new domination of America, people are learning anew about capitalism and imperialism, and about the compradorism of their own ruling elities. The question of an alternative is back on the agenda, and in different shapes and forms, in however confused or muddled a manner, anti-capitalist struggles are being resumed in different parts of the world. These struggles may not produce a re-make of the previous century. History does not repeat itself, we are told. But 'history is more imaginative than we are,' Marx had said. History certainly has its surprises—and revolutions by the oppressed and exploited are among them.

Revolution is not only armed struggle or insurrection, though these still cannot be ruled out. It does not at all help to see revolution as a punctual moment in history or in terms of iconic images like the taking of the Winter Palace or the storming of the Bastille. Revolution is best understood as a complex process—with special complexities of its own in regimes of bourgeois democracy. And however we understand it, we cannot predict the practical and theoretical forms of the revolutions of the future. But we know the surprises that vicissitudes of world history brought us in the twentieth century. There is no reason to doubt that this one will bring more. The inventiveness of masses in revolt has been and will continue to be beyond the imagination of the most sensitive scholar or philosopher.

Revolution is not over. The basic conflicts between classes, between the oppressed and the oppressors, between a new and the old social order will not cease because the Soviet Union has ceased to be and a Fukuyama has announced the 'end of history'. The dynamics and forces which generated the revolutions of the twentieth century remain as they were in the past. The end of 'historical communism' has not put an end to poverty or to people's thirst for justice. The poor and forsaken of the third world still hope for a better life. Not exactly enthusiastic over revolutions, past or future, Fred Halliday, in his recent study on the subject, has yet pointed to 'the enduring inability of those with power and wealth to comprehend the depth of hostlity to them' and 'the ability of history.... to surprise', and written: 'The agenda of the revolutions of modern history is still very much with us because the aims they asserted... are far from having been achieved'. This leaves revolution still on the agenda of history. Revolution remains the vital truth, the unfinished story of our times—in whatever shape or form and over however long a period the rest of the story may be told.

This, however, has not prevented scholars of different persuasions and calibres from preaching that revolution is over. Along with men of 'science' of Marxism, in Russia and outdside, they have even been asking if Russia would not have been better off without the October Revolution, as if Lenin or the Bolsheviks, or the Russian people, had any other choice. The question is in any case irrelevant and not worth discussing. But there is a point I would still like to make about these scholars' failure to understand the October Revolution and, for that matter, any other revolution or revolutionary process.

Revolutions have their historical causation. But they don't happen because of neat economic or political, personal or social calculations, or as a result of someone's 'scientific' theorising about it. Even Lenin's formula, 'revolutions occur when those below do not accept any longer to be ruled as before' does not capture—and, in my opinion, was never meant to capture—the full reality of what happen, nor does 'this consideration', as Dr Johnson once put it, 'that if the abuse be enormous, nature will rise up and claiming her original rights overturn a corrupted political system'. Revolutions happen because an oppressive system has become unbearable and there are people ready to bring it down—people with the dream of a better life, 'Traum', Marx had called it, who are willing and prepared to lay down their lives for it. Drawing attention specifically to the latter aspect, Teodor Shanin has observed : 'Social scientists often miss a centrepiece of any revolutionary struggle—the fervour and anger which drives revolutionaries and makes them into what they are. Academic training and bouregeois convention deaden its appreciation. The "phenomenon" cannot be easily "operationalised" into factors, tables and figures... Yet, without this factor, any understanding of revolutions falls flat. That is why clerks, bankes, generals, and social scientists so often fail to see revolutionary upswing even when looking at it directly. At the very centre of revolution lies an emotional upheaval of moral indignation, revulsion, and fury with the powers-that-be, such that one cannot demur or remain silent, whatever the cost. Within its glow, for a while, men surpass themselves, breaking the shackles of intuitive self-preservation, convention, day-to-day convenience, and routing'. I would only add that the essential thrust of Shanin's observations holds, irrespective of how revolution or revolutionary process is understood or visualised.

III

Capitalism has indeed shown remarkable resilience and survived beyond what can be described as its historical time. But its survival has now put a question-mark over the future of humankind. Hobsbawm has written : 'If humanity is to have a recognisable future, it cannot be by prolonging the past or the present. If we try to build the third millenium on that basis, we shall fail. And the price of failure, that is to say, the alternative to a changed society, is darkness'. 'Darkness' yet does not capture the full gravity of what lies ahead. Caught in a global structural crisis, capitalism has become more creative than ever in unleashing its destructive potential. Its accumulative logic and America-led global politics are threatening humanity with unheard-of ecological disasters and nuclear exterminism. With capitalism, humanity is indeed headed for a collective suicide and destruction of the earth itself. Socialism, therefore, is not just 'a changed society', a superior social order, it is today the necessary defence of humanity and our planet earth. This in its own way makes socialism all the more possible as an alternative to capitalism. Alternatives are discovered or invented, or even recovered when it becomes clear that we cannot survive without them. So it is now with socialism. Pointing to the human tragedy that capitalism's continued existence now portends for humankind, this is how Chomsky has put it in his characteristically simple manner :

> At this stage of history, either one of two things is possible. Either the general population will take control of its own destiny and will concern itself with community interests, guided by values of solidarity, sympathy, and concern for others, or, alternatively, there will be no destiny for anyone to control.

Socialism is necessary and also an 'objective possibility' defined by the socio-econoic conditions of capitalism and the alternative people may come to seek. But this does not imply its inevitability. Socialism is no inevitable product of any economic laws or something decreed by supposedly inexorable 'dialectics'—interpretations the critics have often foisted on Marx. There are no inevitablities or guarantees or victory in Marxist theory of transition to socialism. It is the subjective factor, the conscious political intervention which is decisive in the actualisation of the possibility of socialism. Marxist socialists have never deemed inevitability or certainty of success indispensable for their struggle. As in the past so now, the possibility of socialism is spur enough for them to act and the perspective remains on the one hand of a long march guided and fired by the vision of a radically different society and on the other of a movement which learns and becomes more conscious as it advances and whose members do not mix up their own mortality with a timetable for the achievement of socialist goals; they know that history does not always deliver victories within your own lifetime. Daniel Singer has written:

> If we want to recover the dialectical link between the movement and its objective, we must draw clear distinctions between actuality, necessity, and inevitability. Socialism may be a historical possibility, or even necessary to eliminate the evils of capitalism, but this does not mean that it will inevitably take place. This departure from the fatalistic conception is, in a sense, a return to the more distant past, when socialism was not considered as bound

to happen, since there was always the possibility, to quote the terms of Rosa Luxemburg, that barbarism would win out. Above all, uncertainty as to the ultimate result should not imply passivity, obedience, or resignation. On the contrary, it dictates greater participation, more activity, and more militancy since, within limits of objective conditions, the future will be what we shall make it. And this renewed conviction and activism would be particularly welcome today, because the power of the ruling class and the arrogance of its ideologues is largely due to our weakness, to our surrender, to our acceptance of the established rules of the game.

IV

'Utopian' is the charge that continues to be made against socialism. In a sense, any political project is the affirmation of something that is not here, something, in short, imagined and therefore amenable to the charge of utopianism. But, obviously, this is not what the critics mean. Their real objection is to the nature of the socialist project, the transcendence of capitalism it seeks. There are those for whom any effort to move beyond the confines of apitalism is utopian—a position not too difficult to understand. As Arnold Thurman once put it : 'It may be asserted as a principle of human organisation that when new types of social organistion are required, respectable, well-thought-of, and conservative people are unable to take part in them. Their moral and economic prejudices, their desire for the approval of other members of the group, compel them to oppose any form of organisation which does not fit into the picture of society as they have known it in the past.... Nothing seems clearer than that the attitudes of any given ruling class are so set that all arguments in the world will not change them'. But this obviously does not make the charge of 'utopianism' valid. There is, however, another argument which has a wider acceptance. It questions and rejects the socialist project of a viable, classless and stateless, socialised property-based free and humane social order as an impossible ideal, something that does not and cannot exist, something never done or realised before; we simply cannot do without private property or classes, without a capitalist market or class-structure to make the economy work. This argument does carry weight with the ignorant and the unwary, the so-called 'average' citizens in thrall to the conventional bourgeois ways of thinking. But it is nevertheless a straw argument.

Our growing knowledge in the fields of ethnography and anthropology, about humans' present and past, has much in it that shows this argument to be seriously flawed. Australian aborigines have reportedly maintained for millennia a society in near-perfect ecological balance, with no wars, ruling classes, or exploitation of each other, and with minimal material wants satisfied with a minimum of work and a maximum of creatively used 'free time'. Evolutionist anthropology has generally supported the view that there were thousands of years of classless, stateless, non-patriarchal agricultural societies, some large and complex, before the origins of private property. We can indeed be said to have had the experience of socialism or 'primitive communism' far longer than we have of class societies. This experience, in its absence of private property and classes, had a humane quality to it, something worth reappropriation, of course, in necessarily new forms—which suggests more than just viability of a socialist future for humankind. In one of his imges of the society of the future this is indeed how Marx saw it. Marx thought of socialism/conmunism in terms of a 'process of human emancipation and recovery', 'as the complete return of man to himself as a *social* (that is, human) being—a return become conscious, and accomplished within the entire wealth of previous development'.

This apart, it is a form of myopic conservative prejudice to think that everything which does not exist cannot exist. With the same 'logic' one could have stated that slavery was the only possible form of large-scale agricultural and handicraft production (in the first century AD); that monarchy was the only possible form of government (in the fourteenth and fifteenth centuries); that parliament could only be elected without universal franchise (in the eighteenth century), etc. Yet slavery finished by being abolished. Republics appeared while monarchies disappeared in their majority. Universal franchise ended by becoming general in all countries opting for a parliamentary system. Not to see what is developing without being already realised is a form ideological colour-blindness often based upon wishful thinking; you don't see what you don't want to see.

Ernest Mandel has argued :

> The platitude that "Marxian socialism" does not exist anywhere in the world today is tirelessly repeated, as in effect an argument against all human progress. But was it utopian to fight for the abolition of slavery, which existed on a large scale for more than a thousand years?... Religious oppression, including the burning of hereties at the stake, was a "fact of life" for at least five centuries. Was it then utopian to try to establish freedom of conscience and freedom of thought?... Why should it be utopian today to try to do away with wage labour and gigantic state bureaucracies, which after all have been central structures of society for no more than two hundred years?... Utopia, in the broad sense of the word, has been one of the great motors of the eventual achievement of historical progress.

Any serious student of history would know that every significant social advance in history has at some point had to conquer the notion that it was impossible or, that it had never been done before. Utopias are what have moved people throughout history to make it a better world. So it is now with socialism.

Theoretically, the possibility of socialism arises from within the contradictions of capitalism. Morally, opposition to capitalism is its own justification since capitalism is today poisoning human survival itself, let alone human happiness. The resolve to overturn this globally dominant system and build socialism does indeed involve 'utopian surplus', as Ernst Bloch once called it. The utopian dimension of the socialist project of course must not translate itself into either 'teleology' or 'messianic eschatology'. We must not be starry-eyed about the future and also need to divest ourselves of the hubris of tying our own mortality to its construction. But we must also not let the historically limited and capitalism-blighted vision of our enemies settle the question of possibilities of the future. 'Utopian' is a compliment and a challenge we should be willing to accept.

V

We, as socialists, are utopian but we are realistically utopian. Our project has its roots deep on the one hand in the reality of capitalism and on the other hand in people's economic, social and political struggles against it. Therefore, even in our optimism about the possibilities of the other kind inherent in the present situation. The fact that our perspective is that of a long march does not mean that we have plenty of time to start moving. Crises are beginnings but they can be endings as well. It is quite possible that capitalism in crisis will begin to unravel at the seams at a time when we are still dishevelled and disorganised and thus incapable of steering the emerging struggles of the people into an effective overall struggle against capitalism. Popular discontent is rising, and if we, as socialists, do not provide rational and progressive solutions, there are plenty of people waiting in the wings with their irrational and reactionary solutions. The absence of an effective alternative to capitalist social order has already much-contributed to 'the flowering of poisonous weeds in the capitalist jungle'—racism, sexism, xenophobia, anti-semitism, ethinic hatreds, relitious fundamentalisms, and things much worse. Fascism's rise to significance in Western Europe in recent years in a waning that the ghosts of the past are not buried for ever, and similar ghosts are appearing elsewhere. The old choice, socialism or barbarism, may still lie in the future. But barbarism of sorts is already with us in the form of a globally degraded and plundered environment, of famine and pestilence in large parts of the third world and refined brutality of commodified existence in the metropolis of the First World, whose technological and cultural sophistication is quite compatible with its growing barbarisation.

Marx had hailed the productive achievements of capitalism. But he had also pointed out the damage capitalism regularly inflicts upon man and nature and warned of its long-term destructive potential. It is this destructive potentiality of capitalism and the threat it poses to human existence on this earth which Rosa Luxemburg later summed up in a prophetic poser: 'Socialism or barbarism?' The threat is now becoming daily more real and can well take the form of a nuclear holocaust or an ultimate ecological disaster. Socialism and barbarism are indeed the alternatives for the twenty-first century. If we are unable to build, and build in time a socialist alternative worthy of the name, what capitalism now promises us is only a future of barbarism. And since the possibolity of the destruction of our world itself cannot be ruled out, it could well be a future of no future at all. 'History is about the most cruel of all goddesses', Engles had once said. History could now be cruel to us in a way that will really be the 'end of history'. But, as Marxism of Karl Marx has it, nothing is inevitable in human affairs till it happens. We can fight back and reject the future that capitalist masters are making for us. In the final analysis, it is how we struggle and fight back that will decide our future. We can still make our future our own way, build it as a society of freedom and equality and a truly rich human life for all—for that is what socialism is about.